ABOUT THE AUTHOR

Mark Swain was born in Singapore in 1958, where his father was stationed in the RAF. He has lived in many countries, and as a young man found it hard to break the habit of a nomadic life, spending a great deal of his youth hitchhiking around Europe.

With a low boredom threshold, Mark has had dozens of jobs and quite a few careers, but only one wife. Studying Graphic Design at Hastings College of Art, he soon joined the Army in search of adventure. At one point he found himself travelling the world on the QE2 as a silver-service waiter and going to the Falklands war.

Training as a TEFL teacher, he went to Tokyo in 1984, where he met his wife Lorna. Between then and now, Mark has run a language business in Barcelona, cut the tops off VW Beetles, trained and worked as a systems analyst and completed a degree in 3D design. Eventually he stood still long enough to set up a risk management and business training company. At 54, when not writing, he still works as a management consultant and trainer for Systems2 Consulting Ltd, the company he founded as Safe Systems in 1998. He sleeps little, yet there are never enough hours in his day.

Mark and his wife Lorna have three grown-up children and live in Canterbury, Kent. He plans to repeat his cycle trip with his grandchildren, when they arrive.

ALSO BY MARK SWAIN

Special Treatment

Winner of The Kinglake Short Story Prize 2010

Published first in *Ten Modern Short Stories 2010*

Long Road, Hard Lessons

A 10,000-mile Test of a Father and Son's Relationship

by

Mark Swain

With candid commentary from
Sam Swain

Tinderbox Publishing

First published in the UK in 2012 by

Tinderbox Publishing Limited

This book is a work of Non-fiction based upon the life, experiences and recollections of the author.

ISBN   978-0-9572002-0-3

Cover design and interior photographs layout
by Caleb Simmons   www.calebsimmons.co.uk

Maps by David Court   www.severnsidestudio.co.uk

Cover photographs by Mark Swain
Inside photographs by Mark and Sam Swain

Front cover: Heading north from Caldiran, Eastern Turkey

Printed and bound by CPI Group (UK) Ltd, Croydon, CR0 4YY

For my father, Ken Swain, who worried about me too much, and for my son Sam, who has taught me how to worry less.

I am indebted to my parents for their kindness in spite of my refusal to conform, to my children for their good advice, to Colin Bowyer for taking the burden of business responsibility from my shoulders and not least to my wife for her support, and for helping me to make sense of my life.

Steve Walsh provided us with a target to aim for, hospitality at the end, advice and much else. Martin Latham gave me invaluable encouragement and advice. There are many more – too many to mention here, but you know who you are. People have always been generous to me regardless of my lack of restraint. Thanks. I love you all. And, by the way, I may never learn to shut up.

Contents

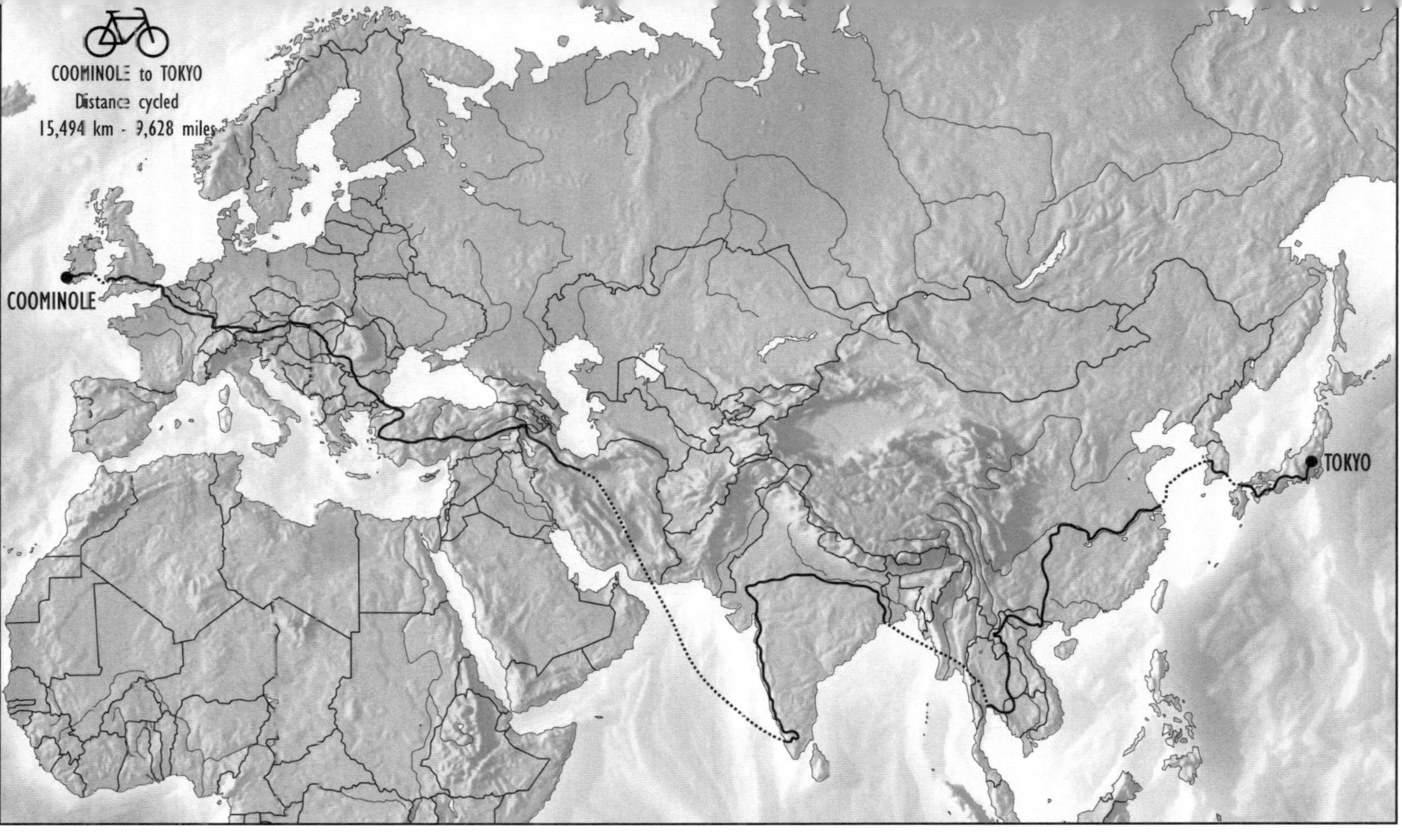

COOMINOLE to TOKYO
Distance cycled
15,494 km - 9,628 miles
COOMINOLE
TOKYO

Introduction

The Seed of an Idea

Wheels are made for rolling; mules are made to pack,
I've never seen a sight that didn't look better looking back.
Lee Marvin, Wandering Star, 1969

As a small boy I remember thinking that song might have been written for me.

"Where did the idea for the bike ride come from?" we were constantly asked.

The story goes back a long way, further than I first thought in fact – back to my own childhood.

I realised at the age of four that a bicycle was the key to freedom. The thrill I felt as I first escaped down the hill from my home has never left me.

In their first few years of parenthood my mother and father realised they had a child with a burning need for adventure. I don't think they saw this as in any way positive. In fact I think they bore it as if I were a child with a kind of mental abnormality. Oh I loved my parents well enough, but this did not prevent me from spending much of my time plotting my escape from them. Years later, with a ten-year-old son of my own, that desire for adventure was reignited.

As we set out on our first long bike ride together, I saw in Sam that same need to be free. Inside me, though, I felt a rising sense of apprehension. Danger lay beyond our front gate. I was his father; it was my job to protect him.

The depths of winter seemed a strange time to go off on a bike ride but I had promised. Sam seemed undaunted by the cold as we cycled away. He looked every bit a boy on a mission. Staring dreamily at the sunrise, I did feel a special sense of occasion about that moment, but I was completely unprepared for the fact that this day was to become a major turning point in my life and in the life of my son.

That night, camping on crunchy frozen grass, looking out into the black English Channel, we huddled inside our sleeping bags. The night before Christmas Eve was the coldest night of the year yet Sam's enthusiasm was irrepressible.

"Dad, would you do a *long* bike ride with me when I finish school?"

"Not the best time to ask," I croaked. "But yes, where did you have in mind"?

"Japan?"

"Do you know how far Japan is, Sam?" I smiled. "It's probably about ten thousand miles!"

"That's OK, Dad, we'd have a year."

COOMINOLE to DOVER
Distance cycled
862 km - 536 miles
ATLANTIC OCEAN
HEBRIDES
SHETLAND IS.
ORKNEY IS.
NORWAY
Bergen
Oslo
Åland
Stockholm
SCOTLAND
Glasgow
Edinburgh
Vänern
Göteborg
Gotland
Öland
Skagerrak
NORTHERN IRELAND
IRELAND
Belfast
NORTH SEA
BALTIC SEA
Dublin
IRISH SEA
Aarhus
DENMARK
Coominole
Boherbouy
Dingle
Ballinamona
Copenhagen
Cork
Rosslare
WALES
Carmarthen
Birmingham
Gdansk
Pembroke dock
ENGLAND
Newbridge
Hamburg
Chippenham
London
Amsterdam
Elbe
Canterbury
The Hague
Liphook
Dover
NETHERLANDS
Berlin
Meuse
Calais
Dortmund
Rhine
Vistula
ENGLISH CHANNEL
Brussels
Odra
POLAND
Le Havre
GERMANY
Leipzig
Seine
Paris
Metz
Frankfurt
Prague

Chapter 1

Setting Off – A Poetic Irish Beginning

May the road rise up to meet you, may the wind be always at your back.

The morning we set off for Japan, I could tell Sam was apprehensive. I thought I knew why. Ten thousand miles felt like a ridiculous distance to cycle and this had been driven home by the reaction of other people. They behaved as if they had misunderstood us.

"You mean you're going to cycle *around* Japan?"

In fact, I now understand that it was not the distance that worried Sam, it was the thought of spending nearly a year on his own with his dad. I clearly underestimated what a pain in the arse I am. I know now – although surely there must have been easier ways to find out.

*

We had originally planned to start our expedition from home in Canterbury, which is located conveniently close to the continent. This would be a more conventional beginning, but it was Sam who pointed out that Ireland is at the western edge of Europe, and Tokyo at the eastern limits of Asia. More than this, the most westerly inhabited point of Ireland is a small town called Dingle, in County Kerry, where we go every year for a family holiday. Over many years, Dingle has become a kind of spiritual home to us and Sam felt that these factors combined to create an overwhelming case for starting our trip there.

"What difference will another 800-odd kilometres make?" he insisted.

This made me laugh. At that stage, 800-odd kilometres sounded like a hell of a lot, but his argument grew on me.

And so it was that we found ourselves setting off from Canterbury on 19 July 2008 with the bikes on the back of the car, heading west for Ireland (the wrong direction). Once we arrived in Dingle, though, it quickly became apparent how much of a good decision that had been.

I had asked my friend John Verling, who runs the local Dingle Phone Shop, to print off some posters inviting locals to come and see us set off on the 26 July at Coominole point. A friend of John's, a colourful local character named Colm Bambury, had contacted people he knew in the Irish media to persuade them to cover our story. I spoke with Colm on the phone the day we arrived.

"OK now, how famous do you boys want to be?" he asked.

By the following day the phone calls had started to come in. Interviews were set up and I had a conversation with a pressured Paschall Sheehy, news producer at RTE, Ireland's main television station. This attention introduced an unexpected and somewhat unwelcome element of urgency into the week leading up to our departure, but on balance it proved worthwhile.

This was a slightly nerve-wracking time for me, but less than it might have been, since we would be calling in at home around ten days after departure. The rest of the week was a combination of a few short training rides around the peninsula, interviews with journalists and celebratory drinks with some of the good friends we've collected there over the years. It was not exactly good healthy training for the ride and we tried hard to restrain ourselves. Anyone who knows Ireland, however, will understand that this was a strategy doomed to failure.

*

Late the night before our departure, my new business partner Colin arrived, having ridden over by motorcycle to see us off. He said he was checking that I was really going. Colin was the final critical part in the jigsaw that had allowed me to make the trip. I met had him just over a year before at a time when I was extremely stressed, with it looking as though my only way of going was to close the business.

Colin took to the challenge of running things like a Gurkha takes to battle. Somehow it felt like fate to have met someone as madly optimistic as myself just at the right time.

Sam spent the final night with friends at the Rainbow Hostel campsite. About half a dozen of them had come over from Canterbury to see him off. He promised to take it easy of course, but I felt sure he would be good for nothing the next morning. I was not much better myself, but managed to get away from McCarthy's bar just before midnight, in time to get a bit of sleep before the early start demanded by the television crew. They wanted us there by 7am – two hours before the start time – so they could film us for the evening news without interference. It was a tough call for us, but harder for them since they had to drive all the way from Dublin.

*

We arrived at Coominole just on time for a briefing from Paschall and his team. It was a windy morning with angry clouds looming over the Blasket Islands and the Ring of Kerry. By our planned 9am start deadline, we had already cycled around 25km up and down the road around Slea Head and were feeling a little weary. In that two-hour pre-start session, Paschall and his team filmed us from the back of a moving 4x4. Cycling along the same stretch of road numerous times in a howling gale, we began to realise why people come to resent media attention.

Eventually the time came for our departure and we returned to our starting point – the small car park at Coominole, above the beach where the main scenes for the film Ryan's Daughter were shot. Here, we found a car park full of wind-battered well-wishers with flasks of tea, along with members of the press. More delays, as newspaper and radio reporters took their turns with us, with our family and friends not getting much of a look-in. Ah the price of fame!

My newly fitted bar-bag – now filled with snacks, maps and a few tools – had decided to follow the way of gravity. It spun around awkwardly at the first bump and engaged the front brake. I attempted to tighten it, while the continued questions from the journalists at my shoulder began to draw increasingly sarcastic responses.

"Will you have a support vehicle?"

"No, I'm not Ewan McGregor."

"How much training have you done for this trip?"

"None, mate. We'll train on the way."

It was time. No time for the bar-bag now. I bodged it with some matchsticks to tighten the cable mounting and wheeled over to the start line.

"What kind of planning is this for a 10,000-mile trip?" I muttered to myself.

A man from the Irish Sun heard me and began scribbling in his wind-ravaged notebook. My wife Lorna heard too. She was already worried about this uncompromising, self-flagellating tendency in me. She shot the reporter a withering look and he moved back a few paces.

"A few things are bound to go wrong; that's not a failure," she told me. "Remember you *are* allowed to enjoy this!"

She was right, of course. We had agreed that we were making this trip for pleasure, not to break records or prove anything to anyone. I could see I would need to constantly remind myself of this.

*

One of our preparatory rides from Canterbury to Brighton had already highlighted my issues in this area. We were nearing the end, heading to the house of some friends, when I insisted on stopping to get some wine and cider from an off-license. On the last stretch, one-handed with the brakes hampered by a carrier bag of bottles, I nearly missed the house. Swerving sharply, I clipped a wall and the bag ripped, sending its contents crashing to the ground. We arrived at our friends' house with only two hissing bottles of cider, the tops half off. After 75 miles without mishaps, we'd crashed and burned 100 yards from our destination. I was hard to console, although Sam tried valiantly. In my mind, I had failed.

*

Back in stormy Coominole, we positioned ourselves at Lorna's start-line.   As always I was worrying about the time, but managed not to show it too much, I thought.   I forgot all about everything else, though, when my eldest daughter Alex emerged to sing the most beautiful song for us, followed by Lorna reading a poem.   Their words, buffeted around that rocky outcrop by the roaring wind, seemed to stop time for a moment.   It was an intensely moving experience.   Unforgettable.

Following a couple of annoying imitation starts for the cameras, we finally sped off along the Slea Head Drive at about 10am.   We felt shaky at the knees from the emotion of it all.

"Shit, we're doing it!" I said.

After nearly being blown off our bikes as we turned and waved at the first bend, we made our way along the tiny road beneath the towering cliffs of Mount Eagle.   Solitary beams of sunlight broke through the clouds and shone down like angled towers of light onto the raging sea.   The storm-battered beaches stretched out westwards into the distance, with the Blasket Islands surrounded by huge white waves.   What a place to start!

Rounding the headland to face south, past a lonely statue of the Madonna looking out over the Ring of Kerry and towards lands afar, we stopped to take a photograph.   We were eager to get going but this dramatic scene needed to be captured on camera as well as in our minds.

From that point on we had some company.   A group of three local cyclists had turned out on their racing bikes to do the first 20km leg back into Dingle town with us.   This was a nice surprise; cycling through stunning scenery with a few local Kerrymen.   It was good to be away from the crowds, chatting to them on the open road.

Jostled by the wind, thankfully at our backs, we were passed by friends on motorcycles who whizzed by with a wave, soaking up the scenery, dodging sheep and dry-stone walls, weaving around the tight curves.   We would see them again soon.   We were heading for historic Currain's Bar in Dingle Main Street and yet another send-off.

Currain's is one of the few remaining genuine hardware-store bars in Ireland (some are little more than reproductions for the benefit of tourists).   During the great depression in Ireland, the government allowed many hardware stores to adapt themselves to also serve alcohol (and some vice-versa) as a means of making ends meet. Those that remain have done so only by managing to stay continuously in business since then, as the law prohibits them from reopening as licensed premises once they have closed down. We felt very much out of place standing in the small shop in our lycra shorts and cycling tops, supping Guinness with elderly farmers at the counter. Our supporters, not ready for Guinness at 10am, waited outside. We had picked a good morning to stop here. The bar was full of people, none of whom knew we were coming. Old oilcloth coats predominated, smelling of sheep. A line of pint glasses half filled with *settling* Guinness stood framed by shelves of Wellington boots, farmers caps and horse blankets. Wizened old men with long grey beards and twinkling eyes looked us up and down.

"Do you not think you'd have been better with decent sweaters, lads?" asked one. "Young James behind the bar will be happy to sort you a couple out if you ask him like."

Young James, all of 65 years old, stretched across to pass me two pints.

"On the house, lads. Have a safe journey."

We thanked him, wondering how he knew.

"What about us?" called an old man, whistling through his tombstone teeth. "We walked all the way here from fekin Milltown!"

"Ah, but you haven't the silky shorts, Michael now," said woman with a red face and a headscarf.

"If that's the price of a free pint," said Michael, "I'll buy me own and stick to wearing trousers – if you don't mind!"

It might seem to be asking for trouble, stopping at an Irish bar 20 minutes after starting our trip but it was not for the Guinness we stopped.

The atmosphere of this place sums up Ireland. It's an incredible microcosm of traditional Irish life, like a living museum: old lined faces full of character, the years of happiness and hardship there for all to see; lean, tobacco-stained men wearing battered old hats that told of harvests, rounding up sheep in a storm and falling drunk into peat bogs; laughing old women who were once chased after by half the young men in town, now toothless and aged by child-bearing or saddened by the inability to give birth; a young man propped up at the bar so in love with drink he will never marry; and pushing in behind us, a small child with a lollipop and sticky face, which she wiped surreptitiously on the tail of the local barrister's cashmere overcoat.   Here was old Ireland, condensed into one 14-foot square room.

After drinking in the atmosphere and a pint of Guinness each, Sam and I emerged from Currain's, into the arms of our well-wishers and began saying our goodbyes.   We were feeling good, but it was a genuinely tearful farewell, which we were not prepared for.

"Sam, a stroke of genius your idea to start the trip here," I said. "Well done."

These people had taken us and our quest to their hearts – of course they had, they were Irish!   The elderly lady owner of Ventry village post office shop epitomised their spirit when asked by our friend Colm to put up one of our posters for a week:

"It will go up here on the counter window Colm, where everyone will see it, and it will stay up there *pairmanently*."

Outside Currains, press photographers asked us to stand for a few more shots.   Linda, a lovely dentist from a few doors along, ran down the street to us and gave us a little dental hygiene travel-pack to pop in our bar-bags.   We were just about to go when a French lady from the Goat Street Cafe across the road, ran over with the name of a miracle injury healing cream we could buy in France.   We kissed a lot of people before we finally began moving.

As we headed out of Dingle along the peninsula, past the beautiful four-mile sandy beach at Inch, we thought of all the days we had surfed there over the years and felt a chill as we read the famous inscription on the wall of the beachside shop.

Dear Inch, must I leave you
I have promises to keep
perhaps miles to go
before my last sleep.

Despite having seen it dozens of times, this inscription, of unknown origin, had never meant as much to me as it did that day. We cycled on silently, deep in thought about what lay ahead and what we were leaving behind.

Later we stopped briefly for a picnic lunch at the roadside near Faranfore, we got quickly back on the road and were passed by Lorna dropping some of Sam's friends out to the tiny local airport. It felt strange to seeing her now we had set off.

*

I met Lorna in Japan when we were both teaching English in Tokyo. Sam says that as a small child, he heard stories about when we lived there, and that as a result it held a kind of mystique for him. He also knew that it was on the other side of the world. These two factors made Japan an obvious choice as a special place to cycle to, although at the time he had no idea of how far away it actually was. This is my version. Sam tells me now that he thinks his main motivation had been one of wanting to please me, since he realised that Japan had been an important place and time for me. Anyway, it was the place I'd met Lorna and was therefore the reason he existed.

Lorna always felt that this trip was a family effort, even though it was only Sam and I who would do the cycling, so she and the girls were almost as excited about it as we were. She was aware that it presented her with an opportunity to prove to herself that she could survive perfectly well without me, dealing with things that up to that point I had always taken responsibility for. Doing all this while holding down a very emotionally demanding job was not going to be easy, especially since she is seriously inclined towards perfectionism. She has never had a problem with being on her own – although she did have Scarlett and a dog for company – so she was not concerned about the lack of my physical presence. In fact she was looking forward to having the house and her time largely to herself. Growing up abroad in the world of the oil industry, she was also used to living in a family where the father/husband was frequently away.

*

Making good time along the straight single-track peninsula road, we received a text message from Colm telling us that we were to be on both the RTE and TG4 (Irish language) national news at 6pm and 7pm, so around 5:30 we started to look for a pub to have dinner and watch the news. We found just the place in Bally Desmond and asked the landlord if he would put on the TV. We felt uncomfortable asking as the place was pretty packed, but everybody gathered round to watch when the news came on and big cheers went up after each showing. A minor party atmosphere developed. We would need to be careful here, I told myself. In Ireland a situation like this could easily end up with the expedition being held up for two days while good luck is showered upon the travellers along with quantities of drink. I hesitated as we were bought Guinness and had our photographs taken with several groups of ladies who were on their way home to Cork.

By the time we managed to leave we had been given about 50 euros for our chosen charity (The Rising Sun Domestic Violence Project) and felt like we were being carried along by a magic carpet of Irish good fortune.

In the 25km from the pub to the small town of Boherbouys, we had many groups of people wave to us from gardens and cars, shouting things like, "Saw you on the news, fair play to you lads!" Around around 9pm as we came into Boherbouys, a car overtook and pulled up sharply in front of us. I felt my pockets to see if I'd left anything at the pub. A man got out saying that they had just seen us on the news and his wife had told him to get the car out so she could shake our hands. After prolonged shaking of the grinning lady's hand we were asked where we were heading for, as it was now dusk. We said we were looking for a place to camp.

"Oh no, you don't!" said the man (whose name was Gerry). "You see that cottage over there, that's our rental place and it's been empty since Christmas while we're doing it up. There are sheets on the beds and milk in the fridge for tea, so here's the key now. Just pop it through our door across the street when you leave in the morning."

How much more good fortune could this country shower on us?

Sam was feeling pretty tired (drained from the night before) and was thrilled to see a working TV and a comfortable sofa to slob out on. We cleaned up and bought some provisions at the local Spar shop. Returning to the house, a drunk tried to accost us as we fiddled with the front door lock.

"Hey, what d'fuk you doin' going into dat house?"

Propped against a fence, he tried to run towards us but tripped several times and ended up getting himself caught on the garden fence. Grimacing, he had already given up before we managed to close the door on him. We went into the front room and looked out from behind the tattered net curtains. He had now dragged himself over to Gerry's house and was speaking to Gerry at his front door. We waved from the front window. Gerry signalled back with a thumbs-up.

The next time we looked out we saw Gerry shooing him out of the garden with Gerry's wife looking angrily out of the window. The drunk now despatched to the street, Gerry went back inside, but the guy soon returned and lay down in Gerry's front garden. At that point we lost interest.

Upstairs in the darkened bedroom, tired after a challenging day, Sam was straight to sleep. Half an hour later, though, he began murmuring:

"Maybe he was a friend of Gerry's, y'know, or a relative. He could be Gerry's brother – the black sheep."

*

One good night's sleep later, we headed off in the early morning light, depositing the keys and a bottle of wine at Gerry's house. Sam did his best to disguise the bottle behind a small pot plant in case the Black Sheep returned early.

"He won't be up until late anyway," I assured Sam. But just as we rounded the corner into the main street we saw him trudging down the hill. His gait was unmistakable. Barrelling along, tripping at various points, both arms were held out like a man about to go into a rugby scrum. People coming up the hill crossed the road when they saw him coming. He saw us as we coasted past, swung around and growled something incomprehensible. Looking back, we noticed that at some point in the night he had collected a large gash down his face.

"Perhaps Gerry's wife walloped him with a frying pan," Sam suggested.

I had wanted to start early on this second day, mainly because I held onto a faint but stupid hope that we might make it the whole 104 miles to Waterford that day. We had arranged in advance to stay in great comfort with some Irish friends from Canterbury who were there on holiday, although it did seem a tall order to do it in one day. Sam asked over breakfast where we would stop the night. I said we would wait and see how we felt and how far we could get. He was suspicious from that point on.

"I will not be able to make it to Waterford by tonight!" he assured me curtly when we stopped for a picnic lunch.

I consoled myself with the knowledge that people often tell themselves they cannot manage things, but with a little encouragement and good fortune they can surprise themselves.

It was by such devious means that Sam later found himself only 25km from Waterford, eating an early supper in a pub on Dungarvan seafront. He was shattered but – looking at me with accusation – grudgingly agreed that it was worth making the effort to do the last 25km to reach our friends' house that night. The little coast road from Dungarvan to Tramore was beautiful. Perhaps 'spectacular' is a fairer description. Unfortunately, it rose up and down between each tiny bay like a crazy switchback at a fairground. Halfway to Tramore Sam did not even have the energy to lift his leg over the crossbar to take a five-minute break.

"Dad, I really can't go any further," came a faltering voice from behind.

Still trying to manage him, I told him I totally understood and that we would look for a field to camp in, then do the last 12km in the morning. I was quite confident that this would not happen. Smugness was not far from the back of my mind. Nevertheless, we cycled along looking for a suitable field and before too long we came to a café where we ate some greasy sausage and chips with some lurid coloured fizzy drink. This arterial glue boosted Sam slightly, enough for us to reach Tramore and some B&Bs anyway, I thought. I was just preparing my next persuasive statement in my head when, at the first roundabout, Sam signalled that we should continue on the Waterford road.

"Hah!" I said to myself. "Right again!"

Sam was silent in his determination to complete this gruelling day of never-ending steep hills. His silence barely masked his fury with me. He was almost on autopilot now. His body was running on some final hidden reserve of energy after which it would go into coma – or so it seemed at the time.

We had only about 8km to go now so I knew that, barring disasters, we would be there in half an hour. Following the directions we had been given we reached a junction where there shouldn't have been one and we had to stop at a house to check. Puzzling over the poetic Irish instructions, we headed up a long steep hill for a couple of miles expecting to find the house near the top, but it did not materialise. In desperation I flagged down a car and asked. We were miles in the wrong direction but the driver knew the right way. Sam's eyes burned holes in me. I had to save the situation. Darkness was descending upon us so I phoned our friend Dee and was given strict instructions to wait at a roundabout at the end of the lane. Meeting her there, I was stunned by the nearly catatonic Sam's refusal of a lift in her 4x4.

"We're fine, we'll follow you," he said, adopting a cheerful demeanour.

Ten minutes later we reached the house. Naturally, it was at the top of a steep hill and Sam's chain came off half way up it, but we got there and were welcomed by a whole bunch of cheering children with a big banner. It all seemed worthwhile to me then. And this was only day two!

I tried to justify my dastardly plan to Sam later that evening after he'd been warmed by T-bone steak with roast potatoes, copious wine and endless kindness.

"You see, Sam, at 6am you couldn't see any way you could do a hundred miles to Waterford, and by lunch you were sure you couldn't. Then by 7pm you thought you were going to die, but by 8:30 you'd made it. Now we can have *two* nights here in comfort and you've learned that you're always capable of much more than you think you are."

Stupidly, I was pretty pleased with what I had taught him. It would serve him well for the rest of the trip, I told myself. But Sam was not impressed. All he'd learned, he felt, was what an idiot his Dad was. He felt tricked and said that although he felt proud of his achievement, he would still rather have stopped after 100km as per our original daily target. Now, feeling rather less self-righteous, I had learned something to serve *me* for the rest of the trip too.

*

I felt uncomfortable during those two days outside Waterford. I lay awake thinking about it in bed the first night. Surely the right thing to do was to make the first week a succession of easy cycling days so that Sam got back to Canterbury feeling positive about the road ahead. Instead I had convinced him that every day would be a living hell. It seemed unbelievable to me that I would intentionally subject my own son to the very thing I railed against as a child – being forced or manipulated into doing something I didn't want to do. And then to think I could get away with it?

Sam has always been the quieter member of a family dominated by people who have a lot to say and plenty of determination to say it. Like me, he always had a dreaminess about him as a boy, with a tendency to be over-sensitive. We frequently groaned at Sam for not noticing what to the rest of us was obvious. On several occasions after we'd all been talking about going on holiday for weeks, we would pack the car, get up early and head off excitedly for the airport or ferry port. Then, half an hour down the road, Sam would ask where we were going. We found this an endearing quality. He felt not knowing about it was perfectly natural.

Sam's alternative way of seeing the world extended to many other things in our lives. He often seemed to have totally missed the point in discussions or in his answers to questions, but what often transpired was that he had a far more profound insight than the rest of us, often expressing his ideas in what I would have to describe as poetic terms. It was fascinating, moving, and sometimes quite shocking.   Unfortunately school does a good job of trying to knock this sort of alternative approach out of you, but he still retains it as a character trait thank goodness.

Sam's behaviour as a young boy may have encouraged me to think I could push him to cycle further than planned, since it included him having no sense of any practical challenges being difficult.   For me this was really admirable, although I think it worried Lorna, since I myself have an *anything is possible* approach to physical challenges that she regards as extreme.   With increasing maturity, Sam has learned to be more reasoned in his expectations, whereas I still persist doggedly with blind faith.   It was this I had failed to account for that second day, and I think the misjudgement knocked my confidence more than his.

*

After two comfortable nights we continued on our way, crossing the Irish Sea between Rosslare and Pembroke Dock.   Again we met with cheers, free Guinness and encouragement from people who'd seen us on television.   Our ferry docked in Wales and we were friends again, with big smiles on our faces.

One of the questions the Irish Press had asked a lot was which country we were most worried about cycling through: Iran, China, Cambodia?   Each time, I replied, "Wales." I knew what some of the roads were like there.   Instead of going around hills they go straight up and over the top.   The comment was supposed to be humorous, but the joke was on us.   Once we turned east from Carmarthen, the hills became like a small child's drawing of tall peaks with little houses perched on the tops.   Some of the hills were so steep that the terraced houses beside the road were stacked with the roof of one at the same level as the front door of its conjoined neighbour.   At the tops of these rain-beaten villages in the sky, solemn brass bands practiced in damp village halls.   There used to be a Hovis bread advertisement on television with similar villages, but that was far less extreme.

We passed through about half a dozen of these *pinnacle villages*, enduring pouring rain for most of the day until we reached a small hamlet called Llannon. I could see a town named Pontarddulais on the map and I felt there would be a B&B here. Not seeing any road signs for Pontarddulais, I entered a pub and asked a man inside the door for directions.

"Could you tell me which road to take for *Pont Ardulais* please," I said, assuming from the spelling that the name was of French origin.

The landlord (Dick), a leather-tanned man of about 55 wearing a t-shirt and a pair of very short shorts (as men this age sometimes do), sniggered to himself. He seemed fixated upon my tight lycra cycling shorts – a little unnerving.

"Well now, just follow me a minute and we'll see if any of these gentlemen know," he said ushering me inside. "Hey lads this chap's cycling and needs directions. Where to you for mate?"

His Welsh sentence construction amused me. "Pont Ardulais," I said with a smile and an exaggerated aristocratic English accent, happy now to enter into the joke.

They all fell about laughing of course and after asking me to make several more attempts for their entertainment, explained the correct local pronunciation – *Ponta-doolis*. I asked Dick, who then called Sam in and welcomed us both hospitably, whether I might find a campsite or B&B in *Ponta-doolis*. He and the men at the bar made serious *oohing* sounds, lowered their eyes and shook their heads.

Was Pontarddulais not the best place to stay nearby?   I asked.

"Well," said Dick sternly, "it's all right if you want to get mugged or raped."

He mouthed the words with relish and opened his eyes wide like the teller of a children's ghost story.   The locals at the bar seemed to agree, so I asked where we could find a better alternative.   Dick, who had clearly missed his vocation as a theatre actor (or pantomime dame) breathed deeply and struck a serious pose at the bar.

"Well, the workhouse is closed down, look you   Daffyd here has a shed but he's got ferrets in it now.   Gwyn's got a spare room but his wife's kicked him out.   Normally I'd have said have our bath, but I'm in there since the wife moved her toy-boy in.   So no, you've come on a bad day, like."

His performance over, he kindly gave us directions to a very good B&B along the country lane.   Thanking him, we remounted our bikes and headed off down a manure-splattered lane, agreeing to return for dinner and more entertainment by the 9pm kitchen deadline.

At the B&B we were informed shiftily by the English patrons that they were full.   It was 8:20pm and there was only one vehicle in the car park so this seemed unlikely, but no amount of looking exhausted or explaining that we had just cycled from Ireland thawed their resolve.   We headed back along the lane to a field we had passed on our way there.   After pitching the tent behind the hedge, where we might not be seen, we quickly made our way back to the pub for dinner before the restaurant closed.

Revived by a truly delicious dinner, we discovered from Dick, that he came from the same town as Lorna's relatives on the other side of Wales – our next planned stop in fact.   Miraculously, he knew Lorna's uncle and cousin well.   A day later, when I checked with Lorna's cousin, we discovered that he was once a notorious modern-day highwayman of sorts, who had spent time at Her Majesty's pleasure before escaping to Spain.   Nobody had seen him since.

Returning to our field, we climbed the gate and found the tent undisturbed.   It was beginning to rain so we fastidiously cleaned our teeth and got straight into our sleeping bags.   After such a hard day's cycling we were quickly asleep.   Around an hour later, I was awoken by Sam nudging me.

"Dad, there's someone walking around outside the tent," he whispered.

I listened and said that I thought it was the wind getting up and raindrops that were just starting to fall.   Sam went back to sleep, but lying there quietly afterwards I heard the footsteps he had been talking about.   From the sounds and some careful deduction I felt pretty sure that it was a large farmer in Wellington boots, probably with a dog, and he was walking around the tent in ever-decreasing circles.   I waited for the sound of a shotgun being cocked.   By now there seemed no point in hoping that he wouldn't see us, so I boldly unzipped the tent and looked out into the dark to greet him.

What I saw horrified me.   A large group of cows had encircled the tent.   They looked half-curious and half-annoyed at the intrusion. One even scraped the ground with its hoof as bulls do in Spain before they charge at a Matador.   I had checked that there were no livestock in the field before we pitched there, but these ladies must have been let into the field after milking.   I shook Sam.

"We have to move the tent.   Cows aren't aggressive but they are curious, and they'll probably trample the tent and us inside without meaning to."

For once Sam did not take his time getting up.   Climbing out into rain that soon became a thunderstorm, we unpegged the tent with everything still inside.   Trying our best to laugh, we zipped it up then carried it carefully over the gate and down the lane in the pitch-black until we reached the road junction at the foot of the hill.   There we quickly repitched it behind a hedge and ran back up the lane to get our bikes.   Back down the hill we climbed into the tent, drenched and muddy, intermittently cursing then laughing at our plight.   This seemed a little extreme even for Wales.   If it was this bad so close to home, how would we cope with the more inhospitable parts of the world we were planning to cycle through?

Woken early the next morning by the sound of a tractor, I heard a man's voice: "Gwyn, those f'ing Swampies are back. Give Sergeant Pryce a call when you get back up the house!"

I got Sam up as quickly as I could.

*

The rain continued to fall on a miserable South Wales and we were happy to reach Lorna's aunt and uncle's house by evening for some home comforts.   We arrived to Welsh-cakes straight from the oven and followed that with a trip to the rugby club with Lorna's uncle. Here we were entertained with stories of Dick, the notorious local highwayman.   The misery of the day before was soon forgotten in the midst of warm Welsh hospitality.   We would happily have stayed longer but Sam was eager to see his friends.   Fortunately, though, we did delay the following morning to visit the then semi-derelict Newbridge Miners Institute.   Sam and I were given our own private tour of the place, with its sadly fading regency theatre, the *green room* with dusty old armchairs and smoke-stained old posters of postwar stars still pinned to the walls.   It was a perfect film set waiting to be discovered.   Like Currain's bar in Dingle, the place seemed to encapsulate something of traditional local life. Looking down from the lighting control room onto the dusty banks of theatre seating and panelled walls, I could imagine what it must have been like filled with miners and their wives. The atmosphere, the look and the smell of the place, constructed to provide some pleasure and dignity to people living in hardship, is as vivid in my memory now as it was the day we stepped inside.

The heavy rain returned to persecute us all the way into the west of England later that day. The comforts and hospitality of Newbridge had been left behind. We cycled for an hour waiting for a suitable lunch spot. The cigarette-butt-strewn vandalised bus shelter we found (the only dry place) hardly did justice to Auntie Margaret's hearty sandwiches. But at least we needed no encouragement to move on.

Crossing the enormous Severn Bridge by bike was pretty exciting. The rain held off for a bit as we wound our way through pretty villages north of Bristol until our arrival at a sleazy B&B in Chippenham. It was a strange place, used mainly it seemed by travelling workers. It was run by a jovial Asian man, who was interested in our trip and asked us about our route. He then gave us a tour of framed posters in his reception. These were pictures of him shaking hands with various celebrities. President Reagan, Prince Phillip, Muhammad Ali the boxer, Elizabeth Taylor – this guy seemed to be very well connected for the owner of a seedy B&B in Chippenham. It was only on closer inspection that it became apparent that these were photoshopped montages. The exception was the one with Muhammad Ali, which we realised, had in fact been taken in Madame Tussauds waxworks museum.

Having hung up our tent to dry in the bathroom, Sam and I went off to find some hearty food to warm us up. Midway through our sausages and mash, sitting in the window of a pub down the road, we witnessed a complete deluge and watched an endless parade of buxom mini-skirted girls strolling casually by as if taking part in a Club 18-30 wet t-shirt contest. They make them tough in the West Country.

*

Making our way across country into Hampshire, Sam suggested that we dispense with the planned rest days on our journey to Canterbury – partly to test our stamina, but mainly so that he could have more time with his mates back home before we left for France. Privately, though, I knew that one of them had become more than a friend since Dingle and that he was eager to see where things might go with her. Lorna, incidentally, felt that this showed a typical case of teenage lack of foresight – waiting until just before he was about to leave was bad timing, as it meant that he would be less able to focus upon the trip. Sam at least pretended he didn't mind one way or the other.

Without the rest days, we prematurely found ourselves approaching Cranbrook in Kent, near to where Lorna's brother and sister-in-law lived. After texting them to say we were unexpectedly in their area and in need of a bed, arrangements were made for intruding upon their evening and we pushed on. At around 5pm, we stopped at the cashpoint machine in Cranbrook centre. I may have been distracted by the prospect of the known long steep hill out of town, I don't know, but as I remounted my bike I lost my balance and lazily allowed myself to topple over. Getting up, I was aware of a dull pain above my inner ankle. I looked down and Sam followed my gaze. Blood was flowing. I ignored it and continued in my determined pursuit of the top of Cranbrook Hill. In my mind, I was already in a hot bath in Glyn and Sylvia's house. The gashed leg could wait.

At Glyn and Sylvia's we found the key as arranged, over-rode the solar water heating as instructed and ran the bath. After examining my injured shin, Sam pronounced with concern (tinged with amusement) that the bone was visible. Laughing idiotically, I reassured him that the flesh is thin there and that I heal quickly. Taking the second bath, I washed the gruesome injury clean, and we headed over to the pub opposite. Here we waited for Glyn and Sylvia to return from a Jazz in the Park event. The Bell and Jorrocks was just the right kind of pub for that moment, and Sam and I sat happily drinking local Kent cider, listening to eighties classics for a couple of hours until they arrived.

There followed a pleasant, restful night, although I ruined a perfectly good sheet by oozing blood all over it. In my world, ignoring something makes it disappear. This puts me in mind of a superb Sociology teacher I had at boarding school. Helpful and succinct, this man was also a communist, who insisted we call him Stu rather than Mr Cole. Once, struggling to understand existentialism I asked him for help.

"Stu, what's existentialism?"

"See that chair over there?" he said.

"Yeah."

"OK, turn around."

I complied.

"Now the chair doesn't exist."

He walked away. Enough said. I liked this philosophy. Now, however, although I avoided looking at this wound on my leg, I knew it existed. It hurt. Explain that one, Stu!

*

Riding back to Canterbury the following afternoon, we were accompanied by Sam's oldest friend, Luke, who we met at the foot of Charing Hill with his latest carbon-fibre race bike. This long local hill was familiar to us. As jaded as we were, though, Luke spurred us to our fastest ever 15-mile stretch.

Climbing that long hill together, I thought back to when he and Sam were eleven and we had gone on a dads and sons cycle trip to France. Cycling back along the coast road from Quiberville to Dieppe over some big hills, Brendan and I had been impressed by the grit the two boys showed in leading us up the biggest climbs then the thrill they felt powering through the downhills. Back on the ferry to Newhaven, Brendan asked them which bit of our five-day trip they had enjoyed the most. Both said that their favourite bits had been the hills.

"What, the whizzing downhill bits?" we asked.

"No, climbing up those big steep hills!" they insisted.

We reached Canterbury in no time at all. By 6pm Sam had showered and gone off to play a Championship Final game of five-a-side football (which they won). With the first 815 km under our belts, Sam's confidence was high. Having arrived home four days early, I think we both felt more positive about the physical challenges that lay ahead.

SAM'S POINT OF VIEW

The key thing at this stage has to be my mum (Lorna) saying to my dad, 'Remember you're allowed to enjoy this.' It would have proved useful if she'd reminded him later on in the trip, when tensions between my dad and I had risen beyond boiling point. Unfortunately she wasn't around. You can imagine two blokes trying to communicate in such extreme circumstances; it was mind-blowing. To be fair to my dad, though, he's not as annoying as he thinks. I gave him a lot of stick at the start because I was so upset about leaving my friends and being taken around by my dad. At 18, I'd guess most guys are craving independence, so I didn't feel I was heading in the right direction. In retrospect, that was so naive.

Setting off, my general mind-set was to take everything in small chunks. Really small! For the first month I'd aim to make it to lunch, then dinner, then the next day and so on. This explains why food became such a dominant feature.

The second day's cycling across Ireland left me with mixed feelings. I was proud that I'd managed such a massive distance. This helped me prepare mentally for tougher challenges ahead, but I was angry. It was typical of my dad to go way beyond the agreed distance. I felt powerless, and that I was being pushed. This was 50% about me giving in to my dad too easily, and 50% him being excessively persuasive. He's just too 'driven' to ever give up. Many have said he'd make an excellent lawyer; they'd be right!

Arriving home after the first leg did feel great. I knew then that I could achieve what was in front of us. I never really thought that the cycling was going to be the hard part. We both knew that being in close proximity to each other for so long would be the toughest mountain to climb. I wondered how healthy this would really be for our relationship.

CALAIS to ISTANBUL
Distance cycled
2,913 km - 1,810 miles

Dover
NETHERLANDS
Calais
Menneville
St Quentin
Le Havre
Laon
Paris
Metz
Seine
Meuse
Rhine
Dortmund
Brussels
GERMANY
Berlin
Warsaw
Pripyat
Bug
Odra
POLAND
Vistula
Leipzig
Frankfurt
Prague
CZECH REPUBLIC
Krakow
Vistula
Kiyev
UKRAINE
L'vov
Dnestr
Stuttgart
Inglostadt
SLOVAK REPUBLIC
Strasburg
Sigmaringen
Donau
Donnaueschingen
Passau
Vienna
Bratislava
MOLDOVA
FRANCE
Munich
Petronel Carnuntum
Gyor
Budapest
Odessa
Prut
Loire
LIECGTENSTEIN
SWITZERLAND
AUSTRIA
Graz
HUNGARY
Csongrad
CARPATHIANS
Zurich
Lyon
MASSIF CENTRAL
Rhône
SLOVENIA
Milan
Ljubljana
Zagreb
Timisoara
ROMANIA
Caransebes
Po
CROATIA
Bucharest
ITALY
Bologna
SAN-MARINO
BOSNIA-HERZEGOVINA
Sarajevo
Belgrade
Orsova
Nice
MONACO
Marseilles
ADRIATIC SEA
Calafat
Danube
Kozloduj
BULGARIA
Corsica
Elba
Tiber
YUGOSLAVIA
Stara Planina
Sofiya
Ajaccio
Sardinia
TYRRHENIAN SEA
Rome
Naples
ALBANIA
Skopje
MACEDONIA
Tirane
Star Zagora
Istanbul
Serrai
Ipsala
Minorca

Chapter 2

Western Europe – Moving away from home

As a man with daughters, I never trust young men on bikes. Something with hoofs or an engine – they're harder to sneak about with.

Arriving back home just eight days after setting off on a 10,000-mile trip was a bit of a challenge psychologically. We knew, however, that it made sense from a practical point of view and had deliberately planned it that way. It gave us a chance to get fit and test our equipment, then change things once we got home if needed. We were also able to service and readjust the bikes, as well as sort out my bar-bag mounting. In most respects it worked really well, but waving goodbye again after a second leaving party still felt odd.

The five-day break at home also gave me a little time to reflect upon the first leg. There had been one glaring error: my belief that I could use devious means to trick Sam into covering a hundred miles on day two had not been vindicated by Sam being grateful for it later. Despite agreeing that it was good to know what he could do, resentment towards me for manipulating him was still very evident. It seemed my plan had been more obvious than I had believed – utterly transparent, in fact. On the positive side, though, I had seen how a challenging expedition like this presents an opportunity for such personal faults to be addressed. After uncomfortably owning up to my trickery and criminal hypocrisy, I felt a long way towards putting it right, and I already felt much better for that. Nobody was more relived than Lorna. Of course, she had been putting up with it for years. *Change the record!*

*

When Sam and I made our first bike trip, back when he was only ten, it had been him who pushed me to do more. I took this as an indication of his character, assuming that he was taking after me. Later on, after we had returned home from Japan, he told me it had all been about wanting to please me and trying to encourage me to do more things with him. I can see it did lead me to labour under a false impression all those years. Or perhaps it was just an impression of him that suited me.

I think the desire I felt to escape from my parents that I talked about at the start of the book was a cause of worry for me with my own children. I always worried that they would be as difficult as I had been, and this was especially true of my son. Assuming he would feel the same things I had, I tried hard to encourage him to do adventurous things with me, in order that he would have less determination to do them alone – less desire to take crazy risks.

Crazy risks of course were my stock-in-trade as a child, and this continued well into adulthood. My parents must have been in a constant state of stress about what I might do next. I came to see how every news report about some tragic accident involving a child plunged them into thoughts about how long it would be before that was me. It was written on their faces.

Around 1961, after I had already demonstrated my determination to escape the confines of home by the age of three, an era of conflict ensued within our family unit, with my mum nervously trying to keep me safe and my dad, like most fathers of that time, seeing his role as one of needing to instruct wisely and then be obeyed. I didn't mind that; in fact, I relished the challenge. My bike became a regular feature in my spirited breaks for freedom, and its withdrawal became my regular punishment. This made for a volatile family dynamic that stretched us all to the limits. Years later, when I had children of my own and my father was long dead at 37, I was determined not to repeat the wrongs my father and I had perpetrated upon each other. I hoped this trip might help me to make sure of that.

*

As we prepared to leave Canterbury, I felt eager to get back on the road and continue our ride to Japan, but I was a little sad to leave Lorna.   Up to this point, I had not felt I would have a problem being away from her.   I had felt secure.   The fact that she also seemed unworried by the prospect of my absence had helped me not to be concerned, so my moment of sentiment took me by surprise.   I consoled myself with the fact that we had agreed Lorna would fly over to meet us for a few days in Istanbul about six weeks later.   It seemed like a good arrangement.   We were going to need to be there for a few weeks to obtain our Iran visas, since trying to get them in England had all gone wrong at the last minute.   But it was also reassuring to know that if we forgot anything, Lorna could bring it over.   Also, she would hopefully be able to see for herself that we were not on death's door or ready to strangle each other.

These kinds of contingency arrangements had been worked out from the practice trips we had made over the eight years leading up to our start and in general they served us well.

Lorna was key to the success of the trip.   She persuaded me of its value, bolstered my confidence about being able to take the time off, readily took on the running of all family and financial management tasks, and even looked after my personal financial affairs.   She did all this without complaint and contacted me about such tiresome things during the trip only if it were absolutely necessary, as she didn't want me to be stressed.   In the eight-year buildup to the trip, Lorna regularly had talked Sam through his anxieties about it – in particular, putting up with his dad 24 hours a day for ten months.   And for all of this she asked for very little praise or payback.   Luck has no part in this really.   Yes, I feel lucky, but in our family we believe in helping each other to achieve our desires rather than competing.   I think I can speak for our whole family when I say that it's well worth the effort.

*

My five rest days leading to our second start were spent getting minor things sorted out on the bikes and making a few changes to the clothes I would take.   As expected, I felt I needed less, although most people felt we were already taking remarkably little. Clothing could be bought en route. Besides, Lorna could bring things or take them back from Istanbul. During this time, I was disappointed more than annoyed that Sam spent every day sleeping until the afternoon, and every night out partying with his friends until the early hours. I did not begrudge him time to celebrate with his friends – after all he was embarking on a major expedition and would not see them for nearly a year – but I had hoped he might show some interest in getting things prepared. What I was conveniently forgetting, of course, was how scarred he had been by the 104-mile journey on our second day out of Dingle.

The whole period of time in Canterbury had a strange sensation about it. I really didn't feel we should be there. I would even go as far as to say I resented the interruption. In my mind, we had already begun the trip, so hanging about at home in relative luxury just felt wrong. I was not alone. Friends phoned to speak to Lorna and were surprised to find me there. *Had there been a problem?* It was all very annoying having to explain that we had planned this but arrived back in Canterbury quicker than expected. The extra time was the crux of the matter. A couple of days would have been manageable, but five days' rest at this stage was like mental torture. I remember mentioning this to Sam the day before we left. He just looked at me as if I were speaking a foreign language.

*

Saturday 9 August was another rainy day, but a large and enthusiastic crowd of friends, plus a few newspaper reporters, saw us leave home in good spirits. Sam was in a familiar morning-after haze. As in times long past, it seemed as if he were not exactly sure where we were going. Our friend Brendan escorted us by bike as far as Dover, where we were to catch a ferry to Calais. Brendan and I chatted as we rode along the cycle path, remembering a bike trip to Rouen with the boys (Sam, and Brendan's son, Luke) when they were eleven. Most of all, we recalled how he and I had over-imbibed with Calvados one lunchtime and I had pushed us along too hard in the afternoon. After arriving at the campsite, Brendan had lain down for an hour, thinking he was having a heart attack. At the time I had thought it was a joke, but he assured me it wasn't. Back then, we had talked about the idea of the Japan trip and it seemed surreal that those vague ideas were at this moment becoming reality.

Our hilarity and comfortable sense of well-being were short-lived, however. Sam's fuzzy state and my nostalgic conversation with Brendan had resulted in Sam falling behind and getting lost. As I began to worry about missing the ferry, Brendan noticed stress creep into my voice. It seemed perverse that Sam could get lost in his own backyard and drop behind so soon in the proceedings. All was well soon, however. Thanks to Nokia mobile phone technology, we were quickly back on track and flying down the long hill to Dover docks. Brendan saw us off, then headed back as the rain began to gently fall.

"Don't worry, Sam, once we're into southern Europe it'll be sun every day," I said, attempting to raise some enthusiasm in my still dormant son.

"I wasn't worried," he muttered gruffly. He seemed offended.

It was only a short wait until we boarded the ferry, but during that time a number of people wandered over to speak to us.

"Are you cycling far once you get to France?"

"Only to Japan."

"Blimey, how long's that going to take?"

"Around nine months, give or take. We'll be back in ten months."

"Ten months! Where's your luggage?"

We boarded the P&O ferry as special guests, arranged for us by our friend Nigel, P&O's chief purser. On leave that week, he had arranged for his deputy to look after us on board. This taste of life as minor celebrities cheered us both up, and Sam even began to show signs of awakening from his dormant state.

After a delicious lunch, we hardly minded the heavy rain that greeted us as we coasted onto French soil.

Heading out of Calais, we followed directions given to us by Alain, another cycling friend, whose house 50km to the south we were to stay at that night. It was not great to be beginning our journey under grey skies, but we felt confident and full of enthusiasm for the trip ahead. I was ultra-careful on the road, though. In the years leading up to the trip, I had read Chris Smith's excellent book about cycling to China, *Why Don't You Fly.* He had suffered a nasty crash on a wet road in Calais at the start of his journey and nearly had to abandon his trip. I didn't want that happening to us.

The rain had awoken Sam and we were now having our first minor disagreements about directions. To lighten the mood, we talked about how moving it had been to have all those people (well over a hundred) at our house to see us off and what the scene must be like there now. A few stragglers would probably be drinking up the remains of champagne and beginning to think of the canapés as an early lunch.

*

We also remembered that the last time we had cycled through Calais was on a winter trip to Gent in Belgium when Sam was about fourteen. After this point in the eight-year buildup, Sam abandoned the Japan trip idea for a while. I think it is worth recounting the story since it helps to explain where I got some things badly wrong with him.

A typically contrary teenager back then, Sam had insisted he would pack his stuff in the early morning before we left, rejecting my suggestion that he would not be able to focus at such a time. After setting off, and in a rush to get to the ferry, I noticed that he was wearing his sister's miniscule woollen gloves. When asked what had happened to his waterproof cycling gloves, he grunted something about not being able to find them when we left. This scenario will be familiar to most parents.

My particular *dad* philosophy is that after children are a certain age you make them responsible for remembering their own coats, gloves, etc. If they don't bother, they learn from painful experience. I was to learn the downside of this philosophy that morning as the weather turned colder and sleet began to sting our faces. Sam's joke gloves became more of a liability than a benefit. His hands purple from the cold, I realised the trip could not continue if I didn't get him some new gloves. We eventually found a motorcycle shop, where I was forced to buy him an overpriced leather pair that allowed us to reach St Omer that night.   We reached Gent the next day, but I had needed to push Sam in order to make up the time the glove fiasco had lost us.   Needless to say, Sam saw this as entirely my fault, not his, much like the driving sleet that cut into us all the way back again over the following two days.

To a resilient adult, this kind of experience might have been fortifying.   For a 14-year-old, however, it was too much.   When we finally arrived frozen at Dunkirk, our bad luck on that trip culminated in being turned away from the port, due to a broken dock, and having to ride a further ten miles to Calais.   Sam, who seemed to take a week to thaw out, told Lorna privately upon our return that he no longer wanted to do the Japan trip.

I did learn that taking cycling trips in the depths of a North European winter was probably unwise as a confidence-builder for a 14-year-old boy.   Unfortunately, though, I had still not understood that Sam didn't enjoy those punishing expeditionary experiences in which you endure pain but eventually overcome seemingly impossible obstacles to arrive at success – at least, not in the same way I did.

Fortunately, Sam did get over that crushing experience and I would still argue it made us mentally stronger.   It also taught us some valuable lessons about planning and contingencies.   Now, cycling through Calais docks again four years later, I felt we would benefit on this trip.

Chilling memories of the Gent trip continued to nag in both our minds all day, but they were forgotten once we reached Alain's house in Menneville.

*

Fran, Alain's wife, made us feel at home in their farmhouse, creating a positive ending to our first day in France.   An excellent dinner and a really good first night's sleep certainly put a good complexion on our second morning, as did the lovely French breakfast I ate while I waited for the rain to abate.

Deep in thought, I passed the morning conversing with the donkeys in the garden as I waited for Sam to come down.   He had a lot of sleep to catch up on and I was already beginning to feel I needed to be more relaxed about scheduling. I patted the donkey's noses, telling them I was determined not to spend the trip getting annoyed with Sam for not being up early. It was not a race. As Lorna said, we were allowed to enjoy it.

The wait was fortuitous. By the time Sam was ready to go, the rain had stopped and there was an invigorating aroma of sun drying rain on pine trees. The calming sound of cowbells accompanied us as we cycled due south through green hills and lush valleys.

Reaching St Quentin by lunchtime, we called at a convenient roadside snack bar on the outskirts of town. I was not crazy about the fastfood menu, but Sam was keen on trying their maxi-burger, so we went in. The food was better and more generous than expected and Sam's burger actually filled a full-sized dinner plate. Most of the other customers looked like freaks – circus performers, perhaps. Seeing the bikes and our cycle clothing, they asked where we were cycling. "Tokyo, *Japon*," we answered casually. This caused a bit of a stir.

Someone went over to explain to the owner. At the same time, a small bald man wandered outside to look at our bikes.

"Human cannonball," I told Sam.

"Or lion-tamer," he laughed.

A man came out of the toilet and tripped over his own oversized feet.

"Clown," we mouthed at each other in unison.

The man bumped into an empty table, dislodging a glass that bounced off his hand when he stretched out an elongated arm, sending it spinning in the air. After fumbling desperately, he managed to catch it in his other hand. Relieved, he replaced it on the table but kicked the table leg as he walked away, nearly sending everything cascading onto the floor. He smiled at us as he passed.

"Juggler," we agreed.

A cheerful-looking lady at the next table heard us and translated for her small children. The children roared with laughter and began trying to juggle with their French fries, one small boy proving most adept at tossing them into the air and catching them in his mouth.

"Arête, Christophe!" she insisted. *"Arête, ou pas de desert."*

The boys beamed when they saw Sam smiling.

The commotion brought the rotund owner out from behind his counter. Boasting a hefty physique and curly-ended moustache we supposed could belong only to a former strongman, our host remonstrated with the big-footed clown. We almost expected fake tears to squirt from his glasses. The strongman ducked down behind his counter, then returned with a small camera to have his photo taken with us, saying he would have it made into a big poster and put on the wall. He asked what we had eaten and promptly insisted on returning all our money. Good luck seemed to be following us.

That night and the following five until we reached Metz, we camped at small *camping municipal*. We settled into a healthy daily routine of cycling over hills, staying at small country town campsites and eating fresh local food. Sam and I were getting on well now, my French had returned after the first few stumbling days and summer sun had replaced the rain, so life was sweet. At this point, you would expect something to go wrong, but it didn't.

Metz was more beautiful than I remembered from passing through years before. We also had the unexpected pleasure of being shown around the city by a young university lecturer who I had contacted, as I had Alain, via a cycle-touring website.

*

It had become apparent to me around this point that Sam seemed rather more quiet and pensive than usual. His relationship with Hannah had begun to develop further in Ireland and then moved on quickly back in Canterbury. It now seemed to have been put pragmatically on hold, but I concluded that it must be what was troubling him. But when I asked, he said that was not exactly the problem.

He was finding, he said, that having so much time every day to think on the bike was making him inward-looking and rather self-conscious as a result. He was starting to wonder about what he was really like as a person and whether the great relationships he had enjoyed with a wide circle of friends were based upon anything real or whether he was popular for primarily trivial reasons.

No amount of gentle reassurance from me that these were very normal and healthy concerns for someone his age seemed to make much of a dent in the problem. In fact, I often seemed to say the wrong thing and make him feel worse.

Certainly, I think it was during this time that I realised timing played a critical part in determining whether conversations with Sam were successful or not. He was always quiet in the mornings and although he could cope with the odd short essential question, he responded badly to any invitation for a discussion. It was at this point I made a rule for myself that I think might benefit most parents dealing with teenage children:

Never attempt to engage a teenager in conversation before lunch.

Sam dismisses the validity of this, but it has worked well for me ever since.

I was missing the help that Lorna and I have always received on such matters from Alex, our eldest daughter. From quite an early age, her precocious insight into human relationships made her a valuable source of advice and good sense with both her younger brother and sister, and even with issues we were trying to resolve for ourselves. In her final year of training as a contemporary dancer, she was away studying hard in London most of the time during our trip but visited home more to support Lorna and still maintained her regular family role with Lorna and Scarlett. Sam and I, though, were limited to periodic emails.

*

After three days' rest in Metz we cleaned and lubricated the bikes then headed off east towards the German border and the Rhine.   There, we planned to continue east towards Budapest. We had agreed to give Lorna a date to come to Istanbul once we arrived in Budapest and had a better idea of our realistic pace. A week out of Canterbury, we were already managing well in excess of our planned 100km per day average and this pleased me. Sam said he was happy with our pace too, but past experience still made me anxious not to be seen to be pushing him.

It was a great pleasure to see that Sam was enjoying France. He loved the change of culture, new people, new language, and in particular the food.   So it was with mixed emotions that we began to notice the small towns between Metz and the Rhine becoming gradually more Germanic.   The architecture began to resemble that of Bavaria and people were up and about earlier.   One morning, stopping for a breakfast croissant, we watched an elderly lady energetically sweeping up a single leaf from the pavement outside her immaculate house.   No doubt this had fallen since she swept the pavement the evening before.

On the other hand, it is generally true to say that we were always eager to move on to the next country fairly soon after getting used to the one we were in.   A new way of life was always calling us, especially Sam, for whom increasingly these regions were a first taste.

Not all our experiences were positive, though.   Unable to find a campsite or affordable guesthouse in the French town of Bitche (near the German border), we decided to camp in the forest.   The spot was well hidden but within easy cycling reach of a spa-resort and a restaurant for dinner.   After pitching the tent, we made our way back to the forest road and to the restaurant, where a surly waitress told us they were full.   We pointed to some free tables outside, where others were also eating.   Tutting loudly, she conceded that if we were happy to eat outside, we could please ourselves.

We sat down and perused the menu, then spent some time trying to attract the attention of the waitress again.   She seemed to be constantly muttering to herself and sneering.   I imagined the terrifying possibility that if we waited too long she would say it was now too late and they were closed.   At that point, I spotted her earpiece and realised the muttering was in fact being addressed to someone at the other end of a mobile phone conversation.   When our persistent expressions of concern finally persuaded her to leave her conversation, she came over and we asked for two set meals.

Hands firmly on hips, the woman masticated her chewing gum loudly.   A hairy belly button peered at me through the strained fastening of her blouse.   It was at my eye level, so I could hardly avoid noticing the large amount of black fluff lodged in it.

Today was a *fete* day, we were told (it was not), so the set menu was off.   Had we wronged this woman in a former life, I wondered. We asked if she was sure.   Of course she was sure!   Reluctantly, we chose two pizzas off the a la carte menu and two beers.   The woman wandered off mumbling.

Forty minutes passed easily as we fell into a discussion about saddle sores and forgot about our poisonous waitress.   Having explored all facets of saddle-related issues, though, we realised there was no sign of our waitress or the pizzas and Sam went to look for her.   He found her slumped by the back door, phone pressed between shoulder and ear, painting her nails.

Angry at the disturbance, she waved him to his seat.   After 15 more minutes, the pizzas arrived, cold and decidedly crisp.   The woman stood at a short distance glaring at us, as if daring us to complain.   There were by now only two further customers, others having left without eating it seemed.   The woman returned to her nails.   The varnish, a putrid shade of pink, clashed horribly with her orange blouse.

When we asked to see the dessert menu, it was as if we were deliberately trying to antagonise her.   She threw the menus onto the tables, adding *"pas de flan,"* and disappeared back inside.

Sam and I found these antics rather amusing and began theorising about what might have caused her bad temper.   I felt certain it had to be caused by a man, probably her husband, who paid too much attention to her sister.   Sam suggested it was more likely a dispute with her employers.   Perhaps she had objected to wearing the vermilion-coloured uniform.   Her boss insisted, so she put on the pink nail varnish to clash with it deliberately.   Robbery was added to the list of possibilities, along with the idea she had received a call saying she had won the lottery only to discover it was a hoax.   As hard as we tried, though, excusing her behaviour was not easy.

Determined to try and salvage some enjoyment from the meal itself, Sam went inside to ask for two fresh fruit salads.   There was, of course, a certain amount of provocative mischief involved in this. We did not have to wait long for the fruit salads.   Unfortunately, though, we felt unable to eat them, after discovering a very characteristic type of body hair in one of them.   We paid and got up to leave.

As we mounted our bikes, we heard the woman mutter something to the effect of "thanks for the tip."   It was an interesting evening but one that we could have done without.   Making our way through the dark forest back to our tent, we talked through crazy possibilities that might have caused the behaviour of the waitress. Finally, we conceded she was probably from a long line of women who perhaps had earned the town its name.

*

The day after Bitche, we were treated to a downhill run through a misty valley and past orchards where we stopped to pick a few large apples.   Sam tucked into one and had started a second when I warned him how ill too much fruit can make you.   He seemed unconvinced but decided to save the others for the next day.

By lunchtime, we had reached the Rhine, which forms the French–German border, and were puzzling over whether we should head north or south to the next bridge when an elderly couple on Brompton folding bicycles approached us.

"Do you need directions?" the man asked in a good English accent.

I explained that we were cycling to Japan by way of Budapest. It seemed almost as if they had been stationed there just to help us. They were from nearby Baden Baden and knew plenty of touring cyclists.   They suggested we head south to Strasbourg that night and from there to Freiberg before a short hop through the Black Forest to Donaueschingen – the source of the Donau (Danube).   From there, we could cycle along Danube Cycle Path all the way to Budapest. Some friends of theirs had done it the year before and said that it was downhill all the way.

I had heard great things about Danube Cycle Path before, so I was happy to follow their advice.   Sam agreed, although he'd been quiet for some time during this exchange, busy eating another giant apple, I now realised.

Heading south along the Rhine Cycle Path through some lovely countryside, we passed groups of happy cyclists and joggers. We took the next bridge across the Rhine into Germany and stopped at a *schnellimbis* café for a basic lunch.

Sam's bike toppled over, breaking the rear-view mirror. Since he was already feeling a little out of sorts, this seemed to him like a harbinger of bad luck. I didn't understand why at that point but remembered my pledge not to discuss anything with him before he'd eaten lunch. The bad luck continued after lunch, when the towpath on the German side petered out into a quarry and we were left zigzagging across fields of cabbages. After two hours of wasted time, we crossed back to the French side and cycled on to Strasbourg, finding one of the very reasonably priced Formula1 motels just as we arrived. The day had finished well in the end, or so it seemed.

On checking in, though, Sam rushed to the toilet and stayed for an hour. When he came out, he said he didn't want supper and I should go and eat alone. He looked dreadful. When I returned later, he was still in the toilet, and spent much of that night there.

"Do you think it was the apples, Dad?" he asked weakly.

I indicated sympathetically that it probably was. It was another of Sam's lessons in life. I knew that under the same circumstances I would have taken no notice of my own father either.

*

Sam did not want to talk that evening and the solitary interlude led me to wondering how things were going with Colin running the business. I ran a risk management consultancy, something Lorna had always considered counter to my nature as an inveterate risk-taker. In fact, the key to my modest success in the business probably stemmed from my lifelong attraction to hazardous activities, while at the same time managing the risk, to avoid killing myself. Even at 50, I was the opposite of risk-averse.

With a psychologist as a wife, I have had to recognise in recent years that I am a terrible control freak – the very thing I have resisted in others all my life. Like my father before me, I feel very vulnerable if I'm not in total control of my life. That extends to the lives of my immediate family, since like most fathers I see their wellbeing as my responsibility.   This has caused untold conflict in my family and was already proving the greatest challenge for me to face during this trip.

Sam had been happy enough for me to do all the planning and preparations for the trip.   At times, though, he really resented it, feeling I was subtly trying to have everything my own way.   This left plenty of potential for conflict and he found this prospect worrying as the start of the trip drew closer.   I believe the rest of the family shared his concerns, but my blind faith in my own plans kept me in ignorance of this.

*

When morning arrived in Strasbourg, Sam was better and ready to get going again.   I was glad, particularly since I didn't feel it was a place I wanted to hang around.   He was astounded that a couple of simple apples could make him so ill.

We continued down the French side of the Rhine and then crossed over to Freiberg, where we took a 40-minute train ride to Donaueschingen, as advised by the Baden Baden couple, who warned us that tunnels on the road are very risky to cycle through.   After a bit of dithering around in the early evening traffic outside town, we eventually made it to a large campsite by dark.

Some people have since remarked that taking a train ride was *cheating*.   They are missing the point.   Who or what were we cheating?   We were making the trip for pleasure and experience, not to try and break any records or prove anything.   The fact that we cycled a total of 9,570 miles is not nullified by a few short train rides at points when good sense dictated it.   Better that than to do 900 miles only to get flattened by a truck – then someone might have been cheated!   I feel sorry for people who cannot see this.   It is no coincidence that they are most often the kind who cannot be bothered to make any effort themselves.

The next morning we cycled back into town to the tourist office for details of the cycle route.   The staff kindly directed us to a great bookshop opposite, where we bought an excellent waterproof cycle

41

guide.   Having stocked up with food for a picnic lunch, we headed off on what we could now see was an excellent path, with signposting of Germanic efficiency.   We could already sense how much we were going to enjoy it.

*

Danube Cycle Path proved to be the surprise gift of the trip.   It runs all the way from the river's source in Donaueschingen at the edge of Germany's Black Forest to Budapest in Hungary.   On its way, it winds through Germany, Austria and Slovakia. From there, due to the increasing popularity of cycling and cycle tourism, further sections are being developed in Rumania and Bulgaria.   The countryside was beautiful, enhanced by the good weather, and we had the convenience of a good path with amenities always nearby.   It was really exciting for us to find this so close to home and we agreed we should try to organise a family trip, maybe the following year.   The scenery as you pass along this great river is stunning and I cannot recommend the area highly enough to visit, especially for a cycling holiday.

Sam and I soon got into a routine suited to this section of the ride.   In cities or on rest days, we generally stayed in guesthouses. In between, we tended to camp.   The Danube route is so well served by campsites, cafes, restaurants, *gasthoffs* and friendly hotels that we were seldom short of choices for a place to stay.   Despite it being August, we never booked ahead, yet we were rarely disappointed.

A cycle hostel we found conveniently situated above an artisan bakery next to the main railway station in Passau was one of our best experiences on this part of the trip.   Seeing a poster for it on a lamppost was a real stroke of luck.   The smell of bread and cakes wafting under the door on our first morning really started our rest day on a high.

On that first day, we went for a walk around the city then called into a supermarket for some food and supplies.   Back at our hostel, we found an ideal picnic area by the washing lines behind the building.   Attractive flowering weeds grew out of the cracked concrete and a small tree provided some dappled shade where we ate a delicious leisurely meal, drank local wine, and were entertained for

42

hours by the comings and goings of passengers, trains and baggage on the adjacent station platforms.

To enhance our pleasure, groups of elderly tourists were periodically delivered onto the platforms by sleeper trains. At one point, some well-heeled Americans wandered past on the other side of the fence, looking like they had been dropped on another planet.

"What's here, Winifred?"

"Well, I think the guide said it was *the* place to buy hats and walking sticks."

"Oh, fancy that! My niece asked me to buy one of those French hats Napoleon wore."

"If I'm not mistaken, Cissy, this is Germany – or maybe even Austria."

"Oh well. I think Napoleon came here too."

"D'ya think?"

After the passengers had gone, tour staff began removing their expensive baggage from the train. There was plenty of it – these people certainly didn't believe in travelling light. The porters grumbled to each other about it.

"Must have a body in this one!"

"Could be a live one. Maybe we'd better check. Might have sneaked on an extra passenger. Granddaughter maybe."

"Or a toy boy."

Sam and I lazed around there for most of the afternoon. It wasn't any kind of hardship. The sun beat down on the cedar weatherboarding, creating a soothing aroma that combined well with our cheese, salad and dates. The local red wine was surprisingly good despite having to drink it out of plastic mugs. We imagined ourselves as being like a couple of hobos living it up after an unexpected windfall. *This* was how we wanted our trip to be.

*

The only minor blemish I can recall along the 1,200-kilometre Danube Cycle Path was a plague of aggressive mosquitoes on an Austrian campsite in historic Petronell Carnuntum. Even our super-strength

43

Deet repellent failed to deter the monsters.   At the same time, we still managed to find a positive side.

The site was located around some small lakes a short distance from the river, on the edge of the picturesque little town.   We arrived in late afternoon to discover a nicely appointed place with a restaurant, bar and games facilities.   Soon after putting up our tent, noticing the insects biting, Sam and I zipped everything up and took refuge in the site's restaurant.   Here, we were able to sit in comfort with cool beers, while through the window we witnessed the antics of our fellow campers.

Most of the people seemed to have arrived recently and were determined to take an evening shower after the heat of the day.   This seemed a crazy idea to us.   Surely these people knew that mosquitoes bite mostly at dusk?   But the pale-skinned holidaymakers trooped into the shower block.

Sam and I sipped our beers and waited for the inevitable.   We did not have to wait long.   One by one, the freshly showered pale apparitions emerged and soon began running from the shower block to their tents, calling out in pain as they went.   The mosquito population were quickly alerted and before long a dark cloud of them seemed to be hovering over the shower block.   Those inside behaved like soldiers on a battlefield, running for their lives from refuge to refuge, dodging the enemy attacks.   Some tried wrapping themselves in towels or draping them over their heads, causing them to trip and fall as they ran.   Others foolishly delayed on the way, trying to swat the enemy as they ran.   These early combatants paid a high price for their mistakes.

Eventually, the remaining eight or ten people decided they stood a better chance if they all made a run for it at once.   Maybe they could split the swarm or cause some confusion?   There was a lull, then a sudden mad rush, as men, women and children ran screeching and whooping in a last desperate headlong dash for the tents. Unfortunately, the mosquitoes were ready for them.   The cloud split into packs, descending upon their prey in a final feeding frenzy before retiring for the night.   The wounded dived headlong through the doors of tents held open by terrified partners.

The sound of a dozen tent zips being rapidly closed was quickly followed by the hissing of insect sprays. The pitiful whimpering of the wounded could be heard from many of the tents, punctuated at times with the crack of swatting and cries of murderous satisfaction.

It had been a sight to behold. We agreed it was almost worth staying an extra night to witness it again tomorrow. At this point, we still had to make it to our own tent after our dinner. In theory, we hoped, the swarm would have subsided by then. Fortunately, we were right.

It did seem cruel, gaining such amusement from seeing people under attack. We felt, though, that any of the victims would have been hard pushed not to have laughed to see the spectacle for themselves.

The nightly battle was very much a serious affair, however, for the elderly couple who ran the campsite. They told us they had been unaware of the mosquito problem when they paid a hefty lease on the place at the start of the season.

"*Ja*, we have been tricked by the owner," the man told us. "People stay only one night. They leave with bite wounds and much anger. We can do nothing because the nature wardens do not permit to put insecticide in the water. It is *verboten*!"

*

Along the German and Austrian sections of the river, so many considerations had been made for cyclists that there were even small cycle ferries to cross where there were no bridges or when the path was being repaired. As if this was not spoiling us enough, we found cycle tools on cables next to carved wooden maps at various junctions along the way. This was a cyclist's paradise. By this point, we had accepted that the *downhill all the way* report from the helpful Baden Baden couple was overselling it somewhat, but their friends were no doubt remembering it in the same golden light that we now do.

Food is an important part of any cycle trip since, as I have said, it represents the fuel element. We were finding that it occupied our thoughts for much of each day. We liked the way the food gradually changed along with the predominant culture as we progressed, and this was a noticeable feature as we made our way along the Danube. There were plenty of supermarkets and village shops along the banks. For us, this generally meant an early breakfast from a bakery eaten beside the river.

Typically, after some steady effort during the mornings, we followed with extravagant picnic lunches accompanied by local beer, wine or fruit juice at the benches and tables provided all along the path or on benches in village squares. It meant we could happily splash out a bit on dinner in a restaurant, with a sense of having earned it after the day's exertions.

Sam agreed that starting early was the best plan. We were boosted by getting two-thirds of the day's cycling done by lunchtime. But more than this, the weather was hot and we were in the busy holiday season. Starting early meant we had the advantage of cycling at the coolest time of day and when fewer people were on the path. It may have been counter to Sam's normal body-clock, but over these early weeks he gradually became convinced by the benefits and quietly adjusted. Surprisingly, he almost never made me feel bad for waking him early – something I had been worried about before the trip.

The purple patch of the Danube route was unquestionably a section of nature park from Fridingen to Beuron (near the town of Sigmaringen). Access by motorised vehicles seemed to be prohibited on this 30km section (unless you drive a tractor), so only cyclists and intrepid walkers made it this far. It was well worth the effort. Buzzards soared overhead, looking down on lush fields with abundant flowers, farm animals and wildlife. Cycling quietly beside the river, we were framed by towering chalk cliffs topped with castles and a monastery. A gentle breeze blew down through steep forested hillsides and filled our heads with the scent of pine. I do not exaggerate when I say that the stunning day we spent cycling calmly through this beautiful section is forever burned into our memories.

Couples, families, pensioners and small groups of casual local cyclists (the lycra-free variety) greeted us as we progressed along the Danube, mostly making their way in this cycling nirvana to simple riverside restaurants for a long lunch before cycling home in the afternoon sun via a farm-shop or vineyard. There were a few commuters at peak times but the atmosphere was always relaxed and the path rarely overcrowded. Thankfully, Sam and I found these blissed-out locals to be a reliable source of directions and information on places to eat or sleep. It seems surprising that after cycling through so many more exotic locations on our way to Japan, we still look back on Danube Cycle Path as one of the best parts of our route, despite it being in our own backyard.

*

Passau (with the excellent cycle hostel above the bakery) was our midpoint rest stop on the Danube trail. It was a rather quiet, genteel city but a very pleasant one to rest for a few days. We found a good internet cafe and brought our blog up to date. This seemed a good point to re-evaluate our general day-to-day strategy.

By now, we had found that our plan of breaking the cycling up into five-day stints with two days off in between was unnecessary. One day off after every five was plenty. This allowed us to take a four-day break when we reached a special location such as Budapest. We much preferred this arrangement, which gave some flexibility if we were tired or encountered something special on the way. There were also times when we felt it worthwhile to continue for eight or even ten days without a break, in order to have even longer at the next main location. This was possible but not always wise. Especially due to the wear and tear on your bum!

People we met began to ask us about the physical effects. After a couple of months of cycling your legs feel very little pain, however long or steep the hills, but your bum always aches after a few days. Despite padded lycra cycle shorts, damage to the skin through chafing starts beyond five days. Squidgy gel saddles can actually make this worse, despite feeling luxurious at first. They are really only a benefit for shorter rides. Our traditional Brooks saddles were serving us well. It seemed the research I had done – finding that many long-distance cyclists recommended them – had been worthwhile. When we overdid things, our pot of Sudocrem (a common antiseptic nappy rash cream in the UK) became invaluable. This doesn't contain

47

anything nasty like cortisone but works wonders on any raw or inflamed skin. We know nobody then or since who has found anything better.

*

Moving on briskly through Austria and Slovakia, we went through the usual mixed feelings as we reached Hungary. As with France and Germany, Sam in particular had really enjoyed the food, the people and learning the languages, but his enthusiasm for what was to come seemed to pick up noticeably at signs of Western Europe giving way to the East.

Lorna and I both grew up abroad for significant parts of our earlier lives – her in the Middle East and me primarily in Singapore, Malaysia and Germany. Although my formal education certainly suffered by moving every two or three years, we feel that these experiences have really enhanced our lives and we were worried about our own children missing something by largely being brought up in the safe, conservative environment of Canterbury. I think my sense of anything being possible, although there from birth, was encouraged by living in various cultures and distant parts of the world at a time when relatively few people travelled that far. So for Lorna and I, this trip also represented an opportunity to fill a gap in Sam's education.

I had been thinking about this a lot since the Bavaria and Austria section of the trip, as it brought back happy memories of family holidays with my parents and younger brother when we lived in Germany for a few years. Sam had seemed particularly interested and asked a lot of questions about what my dad was like and my relationship with him. I knew he was comparing what I told him with what he was feeling about our own relationship. Although talking to Sam about it made me happy, I felt slightly nervous. I suspected that everything I maintained was difficult about my father was proof to Sam I had not learned to avoid doing the same with my own children. I very much wanted to avoid that and realise now that I could have asked him to help me with this. At the time, however, it didn't feel fair to burden him. Not when he had problems of his own. Of course, the truth is that me asking for his advice would have helped him with his problems, but I could not quite see that then.

My own parents – young and new to the job – had struggled to deal with my rebellious nature, employing techniques that varied between reasoned loving requests at one extreme and rigid discipline at the other, all with little success. This escalated soon after school began as I became incensed by people I saw as mindless authority figures. My defining instinct became a determination to resist any attempt to condition, manipulate or subjugate me. In time, I became preoccupied with attacking authority at its foundations – with my father as my daily opponent. I really was very difficult. As I have said, when I became an adult I worried about having kids of my own for fear they would be as rebellious as I had been. I needn't have worried.

It seems to me now that strict, conservative parents produce teenagers who rebel by being very liberal themselves, whereas teenagers of more liberal parents rebel by being more conservative. Why on earth does that surprise me?

As with most of us at some stage, I do worry about the tendency of children to repeat the behavioural traits of their parents. I was determined to use this trip to try to exorcise any negative habits I had obviously picked up from my dad, and to avoid passing these and any other negative traits on to Sam. Of course, it goes without saying that many positive traits were also passed on.

Seeing Sam struggling to be his own person, trying to resist simply falling into the stereotypes that his parents and even his friends had set up for him, couldn't fail to make me wonder about those old battles I fought with my parents, or to notice how I still had so much to resolve. It is obvious to me now that this trip presented an opportunity for each of us to help the other in this respect. But again, at the time, I remained patronisingly convinced that my role was simply to help Sam.

SAM'S POINT OF VIEW

This was a difficult time for me. On one level I was excited about beginning the trip, but on another I was filled with anxiety about how it was going to pan out. In the period after finishing school I was happiest when I was hanging out with my friends, drinking and lazing around in parks during the day, playing football and chatting with new people. I was happy in Ireland doing the same thing, but the cycle back to Canterbury was miserable. It wasn't a pleasant position to find myself in.

During the pre-start time spent with my dad I was often quiet and moody. It became hard to find the energy to make any effort in preparation for the trip, let alone get enthusiastic about it. But it seemed the only option for me was to continue. If I had called the whole thing off I knew I would have felt disappointed in myself. Other people would have felt the same – it would have crushed me. I felt totally trapped really.

Heading off again from Canterbury began badly. Within half an hour of setting off for the ferry at Dover, I managed to get lost. My dad's way of dealing with it was really awful.

"Sam, how on earth did you manage to get lost?!" Not the best thing to say to an 18-year-old searching for his own independence.

I wanted to be anywhere but with my dad at that moment. Sadly, he didn't realise that. He wouldn't remember that he lost his temper. He just isn't aware of how he comes over to people. Most commonly, he'll throw you a screwed-up confused look as if to say, "What the hell are you on about?" He'll swear blind he doesn't do that, but he does, and I'm still certain to this day that those expressive looks indicate his true feelings. I think they do with all of us. We all have a closed off world where we make critical judgements and romanticise dark, often unkind thoughts. What can be hard is that my dad is honest about those feelings. That can be painful. I think it's something he has a conscience about. It doesn't seem right to him to hold back what you are truly thinking. In fact, he deplores what he calls typically English behaviour, where people hide the truth purely to be polite. I've come to agree with him on that. All that traditional English politeness seems to result in is you losing your grip on what your true feelings are. You simply become a slave to a 'correct' way of being. It's not only the English, of course. Travelling really taught me how screwed up many Western values can be.

My spirits lifted once we arrived in France and began cycling. The weather was fantastic and we joked with each other about leaving our women behind. I'd just entered into a proper relationship with a girlfriend at the time. It was probably the first time I felt like one of a pair. And of course there was my mum, who had made the whole trip possible. On reflection, I realise my parents are pretty cool, but it just wasn't the right time for me to enjoy the company of either of them.

Crossing the world, I think the greatest thing for me was the food and it remained that way for the whole ten months. My confidence to express myself and socialise had evaporated, so quite honestly, keeping my mouth full was a help. For me, the further we rode east the better the food was.

It was not all positive, though. The day we reached the Rhine I was horrendously ill. Those who have ever eaten too many apples will understand the pain. For nine hours I lay next to a Formula1 hotel toilet with excruciating stabbing pains in my stomach. Never again – although scrumping for fruit was great fun. German food was really enjoyable. Generous portions and plenty of Wiener schnitzel went down a treat after a hard day's cycling.

It was a shame I couldn't have found the same excitement I did trying new food with the chance to spend time and interact with my dad. It would have really helped if I'd been more honest with him – come straight out and told him when he did anything to annoy me. But how could I? I would have been criticising him all day every day for ten months! It simply didn't seem practical to spend a whole year with someone so much older than me. Not at that stage of my life. In fact, I think a better time to do the trip would have been at about 16, when people expect you to be slightly shy, or when I was older and capable of looking after myself. That constant feeling that I was being 'cared for' was tough to deal with.

Chapter 3

Entering Eastern Europe – Internal conflicts

"You cycle for health please, or for pay small money?"
"We are cycling because we experience more that way."
"Ah, yes. But more is good only if more is happy. More pain, more death – not good!"

Reaching Budapest was a classic cycling story of a place that seemed it would never arrive. The hills were challenging. We were out of practice after the largely flat Danube Cycle Path, and the roads had fallen apart. Potholes large enough to lose a bike down threatened to swallow us whole. To make matters worse, we had no map for this section. What with the linguistic challenges in the rural areas, we were not sure whether the place on the signposts we were following (in strange text) was actually Budapest, or somewhere completely different. There was nowhere to buy a map. It made a change after the Teutonic efficiency of the Danube path, although not an entirely welcome one.

The city of Budapest did eventually appear, down below us from the top of a densely wooded mountainside. Hurtling downhill into the fuming cauldron of rush-hour traffic was also our first experience on this trip of inconsiderate heavy traffic. We gritted our teeth and fought our way to the main railway station. Near it, instinct and experience told me, we would find cheap accommodation. The tramlines were hazardous, but nowhere near as bad as the trams.

Unfortunately, any cheap hotels in the station area were well hidden. Strolling into the nearby Hilton Hotel in cycle shorts, face blackened by traffic fumes, I slipped back into businessman mode. The receptionist stretched to look down over the counter. I had forgotten I was not dressed for this.

"Excuse my casual dress," I said, seeing her surprise. "I often stay at your hotels on business, but today I'm cycling with my son so we're looking for something more basic like a hostel."

Other guests studied my out-of-place attire with amusement. My beard was also now starting to look rather wild, I realised. I had agreed with Lorna that I wouldn't shave it until I got home. Itchiness was making me start to regret this.

The lady continued in polite professional mode, making a phone call, then providing me with a map indicating the location of a good hostel around the corner. If she had offered us a luxurious room at hostel prices, I don't think either of us would have accepted. The opportunity to meet other overland travellers, make friends and pick up information in shared kitchens and dormitories is usually more valuable than plush surroundings. We would save the luxury hotel experiences for when we were really shattered and filthy.

The large city centre hostel in Budapest seemed comfortable enough, so we checked in for three nights. We had not had a comfortable night since Passau five hilly days before and we were worn out. Three days in Budapest would also give us an opportunity to email a few people and phone home. We had our first chat to Scarlett, my very determined 13-year-old daughter, who seemed to be missing Sam in particular. In retrospect, I probably underestimated the effect of our absence upon her life. At this stage in our trip, it seemed to me she was so preoccupied with her own busy life that she had hardly noticed we were gone. But later, as the trip neared its end, I came to realise how much she had missed us. For now, though, determined to use the time well, Scarlett told us that she had started a cake-baking business. Lorna seemed impressed with this embryonic entrepreneurialism and was allowing her to regularly trash the kitchen as orders came in. Ever the persuasive diplomat (a dictator in waiting), Scarlett thought she should satisfy what she saw as a likely parental prejudice by asking me whether it was possible to do a degree in baking.

Back to our food fixation: I had often heard that Budapest was famous for good food but up to that point I had missed it on my travels, so Sam and I were looking forward to treating ourselves to some good meals out. Disappointingly, it never quite came up to my expectations. I remember on our first evening in Budapest heading off out after a shower at the hostel, anticipating a plethora of tempting eating establishments. We made our feet sore walking around endless streets, reading menus and peering in through windows, but nothing really grabbed us. Worst of all was the number of pizza and burger restaurants that predominated around the centre. North African waiters attempted to pull punters off the pavement and into fastfood joints. There seemed to be a price war going on, with some places offering slices of pizza at very low prices as a tempter.

Budapest, it would seem, had suffered a surge of Americanisation now the communist era had come to an end. I say *suffered* but realise this was only my point of view. It must never be forgotten that the inhabitants of such countries may be very happy to see these changes. But I do feel that the time will come in the future where they bemoan the loss of their traditional cuisine.

Sam and I did manage to find a few traditional Hungarian restaurants in Budapest, but they were down-at-heel and seemed somehow to be clinging on in the wake of an overwhelming tide of change. It saddened me and I think this rubbed off on Sam. Even so, the sight of the spectacular parliament buildings along the river as we left our restaurant on the first evening was enough to provide at least a temporary lift. Like many others, we sat there on the wall of the promenade staring at the building on the opposite bank for about an hour. It is an absolutely stunning piece of European architecture and may be worth visiting Budapest for on its own.

*

Four days in Budapest was plenty for us and we were happy to move on into rural southern Hungary. The inconvenient side of this was that hotels and formal campsites were fewer and further between, and that far less people spoke other European languages. Nonetheless, the change was welcome.

Sam had enjoyed meeting some young people in the Budapest hostel. I was reminded just how difficult it might be for him, spending all his time with a 50-year-old man and only rarely meeting people his own age. At a couple of points on the trip, people asked Sam whether this was a problem for him and he confirmed that it was sometimes. He was always careful to add, however, that it was not so bad really, because "my dad is quite immature." The first time he said this I corrected his misuse of English, saying that what I thought he meant was *young for his age*. He told me he was well aware of the difference but liked to pretend to people it was an ironic mistake. I had either underestimated the subtlety of his humour, or he was trying to spare my feelings.

What remained evident was that Sam was still suffering from the self-doubt that had begun in France, due to the long hours on the bike contemplating life. In fact, it was becoming worse. He had periods of mild enthusiasm but was not his old happy-go-lucky self. There were extended periods of silence and he often failed to reply to questions, or just grunted. I realised that many parents would no doubt say it was normal teenage behaviour, but Sam had never been like this. It is not something I dealt with very well. Sam seemed resentful towards me but if I mentioned it he said he was fine. I couldn't stand that.

By now, Hannah had suggested that she come out to India with Lorna and Scarlett for Christmas, which had cheered Sam up a little, but only momentarily. I had been expecting confrontation between us at times but not this. What I found very considerate of Sam, however, and rather touching, was that on a few occasions he decided to talk to me about how he was feeling, he apologised for being so quiet and moody. He told me it was not my fault or responsibility to sort this out for him – he would be fine eventually. I really appreciated this. It is typical of his sensitive and caring nature. I'm not sure where he gets that.

*

Although we found fewer places to eat or stay in southern Hungary, the people were friendly enough and we found some places that stood out.

In Csongrad, we arrived after a day of over a hundred miles on the bikes due to our planned campsite being closed. This had felt unfortunate, but we were well rested after Budapest and in the lovely sunny afternoon weather, we had enjoying the views of simple farms, red-faced farm labourers and unspoilt countryside.

With dusk approaching and feeling somewhat saddle-sore, we finally passed a sign telling us we had reached the rural outskirts of Csongrad. The road went through a wood where large trees overhung the road.

The town must arrive soon, we thought. Was it going to be one of those days?

Eventually, we emerged into the dying sunlight and saw a queue of stationary traffic ahead. Coasting slowly past the cars we saw that people had begun to get out to smoke or chat with people in adjacent cars.

"Bloody great! What's this then? An accident or level crossing?"

"Calm down, Dad," said Sam. "Don't get yourself into a negative mood. It won't help."

Approaching the front of the queue we saw a river. There was no formal barrier, just a faded white line before a casual concrete slipway on a slight incline down into the water.

"Hmm, I wonder how many people have ended up in the river, hitting it at speed – especially at night?" I mused. Sam pointed to a rusty motorbike submerged in the river.

On the opposite bank, about 50 metres away, sat a very basic roll-on roll-off barge connected to a cable across the river. A similar queue of traffic was forming on the road on that side. Nobody seemed in any hurry. I remembered Sam's advice to stay calm. Looking for the positive, I reminded myself what a beautiful country scene it was. If I could forget my concern about finding somewhere to stay in the dark, I might even enjoy it.

We asked one of the drivers when the barge made its next crossing.

"One hour." He smiled and made a swimming motion.

Looking over at the barge, we saw the barge operator sitting on the side of his boat, fishing. He had one of the rods I used to make as a boy – a willowy branch cut from a nearby tree. This endeared him to me and made me less cross about him keeping us waiting. Maybe on the end of the short line he also had a hook made from a bent pin, with a piece of squashed dough from his lunchtime sandwich for bait. He was like a grown-up Huckleberry Finn. He certainly seemed determined to enjoy his hour between crossings and nobody seemed to begrudge him that. Perk of the job, we supposed.

After resigning ourselves to our hour's wait, we made the most of the opportunity to rest. We had cycled a long way and felt in need of somewhere comfortable to stay. On the opposite bank, there seemed to be a small collection of wooden houses on stilts. Summerhouses, I imagined, since they didn't look much bigger than sheds – *dacha*, I think they are called in Eastern Europe. Maybe we would be able to stay in one. I imagined spending an idyllic summer holiday in one of these huts with just the basics for living: fishing every day in the sun and cooking over a fire at night, whittling things out of wood and drinking a few beers, cooled in the river. I told Sam I would build one in our orchard when we got back.

"Is that what people call being an incurable romantic?" he asked.

Time trickled by at the pace of the sleepy river. Finally, the man put down his rod and started the motor. It had an ancient, throaty burble that did not seem out of place in the tranquil scene. Cars filed onto the barge and soon rolled off on our side. We boarded the rusting craft, which slowly filled up. Nobody was in a rush. They seemed used to this and were enjoying the early evening as much as we were.

By the time we entered town it was dark. It was not a large place but was bustling with people heading home. After asking a number of people for help, we managed to get ourselves directed to a hotel run by an elderly lady with a fiercely academic daughter. Fortunately, this somewhat cybernetic daughter had English amongst her wide repertoire of languages. Before opening the heavy bedroom door, she turned towards us and hesitated a moment.

"My name is Greta," she said, her stare uncomfortably direct.

Greta was about 20, wearing a rather trendy tracksuit and chic narrow glasses, yet somehow she still managed to look like a young 1950's Soviet woman. Her stare remained fixed for an unnaturally long period of time. Her wide face was friendly enough, although she did not actually smile. There was something a little strange about her manner. I wondered what was behind the door. Eventually, one of her eyes began to twitch and she looked down. With a heavy turn of the key the door creaked open.

Sam and I timorously followed Greta into a large room spookily fitted out with what seemed to be furniture from the postwar era. A shaft of dusty light cut through a crack in the heavy curtains, giving us the sense almost that we had stepped into the past. She drew back the curtains to reveal a large sash window that looked down into a large cobbled courtyard. We noticed a pair of bikes standing against the wall and realised that they were our own. The elderly mother must have moved them, although it seemed unlikely. It all felt very odd. Looking out onto the grand Austro-Hungarian cobbled courtyard, I felt that a horse-drawn carriage, or mounted soldiers with muskets, might arrive at any moment. I looked at Sam. It wasn't only me; he too looked mesmerised.

"This courtyard is beautiful, not?"

Gretta's words echoed in the high-ceilinged room and it was a moment or two before I realised it was she who had spoken. Pulling myself together, I turned to look at her. The full sun on her face had revealed a surprising feature – she had one brown eye and one blue. I tried not to stare. She turned and started to show us the room, opening every drawer and cupboard as if carrying out an obsessively practiced routine.

"It is a *spracious* room, not?"

"Very precious, yes. Thank you."

"Yes, much space. It is our pleasure. We have few stranger guests. We will try hardly to give you comfort."

"We will try hard to be good guests," smiled Sam.

A change occurred in Greta's eyes. There was an awkward silence, followed by a radiant smile. Sam had scored a direct hit. Thank God, I thought. Maybe now we won't be tied up and held prisoner for years in the cellar.

Greta showed us into a large historic bathroom. Over a large rust-stained bath was a device I had seen before, or something similar at least. My grandmother had one when I was small. It was known as *The Geyser*: a huge threatening gas boiler smelling of burning gas, that shook and gurgled when lit, threatening to explode at any moment. The fear I reserved for this monstrous device as a child was still there now. I had no intention of using it.

Greta had become animated and was now eager to talk, asking us what we had seen on our journey and what we thought of her country. She was also very informative.   She sat down at the writing desk and began to give us a potted history of Hungary, while Sam and I were transformed into an attentive audience, perched on one of the beds. In addition to enlightening historical and political facts, Greta provided local information.

"I want to commend you about a very good pizza restaurant near to this establishment," she said before she left.   "It is very marvellous."

This didn't sound particularly enticing to me – commended or not.   Eating there later, however, we found it served not only excellent pizza but also exquisitely prepared Hungarian dishes with very fresh fish and delicious wild game.   It was better than anything we had found in Budapest.   I doubt the town had ever seen more than a dozen foreign tourists.   Surely the cuisine couldn't be just for the benefit of a local clientele of relatively modest means?

*

I have already mentioned that we noticed a progressive lack of places to stay or to buy food as we moved away from Budapest and the larger outlying towns.   There were compensations.   We found our bikes drifting across the road as we gazed in wonder at the wildlife and idyllic rural scenes on either side.   For us, it all seemed so much something from a bygone era, with small carts spilling over with hay or maize cobs trundling along on rickety wooden wheels, pulled by bony but highly prized mules.   Invariably, beside the ubiquitous leather-skinned old farmer we would see a head-scarfed old wife, ready to jump down if anything substantial fell off.   On some occasions, we saw carts unwisely entrusted to teenage boys, who whipped the mules and raced along in a spray of mule saliva, alternately waving or flinging insults at us.   As well as these animals pressed into labour, wild creatures seemed to be everywhere: storks nesting at the top of telegraph poles; hares darting from hedgerows; stoats running through the corn stubble while buzzards tracked them overhead.   Cycling along quietly at speed one morning with the smell of cut hay in our nostrils, we found ourselves being raced along the edge of a field by a deer that jumped small fences to keep up with us, looking across to check we were still there.   It was quite surreal.

Equally unlikely was a rustic scene we came upon very early one Sunday morning.   We were way out in the sticks, miles from the nearest town.   As we cycled along with the heat of the sun just beginning to cause a haze, we noticed a person in the distance up ahead looking back at us.   A rickety old farm truck passed us.   As it drew near, the figure stood back on the verge with a thumb out in hope of a lift.   Even at that distance, we could tell by now it was a woman, from her stance and backcombed bouffant blonde hair.   As we approached, we were astonished to see that she was clad in a black plastic dress with an extremely short hemline and her boobs bursting out of the unzipped top-half.   The Barbie blonde hair was clearly a wig, and it was not on straight.   With huge painted nails, she beckoned us towards her; puckering up lips that were so badly lipsticked they resembled graffiti.   As we came close, she staggered in front of us, teetering on towering high-heels.   Sam and I braked hard.   The apparition began to shout incoherently.   She was either blind drunk or drugged.   We swerved to avoid her, making a quick decision to speed up rather than stop.

Once the woman was out of sight, Sam coasted up next to me.

"What the hell was that all about?   I mean, how on earth did she get out here?"

"Must have been dumped there by a customer, I suppose.   I can't think she'd get much business out here."

Sam and I pressed on.   It was a strange place, we agreed. Beautiful, but something not right.   I felt worried for the woman now, and what fate might soon befall her, but not so much that I wanted to risk going back.

*

Well before lunchtime, Sam and I began to worry about our empty stomachs.   There were no shops or restaurants, so we had been limited to one measly muesli bar each for breakfast and this had not sustained us for long.   We were used to eating a good breakfast by this stage of the journey, but I could not imagine this would happen again for a while.   By midday, we were pretty ravenous, so we began stopping at simple village bars, expecting to find one serving basic country food.   Surely, at the very least, someone might be tempted to boost their income by cooking us something?   But no, each time we were disappointed.   Finally, we resorted to ordering a beer to keep us going.

"It's full of vitamin B and carbohydrate," I assured Sam.

He laughed wryly.   He'd heard that one before.

We were now in a small hamlet and outside the bar I had noticed a kind of public orchard with a bench.   I told Sam that after our refreshment I would rustle up something out of the basic emergency supplies in our panniers.   Back outside after finishing our beers, however, we found the same bench occupied by a group of old men.

Disappointed, we sat down on the grass while I knocked up some tuna, kidney bean and raisin sandwiches.   After a few minutes, when they began slurring their way through some traditional Hungarian songs, it became obvious that the old men were hopelessly drunk. Thankful for a bit of entertainment, Sam and I sat back to observe the proceedings.   It was a scene straight out of the Middle Ages, framed by fruit trees, barns and tiny dwellings with low doors.   Strange-looking heavy horses stood tied to trees.   A boy came by, herding a large gaggle of geese with a long crook.

Congratulating ourselves on our custom of carrying a few items of emergency rations, we tucked into the tasty sandwiches.   Cyclists cannot go far on empty stomachs.   Beyond the simple lack of energy, sense of humour failure soon sets in when food becomes scarce. This was a good lunch, made all the better by the raucous entertainment provided by our elderly neighbours.   After finishing off our meal with a few dusty nuts, discovered lurking at the bottom of Sam's bar-bag, we found ourselves hanging around to see how long the now immobile old men could continue.   All of a sudden, a short, toothless woman in a blood-stained pinafore appeared out of a small house at the back of the park.   She hollered at them, startling the horses more than the old men who were the target of her discontent.

One of them – logically the husband of the harridan with the headscarf and rolled-down stockings – attempted to jump up but spilt his *palinka* (a lethal home-brewed spirit) all over his neighbour. The neighbour leaped up, unbalancing the bench and all three men fell backwards into a heap on the ground. The husband managed to drag himself up, desperately trying to give the impression of sobriety. Leaving his two friends unconscious, he made his way towards his house for a lunch of whatever defenceless creature the woman had just butchered. The short-tempered woman shouted something more and returned inside in disgust.

His wife now safely out of sight, the old man paused to urinate against a ramshackle barn, resting his head against the wooden-slatted wall as he took control of business. After a minute, the flow stopped, but he remained propped at an angle against the wall, penis in hand and fast asleep. Remarkably, he managed to stay in this position for quite some time before his wife returned. Unfortunately for him, she had returned carrying a large metal soup ladle, which she used to give him a crack across his bald head. The sound resounded around the orchard but failed to waken either the husband or his friends nearby. The horses whinnied in sympathy, but the woman had had enough. Leaving her husband shamefully unbuttoned, she returned to the house to eat Sunday lunch alone. Thank goodness some rural traditions survive, I thought.

*

The scenes of a largely pre-mechanised pastoral world continued into Romania. By now, we were the recipients of dark, suspicious looks in the villages we passed through. The landscape had become more rugged and mountainous. Domestic rubbish littered the rivers and grass verges. What food we saw was basic and outside the towns quite scarce – a box of scabby potatoes here, a bundle of wilted chard there. Nevertheless, all this simplicity was a welcome change to the sophistication of Western Europe. Despite their abandon with rubbish, the people displayed a sense of basic honesty that was really reassuring.

We were happy to delay an hour or two in Timosoara, with its surprisingly large, modern shopping malls. Now known for being the birthplace of the demonstrations that finally ousted the tyrant

Ceausescu, it seemed a pleasant city.   We had lunch in Pizza Hut and enjoyed a walk around the shaded malls during the heat of afternoon.

Moving on, we found the roads later that afternoon not so much less sophisticated as less there.   In places, a single-track pot-holed road was the main trunk route across the country.   On one section, after asking a policeman for directions, we were advised that it was too dangerous to cycle further, due to the heavy trucks.   We agreed but said we could not see any alternative on the map.

"Correct, because is no alternative," the policeman said. "Change your plans or die!"

We were told to take a train from the nearby station to the next town, where the road improved.   Reluctantly, we followed his instruction, buying two tickets from Caransebes to Orsova, a naval port on the Danube.   Seeing the opportunity of a few shops, we bought some supplies and found a pleasant graveyard with benches for a picnic supper of bread, tomatoes and tinned fish while we waited for our train.   Graveyards have always been one of my favourite picnic locations.

We were on the train enjoying our dessert when the ticket collector arrived.   We proffered our tickets, which she snatched rudely from my hand.   The lady then asked us something in Romanian and seemed annoyed at our lack of understanding.   Taking me into the corridor, she jabbed her finger towards the bikes.   Were they ours?

"*Da*," I said, nodding in case I had guessed the wrong word.

The woman took on an officious air and it became plain that she was ordering us to get them off the train.   I tried to explain that the ticket office in Timisoara had said we could take bikes on that train, but she dismissed this explanation.   Calmly, I sat back down, refusing to budge.   It wasn't far to Orsova, I thought, so I would play for time.   The woman marched off to fetch the guard.

The elderly man soon arrived and asked for an explanation, which I attempted to give.   I had no idea of Romanian, so I tried combining some Russian and a few words I knew of Serbo-Croat. The man seemed satisfied and began to leave.   At this, the woman exploded, remonstrating with him as he walked away.   I was determined to stay calm and was glad I had managed it so far.

Moments later, the woman put her head around our carriage door, spitefully hissed something at us and wagged a warning finger. I remained unworried, telling Sam it would be fine. We were getting off at the next stop anyway. She was, we agreed, the first unpleasant person we had come across since the bitch of Bitche.

Up to this point , the train had waited about 15 minutes to move on at each small station stop, so it was nearly an hour before we arrived at Orsova. We had put our bikes at the end of the last carriage to avoid inconveniencing other passengers. When the train arrived in Orsova, however, our end carriage was well short of the platform and there was a towering drop to the track. Sam climbed down to the track and I had just started to pass down the panniers when I became aware that the train was moving. It was a gut-wrenching feeling. At first I assumed that the driver was moving the last carriage in line with the platform, but he was not. The speed continued to build, with Sam shouting from somewhere out of sight below me.

"Sam, stay there!" I shouted back. "I'll come back for you!"

I wasn't sure if he had heard me.

I didn't regain sight of Sam. Each second carried me further away from him. I felt numb and powerless. How far would it be before the next stop? Had he kept away from the wheels?

Soon the ticket woman walked along to my carriage and looked in with an evil smile. I could easily have strangled her. Pity for her husband, however, quickly replaced my desire to bring a swift and painful end to her life. Remembering things Lorna often told me about vindictive people, I wondered what kind of childhood had made the woman this way. The feelings of the other passengers towards her were less charitable, shouting at her and making gestures that questioned her sanity. She simply tossed her hair and said something I took to mean, "Tough!"

The other passengers quickly came to my aid. I ascertained that the next station was a full forty minutes away. I tried to phone Sam's mobile, then realised it was in the bar-bag on his bike, which remained on the train with me. As I tried to calm myself, it slowly dawned on me that he had also been left without passport or money.

Rather melodramatically, I felt I had abandoned my child in a hostile place in the middle of the night.

At the next station, Drobeta Turnu Saverin, my fellow passengers helped me to get both bikes and the other bags off the train before the smirking witch-woman blew her whistle to leave. One passenger took me to the policeman at the station and explained the situation. I tried English, French, German, Italian, Spanish and bits of Greek, all to no avail. I was limited to sign language and one or two words of Russian, which I still naively hoped might be similar to Romanian.

Finally, a young student approached. He spoke a bit of French and English. This kind young man explained to the policeman that I was worried about my son and could he call for a policeman at Orsova to go to the station and tell Sam I would be there in a few hours. This he did, but Sam was not at the station. Doom!

I paced up and down the platform in the early hours watching an elderly vagrant woman trying to sleep against a wall by the goods hall. The policeman repeatedly woke her up and, I assumed, kept telling her she had to leave if she wasn't catching a train. Each time, she sat up for a few minutes then lay down again with her bundle, exhausted. This game continued for the hour and a half that I waited, and probably every night after that. What came as a shock, though, was to suddenly notice that her bundle was in fact a very young child.

Eventually, I thought to switch on Sam's mobile phone. I had got a new SIM card for my own phone before we left so I wouldn't receive work calls. Sam had put the number on his mobile but not memorized it. But he would, I realised, know his own number. Thankfully, Sam had the same idea and asked some Hungarian coach tourists if he could borrow a mobile phone to call his lost father. They were eager to help. Sam reassured me he was OK. He had eaten all the food, he said, and been using the time to write a song in his head about the experience. The cloud of doom lifted and I managed a smile.

*

All the time waiting and watching the old woman protecting the child gave me a chance to think. *Why do I seem to insist on seeing Sam as vulnerable and needing my protection? He's virtually a man now.* My mind drifted back to that first bike trip Sam and I made when he was ten – the reason I was standing here now, in fact, on a station in the middle of nowhere.

As I continuing to pace up and down the dusty platform with the odd goods train slowly trundling by, vivid pictures of that time came flooding into my head, accompanied by Sam's ten-year-old voice.

It started very early in the morning: a dark bedroom, silent except for the faint sound of shallow breathing, Lorna and I asleep in bed. Suddenly, I was startled into a state of wakefulness by the silhouette of a figure standing before me in the dark. At first, I thought I was still dreaming, until the small skeletal figure spoke to me.

"Dad, is it time to go yet?"

I began laughing out loud. I saw the policeman by the ticket window look over at me. Embarrassed and unable to explain, I smiled and paced off along the platform again.

Drifting back to the darkened bedroom, I remembered how terrified I had been, waking to see that little figure. The skeleton printed on the pyjamas looked so real in the dark. Of course, I realised it was Sam once he spoke and that we were due to set off on our first proper bike trip that morning, but it had scared me rigid for a moment.

I pictured Sam now, standing forlorn on the station back in Orsova with no idea where his father was or how he was going to get out of this.   If only the train would hurry up, so I could sort it all out. I couldn't get the image of the innocent little boy of ten out of my head, standing there in his pyjamas. I thought of us getting home frozen after that trip and his little voice saying to Lorna the next day:

"And me and Dad are going to cycle to Japan!"

For the hundredth time that night, I reached the end of the platform and glanced over at the old woman and her bundle. She was checking the child. For the first time, I saw its face – a little boy looking so calm and contented, sleeping safely in her arms. Sam would be fine if I could just get back there quickly before he decided to wander off.   It seemed like an unlikely series of events that had brought us to this point.   It gave me a strange sense of it having been meant to happen.

*

My reverie and the pacing up and down ended when the train finally drew up to the platform.   More stress.   Now I had to get two bikes and myself onto the train, alone.   Fortunately, though, someone helped me and I relaxed a little once I was in my seat.   When I eventually got back to Orsova, however, it was around 3am and Sam was nowhere to be seen.   I walked along the platform littered with surly drunk men and began to worry.   Had he tried to walk to the next town?   Had the police taken him?

Thankfully, Sam turned up after a few minutes.   He had been waiting by the riverside, where the drunks would not bother him.   I hugged him, reassuring him that there was no harm done, and that this had been a useful lesson about not taking trains with bikes and making sure we kept valuables in our bum-bags at all times.   We started to pack the bikes.   My happiness was abruptly cut short, though, when I realised one pannier was missing.   I had thrown down three, but he only had two.   I realised it was my pannier with my clothes in it but more importantly with all the documents with things such as visa application details.   A horrible sick feeling overcame me.   We had celebrated too soon.

"Oh my God," I said, catching my breath. "What the hell was in that pannier?   I can't bear it…."

"Keep calm!" Sam called as he ran back along the platform and down the track.   I wondered why he was bothering.   It was futile after all this time.   I watched him walk along to where he thought he had climbed down from the train.

"You're wasting your time, Sam," I muttered. "It was three bloody hours ago!"

Surely someone would have gratefully acquired the bag and its contents by now, even if a train had not driven over it, I told myself.

A drunk shuffled up, staring at me as if mesmerised.   He put out his hand in the ubiquitous gesture of the world's beggars.

67

"And you can F off," I muttered. "If I had any money, it was in that bloody pannier!"

Call it the luck of youth, but Sam soon returned out of the dark clutching the bag – intact, contents undisturbed. I hugged Sam again, thanked him for staying so calm and sensible, and apologised. I was a mess. Thinking everything was about to go wrong, I had behaved like a total prat.

"Sorry, mate," I muttered to the drunk as we turned to leave.

He remained transfixed in wonder as we left the station.

It was now 3.30am and we were pretty shattered – probably more emotionally than physically. I surmised correctly that there would be no hotel or campsite here, so we walked along the main road looking for a park to camp in. Narrow and unlit, with trucks still thundering along it in the night, the road felt extremely dangerous. Our dilemmas were soon over, however, as we found a kind of derelict playpark adjacent to a closed petrol station at the top of the hill.

In the pitch black, it was not easy at first to see what kind of the place it was. By waiting for a truck to pass, though, we managed to identify a broken climbing frame, along with some swings (with no swings) and the remains of a sand pit (long transformed into a latrine). After waiting a few minutes, another truck passed and we saw more. Among the now familiar domestic detritus we identified a few broken old benches. It was the best we were going to find tonight. We laid down in our sleeping bags on the rickety benches for what remained of the night.

Sam and I did not lie around discussing our day as we normally did. We were utterly exhausted. Tired as I was, though, I couldn't sleep. The trauma was over, but I still felt scared. Had we really survived that near disaster? Were we really both here unharmed with our bikes and luggage intact?

I spent most of that night thinking through the evening's events and watching shooting stars. The display in the heavens only added to my already surreal sense of that day. Sam, on the other hand, fell asleep immediately, looking very much the worst for wear. I heard him coughing unhealthily during the night. The benches were uncomfortable and we were disturbed regularly by drivers pulling into the lay-by for a sleep, but I felt fortunate.

*

In the morning, I awoke to a revitalising golden sunrise and a superb view down over the naval docks on the river. I pictured a map of the area and it dawned on me that this was the point at which the bridge over the Danube to Serbia had been pre-emptively blown-up during the recent Bosnian war. It put our overnight troubles into some sort of perspective. Unfortunately, Sam had woken up with a worsened bronchial cough after our night's ordeal. I felt to blame for the whole fiasco, but it had been nothing that either of us could conceivably have avoided. If we had have defied the police and continued on the road, who knows what might have befallen us? As the policeman said, "Change your plans or die."

I knew I was still seeing myself in the role of a father with a dependent child and it was really about time I recognised that Sam was no longer that reliant on me. Before we left home, I had told him that I wanted him to take a full part in the decision-making on the trip and I didn't want to go through it in the role of *the dad*. I thought I needed to say this for his benefit, but I was starting to see it might be me who was finding it difficult to let go of the role.

We ached a little after our night on the broken benches. Mine had been broken in the middle and I'd slept folded at a 45-degree angle. Even so, we felt surprisingly upbeat as we packed up in the glow of the early morning sun. My glass-half-full nature saw the train experience as ultimately a strengthening one – Sam certainly seemed to have sorted a few more things out in his head – but our inner confidence had been shaken.

I cleaned my teeth sitting on my bench and encouraged Sam to do the same. I felt preoccupied with our health. We looked around at the place we had spent the night. It looked like a bomb had gone off in a rubbish truck. All manner of household rubbish and takeaway cartons covered every inch of the playpark. If it had been a theatre stageset for a rubbish tip, people would have said it was overdone. We rechecked our luggage and when we were sure nothing was missing we set off.

That morning was our first experience of cycling through long road-tunnels and it was a rather nerve-wracking introduction. We had managed to avoid this hazard so far, but here we had no other option. On narrow corniche-type roads, there is no room for a cycle lane or pavement inside the tunnel, even if they could be bothered to put one there. Large trucks and speeding cars roar through, never for a moment expecting to meet pedestrians or cyclists. Even with your lights and reflective vests on, they don't see you until the very last moment. The shock visible on the faces of drivers coming towards us was worrying, because those coming up behind us on our side of the road would be even more surprised. It was very dangerous – only a fool would argue otherwise – but sometimes there is no alternative. In fact, we did have an alternative, but the tunnel was certainly not worrying enough to make us get back on that train.

In such circumstances, your best bet is to wait until the road looks quiet as far as you can see, then pedal like hell to get through it quickly, while at the same time listening and watching for lights in your mirror. If you see a big truck, stop and quickly pin yourself and your bike against the wall. That morning, the road was not too busy and also was under repair. The temporary traffic lights broke the traffic up into batches, so we got through without coming too close to death.

*

If the train experience was one of the unluckiest days of the trip, then the following day was one of the luckiest. The rural parts of Romania – which means most of it – deliver some beautiful pastoral scenes. The thatched village of Nicolau Balcescu is apparently a world heritage site but there were no signs of tourists ever going there. We stopped on a hill looking down on the collection of about eighty haphazard thatched houses. Each had a small adjoining barn, a hayrick and a small farmyard with vegetable beds, fruit trees, a few pigs, chickens, goats, sheep, plus the odd cow and a mule pulling a cart. A man in a jaunty cap came along the muddy lane driving an extremely large collection of shuffling geese with a crook. They were reminiscent of a badly trained platoon of old soldiers. It was a scene from a historic film, or maybe Dad's Army. For half an hour at least, we wished we lived there. Then again, there would be no internet access and I doubt their bathrooms were up to much.

After a few steep mountain roads and runs through deep ravines, our stomachs began to yearn for a substantial lunch. Emergency rations mostly gone, we began to worry about not having seen anywhere to eat or to buy food all morning. We stopped at a couple of village pumps to ask locals but came away with nothing save an offer of a few unattractive potatoes and some cobs of maize. Finally, as we cycled through the village of Rosion, we were hailed at the side of the road by a man and a woman shouting, "Coca Cola! *Bierra!*" We waved, continuing on at first, but they were very persistent. "*Manjare!*" they yelled, running along beside us.

Deciding that an Italian offer of food was worth investigating, even if it meant risking being robbed, we pulled over.

The couple showed us where to park our bikes out of the blistering sun and ushered us inside their simple shop. They seemed to speak Italian. It transpired that they spent six months of every year living and working in Verona. We were poured beer from a barrel and found we could converse comfortably, with them speaking Italian and me speaking Spanish. Their teenage son joined us, along with a group of inquisitive village children, who stood in the shop watching the show. Two of the children were sent off by Maria with a few coins to buy fresh bread, luncheon meat and a big bottle of Coke for Sam.

Maria, clearly the matriarch, brought out a huge homemade Feta-like cheese. Marion, the diminutive husband, poured me endless cups of beer from a barrel. I drained them recklessly.

"How much do you think this is going to cost us?" murmured Sam nervously.

I told him not to worry. We had committed ourselves now, so we might as well enjoy it. After half an hour of jovial discussion with beer and food, Maria arrived from the kitchen with chicken drumsticks. She was worried about Sam – such a skinny youth, without his mum to look after him – and piled up his plate. Marion continued to refill my beer and together we soon finished the whole barrel. The premises were basic, but it was the only thing approaching a shop we had seen since Drobeta Turnu Saverin. They even had one of those ultraviolet fly-zappers!

The conversation gave our spirits a great lift. Maria, Marion and their son Daniel were jovial and kind. It seemed they had never seen a foreigner in the village, let alone cyclists, and were determined to make the most of it.

Slightly the worst for wear after an hour or so, and half hoarse from laughter, we were offered a bed to lie down on for the afternoon. By now, we trusted them completely, but we reluctantly declined the generous offer. Arrangements were made for Sam to come to Rosion the following summer to go fishing with Daniel, but concerned about the time and the distance to the next main town, we rose to pay and get on our way.

Sam's worries about being stung with a big bill at the end were reversed. All payment was steadfastly refused. Nothing we said would change it.

"Please do not offend us by trying to pay," Maria warned – or words to that effect. She held up a firm hand. Maria had spoken, and she was clearly not a woman to argue with.

By the time we left, our bikes were overloaded with bottles of drink, bread, cheese, luncheon meat and fruit. Sam agreed to accept a stuffed green bunny-rabbit to accompany us on our journey. Around its neck hung a big sign saying, A PRESENT – MARIA, MARION & DANIEL, FRIENDS FOR ALL LIFE, along with a phone number in case we got into trouble. We managed to leave behind several further stuffed animals.

Sam and I laughed with abandon as we cycled along the road. It was a major upturn in our fortunes, compared to the previous day. Were there really people in the world that generous? Sam wondered. He had been sure the whole time that they would ask for some special favour from us at the end. In the space of an hour and a half, we had made three close friends in a country where we didn't speak a word of the language. I had drunk a large quantity of beer, though, and we still had around 65km to ride in full sun and 40 degree heat. It sloshed around inside me and I snaked about a bit on the road. It was not a great problem here, though; any traffic was slowed to a crawl by the donkey carts along the road.

I was blissfully happy and this amused Sam. He was happy too and his faith in human nature had been restored. We waved to village people as we passed by watching them shelling huge piles of maize and winnowing barley by hand. One elderly maize-sheller called out in English.

"Hey, she wants to marry you!"

We looked over to see one lovely girl but many more toothless grinning old ladies.

"Be warned, Sam," I said. "That's the before and after."

Far from hampering our progress, the over-indulgence in beer seemed to help the afternoon pass with ease. What a contrast to the evening before.

That night was spent in a hotel at the port town of Calafat. The rooms were large but rather bare and the whole place had the feel of a conference centre converted into a makeshift B&B. Calafat had that special age-old atmosphere of a place where everyone is arriving to cross at the port, arriving from the other side, or working in some way to facilitate trade between the two. For me, it's a good atmosphere – life going on almost as it has for centuries.

SAM'S POINT OF VIEW

Cycling through Romania and Bulgaria was fun. Although poor and undeveloped compared to the parts of Europe we had conquered previously, it was significantly different and far more peaceful. It was the first point when I felt we had cycled far from home.

My personal highlight of this period was the family we met in Rosion. We had spent the majority of the day cycling in blistering heat, passing tiny villages where all the farmers' wives and daughters seemed to be sorting huge piles of sweet corn. Stray dogs would idly follow our dusty trail. Maria and Marion were determined to meet us. The area we were cycling through rarely saw foreign travellers. Ravenously hungry, we were given a mountain of bread, roast chicken, salad, coke and cheese. They even had their own lager on draft. I was so full, but they continued to feed us. Maria was concerned that I was too thin. I came to realise that a fast metabolism really isn't an acceptable explanation in Eastern Europe. You're either fat and wealthy, or thin and poor. These lovely people offered us a corner to sleep in but we thought it best to take care about being ripped off. We needn't have worried. They point-blank refused any payment for food and drink and sent us on our way loaded with gifts. The whole experience was really humbling and gave us such a positive feel about Romania. It's a common thing to have locals want to show you how great their hometown or country is, but I don't think we ever met with their level of generosity again.

The road through Romania eventually became impossible to cycle. The Cops stopped us and warned us about the trucks, at which point we decided to get a train to Orsova. This was probably a big mistake (although being squashed by a truck might not have been great either!) Anyway, as you will have read above, when we arrived at the station I was left chasing the train as it pulled away still carrying my dad, the bikes, and my valuables. I can't describe the sinking sensation I felt on realising that my bar-bag contained my phone, passport and money. It seemed like the whole world had turned against me. It was 11.30 at night and I was stranded at a small broken-down station with no other buildings in sight, except a basic dockside and a dark deserted road by a river. The station (which smelled like a urinal) seemed to be a dossing place for drunken tramps. I don't mind saying I was scared. I retreated to the dockside. To pass the time and stay positive, I made up a song in my head. This is what I remember of it:

> *Sitting by the docks abandoned by a train*
> *Don't worry, no hurry, it'll come back again*
> *Gotta sit here and wait and treat it like a game.*

That was the chorus. There were about three verses but I can't remember them – probably for the best really.
Finally, after I had eaten all the food in the panniers, my dad did arrive back. It was a good experience. It certainly helped me gain

a sense of independence, and after being separated in such dire circumstances perhaps it brought us a little closer. Plenty more work needed at this point, though, as you might guess.

75

Chapter 4

Bulgaria – On a rocky road to the edge of Europe

"Oh yeah, let's just do 100 miles a day, Mark Swain-style! Great way to see the world! Dad, you really need to get some help. And I'll be straight with you, I don't think it can wait until we get back."

After breakfast at our cavernous Calafat hotel, Sam and I took a small ferry across the Danube into Bulgaria. We had seen the best and the worst of Romania in the space of 24 hours, but we sailed away with a good feeling in our hearts.

Despite it being a new country, Bulgaria looked similar. It was a little greener and they seemed to have a system for dealing with domestic waste, which was an immediate improvement on Romania. Struggling to get accurate directions after getting off the ferry, we cycled into the countryside before coming upon a promising restaurant nestled on the banks of the Danube, near Vidim.

At the restaurant we met a friendly Swiss couple with small children. They were riding on unusual recumbent tandems with the kids up front and said they had cycled there from Germany over a period of a month. The kids slept a lot of the time on the bikes and they stopped most afternoons to swim. What a lovely idea. They certainly didn't have the stressed look of parents on holiday with small children. It made me wish Lorna and I had done something like that when our children were small.

Before too long, the Danube Cycle Path is likely to find its way this far down, making the prospect of a safe and convenient cycle route all the way from Southwest Germany to Turkey an exciting possibility, if you are that way inclined. Further upstream, it must already be proving a worthwhile source of tourist revenue.

In the town of Kozloduj that night, we stopped at a few shops to ask about guesthouses, hotels or a campsite, but drew a blank each time. Finally, we stopped a police car and asked them for help. This proved more fruitful.

"Follow us, please," they said.

If you were not one of the cyclists, an amusing scenario followed. Sam and I found ourselves pedalling like the clappers behind the police car to a series of hotels and worker hostels, which each turned out to be full or mysteriously not open for business. The cops did their best to persuade people and asked about other possibilities. Each time, we moved on in pursuit of yet another lead. To an onlooker, it must have looked like an episode of the Keystone Cops.

Part one finally came to an end when the cops were radioed to go and break up a fight between two rival gypsy families. A common occurrence, they told us. Breathless, we were deposited at the police station and told to wait. Finally, the chief of police came out on his bicycle saying that his two guys had been delayed and we should follow him to a hotel.

After a 10-minute ride it was apparent the chief was taking us to one of the first places we had tried. By now we were shattered and we had got nowhere. We managed to explain that the hotel we were heading had been full and returned with him to the station. Here, a further policeman was detailed to take us to a luxury riverside resort hotel where a phone call had ascertained there was a room available. We arrived after a frantic 5km ride along a rutted dirt road, only to be informed that the room had now gone. We were exhausted and at the end of our tether. We didn't have the energy to go anywhere else.

"Where can I pitch a tent?" I asked the receptionist in desperation.

The young woman winced, then asked me to wait. Moments later she arrived back with a large, imposing man she introduced as the hotel owner. With his upright stance and barrel chest, he looked more like an Army colonel than a hotel manager. Fortunately, however, this initially intimidating man proved to have a kind heart. He also spoke good English and by chance had a daughter who was studying in Brighton. It seemed to make a difference.

"You are very lucky that Bulgarian police are so kind," he said in his resounding *basso profundo*. "I will find you a room, don't worry. You can relax now. Get yourselves a drink and we will take your bags to the room."

We did as instructed. Eating a luxurious dinner in the large dining room that night, we found ourselves laughing again at our eventual good luck. Quite honestly, by then I didn't care how much it was going to cost.

*

Sam seemed to be going through a slightly more up phase at this point but was still quieter than was normal for him. Meanwhile, I remained unable to get rid of the sense that I was the source of his unhappiness. He seemed to be worse after we had been with other people, and at this stage I had not really worked out why. I had decided back in Budapest that it was best to leave him to himself for a bit and not to question him about how he was feeling, beyond the practicalities of general health, aches and pains, and tiredness. This didn't stop me from continually searching my mind wondering if there was anything I had said or done. After all, like him, I had plenty of time each day to think. But mostly I came back to the conclusion he was thinking about Hannah and how that was going to turn out. I resigned myself to making sure I remained approachable but not to press him about anything. It was probably the best thing to do, although it is not in my nature to be reticent about anything.

The following afternoon, we again struggled to find somewhere to stay. You learn to sense whether an area is safe for camping or not and this one certainly gave us the feeling that it was not. We received a variety of conflicting reports about a motel on the road ahead, but nothing materialised. Just when I had accepted it didn't exist, we found it. Imagine our disappointment then, as we fended off a large dog on our arrival, to be told by an armed man in camouflage that the place was closed for redecoration. He was, we discovered, not in fact a guard but a friend of the owner and was there for a weekend of hunting.

As an international business traveller he spoke some English, which was a bonus. More fortunate for us, though, was that somehow he persuaded the owner's wife to allow us to sleep in a room where the paint was nearly dry. She was reluctant. The bathroom, we were told, was out of action. It was beginning to look like the lady had decided no, when I saw her look over at Sam, who was walking disconsolately towards his bike. She was a mother. She caved in.

"Perhaps the front bedroom might be dry by now," she seemed to say.

"Any room is fine by us," I told Rambo. "Even one with wet paint."

That evening, we found ourselves treated well, seated at dinner amongst an extended family and friends. We felt grateful for our good fortune.   Thank God for mothers, and thank God for Sam being so skinny, I thought.   The world was still conspiring to help us follow our destiny.

*

This part of Bulgaria proved to be an interesting area.   The beautiful countryside seemed largely unaffected by the outside world, despite the towns being relatively developed.

Making our way down through Bulgaria, we passed through miles of rocky hills and lovely pine forested valleys.   The slow pace of life seemed to affect our own cycling speed and we found ourselves stopping to enjoy the countryside more often than we had in Hungary or Romania.   The roads were fairly poor, with broken edges and a rocky surface most of the time, but Sam and I enjoyed this simple life: eating simple food in village squares and talking to a few local people.

The historic town of Velico Ternova was probably one of the more visited spots we passed through, with its houses built in spectacular manner on the sheer rockface.   We noticed a few foreign cars passing us as we approached the town, which also marked our arrival at the central mountain range of Bulgaria.   We had been warned how extreme these mountains were and had spent some time trying to establish the best route through – or rather over – them to the plains beyond.

At this point, our map showed two passes over the mountains. Choosing the smaller road, which was shorter but steeper, we set off towards the winding Trevenska Pass.   I liked the sound of it.

For around 25km in the foothills we made good time. But at the beginning of the pass we saw a barrier, with cars and trucks being angrily turned back. It appeared the road was closed for reconstruction and we all had to drive back to Velico Ternova to take the other road. For a car, that was inconvenient, but for us a 50km detour was more significant. We were delighted, therefore, when the guard lifted the barrier, saluted and said, "Cycle, OK!"

Never celebrate too early, my mother often says. The steep road soon lost its surface and became strewn with giant boulders. Despite these obstacles, however, we remained largely glad to have been allowed through. Further along, we reached the first of many points where we were asked to wait while the rock face was blasted from above and huge slabs of rock crashed down onto the road in front of us. Sam and I looked at each other in shock. We could hardly believe they would allow any member of the public, especially on bicycles, to get this close. The sound and feel of the enormous hunks of mountainside crashing onto the road was terrifying.

"Careful, Sam," I said. "Get too close to that and we'll be going home in a matchbox!"

It felt like a film set. The fallen rock, each piece the size of a large house, had to be scooped up from the road by huge bulldozers before we were allowed through with a few contractors' vehicles. These awe-inspiring interruptions delayed our progress every ten minutes or so, but this was not unwelcome. Apart from the entertainment value, the road was so steep that we needed the breaks. It was tough on our legs, tough on our bikes and the dust probably didn't do our lungs much good either, but we reached the summit after a couple of hours and were lucky enough to find a café serving cold beer.

There is nothing as enjoyable as a cold beer at the end of a dusty mountain climb, and this was one of the best. Dusk was approaching. We had not made the climb in record time, but we felt some pride in having made it through the danger zone without any serious harm to our bikes or to us. We really felt we'd achieved something.

After our liquid reward, Sam and I considered the ride down. From a lookout point in the café garden, we could see the road winding down the mountain below like a ribbon, cutting through steep wooded tracts, over rivers and down to the plains below. The smell of the pines soothed our lungs and we breathed it in deeply, savouring it almost as we had the beer. It looked so undeveloped and beautiful. We couldn't hang about here all evening wondering at the lovely scenery, though. We were losing light. I could see it would be a long, fast ride down and my heart began to beat faster in anticipation. Our legs certainly needed a rest from climbing. Sam had other ideas, however.

"Dad, try to resist your mad urge to press on for a moment and consider the idea of camping here on the mountain for the night. We could make some pasta and get to use the camp stove for the first time. I think it would be even more pleasure to ride down the mountain early in the morning when there's nobody on the road."

I smiled at his diplomacy. It did seem an attractive idea, despite my childlike tendency to want to race down the mountain and reach the next town by dark. So just at the start of the descent, we dismounted and climbed up to a lush green field set above the road. We cut down some branches, placed them in the gaps between the boundary trees so we couldn't be seen by passing traffic, and then pitched our tent. No evidence of cows, we were relieved to see.

After firing up the MSR Pocket-rocket for hot water, then chopping tomatoes, garlic and foraged oregano, it seemed no time at all until we were sitting down to a satisfying dinner of pasta with tinned tuna and freshly made Provencal sauce. We felt we were in a good place both physically and spiritually and it was great to end a day feeling we had earned a prize at the end.

Tired after our steep climb up the rough mountain road, Sam and I went straight to bed after dinner and lay talking for a while. It was at this point that Sam asked me whether I had found him annoying so far on the trip. I said that I hadn't much. I conceded, though, that I had been worried by him seeming quiet and preoccupied, but no, not really annoying. I said that in fact I had found him really thoughtful and that this, and the lack of usual home pressures, had really made me feel calm. At the end of the conversation, I was pleased I had managed to resist asking him about this so far on the trip and that it was him who mentioned it when he felt ready. Of course, he had annoyed me at times, but I didn't want to make him feel bad about that.

I hardly need to say to any parent that this issue of judging the right time to ask things, and when it is better not to, is a challenge with teenagers. This is especially true for someone like me who naturally confronts issues rather than avoids them. It is hard to be relaxed about it. If you say nothing, a kind of stretching balloon sensation results, with the dread of an explosion if the tension is not released gently. I had begun to wonder which of us was finding the interpersonal stuff the hardest. I had assumed that he was, but now I was less convinced. I felt unsure and unable to control things in the normal way, and to be honest I didn't like it. I thought about what Lorna would say if I could talk to her now. I knew she would tell me that learning to rein in my natural impulse to confront issues and tackle them like a dog with a bone would be a great learning experience for me. It was a difficult exercise, but I was already seeing the benefits of it.

Annoyingly, having found such a good location that evening, the promise of a much-needed good night's sleep was spoilt by goats in a field on the opposite side of the road, where they came to drink from the river. The bells around their necks jangled loudly all night and meant that we were woken up constantly, startled into thinking we were back in that cow field in Wales. It was some recompense, though, to have the cool swift ride down through the mountains and valleys in the morning sun. We were soon wide awake and drinking in the pleasure of it. By the time we reached the bottom, our bad night's sleep was forgotten.

*

Over the following few days, Sam and I passed through a number of small historic towns, where we seemed almost to be cycling as time-travelling voyeurs through Byzantine Europe. The main road in, through and out of these towns was frequently cobbled in Romanesque style, and often for many miles up into the hills. This looked beautiful, of course, but was an absolute nightmare to cycle on. I worried about broken spokes. It was a problem many other long-distance cyclists had talked about and I got off to walk on the worst bits. It annoyed me that Sam didn't, although he was lighter and it probably wasn't as hard on his bike.

At one stage, already in a slightly bad mood from several miles of cobbled hills, I was struck hard on the back of the head. More shocked than hurt, I looked up to see a laughing youth leaning out of a speeding van with a large maize stick. I couldn't decide whether to laugh along with the youth – it must have been a hilarious sight – or to roar in fury. At the time, I was convinced that Sam, riding just behind me, derived some pleasure from the incident, although I was probably doing him an injustice. I must admit, though, it did put me against Bulgaria from that point on. Afterwards, I thought about how one negative thing like this can completely colour your view of a country.

Arriving in Star Zagora close to the Turkish border, we discovered that there was another long section of narrow main-road ahead, crowded with heavy trucks thundering their way to and from Istanbul. Having been warned that this was no road for cyclists, we looked at alternative routes. By this stage, though, there was no second choice beyond going all the way back into Romania and east to the Black Sea. I can see this is really something it is worth cyclists checking up on in advance. The feeling of being left with a Hobson's choice – the risk of being flattened by trucks or arrested, or taking a train – can be gut-wrenching.

Given time, and an early lunch in a cafe, Sam and I reached an agreement. In the absence of any other sensible option, and wanting to sort out our Iran visa application in Istanbul before Lorna arrived, we decided to risk taking another train. Perhaps the last one was just a one-off, we agreed.

*

After being told curtly "No!" (with an outstretched palm in our faces) several times by the ticket-office lady, we finally found an English-speaking student to help us. The train was already feeling like a bad idea. Our friend assured us that "No!" meant that we had to wait until 10pm before we could buy a ticket for the 11pm Istanbul train. Not so bad.

Sam and I relaxed and went off to explore Star Zagora, buying food in the bustling markets.   We managed to find a free bench in the popular central park and made sandwiches for lunch.   After the dilemma about taking road or train, this cheered us up no end and there was plenty of activity to keep us entertained while we ate. Sitting there for some time, we noticed that one long line of benches was used only by elderly retired people while the benches opposite were taken up by vagrants and winos.

People being what they are, the two groups were unable to just accept the arrangement, though.   Tension builds over time and territorial challenges inevitably result.

Sam and I noticed that periodically one or two winos would go over to take a space on one of the pensioner benches and an argument would break out.   Before long, this would become a physical fight between the feeble opponents.   At several points, a slightly younger tall man with long silver hair (sitting in the elderly camp), stepped in and diplomatically broke it up.   We wondered if this was his job, a formal local council appointment perhaps, or whether he was doing it out of the goodness of his heart.

"Maybe he's on long-term sick," I suggested to Sam.

As each sortie was diverted or diffused by the diplomatic Silverback, the underlying tension mounted, until finally it boiled over.   One frail old man, attempting to negotiate with a group of winos, seemed to stand on one wino's poorly foot.   The injured man leaped up screeching and pushed the old gentleman to the ground. This drew an immediate response from the elderly side.   Twenty or thirty men of varying degrees of seniority and frailty leaped to their feet and made a slow-motion charge towards the winos.   Walking sticks were raised and in some cases brought crashing down upon the heads of inebriated men, stupefying them still further. The Silverback, trying to keep the two sides apart, caught a walking stick in the eye and was finally done for by a bony knee in his groin.   Surprisingly, we were the only onlookers who seemed to find humour in this spectacle.   Others nearby just looked on with disapproval, as if it happened on a regular basis.   Perhaps it did.

The tragicomic battle between Star Zagora Pensioners and Star Zagora Winos kept us entertained for an hour or more before we headed back to the station to catch the train to Istanbul. It was the most amusing thing we had seen for some time. Almost as funny, Sam thought, as seeing me hit across the back of the head with a maize stalk earlier that day.

We took a surreptitious photograph of the Silverback before we left. We had to, since he bore an uncanny resemblance to a friend back in Canterbury. In fact, it inspired us to start a new blog with photos of lookalikes to amuse people back home. Maybe nobody read it, maybe some were offended, but it certainly gave us some pleasure spotting them, and trying to photograph them without being noticed. There is a man running an antique shop by St Sophia mosque in Istanbul who is the double of our friend John Verling – proprietor of Dingle Phone Shop in Ireland.

*

Unsurprisingly, the train was far from a relaxing experience. First they said we had to buy a ticket after 10pm. Then, after being kept waiting until eleven o'clock, they said we had to buy it on the train. The train arrived two hours late. Nobody seemed surprised. Apologetic station announcements have yet to reach Bulgaria.

On the train the ticket man sold us tickets to Istanbul, but they were only valid to the nearby border, so we had to buy more ten minutes later. None of this was very expensive but it was annoying and unsettling. We had to pay for all four bunks in a compartment so we could put our bikes on the seats, as they supposedly had no luggage van. This was untrue but fine by us, as it was obviously more secure. Then there was the usual two-hour fiasco at the border, buying stamps for visas etc.

"What is your *porpoise* in my country?"

"Fish?" I answered mischievously.

The man wrote this on our forms, stamped them and handed them back with our passports.

After returning to the train, the fun really began. Two brusque guards swaggered officiously into our carriage and asked to see our tickets, quickly. These guys were not interested in ensuring good relations with foreigners. Clearly, they had not been *on the course*.

The tickets were not valid, they said. Judging by their expressions, this was a serious matter. It all seemed strangely familiar. The two men took the tickets away to the office for inspection. They did not return. Some minutes later, after collecting our visas, I found the men in the station office. They denied knowing me; denied ever being on the train in fact, or taking our tickets. I'd had enough. I was tired.

"OK. Police!" I said loudly.

There was a fumbling in pockets and looking under papers on the desk, and then miraculously the tickets were found in one man's jacket pocket. Later, back on the painfully slow train, we discovered that the tickets were not exactly the same ones – they were a day out of date. It was a con-trick I had heard of before. Fortunately for us, the guard who inspected our tickets before arriving in Istanbul chose to ignore it.

All this was a reminder to me to sharpen my wits. I had experienced plenty of this kind of thing before in my life, but I was out of practice – grown lazy and comfortable in the relative safety of a decade spent in sleepy Canterbury. There would be plenty more of this from now on, I told myself, and we would need to be ready for it. The train trundled slowly out of the border station. How was I going to explain away the bikes on the seats when that woman ticket collector arrived tossing her hair?

"Sam, make sure you keep your phone, passport and money in your money belt," I said.

Sam was already asleep.

SAM'S POINT OF VIEW

Arriving in Bulgaria, we met with more treacherous potholed roads packed with big articulated trucks. They were hardly able to fit on their own side of the road. From start to finish we had a bad feeling about Bulgaria. Having spoken to other people since returning home, though, I'm willing to accept that we just had a collection of unpleasant experiences that coloured our judgement. The first of these was the boy leaning out the window of a speeding truck and whacking my dad on the head with what looked like a long stem of sugar cane. From my position it was hilarious, although I'm pretty sure at the time my dad would have happily watched that truck crash straight into a cliff face! To give my dad his due, though, there was no lasting malice.

My mood improved in Bulgaria. I think I came close to feeling suicidal before this point. I remember laughing for the first time on the trip while watching the winos and the old codgers in the park in Star Zagora. It wasn't just the battle. As we sat there, my dad concocted a ridiculous story that was utterly hilarious. He said we should tell people we had met a genetic scientist sitting on our bench who told us he was a replacement body parts specialist and that he was currently working on getting a human penis to grow on the back of a rat.

I nearly wet myself when a guy came and sat next to us, and after a bit of conversation, put his hand in his pocket, saying:

"Would you like to see something interesting?"

I was sure he was going to get a rat out of his pocket with a penis growing out of its back. He must have thought I was so strange when he got out a war medal and I cracked up laughing. I just couldn't stop for about five minutes. In the end, I think my dad said something about me being on medication. The man looked worried about me as he left. I felt bad for him, but how could we have explained to him why I was really laughing? He'd never have believed us.

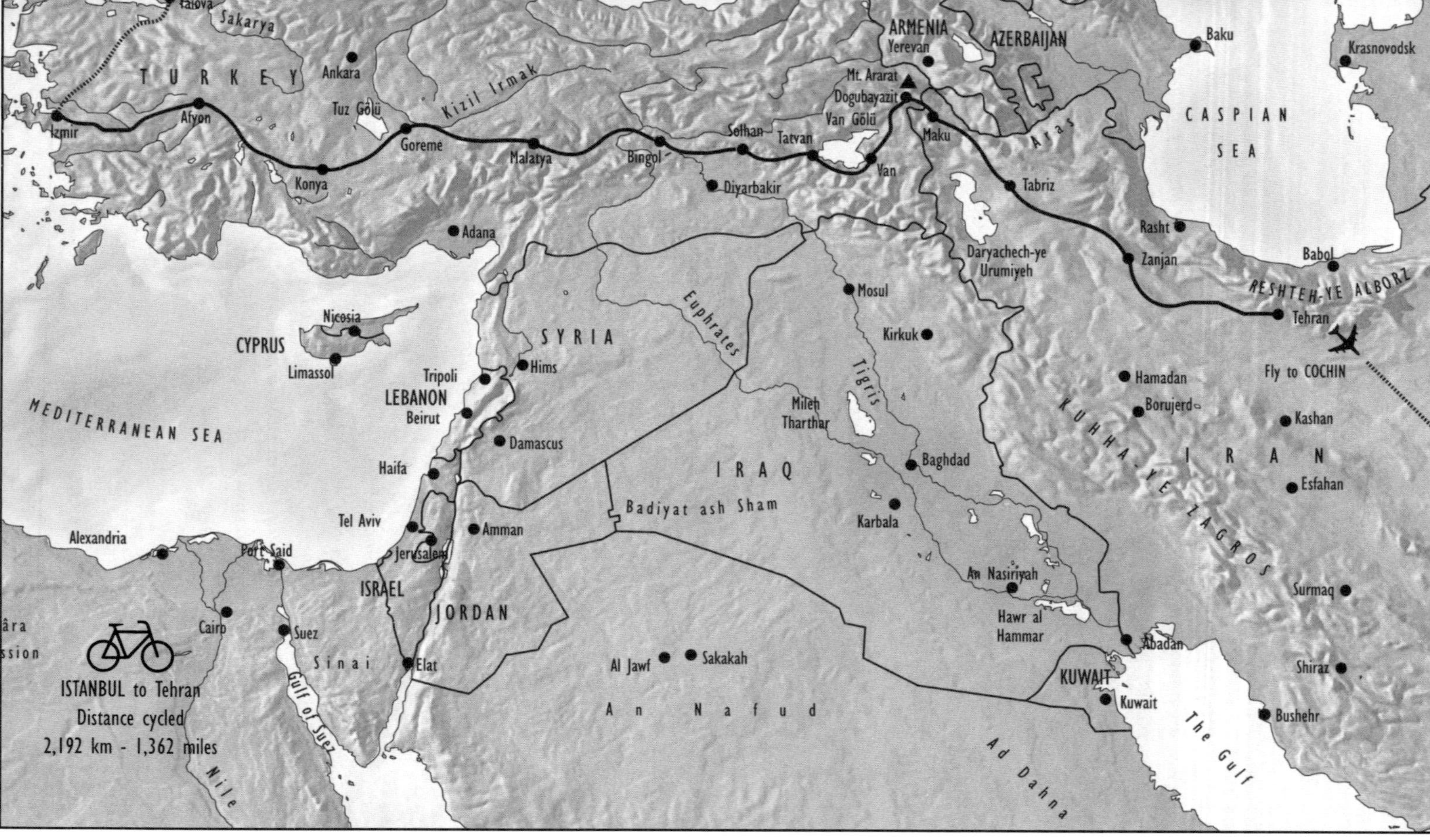

ISTANBUL to Tehran
Distance cycled
2,192 km - 1,362 miles
tatova
Sakarya
TURKEY
Ankara
Izmir
Afyon
Tuz Gölü
Kizil Irmak
Konya
Goreme
Malatya
Bingol
Diyarbakir
Solhan
Tatvan
Van Gölü
Van
Dogubayazit
Mt. Ararat
ARMENIA
Yerevan
AZERBAIJAN
Maku
Aras
Baku
Krasnovodsk
CASPIAN SEA
Tabriz
Daryachech-ye Urumiyeh
Rasht
Zanjan
Babol
RESHTEH-YE ALBORZ
Tehran
Fly to COCHIN
Hamadan
Borujerd
Kashan
Esfahan
KUHHA-YE ZAGROS
IRAN
Surmaq
Shiraz
Bushehr
Adana
Mosul
Kirkuk
Euphrates
Tigris
SYRIA
Hims
Mileh Tharthar
IRAQ
Baghdad
Badiyat ash Sham
Karbala
An Nasiriyah
Hawr al Hammar
Abadan
KUWAIT
Kuwait
The Gulf
CYPRUS
Nicosia
Limassol
MEDITERRANEAN SEA
Tripoli
LEBANON
Beirut
Damascus
Haifa
Tel Aviv
Amman
Alexandria
Port Said
Jerusalem
ISRAEL
JORDAN
Cairo
Suez
Sinai
Elat
Gulf of Suez
Nile
âra
ssion
Al Jawf
Sakakah
An Nafud
Ad Dahna

Chapter 5

Western Turkey – Punctured optimism

I tell you, my friend, most of dogs in Turkey are descended from beasts that were trained to attack English knights during Crusades. You are paying for sins of your forefathers. Do not take it personally.

Our train having left the Turkish border at around 3am, we managed to get a little sleep.   When I awoke later, I realised with a sense of nostalgic anticipation that we were rolling into Istanbul.   Yawning people in grimy suburbs drew back their curtains to let in the morning sun.   I slid open our window for air and caught a whiff of the city I remembered from my youth.   Rubbing my eyes, I sat watching at the window.   Sam grumbled at the disturbance from the daylight and turned over.   There seemed no point putting him in a bad mood for the day.   I closed the curtain and decamped to the corridor.

My view from the train gave me a unique perspective into the world of Istanbul's outer reaches as we passed slowly through, preparing me for the changes since my last visit.   Modern apartments had been built right up close to the tracks, allowing train passengers a close view into people's simple lives.   Most were in the process of getting up, eating breakfast and making their ablutions in bathrooms overlooking the tracks.   The fact that we were only given brief glimpses left an open-ended potential for numerous interpretations.

A fat man in a vest shaving at his bathroom mirror seemed to flinch as he cut himself.   Through a bedroom window a heavily pregnant woman was poking or stretching at something high up with a long stick   Was she trying to hook something off a high shelf? Painting the room as a nursery using an extended roller?   Was she removing cobwebs, or perhaps trying to persuade a reluctant schoolchild down from a wardrobe?   So many possibilities – it was a shame Sam was missing this.

At one point there was a break from the apartment buildings and the train slowed.   A moment later, I was startled as the train passed a man who had set up home in a crevice within a section of broken concrete wall.   He was positioned close to the tracks so I saw him quite clearly.   I guessed an electrical transformer box might have been there at some time.   A busy pavement ran directly over him forming a roof above his little nook, so he was only visible to those on passing trains.   This man was clearly no run-of-the-mill vagrant, though.   Neither did his home inspire pity.

Standing for a clearer view, I saw he had a mattress, clean bedding and a piece of velvet curtain, which gave him some privacy when he desired it.   He laid there in shorts and a t-shirt, like a cat happily warming himself in the glow of the rising sun.   As my carriage began to roll, denying me a clear field of view, I noticed, fixed to the crumbling concrete wall, a number of homely pictures, beside which he had turned a box into a small makeshift bedside cabinet.   There was a candle placed on top of it.   I swear I also glimpsed a portable television, but I may have imagined that.

I often think back to that man, wondering if he is still there and what he does with his days.   I sometimes envy the simplicity of his life.

*

I had spent a few weeks in Istanbul as a 20-year-old backpacking student, and I had really positive memories about it.   Dismounting from the train, we pushed our bikes down the long platform towards the street, stopping at the information desk to ask about hostels. Although I felt fairly confident, from a distant memory, that Sultanahmet Square was the place to head for, I wondered if that might have changed.   The station was busy, but a kind-faced old porter stopped to ask what we wanted to know.   I told him, but he just smiled and said,

"Don't waste time in queues.   Istanbul is a beautiful place, enjoy it.   There are hostels everywhere.   Just go up this street."

Expecting at first to be hustled, we felt instantly charmed by this lovely man, who was not seeking tips or anything for himself, only that people enjoyed his city.

Sam and I walked our bikes most of the way to Sultanahmet Square, a little disorientated by having been on a train, but we soon felt brave enough to cycle through the manic traffic and the treacherous tramrails. Walking through the square, already busy with tourists, we found our way to the excellent Nobel Hostel in the shadow of Santa Sophia mosque. The staff, and everyone we had talked to on the way to the hostel, seemed jovial and friendly. They still had that city sharpness I remembered, though. Something that made you feel they might be trying to make a fast buck out of you. But the feeling was based on experiences in Istanbul 30 years before, and it proved to be largely unfounded.

We felt at home in Nobel Hostel, and talked more to other people than we had in weeks. Except for the inconvenience of a champion snorer in our dormitory, with deadly smelling socks, we were really comfortable. Fortunately, the snorer left on day two. We really enjoyed the salad breakfasts served on the roof terrace by motherly Turkish ladies who totally spoiled Sam.

The roof terrace was a lovely place to sit and meet other people. It also provided a stunning view of Istanbul, with St Sophia on one side and the sea on the other. Large cargo ships could be seen anchored off the coast waiting for permission to round the Golden Horn. It was a constantly changing vista that filled us with a sense of being at one of the world's great crossroads. We knew that applied to us more than most people at that moment; lodged there at the end of our trip across Europe, waiting to embark upon the next leg of our journey into the Middle East. It was a similar feeling to the one Sam and I had enjoyed looking east from Coominole the day we left Dingle two months before.

Sam seemed happy to meet some backpackers who were nearer his own age and went out with them a few times without me. I was relieved to see this, but he confided in me that it wasn't solving his problem. He found some of the younger people (older than him) a little naïve. They seemed to think they had seen the world when what they had done was go from one tourist city to another with other western backpackers. He found us middle-aged people more interesting, he said, but he felt unable to say anything he thought they would find worth listening to. In fact, he said he felt he could tell that we were all sniggering inside, thinking how naïve he was (which we weren't, of course).

I tried hard along with other new friends to explain that people my age like to hear the opinions of young people, since there are more surprises to be found there than in listening to people one's own age. Sam was not at all convinced by this. He felt that he could sense our embarrassment on his behalf. I suggested he ask questions rather than feel he had to know anything, but it seemed nothing I said really helped. Sadly, he was resigned to his fate. He would, he surmised, be a passive onlooker for the rest of the trip.

On day two, we set off in the morning with a sense of purpose to the British High Commission. Here we hoped to get a letter of recommendation for the Iranian Embassy so we could put in our visa application the following morning. There was a Moslem public holiday (Eid) coming up and it felt by no means sure we would be granted visas. Istanbul veterans at our hostel, however, told us not to worry. It certainly seemed true that Istanbul was a place where visas were easier to obtain. After a short debate, Sam and I agreed that the two-week advised wait would be worthwhile. We submitted our visa application the following morning, already feeling that two weeks in Istanbul would be a pleasure, regardless of the outcome.

*

Lorna arrived from England after we had been there six days and I temporarily moved around the corner to the four-star hotel she had booked with her flight. Four-star hotels were of no interest to me at this point, but I did feel she deserved a place she would enjoy after all her sacrifices and hard work on our behalf. The hotel was OK but certainly didn't seem to justify costing eight times more than our friendly hostel. In retrospect, Lorna agreed.

Sam was happy staying on his own at the hostel. It gave some independence and a bit of a break from me. It also meant that I had some time alone with Lorna to talk about Sam's issues, and also try to find out why she had been missing me so much more than she had expected. I had talked to her on a weekly basis on the phone and she had seemed very down on most of those occasions.

Our first day together was really lovely and it just felt great to be together. Very quickly, however, we found ourselves in conflict over how we wanted to spend the five days. Without wanting to generalise too much, I would say that Lorna wanted do *holiday* things, whereas I was in *expedition* mode and wanted to keep things practical and basic. The idea of sitting in an open-air café alongside loud tourists smoking *sheesha* pipes, or being pestered by waiters to take tours, was complete anathema to me. Lorna, on the other hand, took it lightly as part of the local entertainment. Sam was far more able to go along with her wishes, so I went elsewhere, increasingly irritated at our expeditionary lifestyle having been derailed. I tried not to mind, but I found myself ranting inside my head. It felt almost corrupting.

After a further day, Lorna's corrupting cafe preferences were extended to a desire to visit hammams, souks and even mosques. Yes, *extreme* is my middle name, and I would ask for numerous similar instances to be taken into consideration. Memorable uncompromising examples that come to mind are: my insistence that a tent you can stand up in is not proper camping; trying to ensure that my first child ate nothing containing refined sugar for the first three years of her life, and refusing to ever give my wife *empty cliché* gifts of chocolates or cut flowers.

After talking our feelings through and recognising that it was simply a matter of considerate compromise for five days, we did thankfully return to our previous happy state. Sam was a very helpful counsellor and I was happy to give him the opportunity of a reversal of roles.

I do feel I learned a valuable lesson from this experience. I also surmised that there are sound reasons for the fact that explorers rarely met up with their families midway for holidays. The same applies to touring bands and athletes. It is a matter of focus – of needing to stay disciplined and determined until the end. If the purpose of the expedition becomes blurred, impetus can be lost. Someone like me reacts particularly badly to any sign of that happening (anxiety neurosis, I am told).   So yes, although it seems hard for some of my friends to believe, I am a very difficult person to live with sometimes.

It was fortunate that during the last few days of Lorna's visit, I agreed to go along with a bit of tourist activity.   Our trip by boat out to the Princess Islands was a memorable day, as was a concert we went to with some new friends to see the Gipsy Kings at the Besiktas football stadium in Taksim.

With its narrow covered backstreets and excellent restaurants, Taksim became the favourite hangout of Sam and I towards the end of our time in Istanbul.

*

Once Lorna had gone, Sam and I began to discuss our options from Istanbul onwards.   We were not at all sure of what we should do from here, and this played on my mind as we approached the time an answer on our illusive Iranian visa was due.

While visiting the British high commission for our letter of recommendation, I had got into conversation with the member of staff who dealt with it – an American, strangely.   We talked about our trip and where we might encounter problems along the way.   Iran, he had said, was not too much of a problem at the moment, but Pakistan was. Although nothing too public had happened there for a while in the way of terrorism, he assured me that their intelligence said it would do soon, and that we would have difficulties getting a visa to enter.   I asked about alternative routes, up through Georgia and Uzbekistan, etc.   He assured me that despite the recent minor war in Georgia it was a relatively safe option.

This left us in a bit of a confused state.   Which was the best route?   We would have to make a decision soon, but there were pitfalls with both the Iran and the Georgia options.

Over the coming two weeks in Istanbul, desperate for some surety and not knowing whether we would finally be given Iran visas, we talked to fellow travellers and slowly began to have confidence in Iran as our preferred option, with the other routes as fallbacks.   How likely those fallback options were to be implemented, though, was a constant cause of concern that kept me awake at night.   What troubled me most was that if option two were needed, we would have to apply for new visas, and that would take time. Much as we had grown to love Istanbul, we were eager to move on and a longer stay was not something we would be happy about. I could see us cycling on, then leaving our bikes in Dogubayezit while we scooted back to Istanbul by train to collect visas – possible, but a major hassle.

Sam was content to leave me to do the research on travel route options. This was largely a blessing and I took advantage of the free internet access at Nobel Hostel and combined this research with further questioning of other people at the hostel. Sam played his part by asking people he talked to for their opinions. Periodically, we pooled our thoughts and information and slowly we worked towards some kind of concrete plan.

Suggestions were offered by a number of people about avoiding Pakistan by taking a boat from the south of Iran to Oman and from there to Bombay. It lifted our spirits for a day, but after some long and tedious research, I eventually discovered that all passenger boat routes had ceased to operate due to competition from low-cost flights.

Further disappointments came when researching the Georgia-Azerbaijan-Turkmenistan-Uzbekistan option. I discovered that we would be unable to get over the Himalayas into India in the winter without flying, unless we took the crazy risk of going through war-torn Afghanistan and the Khyber Pass. This route was, I heard, theoretically possible by hiring a taxi at the Turkmenistan-Afghan border and being driven (under a blanket) to Kabul. From there, I was told, it might be possible to get a military escort through the Khyber Pass into Pakistan. Even so, the bikes on the roof of the taxi would be a bit of a giveaway. When I asked a few friendly Afghan people (who I reached via Lonely Planet's Thorn Tree forum), they all said I was crazy to even consider it. We dropped the idea.

My head was in a spin. I had to have some sort of plan. I asked Sam if we could discuss the issue the following morning over breakfast and come to a resolution. He was happy to do this, which was a relief in itself and I slept better that night. The next morning, Sam and I agreed that if we got our visas, we would cycle to Tehran and then check the latest situation there. This still left our plans uncomfortably fluid beyond that point but at least our next step was agreed. I also used this time to get our India visas, which in Istanbul was a very easy, even pleasant, experience.

Without actually saying anything we could both already see that the easiest way out of our problem after Tehran would be to take a short flight over Pakistan to Amritsar in India if we couldn't go overland. Neither of us liked this idea, though, and felt that it should be our last resort. Not only would we be adding to the global-warming problem but flying with the bikes would be a bit of a nightmare. It would also mean a sudden jump to another culture, rather than the gradual change we were accustomed to. I think we both kept this option in mind, though, without actually admitting it. Our extended breakfast ended that morning with Sam casually declaring himself happy to go along with whatever I decided.

Sam was more focussed on enjoying a more teenager-oriented period with young people newly arrived in our dorm than planning our route. I wondered what the situation might have been like if he'd found himself here on this trip with a friend his own age, and what decision they might have made about the way forward. He was certainly still keeping me in the role of the dad. It was not what I had planned and I resented it. Not only might he later accuse me of railroading him but he would gain less from the trip if it stayed this way.

*

Our time in Istanbul was a real change of life for us. No cycling to get up for every morning, no picnics, the same hostel every night, making day-trips to surrounding areas by ferry and metro, going to an international football match at Fenerbache stadium. It felt like an interim holiday. It also meant that we got to know quite a few people staying at our hostel. Some moved on after a week and then returned a week later to find us still there. It was a really enjoyable time and it had come to feel like home.

After two weeks of enjoying ourselves, our patience was finally rewarded by the receipt of our Iran visas. The man at the embassy presented them to us like special awards.

Just a day before this, I had done a Google search for my old Turkish head of department when I was studying 3D Design in England.   I wanted to contact him in case he was back in Turkey or could recommend things for us to do.   Miraculously, he came up as dean at Izmir Economics University and within minutes he returned my email with a call to my mobile phone.   Tevfik was now married with a young son and encouraged us to come to Izmir that week to visit them before they went away on holiday.

Sam and I discussed this new idea and how it might fit in.   The previous night, we had met two cyclists who had just arrived via the Black Sea coast route – the route we were planning to take.   They had made it sound a very unattractive prospect, with tales of narrow roads and trucks blasting through with abandon.   There were also, they said, a lot of long road tunnels without pavements or cycle lanes. Meanwhile, Jimmy, one of the hostel managers, told us that the weather would now be turning stormy in that region.

"You should be better to take my advices, my friend, and go south side of big Turkish mountains."

Weighing all this up, Izmir looked like a blessing in disguise.   It meant taking the bikes on the bus, since Tevfik needed us to be there that week.   But on the plus side, it also meant we were heading back west and adding about as many kilometres to our total journey as we had lost by taking the train from the Bulgarian border.   This seemed to make sense, so we checked the bus situation and then called Tevfik.

The very next morning we checked out of Nobel Hostel, promising Jimmy and Mustaffa we would return soon.

*

Getting to the huge national coach station was a logistical problem, as most people went by urban expressway (no cycles) or by metro.   We found this a common problem in cities outside Europe   Sam and I agreed that the thing to do was just to set off and find a way.   Eager to be moving on now, we cycled along dodging mad traffic and the treacherous tramlines before finally getting on the metro with our bikes for the last bit.   We half-expected to be turned away at the barrier, but the staff and passengers were so helpful.   That always makes you feel positive when beginning a journey. People even helped us to stand our bikes on end to fit them in the carriage.

At the huge modern coach station, they loaded our bikes carefully into the cavernous luggage compartments of the Izmir coach. We were really surprised by how high-tech this place was and what excellent modern coaches they used. We had a smart young coach steward who served drinks and talked to us as we began the journey. Little did he know when we photographed him that it was to put him on our lookalikes blog. He was the image of a young Sean Penn. No, really!

On the short ferry trip across to Yalova (cutting the corner) we sat on deck enjoying the view. The relative tranquillity was disturbed by a stocky Turkish businessman on the open car deck just below us shouting at someone on his mobile phone. The man waved his free arm around wildly as he propped himself against the rail, gesticulating across the bay to where he assumed the recipient of his call to be. The reception out at sea must have been bad because the call kept breaking up and cutting out. Each time he had to call back he got angrier, until finally he smashed the phone on the railing. He did this three or four times until the mobile was in pieces and then tossed it into the sea with a volley of curses. Finally, he strolled off to the café to buy a coffee.

Most of our fellow travellers were calm. We were charmed by the friendliness of those on the coach and by their help when we arrived at Izmir bus station late that night. The university (where Tevfik had arranged for us to stay) was quite a way out of the centre, so they persuaded a driver to squeeze our bikes into one of the minibuses that run to outlying areas. The other passengers told the driver to take us there first in case they locked the university gates early. I just couldn't imagine passengers being so generous in England, but perhaps I'm being uncharitable to the English.

After a brisk drive along the seafront and through the back streets, we were dropped right at the university gates. Fortunately they were expecting us and we were put into a comfortable, well-equipped student room with cable TV and a kettle. We couldn't see much of Izmir in the dark, but we had a sense that our decision had been a good one.

Sam and I spent a lovely week meeting staff at the university and getting to know Izmir. We took Tevfik's advice and visited historic Ephesus, joining groups of Japanese tourists with their audio-tour headphones. Over the weekend, we visited Tevfik and his family and went out with them to a lovely country market, meeting up with some of their friends for lunch and experiencing a little of Turkish life.

Izmir is not too affected by tourism and this was one of its most attractive features for us. It was a taste of what we took to be *real* Turkey. We read in the Lonely Planet guide that there was no reason to stay here beyond visiting Ephesus. I wondered what kind of people wrote these guides, and if in fact some of them ever ventured beyond the station café in the places they visited. From our experience, it couldn't have been more misleading.

Sam had been suffering since leaving home with blocked sinuses and throat congestion. It had not bothered him too much up to this point, but in Izmir it seemed to worsen. I hoped that a bit of time staying in a comfortable room and some good food would improve it, and to a certain extent it did.

We found plenty to do in Izmir and enjoyed the fresh air after polluted Istanbul. Balcova, where we stayed, was up on a hillside looking down over the huge bay and impressive harbour. It had a lively, invigorating feeling about it.

Despite our enjoyment of Izmir, as the time approached to move on, Sam and I both felt ready to get back to some solid daily cycling. We knew that one of the most mountainous parts of our trip lay ahead. After three weeks of walking around, we expected to need a few days to get back to our previous levels of fitness. One unfortunate oversight was leaving our pot of Sudocrem at Nobel Hostel. This had become indispensable to us and unfortunately proved impossible to find outside the UK. We accepted we would have to make do with an alternative until Lorna came to India.

Sam particularly benefited from our stay in Izmir, I think – getting some good sleep, watching some TV, learning more Turkish and spending a day or two with a family. He seemed a little more upbeat. Even so, conversations in the evenings at what became our favourite restaurant (UFUK) told me that beyond simple sinus congestion he was still struggling with things in his head. I had to fight with myself to avoid asking him what he was so preoccupied with, just wishing he would just unload it all on me. This was making an assumption, however, that what he was preoccupied with was something directly related to me, which it might not have been. It was a dilemma. Sometimes I felt I might be guilty of being too careful with him. Maybe, I wondered, it might be better just to confront him with it – tell him I'd had enough of it, even? That seemed a big risk to take, though. On balance, I decided I was better off keeping my thoughts to myself, as he was doing.

*

Setting off from Izmir on 29 September, we headed straight onto a large main road with heavy traffic. Turkish road manners seemed like another big traffic leap towards craziness, although we suspected there would be worse ahead of us.

The road out of Izmir was frightening in places. It certainly didn't seem safe for cycling, although there were no signs forbidding it other than at flyovers so we continued. We were relieved when within an hour the flyovers faded into the background and we reached countryside.

The first rain since France fell as we tucked into yet another kebab and *corba* (thick Turkish soup) at lunchtime. It stopped just as we scraped the last dregs from our bowls. Sam and I quickly checked the bikes over before heading off along the hard shoulder of a straight, steep dual carriageway. We ached a little but we were glad to be making good progress and by late afternoon we had caught our first sight of the towering Anatolian mountain range. We had been forewarned.

Not wanting to overdo things, we allowed ourselves an easy first day back in the saddle by stopping early in Salihli after only 107km. Sam reminded me that this was still over the hundred kilometres a day that we had originally planned.   I agreed and tried not to feel too bad about it, but there was torment going on inside me.

We managed to find a reasonably priced hotel.   To make things even more fortuitous, they welcomed our bikes into their foyer just as a heavy rainstorm blackened the sky and began to drench the busy streets.   The omens seemed good and this continued as we found Premiership football on the TV in our room.   Leaving the hotel an hour later, though, our luck seemed to have turned, when we found all the restaurants in town packed to the gills.

I note that my diary betrays a slight obsession with good and bad fortune at this stage of our expedition.

After nearly half an hour of dodging rainstorms, we were given a place at a table.   Looking at our fellow diners, it dawned upon us that we were in a predominantly Moslem area.   It was Ramadan, of course, when hungry Moslems rush to restaurants as soon as the sun is down and their fast ends for the day.   This is always a lively and happy time to eat out in a Moslem area and it made for an excellent atmosphere at dinner – a great end to our first day back in the saddle.

Sam had enjoyed being back on the bike, it seemed, but I could see he was not feeling strong.   He had been eager not to cycle too far on the first day.   A sensible idea, of course, but one that seemed to have been motivated more by physical discomfort that by restraint.   I had seen him rubbing his knee joints during lunch and at the end of the day.   Perhaps it was just a matter of his cycling muscles being out of condition, but I didn't think so.   He seemed a bit lacking in energy or enthusiasm for getting some miles on the clock.   It worried me a little.   Was it leading up to an injury, or a worsening of his sinus problem perhaps?

*

Moving on steadily across an increasingly mountainous south-central Turkey, we stopped at a succession of large towns including Usak, Afyon, Aksehir, Cengelti and Aksarai.   What we enjoyed about the route was the fact that these towns were rarely visited by tourists, so we were able to feel part of local life and practice our Turkish.   It was tough cycling up the long, steep, sunbaked roads over endless rocky passes, and there were times when we were both hampered by aches and sharp stabbing pains in our knees.   These kind of pains are always a worry because sometimes they can completely stop you cycling, we had been told, necessitating long periods of rest.

The down side of the locals having little idea about tourists or cyclists was that when we asked about hotels, they tended to stare open mouthed and assure us there were no hotels for 100km.   Their assumption was, we later discovered, that we were looking for five-star accommodation.

To accompany the wilderness environment, dead dogs littered the roadsides each day and I began to keep a tally of the numbers. Three per day was about average.   The aggressiveness of Turkish dogs made me think that they were probably run down intentionally. Unfortunately, they seemed to have a particular blood lust for cyclists, and we began to dread rounding bends for the chance of meeting a vicious dog preparing to attack.

As we penetrated deeper into the Anatolian mountains, we noticed the spaces between towns becoming more barren.   The hot sun beat down on us and we found few places to shelter.   Villages between the towns became few and far between and we seemed to be constantly climbing.   We worried about breaking down out here and were always glad to see the outskirts of towns, where for a while we would be back to running water, plentiful food and comfortable beds.

Time seemed to drag in the wilderness and I felt eager to progress more quickly.   Continued episodes of knee pain for both Sam and I, however, warned us not to rush.   The roads were steep and the sun caused us to dehydrate quickly, so we knew we had plenty to take care.   Over-exertion now could mean disaster, or at least a lengthy spell of recuperation, beside which, Sam still did not seem at full strength.   I had become used to him being quiet all day on the road, so I could not rely on him telling me if he felt we were overdoing it.

*

When I was studying for my degree, I did an architecture project on the region of Cappadocia in central Turkey.   I remembered Tevfik showing us photographs of an amazing moonscape valley, with volcanic rock (*tuffa*) pinnacles carved out for use as houses. They had been doing this since Stone Age times. I thought about it as we slogged on across the mountain range. I really wanted to visit the place, despite it meaning a slight detour deeper into the mountains. Sam was reluctant but agreed. He had still not recovered any sense of optimism and saw it simply as an unwelcomed extra bit of hard work. I felt guilty, but not enough to miss it. More than anything, I felt sure he would appreciate it when he got there – although I had thought that a few times before on this trip and had being mistaken. I still had doubts that night as I phoned to book a hostel room.

When we finally reached Cappadocia, saddle-sore and tired, we were both unprepared for the beauty of the place. No photograph could do it justice. We pulled over at the edge of a hillside looking over the valley to take a photograph. Hot-air balloons floated in clear blue sky above the bizarre landscape, the blasts of the gas burners roaring high above us in the stillness. We were silent and transfixed.

After some time staring at the view over the valley, Sam and I cycled into the small town of Goreme, where we found our comfortable hostel carved into a 50m-high rock pinnacle. We wondered if this might not have been the inspiration for Bedrock in the Flintstones. I was a little downhearted when I discovered I was not the first to imagine this. There was indeed a tourist hotel named Bedrock in Goreme and another named Flintstone Hotel.

Walking along the small dusty main street the following day, we were passed by a couple of ageing hippies on horses. They may have retained the dress and the lingo of the sixties but they reeked of capitalism.

"Angel, y'see that street corner there – with the mangy dog and the cripple guy? I'm imagining that whole corner and the adjoining shops cleaned up, with terazzo and some swinging Hawaiian chairs outside, and folks drinking cocktails. Are you gettin' me? Man, these people just don't know what they have here!"

*

Goreme did have its downsides, even outside the main tourist season, but it was not enough to spoil the magic of the place for us. We spent two happy nights at the Guven Cave Hotel, wandering through the hillsides and around the surreal cave dwellings, before setting off west again with our batteries recharged. We were heading to spectacular Lake Van, via the towns of Gurun, Alcedag, Malatya, Elazig and Bingol. Along the mountainous route we would often find ourselves cycling further than we wanted to in a day in order to reach a town where we might find a guesthouse. The alternative was to camp at the side of the road on the rocky fields, and this had its problems.

One night near Karatayhani, desperate to stop, we cycled along a goat track looking for a secluded spot to pitch the tent. The track soon petered out but we continued, zigzagging haphazardly across stony ploughed fields, heading for a clump of trees. With light fading, I got off and walked. Sam, on the other hand, continued and failed to notice the large thistles growing in his path. Finally, we found a nice secluded spot, pitched the tent and cooked a tasty supper of bulgur wheat, tuna and vegetables before settling down to a good night's sleep. We agreed the day had ended well in the end, with a safe, comfortable place to camp and a satisfying meal.

In the morning I awoke with the light, got up and made some breakfast before waking Sam. I was concerned about being seen in the daylight.

After breakfast we prepared to clean and oil our chains, but all too soon we noticed that Sam had a flat rear tyre. Checking the tyre, we found it peppered with thistle thorns.

Deflated, we took off both wheels and spent half an hour removing every tiny embedded thorn we could find, and there were dozens. All had gone so well with the bikes until now and we should have been pleased that this was our first puncture, but we were far from happy. We took it as a bad omen. Even so, we both kept calm and managed to approach the problem methodically – Sam in particular, telling me to relax while he fixed it.

To rub salt into the wound and reinforce the bad omen sensation, after checking and finding no thorns in my own tyres, I discovered my luggage rack had snapped near the frame fixing. It felt like we were being punished for doing something terrible somewhere. I tried hard to put such superstitious nonsense out of my head. Following Sam's calm example, I fixed it temporarily with a butchered coke can, wire and a notch cut in the rack leg with a junior hacksaw blade. Meanwhile Sam continued removing thorns. Finally, satisfied that they were all out, he repaired the punctured inner-tube, re-fitted the wheels and we prepared to set off. It had not been that bad, we agreed. But by the time we had the bike upright, the tyre was flat again. We repeated the process, finding several more thorns deeply embedded. The new puncture was repaired and we managed to go a mile or two before the tyre was flat again. Sam repaired it, we removed another few thorns and, sure that this time they were the last, we continued on.

Sam was now feeling very depressed. We were wasting half the morning and getting dehydrated in the scorching sun. We really wanted to make it to Gurun and a hotel where we could wash some clothes and check over the bikes, but that was 150km away and we were now well into mid-morning.

"If only we had continued to the next town with a guesthouse last night," I said. I knew as I said that, it must have annoyed him.

Thankfully, the punctures stopped after about the fourth stop and allowed us to make up some distance, before stopping for lunch after a spectacular 90km of hills. Revived by an overpriced lunch in a coach-stop restaurant, Sam and I pushed it hard up ever-steeper mountain passes in the blistering afternoon heat. Gurun still seemed faintly possible but in this terrain unlikely. Miraculously, though, after around 3,400m of heroic climbing, we started to see signs that we might make it. Just at that moment, however, a couple of doctors in a private ambulance stopped us. Sam joked that someone who had seen us on one of the big hills had sent an ambulance to meet us, expecting us to be close to death.

The sun had just disappeared on the horizon. We were annoyed to have our desperate final kilometres disturbed, but it would be good to have someone to ask about hotels, we conceded. We stopped to talk. It transpired that the two men were cyclists and wanted to ask our opinion about the practicality of them cycling from Bingol to

Istanbul. We gave them some encouragement and were elated to be told that the final 20km into Gurun was all downhill.

Our new friends offered us a lift with the bikes in the ambulance, but both Sam and I were determined to enjoy the 20km downhill under our own steam. We couldn't believe that we were going to make it. We almost didn't. Hurtling down the hill as we approached town, I suddenly spotted a large broken bottle right in our path. I swerved and shouted behind me to Sam, who just missed it. It is always the most dangerous time – just when you think you are there and are singing *nothing's gonna stop us now*.

*

Despite the basic nature of the accommodation, Sam and I were delighted to spend a night in a cheap workingmen's hostel in Gurun. Leaving the following morning, we felt rested and pleased to have avoided being eaten by their big angry dog.

Immediately upon rounding the corner at the end of the street, we found ourselves climbing up another steep extended mountain pass – this time towards Alcedag. The climb was tough and beautiful in equal measure. None of these things were unexpected, though. Both feeling back to full fitness after our Istanbul and Izmir break, we felt more than capable of taking anything this terrain could throw at us. Unfortunately, our confidence was about to be dented. Sam suffered another morning of thorn-induced punctures – this time in the front tyre.

It is unavoidable that once you've had one puncture on this kind of road, you tend to ride along in a state of constant trepidation, pessimistically awaiting the next one. It takes a while before you can let that feeling go. Finally, after about the fifth puncture that morning, Sam collapsed at the side of the road in a state of utter despair. His rear tyre had now punctured again too. Seeing Sam's normal calmness broken, I felt the time had come to use one of the two spare inner-tubes.

"It'll be fine now, Sam," I told him positively. "This will bring an end to the problem."

When I inflated it, however, the tube burst at the valve seat. It was rendered useless – irreparable.

Things were going quite badly, I felt. Determined to remain calm in the face of such unbelievable bad luck, though, I put in our last spare tube and inflated it gingerly. My confidence grew along with the tube. On the last pump stroke, however, still quite soft, it burst in the same way. Sam was inconsolable.

"I really don't think I deserve this!" he pleaded, falling to the ground.

Hopelessly irritable and negative in small crises, I always seem to respond better when someone else loses it in a big one.

"Don't worry, Sam," I told him with a kind of mania-induced cheerfulness. "We'll walk to the next restaurant, get lunch, then we can get a bus to the next town and sort it out there – or we'll buy new tyres, it's really not a problem."

I wondered where those words had come from. I had surprised myself. But it was absolutely true, of course. I was learning.

Sam helped me to put the old patchwork inner-tube back in after I had repaired it. I inflated it and waited for it to burst, but it held. Cautiously we cycled along the road, with me trying to cheer Sam up. Thankfully, just around the next bend we saw a nice roadside café. Once I knew it was not a mirage, I allowed myself to be pleased. A romantic optimist I may be, but I think we were both quietly sure the tyre would be flat again by the time we'd finished lunch. We agreed, however, that we would worry about that then. There were taxis in the car park anyway.

The basic roadside café we came to remember as the Mirage Café was full of friendly locals and the food was good. We needed a damned good lunch and fortunately that is what we got. Out of the window, we watched people getting onto a succession of small buses, but by the time we finished our lunch we felt happy to try to reach the town of Alcedag by bike.   Miraculously, the tyre was still firm.   We had suffered enough disappointments by now that we were doubtful of the inner-tube lasting, but we set off up that next long mountain pass determined not to let that turn us into defeatists.

It was baking hot and I spent the next few hours nervously waiting for Sam's familiar call to say that it was flat again.   Had we done the right thing, I wondered.   Well, we could always flag down a bus.

That old patchwork inner-tube lasted the day but our legs didn't. After 100km of extreme hills and heat, we decided we needed to find a place to camp while there was still a little light.   Sam seemed utterly shattered and I wanted him to get a long recuperative sleep that night.   The roadside was so rocky in this area, however, that it offered nowhere viable to pitch the tent.   Finally, in the dark, we found an orchard adjoining a small farmhouse and decided to just pitch the tent between the small trees.   This was wild country now, where the locals seemed suspicious and nervous of us, so we didn't want to chance a bad reception by knocking at the farmhouse door. Treading carefully, avoiding the thistles along the orchard path, we pitched the tent quietly without using the torch.

Inside, I prepared a light supper of stale bread and dates, along with tinned *pate de foie gras* (the nostalgic remnant of a Christmas hamper from years ago).   We consumed this feast quietly from the comfort of our sleeping-bags.   I doubt either of us will ever forget how delicious that meal tasted.   Sam's face still lights up years later when I talk about it.   A small tin of pate de foie gras is now on my list of essential emergency rations, for future expedition.

Getting to sleep that night after such a tough day was not difficult.   Unfortunately, though, during the night we were disturbed by the sound of a dog barking outside the house and footsteps close by.   We remained undisturbed, however.   We had seen the size of some of the local guard dogs chained outside houses, so we certainly didn't wish to be caught by one on its own territory.   Maybe it was common practice here to leave them hungry (angry) until morning.

*

At first light, Sam and I got up promptly, took down the tent and were back on the road by 6am, scaling another huge long hill. Sam was his usual catatonic early-morning self. Despite setting off thinking we had many miles to get to a town, it seemed that in no time at all we rounded the rockface at the summit and found ourselves looking down through the early morning mist onto Alcedag way below. There was a chill in the air hinting at impending autumn as we sped down the winding mountain road. Arriving at a teashop for a breakfast only half an hour later, we ordered sweet black tea and bought rolls from a smoky wood-fired bakery opposite.

Sam did not say much over breakfast. At the time, I put this down to the early hour, but it turned out he was rather quiet all day. I began to realise just how much the puncture experience had broken his spirit. He had recovered enough confidence to carry on, but there was a numbness about him that told a story of a crushing experience. I could see it in his eyes and felt really sorry for him. I wondered if it might do him good in the long run. I was not sure, but for now he obviously found it hard to get excited about anything. I concluded that after cycling the first 5000km, he was probably wishing he had never suggested this stupid trip in the first place. I felt an overwhelming desire to make everything all right for him, yet I knew that this was treating him as a kid. He needed to face this challenge and beat it. The best solution, I told myself, must be to encourage him without actually trying to put things right for him.

After an easy half-day's cycling, I suggested to Sam that we stop in the large town of Malatya, where we would find a decent hotel and might be lucky enough to find some new inner-tubes. Relief filled his face. Stopping at the first set of traffic lights moments later, I asked a businessman in a car where we could find a hotel. Having explained that we were looking for a cheap hotel, we followed him to a rather plush establishment in the town centre. Although the place was far from cheap, it seemed friendly. I felt Sam deserved a little luxury with cable TV and a buffet breakfast, so we parked up and followed our Good Samaritan into the foyer.

It took a little time to persuade the porter that our bikes were too valuable to be left in the street. Despite his early intransigence, however, he eventually showed his good side, helping us to deposit them in the basement. Our room was pleasant and I saw Sam's face brighten slightly. We checked what TV channels we had, took a shower, did our customary clothes washing and then went out for lunch. It was all reassuringly familiar and lifted our confidence a great deal. Sam's certainly couldn't have gone much lower.

After a lunch with minimal conversation, Sam and I walked around the streets of Malatya and found a cycle shop where they said they could get us some 700c-sized inner-tubes. I was doubtful of the validity of this statement but it was reassuring that these people wanted to help us. After a relaxing half an hour of drinking tea with the owner, however, the tubes did turn up. Unfortunately, though, the tubes had larger Schrader valves and so would not fit. This came as no surprise, despite having emphasised our needs in the first place. Tubes with higher-specification Presta valves are hard to get outside Europe/USA and I cursed myself for not getting the holes drilled bigger, as I had originally planned, before we left.

I found it hard to see any humour in my recollection of a grumpy Irishman (they do exist) parking an old grid-iron of a farm bike outside Currain's bar as we left Dingle the first day. After pushing past the press photographers to get into his local pub, he'd muttered, "You won't get far with those bloody valves."

Looking at his bike, I had discounted his opinion at the time. What the hell would some grumpy farmer in the west of Ireland know about it?

"It is not a problem, sir," said the Malatya bike shop man. "This boy can break the valve holes bigger with this screw and a big hammer."

Deciding not to risk letting the shop guys bash holes in the rims with their crude-looking tools, we took the Turkish tubes. Sam and I quietly agreed to get them drilled at the next decent workshop opportunity.

*

It was a pity that the physical recuperation we enjoyed in Malatya was not accompanied by a solution to our inner-tube problems, but I shouldn't even have hoped for it. We were no longer in Europe and the stupidity of having not found time to drill out the valve holes in our wheel rims back at home was costing us dearly. It meant setting off in the morning with that same sense of precariousness we had come to know since the morning we woke up to find Sam's tyres full of thorns. I reminded myself how fortunate I was and that my repaired luggage rack seemed to be holding up better than expected. Bad luck was not finished with us, though. It returned to dog us again later that day.

Feeling more upbeat after no further punctures and finding a very good hotel in Elazig, Sam and I went out for a meal in a decent restaurant. There was a good atmosphere there and we ate a good dinner. After settling down to watch a film in our room later, however, I succumbed to a terrible bout of vomiting that lasted all night. Reluctantly, the next morning I had to agree with Sam that we needed to stay an extra night.

This unpleasant delay gave Sam a chance to catch up with friends online and seemed to cheer him up. More than that, being in a position to look after me seemed to help him. He also spent a bit of time out and about on his own. So when we set off for Bingol the following day, Sam appeared at least to be back to how he was before his puncture-fest. This should have been a firm indication to me of what a lad Sam's age needed. Fine, but in the real world it took much longer to sink in.

I remember the day we left Elazig as a good one. I felt great after a rest with no food for 24hrs and we enjoyed the morning cycling along the shore of the huge Bingol Lake and dam. The views were spectacular and we found an excellent roadside restaurant for lunch, with friendly staff and good food. We ate some powerful corba, followed by lamb *kofte* (meatballs) with tomatoes, peppers and rice then some *kadayif* (Sam's favourite pudding). Sam did spend lunchtime talking more about how immature and naïve he was feeling around older people, but at least he seemed to be talking about it in more positive tones.

I suggested that this perception was actually an indication of growing maturity. Before we left England he had seemed confident and pretty mature for his age, but having been out into the world, he now realised that he didn't know as much as he had thought. Sam cautiously agreed that he should be pleased about that.

I really felt like I was walking a tightrope with Sam's emotions a lot of the time. The slightest misplaced comment might deflate him, sending him into a depression or even anger. I'm sure this will be familiar to many parents of teenagers. I found myself resorting to the techniques of therapy I had picked up from Lorna, asking questions rather than offering solutions, trying to show I cared without patronising. It usually seemed to help.

*

Arriving in Bingol, a rather scruffy industrial town with slightly surly people, we found a decent hotel and got a good night's sleep before preparing to head for Van the next morning. It had been a tough journey so far and it was a relief to feel we were nearing the end of this leg. Not that I should have felt relieved, of course. In reality, once we got to Van, more arid mountain country lay ahead of us and before long we would be crossing into Iran, which would not be easy.

According to my diary, I slept badly during our night in Bingol. I was preoccupied with the bikes not being safe in the hotel's car park. Insecurity about the bikes seemed to plague me at this stage of the journey. Looking back, I think the inner-tube problem had made me realise how vulnerable we were in mechanical terms now that we were out of Europe.

The bikes were fine, of course. I remember watching the news on television that night thinking how lucky I was that punctures and the possible theft of our bikes were all I had to worry about when people back home were facing ruin with the early effects of an impending economic recession.

SAM'S POINT OF VIEW

Turkey was awesome. It was a pretty rapid change in culture and this was exciting, along with the thought of meeting my mum, Lorna.

At last I had a chance to talk with someone else who understood me and the difficulties I was experiencing.

On her arrival we had a quick chat before her and my dad went off to check into their hotel, while I remained at the hostel. I tactlessly decided to check in on them a bit prematurely. Knocking on their door, I heard them scrambling around before my dad opened the door. 'Nice room,' I said casually. The two poorly dressed, flustered parents were never less happy to see their son. Mum tried her best to sound pleased. My dad tried to act casual, laying there, arms folded, pretending to be trying to work out the TV remote. Subtle! I felt bad at the time, although I think it was justified. That's what you buy into when you have kids, I'd say. (Let's hope this little gem slips through the editing process, eh?)

We spent a long time in Istanbul trying to sort visas for India, Pakistan and Iran. It was great to have an excuse to stay put for a while and enjoy the surroundings rather than constantly racing to get to the next place – a mode of cycling solely the preserve of my dad. Manic!

Although that wasn't my preferred style of travel, it did mean we made good time. In fact, the length of time we spent in Istanbul wouldn't have been possible without my dad pushing us. At the time, though, I felt like I'd been rushed against my will. I was unsure what style of cycling I would have preferred, but what I can say in retrospect is that covering such big distances early on in the trip was a major benefit. The time spent in India and almost everywhere east of there was awesome. I wouldn't have wanted to cut any of that short. I seem to remember claiming that almost every new country we entered was my favourite so far.

We took a detour south by coach to Izmir to meet my dad's friend Tevfik Izmir was probably my favourite city in Turkey. Afterwards we cycled across central Turkey. It was far more mountainous than we'd been used to, although the previous month's cycling and a break in Istanbul had more than prepared us. The landscape was pretty derelict and mostly wilderness between major towns or cities, but it was impressive nonetheless. There were regular springs, where fresh mountain water was funnelled off the mountain. Here we could stop and refill our water bottles, and even wash. The water tasted great and in the hot weather it really helped us to re-energise.

Unfortunately for me, the most memorable thing about Turkey was my punctures. I suffered around 13 or 14 in about 7 weeks – most of those within the space of one week. It was a disaster for my confidence. There I was, cycling along a farm track trying to find a nice camping place in the dark, not realising I was cycling over hundreds of thistle plants. My dad (smug bastard) had already got off his bike, of course.

The following morning was agonising when, hoping to escape before the farmers saw us trespassing on their land, I found I had flat tyres. The thistles embedded in my tyres were almost impossible to see, but we removed dozens of them. After repairing the two flats, we soon discovered that pretty much any bump would push more invisible thistles into my tyre and re-puncture the tube.

I was eventually reduced to tears by the number of times we found ourselves at the roadside pulling out more thorns and repairing the numerously patched tubes. The sense of 'deflation' each time it happened became unbearable. At that point I just wanted to go home – and there seemed no chance of that, stuck out in the wilderness. At times like this there was no choice but to carry on. But I did get through it and this was a good lesson to me later. As my dad often told me (too often), eventually you realise that you can overcome any obstacle – nothing is impossible (unless you believe it is). The Mark Swain path to enlightenment!

'Road kill' abounded throughout Turkey. We even witnessed a few dogs being hit. It was here that my dad began a 'dead dog tally' in his diary. Not sure what the total was for Turkey but the amount must have been startling.

There were even more dogs in the east of Turkey. In most villages we cycled through, we were chased by large packs of them. To make matters worse I was always behind, so the dogs would turn around after chasing my dad and face me head on. Very scary! On the decent into Dogubayezit I almost cycled off a cliff edge as I swerved to miss some lunatic dogs. They looked pretty surprised too.

No wonder there was so much road kill in Turkey; they're all clueless about road safety!

Turkey is surprisingly mountainous. I well remember the feeling of having cycled for a morning from sea level, seeing a sign saying we were 2000meters up. It makes you feel pretty invincible when your legs don't hurt and you haven't even broken a sweat. Cycling downhill for up to an hour was superb – a bit like having control of a rollercoaster. The views were fantastic.

Dogubayezit was beautiful. It was quite small and mainly consisted of shacks and market stalls. It was an interesting place to meet other travellers, staying there before or after crossing the Iran border. The view of Mount Ararat from our hostel was breathtaking. A vast snow-topped mountain (an extinct volcano) surrounded by flat wilderness. There are still arguments today as to which country the mountain belongs. If you see it, you will understand why.

Chapter 6

Eastern Turkey and Iran – Biblical landscapes

Listen a hundred times; ponder a thousand times; speak once.
Turkish proverb – Author, take note.

The morning we left Bingol proved to be a tough one.   Just out of town Sam and I found the road *removed* for major rebuilding and widening.   The work went on for around 25km and the surface of the temporary track beside it was too rough to cycle on safely.   More irritating were the clouds of red dust thrown up by the trucks and buses, speeding impatiently along the track.   We were literally eating it and would be coughing it up all that evening.   It wore us out.

Although there were some surfaced sections where we rode, we were fed up with walking in the heat and chewing dirt by the time we stopped, looking for a late lunch in a small town.   Here, we were advised that the roadworks continued another 30km to Lake Van, where we were planning to catch the ferry across to Van city.   The prospect of a whole day walking and eating red dirt was about as appealing to us as a day of fingernails screeching down a blackboard.

Abandoning our concerns for half and hour, we enjoyed a good lunch in a fly-infested café.   The place was busy with locals, so after finishing our lunch we made more enquires about the road.   After several glasses of tea, Sam and I were persuaded by a young guy to follow him to one of the many private bus offices along the street. We were reluctant to see bus travel as a strong option, but we agreed that at least it might serve to shed more light on the road situation.

The road, we were told, continued as a temporary track all the way to Lake Van.   In fact, we had yet to see the worst of it.   We looked at each other with saddened faces.

Assured by the manager that a coach was coming in half an hour and that our bikes could be taken in the trunk, Sam and I thanked our friend from the café and accepted another glass of tea from the bus company manager.   We remained outside, however, in order to keep at bay a group of bold street children who seemed unable to resist touching the bikes, which had already fallen over as a result. My rack would not stand too much of that.

It was over an hour later when an empty mini-bus arrived. It was clear that this had been put on especially for us and I caught a whiff of a very smelly rat. I checked the price again and that it included the bikes. The manager consulted the driver. The bikes would have to go on the roof, he said. This was not good, given the red dust thrown up by the temporary track, but we were fed up with waiting, so after consulting with Sam I reluctantly agreed. The driver seemed unhappy about taking us into Van city, but the manager insisted. The unwilling driver eventually concurred and the bikes were put onto the roof and tied down badly with some string. Unhappy with this, I climbed up myself and secured them with some of our own luggage straps.

Why were we still waiting, I asked. The driver pointed to a group of about fifteen people emerging from our lunch café. They piled into the bus. It almost seemed they were coming along for the ride. I was worried but had a written receipt and the bus office phone number. I sighed. Expecting the worst, we squeezed into the packed bus and chugged off up the road.

The road was as bad as had been warned and seemed to take forever. Eventually, we came over a pass and saw the huge expanse of Lake Van below us. I had read about it before, but nothing I knew had prepared us for the enormity of this lake. At 74 miles across, we were unable to see the other side from the shore. More astounding was the reported depth of 1,480 feet (451 metres). I remembered checking out the ferry crossings that ran from this southwestern edge to Van city and thinking that the 12hr crossing time must be a mistake. I could see now it was not. The ferry was not running until the next morning anyway.

Our fellow passengers, a strange selection, used Sam and I to sleep on, but they were friendly enough. Some seemed to be shepherds or goatherds dressed in heavy brown cloaks. The aroma of their animals made them easy to identify. Two girls sat looking at Sam, giggling most of the way behind their hands. A small boy clung to his mother for dear life, seeming certain we were there to kidnap him. Despite his fear, this wide-eyed little chap waved enthusiastically at us from the roadside after they got off, seeming heartbroken to leave us.

Quite a few of the passengers got out on the way to Van, so the bus became progressively less crowded. Not that Sam noticed. He slept soundly most of the way, buried in a huddle of shepherds and toothless old women near the back of the bus. At one point, his face was nestled right between the buttocks of a large peasant woman in a heavy sackcloth smock. Nobody seemed to find this odd, least of all the woman, so I gave up on trying to wake Sam and relocate him.

On balance, we probably made the right choice to take the bus. The road was terrible and I felt quite sick at having been thrown around for nearly four hours. But as we began to see the city in the distance, I reminded myself that Sam had got some much needed rest, and I could see that we would have had to spend a large part of that distance walking if we'd tried to cycle it.

Around 8pm it was dark and nearly half an hour from Van city when we pulled into a small village car park. I was pretty shattered by now and Sam was groggy from his sleep. The driver turned and explained, with a barely hidden smirk, that this was where the ride ended. My blood went cold. I showed him my receipt for two tickets to Van city Ottogar (bus depot). Pointing towards the ground, I reminded him this was not Van city. The driver got out of the bus and returned with another man from a bus office to explain.

"Stay there, Sam," I said. "They're just trying it on."

The two men told us angrily to get out of the bus, but I refused. Sam looked worried but did as I had asked and stayed in his seat. It was pitch black: there was heavy traffic on the road and it would take us at least an hour and a half to cycle.

After about ten minutes of this fiasco, I told the driver to phone the bus office back where we got on, which he at least pretended to do. He returned, repeating that we had to get out here and get a taxi at our own expense. I shook my head determinedly and we stayed put. I suggested he drive to the police station. The office manager looked worried and conversed with the driver. Finally he got in and drove us back to the main road where we stopped at a petrol station. Here he made a phone call and then told us a coach would be stopping in a few minutes to collect us and take us to the city centre. It seemed unlikely. Even so, we got the bikes off the roof just in time before a coach did indeed arrive.

Passengers on the coach stared out of the windows in amazement as the driver hurriedly squeezed our bikes and panniers into the luggage compartments. Twenty minutes later, we arrived in Van Ottogar. No further money was mentioned.

"Dad, how on earth did you do that?" said Sam aghast as we cycled away.

I shrugged. Immovable stubbornness and a hatred of being conned, I thought to myself. Not traits I am especially proud of, but they have their uses.

*

Lake Van and the city of Van itself were a bit of a disappointment, it must be said. I had often read of this city beside a fathoms-deep clear water lake in the middle of the mountains, and it always sounded amazing. I had noticed, though, that nobody we met en route seemed to make much of it. The lake and the surroundings were undeniably spectacular and there were shops, restaurants, etc. but the city had little atmosphere or anything to mark it out as particularly special. As it was primarily a university city, our hotel was very cheap and we found a great luxury cake shop and café. That hardly made the visit worthwhile, though. Maybe it was just that we expected too much after the hardship the detour had caused. Nonetheless, we were happy to book in for a night.

Not seeing anything to stay for, Sam and I got up early the following morning. After stopping at a supermarket to buy some breakfast, we remarked on the chilly air and put on another layer. We felt spurred on   Partly this was due to the lack of anything to hang around for, but mainly because we were now eager to reach Dogubayezit in two days without having to camp in this rocky terrain. That meant having to make it to Caldiran that night. The terrain looked very mountainous, but we felt confident we could do it if we put in some serious effort during the morning. As luck would have it, the road was newly surfaced in parts, so it was less difficult than we expected.

In Caldiran we found only a poor trading post with one filthy set of rooms above a dark, grimy roadside teashop, whose owner didn't bother showing us the rooms.   He simply gave us the key and sent us upstairs to look for ourselves.   Stepping into the room we looked around in disbelief, scanning what lay before us in slow motion.   It reminded me of a scene from the film Midnight Express.   Suspect streaks of brown finger marks covered the walls by the beds.   There were no curtains and a pane of glass was missing, but despite all of that the beds seemed comfortable enough.   We went down and I paid, while Sam locked the bikes and removed the luggage.   Our host kindly suggested that he put the bikes in the café once he'd closed for the night.   Shifty eyes and unshaven faces peered at us from the darkness of the café as we walked through.   It was like being in the boiler-room of a leaky old ship, with steam coming from the tea samovars down at one end and people huddled around a glowing coal boiler for warmth.

Back up in the room, we unpacked some clothes and Sam went to look for the shower.   Meanwhile, I pulled back the ragged blanket to reveal a pair of yellowed, greasy sheets.   I imagined this place having been used as a hideout for bandits lying low after episodes of sheep rustling or revenge killings.   Perhaps the local police had used it to hold prisoners?   The names and other scrawled graffiti on the walls reinforced the impression.

I was scratching some of those blocks of six lines marking off days, with the seventh crossing them off, when Sam returned.

"OK, Dad, the toilet's an absolute no-go zone.   The bathroom doesn't actually have a shower, just a barrel of water to wash in that smells like it gets used by people who can't face going into the toilet!"

I laughed and continued my scrawling.

"You think I'm joking?" said Sam, "I promise you, it's worse! And why are you defacing the walls of this luxurious room?"

Off out for a bowl of corba at the town's only café, Sam and I continued to laugh about the state of the Caldiran Shitty Room.   It was bad but the only place in town, and the weather seemed to be turning cold.   We were lucky there had been a room free at all, I pointed out.   Sam looked at me doubtfully and smiled.

Returning to our teashop in good spirits, we helped our host bring the bikes inside and went up to our cell.   With no television for entertainment, we spent some time reading the scrawlings on the walls.   Our Turkish not yet up to the standard of deciphering the slang, we made up the bits we couldn't understand.

"Six weeks in this godforsaken room recovering from dysentery, I am now close to death.   Kiss my children goodbye," read Sam.

"I did not kill Asil Osman. He died of syphilis, which he caught from taking pleasure with his sheep.   I lie here, blind and dying after comforting his buxom wife," I responded.

"How did he manage to write that if he was blind?" laughed Sam.

"Psychography," I replied.   "Automatic writing.   His spirit wrote it after he died, working through our friend downstairs.   It's obvious."

I took out a pen and wrote a memento in English.

"Sam Swain stayed here, recovering from the oral thrush he contracted by lying between the buttocks of a large shepherdess on a bus."

Tired after the hills of the day, we settled down to sleep semi-decadently in our silk sleeping-bag liners with the threadbare blankets to keep us warm.   Now we had blocked up the missing windowpane with newspaper, it really felt quite cosy with the warmth rising from the teashop below.   I thought about how it would be spending five years in this room as a prisoner.   Could be worse, I told myself.

*

The next morning it was raining – only the second such day since France – but we set off in good spirits, feeling happy at the prospect of a new country and different food.   There is very little culinary variety in Turkey, it must be said.   Away from the bigger cities, your choice is generally *big kebab* or *small kebab*.   We passed a truck unloading the biggest cabbages I have ever seen.   They were about a metre in diameter and too heavy for one man to lift. I wondered who ate them. We had never seen cabbage in a restaurant around here.

This was a tough day of big mountain passes. We were chased by packs of mad dogs in every village we passed through. At one point I just managed to outpace a group of three while hurtling down a steep mountain road. Turning dejectedly to go back to their village, they were nearly run down by Sam bringing up the rear and had to dive for safety into a deep ditch. It was a close call for Sam as well as for the dogs.

Turkish dogs just seem hellbent on attacking foreigners – especially those on bikes. Some whacky guy we met suggested it was genetically inherited behaviour from the time of the Crusades! It was an inhospitable area. We had been severely warned in Istanbul and Izmir about travellers straying too close to the Iranian border and being kidnapped by rebels. This had happened just a few weeks before to some Americans who had stayed at Nobel Hostel. They were to spend quite some time in captivity, we later learned.

Finally, after catching a stunning glimpse of Mt Ararat coming over the last mountain pass and having braved a long chain of mad-dog shanty villages, we found ourselves on a very slight downhill incline and managed to coast the last few miles into Dogubayezit.

Located at the sparsely populated extremes of eastern Turkey and the last town before Iran, Dogubayezit (referred to affectionately as *Dog Biscuit* by travellers) has a special personality all its own. It is a calm place with bustling small trading shops and cafes. Many travellers call in here on their way through and stay longer than planned due to its chilled-out atmosphere. We found a great hotel here (Hotel Tahran), cheap with very helpful management, and met some really nice people staying there too. The view of Mt Ararat at breakfast from the upstairs sitting room was straight out of an adventure tour brochure. It was here also that we discovered how good the Al Jazeera News station was. It provided us with candid news, of surprising quality, for much of the rest of our trip.

Leaving Dogubayezit after two nights in Hotel Tahran, I was reminded at breakfast by a mature Kiwi traveller that foreigners cannot get money in Iran. You could change foreign notes but, although there were ATM machines, you couldn't get money from accounts abroad or use credit cards. Absentmindedly, I had left it rather late and now had less than $300US in cash. I hurried to the ATM in Dogubayezit and withdrew the maximum in Turkish lira (around $250US). This would limit how long we could hang around in Iran and it made me nervous. It had been a long time since I had felt genuinely short of money and I was not enjoying the feeling much now. Sam reassured me it would be fine, but the prospect of having to get Lorna to send us money by Western Union (which takes around three weeks to Iran) was not a happy one.

At the Turkish border we were approached by moneychangers, but I had been told in my hotel to change it on the Iranian side. So having reached the Iranian checkpoint I agreed to change my Turkish Lira. It could not, I was told, be exchanged inside Iran. Naturally the guy tried to cheat us, and with a new currency in denominations of hundreds of thousands of Riyals it was easy to get confused and miss off a zero. The result was a loss of about $100US that we could scarcely stand in the circumstances. I felt pretty gutted and angry at my own stupidity.

"But I have no excuse, Sam. I know those tricks of old, so I should have checked properly."

"The truth is, Dad, you're embarrassed."

I denied this, but he was right, of course.

Sam soon calmed me down. It was good to have him in the *looking after* role again.

*

Being short of money, or perceiving we were, was an uncomfortable feeling. The point, though, was that we were in Iran. Turkey was behind us and everything was suddenly new again – new language, new culture, different food (not so different, it turned out) and different money. We stopped for our first Iranian meal – kebabs! It quickly became apparent that the advice given by the Kiwi at breakfast that morning had been exaggerated – wildly! He had told us that there were no banks across the border from Dogubayezit. In fact, there were dozens and they all changed Turkish money. He had told us that men could not wear shorts in Iran. This was true but he had added that short-sleeved shirts were also banned, which was complete rubbish.   Even the police wore short-sleeved shirts.

It seemed commonplace for travellers talking about a place they had been to go to extremes with horror stories that in fact they had heard secondhand from other travellers.   So the myths are passed on, even though on arrival you find them to be untrue.   After a while, we just stopped believing the stories.

Following the now-familiar hardship of a few hundred miles of empty, rocky terrain and semi-desert, Sam and I eventually arrived in the bustling city of Tabriz.   With a little trouble we found the cheap hotel recommended to us by the owner of Hotel Tahran in Dogubayezit.   It was, as he had said, pretty seedy and institutional, but it was cheap.   With our funds limited to what we had in cash, I felt glad of that.   It was a little like staying in a monastery.   The rooms were austere but clean.   In the foyer, a very serious and strict old gentleman stood all day in his suit at a kind of lectern with a large bound book.   Into this, he entered your name and personal details.

"Police!" he said gruffly, motioning with the book to let us know that he would be passing on our details.   We wondered whether the bandits from our room in Caldiran had come this way fleeing the authorities or a band of brothers whose sister they had dishonoured.

Thankfully, just down the road Sam and I found a number of busy cafes, all of them serving kebabs.   We chose the busiest and enjoyed a selection of side dishes such as chickpeas and aubergine, which we were not expecting, and tea.   As in Turkey, tea in Iran was plentiful.   We sat around in no rush to get back to our hotel, since television was not a feature of that humble establishment.

*

To complete the monasterial atmosphere of Hotel Tahran, Sam and I were awoken early in the morning by people bustling about in the central courtyard.   Eventually accepting defeat, we got up and had a shower before joining the zealots in the breakfast room.   Bland hard-boiled eggs, bread and tea awaited us.   Enthusiastic, nonetheless, we filled up on this simple fare, aware that we were going into unknown territory and had no idea when we would find our next solid meal.

After checking out, we delayed a while to call in at the well known Tourist Information Office for advice about which road to take and what to expect ahead of us. While we waited for the manager to arrive, we called in at a market, buying some dried fruit and tinned tuna for emergencies.

After being shown some large maps and pictures of tourist resorts, we asked about what to expect on the road ahead. Would we be able to find hostels or hotels? Places to buy food?

We were assured that if we stuck to main roads, we would find service stations, hotels and shops every few hundred kilometres or so.

"Every few hundred kilometres?" we asked, sure that he had made a mistake.

"Oh yes, in most cases," he confirmed.

"But we're on bicycles," we reminded him. "In mountainous countryside we wouldn't normally get further than 130 kilometres in a day. Are there places in between?"

He looked doubtful.

"I'm sure you will find something," he said kindly. "But I cannot say for sure."

"We'd better buy some more food," I said to Sam.

Eager to get on the road, we declined his friendly offer of tea in the bazaar and a meeting with two Australian cyclists. Who knows whether or not that was a mistake?

We headed to a shop to buy more tuna, beans and pasta, then headed out of town on a main road from hell. It was very quickly apparent that Iran has some of the worst driving on the planet. It seemed people just pulled out without looking. Others would stop their cars in the middle of a busy road, open their door and step out into the traffic to go into a shop, leaving their car blocking the lane of traffic. The responsibility seemed to be on the other drivers to avoid them and to blare their horns to warn of their presence. This makes for absolute mayhem and a great deal of noise, but in a bizarrely chaotic way it seems to work.

The morning continued with a three-hour steep hill-climb on a road choked with heavy trucks that belched out black fumes and blasting their horns with abandon. Adding to the agony, there were again roadworks. The views into the distance, though, were beautiful, with snow-capped mountains and signs for ski-resorts. But nothing made up for the traffic. For most of the morning at least, it was sheer torture.

What amazed us most that day was reaching the tollbooth of a new motorway and being politely waved through onto the superbly surfaced road.

"Surely not!" I said, waiting to be called back.

During the afternoon, numerous police cars passed and we were simply given a friendly wave. Not much traffic seemed to use this motorway compared to what we had experienced on the road out of Tabriz. We wondered whether the tolls were a deterrent. For us, though, the motorway seemed like a major bonus and not at all what we had been expecting. It gave us an opportunity to cover some decent distance and avoid the smoky old trucks that seemed to have turned off onto the smaller roads through the villages.

Like most motorways, these ones cut through the mountains with long gentle slopes and stayed fairly straight. The biblical panoramas of rocky wilderness, wide-open skies and purple mountains were spectacular, if a little numbing over time – so much light and space and so little evidence of civilisation.

The highways seemed a sensible option for us away from main towns, with dirt cart roads often being the only alternative. The main disadvantage was that having been built fairly recently, there were almost no services. This meant that as cyclists travelling only 120-150km per day, we often didn't reach anywhere we could get food when we needed it. Water was sometimes available from drinking fountains in lay-bys but for food we had to rely on what we could carry from the last main town, and there was a limit to how much we could carry.

Half of what we had bought in Tabriz had gone by the end of our first day. This meant that we found ourselves on several occasions asking truck drivers in lay-bys if they knew where we could next get water or buy food. It was our first encounter with the legendary rural Iranian hospitality. The truck drivers invariably broke the news to us that the next food and water stop was 100km or so away. They then pressed food upon us and refilled our water bottles from their own large containers. It was the only way we survived.

Apart from water and food, the other key necessity for the long-distance cyclist is rest. With so much wide-open space on all sides, you would think this would have been the least of our problems, but that was not the case. Firstly, wide-open space is a problem for camping if there are inquisitive people about. Anything manmade stands out for miles. Even when you think you are a long way from civilisation, more often than not you will wake in the early light with the sound of someone snooping around outside your tent. Secondly, the ground was mainly solid rock, with thorn bushes fighting their way up between the cracks. This gave us very few options for pitching a tent. Generally, we went for the edges of cultivated vineyards or olive groves, when we could find them. These fields were still stony but flat enough for our needs and meant that we were slightly hidden, at least during the night.

One memorable day we were in the middle of nowhere when we came across a large truck stop. There were no facilities, just a lay-by and about ten large trucks. The drivers seemed to have a system of cooking food and brewing up for tea that involved laying a small circle of bricks or stones and then setting the asphalt on fire in the middle with diesel. A metal grill was then put across the bricks to set their pots on. It left big craters in the road, of course. In this layby, they threw their rubbish over the edge of a slope, which being out in the sticks, was never cleared away. Just picked over by vultures, we supposed. We stopped here to make a tuna sandwich. As we sat on the crash barrier looking over the vast panorama, we heard clanking from below and looked down to see a tramp picking over cans and packaging on the rubbish tip. He wore a shredded old grey suit with no shirt and a piece of string for a belt. With long matted hair and a beard, he looked barely human. He was like an exaggerated version of a tramp from a theatre of the absurd production.

Shoeless, the man worked his way up the slope and put his hand out for money. I wondered what use he had for money way out here but gave him some change, if only to stop it making holes in my pockets. He looked at it in his hand wide-eyed and grunted. He was feral all right. A few moments later, one of the truck drivers came over and chased him off with a big stick, and he returned to his tip.   We watched him drinking something from an old can as we rode away.   It seemed bizarre that he might actually live out here.

*

After days of empty wilderness, it was always a bit of a culture shock when we got to a town.   There seemed to be little in between the larger towns.   I had thought that the lack of any villages and small towns marked on the map between the larger towns was a matter of the map's scale.   But in Iran there really was nothing in between, so we went from days on a desolate highway with very little traffic, straight into a bustling town clogged with hooting vehicles, animals, markets, shops and clamouring people.   It was reminiscent of old movies with caravans of camels crossing the empty desert for weeks and arriving somewhere like Timbuktu to clean up, re-stock with supplies and get a good meal – romantic to onlookers, but a bloody hard life for those involved.

On one of our days out in the wilderness we rode uphill for a whole day: 125km with a bland picnic of sauerkraut and dry bread in the middle and then a stony field for a bed at the end.   Our emergency food stocks were at this point completely depleted and we hadn't seen anywhere to replenish them for days.   We were high in the mountains and there was frost on the tent when we got up in the morning.

At around 5pm one day, after another full day of endless wilderness, Sam said he'd rather stop than kill ourselves getting to Zanjan.   A fairly large town, it was still another 45km away and we had already slogged our way through a mountainous 130km that day, so I could see his point.   I was sceptical about the likelihood of finding any life out here, but seeing a small track running under the highway towards what looked like a military compound, we clambered down the bank and headed along it, hoping at least to find a small hamlet servicing the military camp.   Perhaps here we could get a kebab or restock our provisions.   Within a kilometre we met an old man on a donkey and asked him about food.   He pointed east, and signalled *a long way*.

"Zanjan?" I asked.

"Zanjan," he nodded with a toothless smile.

We had a drink of water, noticing that we were both running low, and were about to set off back to the highway when a man approached on a motorcycle. He stopped. I asked him about food and water. He pointed west, up the track. I sighed. This was the norm when you asked for directions: each person you ask says something different, so finally you have to decide who seems the most credible. An amusing game sometimes, but not when you are tired, hungry and running out of water. Agreeing that the guy on the motorcycle seemed more *this century*, we headed off towards the compound where he had assured us we would find food and water.

At the large gate, we approached the guardhouse and tried to explain what we needed. For some reason, I was expecting hostility. It may have been something to do with the 20-foot fence topped with razor wire. The guard was friendly, though. After phoning someone, he asked us to wait. A few minutes later, a group of men in overalls arrived with a jovial chap in front who seemed to be in charge. We explained who we were, that we had cycled from Ireland and were on our way to Japan. In these situations, one somehow resorts to pigeon English with a few approximated local words and gestures. It was comic, but they seemed to understand. The boss-man was moved by the fact that we were father and son and asked us to follow him. We left our bikes by the gate with all our money and valuables, but it felt safe to do so. The man standing by the gate with a big gun gestured that he would look after them.

The camp seemed to house an educational establishment for women. We deduced it was some kind of Koran school, as the students were walking around reading as if memorising something. They seemed too happy for it to have been a penal colony.

At the cookhouse, we were introduced to the ubiquitous chubby chef. They asked if we wanted bread and we indicated anything was fine. The other men took us to sit down on the wall outside to fill our water bottles and ask about our trip, our family, jobs and so on. After about twenty minutes, the chef called us back. We were ushered through the cookhouse door and he ceremoniously handed us a huge parcel, like a large pack of laundry. This was warm and heavy and contained hundreds of layers of water-thin Iranian bread.

We indicated that five would be plenty but the men laughed and said we must take them all. When we tried to pay, we were refused point-blank.

"Here, money is no good," the chef mimed.

We loaded the bread across the rear panniers of my bike as a cowboy might sling heavy packs over a mule. This was not what we'd had in mind, but we felt extremely lucky. What our supplies lacked in variety was certainly made up for in quantity and they would keep us alive.

Leaving the gates and thanking the man with the big gun, Sam and I noticed the sun beginning to turn red close to the horizon. The daylight would not last much longer. Above the track near to the highway, we found an ideal place to camp with a view over the rough plains to the next range of mountains. Zanjan nestled somewhere in between.

We quickly pitched the tent and began to think about eating. I found some honey and a last tin of tuna we didn't know we had, so we now had the makings of a substantial two-course meal. I was glad to have found a camping spot so easily. Sam's hip had been aching badly all day and he had begun to feel really weak. We sat down on a rock and ate our supper looking over the miles of nothingness in the glow of the sunset. It was a beautiful sight, made all the better for the filling meal and promise of a comfortable bed for the night. We wondered where that tramp was sleeping.

*

Inexplicable things happen on a journey like this that you just learn to accept without being able to come up with any rational explanation. One is that at the end of a day's cycling, there always seems to be a steep uphill, even when there hasn't been a hill in sight all day. This happens too often to be a coincidence. Another is that when you only have a short distance to ride in a day, it seems harder to get there than when your destination is a long way off.

The next morning, Zanjan was only 45km away. We knew we could do it in around two and a half hours, but it seemed to drag on forever. We had seen the town from our camp-spot, so we knew the road was a fairly flat, but once we were on the move it seemed to be uphill most of the way. The only logical explanation is that the mind plays tricks on you when under pressure. You think you are riding uphill when in fact you aren't. You know this, but it still continues to deceive you.

There were various turnings into Zanjan. We asked people we met along the road, but nobody seemed to be able to agree which one went to the centre. In fact, the notion of the *centre* of a town or city seemed to be alien to people once we got outside Europe. Here, as in the future, we learned in the end to ask for the main railway station, which usually worked if they had one.

After restocking with supplies and treating ourselves at a few restaurants, Sam and I moved on in the same doggedly monotonous fashion, through the wilderness to the next town of Qazvin, before finally reaching Tehran. Fortunately, Sam's hip got better during this section, or at least no worse, so we made reasonably good time.

We were delighted to reach Tehran. The desert and the miles of openness had begun to play tricks on our minds. Iran's capital is huge in comparison to its other urban centres and the traffic is unbelievable. The day we arrived, we hit the evening traffic heading home, or heading out on the town to nightclubs. It came as a shock after all the days of solitary wilderness, where the odd tooting truck was sometimes all the humanity we would see in a day.

At first, it seemed that the traffic ignored red lights and oncoming traffic. After five minutes of fighting our way through, though, it felt more like the vehicles attacked anything that moved. All around us, they hurtled towards one another like charging bulls about to clash head on. Then, at the last moment, one or the other would veer off or brake sharply. Motorcycles without lights travelled at speed the wrong way along congested streets, sometimes along the pavements, dodging pedestrians. Police stood at junctions witnessing all this and treated it as normal.

We were terrified initially but eventually just began to laugh. It was like a circus. It was the craziest driving I had ever seen in my life, but somehow it worked. Miraculously, we hardly saw an accident in the whole five days we were there.

Sam and I had been given a number of recommendations for cheap hotels in Tehran and they were all for the same place, so we were relieved finally to arrive at Hotel Fironzeh and find they had a room for us.   It was another of those rather institutionalised hotels for working men that had adapted itself to the demands of western backpackers.   I was disappointed to be told at the reception that their rates had increased fifty percent in the last year.   But it was still cheap, very central and the rooms seemed comfortable.   Fortunately, they had free, if slow, internet access, so we could start looking at where we would go from here.

I was uncomfortably aware that we had reached the point after which we had no fixed plan.   After getting on the snail-net and checking the British Foreign Office website, embassies and travel forums, we had to accept Pakistan looked very doubtful.   This was confirmed the next day at breakfast when we met some English travellers who had just come the other way.   There was no *maybe* about it, they said.   They told us stories of people visiting embassies day after day to apply for Pakistan visas that were refused; foreign embassies refusing to issue letters of recommendation; motorcyclists having to have their bikes air-freighted to India at great expense.   It was chaos, they said.   Apparently, even before visa stopped being issued, there was specific advice about not cycling in the south and even not taking trains or buses in this area.   All our options involving Pakistan seemed to be blocked.

Over the next day, we talked to more people and spent time on faster internet in a nearby deluxe hotel.   Finally, we accepted that the only sensible option was to take a short flight over Pakistan to Amritsar.   I agreed with Sam to book this the next morning, but over dinner I hit on an exciting alternative.   If we *had* to take a flight, why not fly to the south of India and make a long detour to compensate for the distance we were missing in Pakistan?   We had both wanted to go to Kerala and to Goa but agreed at the start that it would be just too much to fit in and to leave it for another time.   This idea put a different complexion on things: our bad luck over Pakistan might be good luck after all.   I like that kind of psychology.

By breakfast time the next morning, we had a flight booked to Cochin in Kerala and had managed to pay for it online with a credit card. We thought were in heaven – or soon would be.

The next few days in Tehran were all the more enjoyable for the knowledge we were going to Kerala. Also, I could now stop worrying about spending money. We splurged on a few luxurious meals out to celebrate and spoilt ourselves with ice cream sundaes and special Iranian cakes. Tehran was not at all the place we had expected. Far from being serious and austere, it seemed to be a vibrant and exciting place to live. Restaurants and cafes were busy with people sitting laughing and joking together. The people we met seemed happy and friendly. Sam and I spent most of our days walking around the streets seeking out interesting places. We never for a moment lacked things to do.

While in Tehran, I emailed Colin and suggested I carry out an audit at the offices of one of our clients. This gave me a whole new perspective on the place. Although I had been to the office a number of years before, this time I had not arrived on a jumbo jet.

Getting close to our departure date, I picked up some polystyrene packaging in the street to protect our bikes in transit. Sam laughed.

"Still looking for something to worry about?"

Before long, we were cycling out of Tehran towards the airport. Sam's mood seemed to have soared at the prospect of cycling through southern India. Getting our bikes on the plane was my only remaining concern. I tried to disguise it. What if they just turned us away? As we rode, I became more certain of problems to come.

At the airport, though, my worries were soon dispelled by the helpful staff who arranged for the bikes to be shrink-wrapped.

Boarding the plane for Cochin (or Kochi), we were pretty ecstatic. I had high hopes that Sam's confidence and general state of mind would take a major turn for the better once we arrived in India I also knew I would feel more at home myself, entering a region of the world where the culture was reminiscent of the happiest part of my childhood. It gave us both a really heightened sense of anticipation as we left Iran behind.

SAM'S POINT OF VIEW

The border crossing into Iran wasn't made easy for us.   There were many tales of it being impossible to get money inside Iran.   Between the border posts, we were 'assisted' by a professional hustler, who almost walked away with an inflated cash exchange.   That was before we checked the amount and realised we needed ten times the amount we'd been given.   Then, after passing through the border, we found that there were banks everywhere and that we'd still been short-changed.   My dad was so pissed off at being conned.   I think he felt embarrassed in front of me.   I felt a bit sorry for him and did my best to make him forget it.   He seemed to appreciate this, which did make me feel good.   I really wanted to feel like I had something to offer rather than just being along for the ride.   He did try to give me responsibility for things like route planning, but I felt reluctant to take it on at the time.

You couldn't get money from cash machines or with cards in Iran. Once you had exchanged all your US dollars and other foreign cash, if you needed money you had to send home for it.   It made our time in Iran pretty tough, along with a number of other factors:

1. The weather was blistering hot and finding water was near impossible – sometimes for hundreds of miles.   On a bicycle, this is dangerous and it is near impossible to carry enough.

2. We always had to cover our legs, in keeping with Moslem requirements.   Due to the heat, you sweat a lot.   We would go three days or more without finding a shower or a place to wash, so unpleasant saddle sores and rashes began to plague us.

3. Our visa had a 30-day limit, so there was no waiting around; we had to cycle fast through some very mountainous terrain.

4. Our money was limited; we couldn't afford to treat ourselves in case of unexpected expenses later.

5. There was nothing to treat ourselves with anyway! All that the food shops had were sweets, a crappy excuse for crisps and occasionally wafer-thin bread. We survived on bread and jam every day, which is tough during strenuous bouts of cycling.

6. Although we met with great kindness in places, there were many unfriendly locals. The usual scenario was a teenage boy and a younger boy who run next to you calling "money, money!" – then throwing rocks or hitting you with sticks if you refuse.

Despite the negatives I have highlighted here, Iran wasn't all bad. The desert terrain was unlike any other. My dad called it 'biblical' and I could see what he meant. I could imagine the parables played out in that scenery: a sacrificial goat tied to a stake and left to perish in the heat; a 'Good Samaritan' finding a couple of cyclists who'd been attacked by bandits at the side of the road. It seemed almost stone age, with thousands of miles of treeless rocky mountains. The rock seemed strange – brown with the occasional strata of red, orange or even purple thrown in. It was very impressive.

Some of the locals were very hospitable. We passed a woman's university miles from anywhere, which was protected by high security fencing. Arriving at the entrance, asking where we could buy food, we were given what must have been a week's supply of flat bread. It was too much to fit into our panniers, so my dad laid it across the back like people do with mules. The chef was annoyed to have his time taken up, but the boss insisted. We were so hungry we didn't protest.

I seem to remember feeling more positive about cycling at this time. We were really making headway, although I was still grumpy a lot of the time. Intense daily exercise is tough, but to be in the middle of Iran with no choice but to carry on really drove me forward. So did the sweat, the sores and shortage of food and water, along with the tantalising idea of a shower, a comfortable bed and a good meal at the end. Water never tasted as good as in Iran when we ran out and had to cycle miles in the heat before finding a place to fill up. It was agony but I can still remember how fantastic it felt when that water finally touched your tongue.

Tehran was so worth striving for, and arriving there in the dark was unbelievable. I've never seen worse driving in my life. Traffic rules were non-existent. We felt so vulnerable. No room to move, horns blaring, motorcyclists racing along pavements – it was like a vision of hell. To top it all, there were traffic marshals flailing their arms about as if to mimic other traffic marshals they'd seen, but in reality having absolutely no idea or any effect at all. We certainly knew we were a long way from home.

Indus
Sutlej
Lahore
Amritsar
Multan
Bahawalpur
PAKISTAN
Bikaner
Ambala
Delhi
Jaisalmer
Jodhpur
Jaipur
Ajmer
RAJASTHAN
Yamuna
Agra
Etawah
Lucknow
Kanpur
Bhognipur
Kesariyaji
Udaipur
Varanasi
Allahabad
Ahmadabad
Lunawada
Ganges
Son
Patna
BANGLADESH
Vadodara
Narmada
Dhanbad
Dhaka
nagar
Surat
I N D I A
Jamshedpur
Calcutta
Fly to BANGKOK
Nagpur
Raipur
Cuttack
D E C C A N
Mahanadi
umbai
Kihim
Khed
Godavari
Puri
W E S T E R N   G H A T S
Solapur
Talere
Naka
Kolhapur
Hyderabad
Vishakhapatnam
Krishna
Arambol
Vijayawada
Panjim
Hubli-Dharwar
Kurnool
E A S T E R N   G H A T S
Palolem
Cancona
B A Y   O F
B E N G A L
Nellore
Mangalore
Bangalore
Madras
Mysore
Kozhikode
Ooty
from TEHRAN
Shoranur
Pollachi
Tiruchchirappalli
Palani
Kodaikanal
Cochin
Munnar
Madurai
Jaffna
Thiruvananthapuram
Gulf of Mannar
Kanniyakumari
Trincomalee
SRI LANKA
I N D I A N
Colombo
Kandy
O C E A N
Galle
Dondra Head
H I M A L A Y A
GANGDISE SHAN
Annapurna
Xigaze
NEPAL
Mt Everest
Katmandu
BHUTAN
Ghagara
COCHIN to Calcutta
Distance cycled
2,919 km   1,813 miles

Chapter 7

Incredible India – Sam's growing confidence

But, sir, you are rich gentlemen.   Where is your car?   We Indians are perplexed, sir.   Why to travel by bicycle when you and your son could use your Mercedes?

The big difference with flying somewhere rather than going overland is the sudden change of culture and environment that meets you on arrival.   It can be quite disarming if you are not expecting it.   Until now, on a bicycle, these changes had occurred so slowly that we absorbed them calmly.   This, we realised, is certainly an advantage to your mental state.

Sam had travelled a fair amount as a boy, but he had never been anywhere tropical and he seemed really mesmerised by the landscape, the smells and the wildlife of India, along with its people.   He loved it from the moment he arrived.   Looking back, he says he is glad that his introduction to India was in Kerala, because it remains his favourite place.   For me, I did feel a subliminal sense of returning home, as I suspected I would.   I was born and brought up in Singapore and also Malaysia for quite a while as a child.   Both had been full of Indian people driving taxis and running little barrow shops on the streets around where I lived.   We used to stop over in India in the days when you couldn't fly to Singapore in one hop.   I had also been back to India when working on the QE2 in my early twenties.

Kerala felt very similar to 1960s Malaysia at this point in its development.   It did feel like bad luck to have had to fly, but we accepted that without that bad luck we would not have got to heavenly Kerala (as advertisements call it), and that would have been a travesty.

A sudden downpour on our way from Cochin airport failed to dispel our sense of good fortune.   When it rains in India, it really rains.   The rough roads quickly turned into muddy rivers and we were soon soaked to the skin, but we didn't care. Somehow, even the rain was beautiful. What did deflate us was Sam getting yet another puncture. The Indian roads were potholed and strewn with debris. The potholes were mostly hidden under muddy water that swamped the entire road and it was hard to avoid what you couldn't see. It was a slow puncture, so we were able to reach the outskirts of Cochin by stopping to pump it up every five minutes. Sam tells me he remembers feeling very depressed about it. I remember being slightly annoyed, although Sam probably saw this as fury.

In the end, we stopped and were directed to one of the many *puncture-wallahs* who line all roads in India. It was our first experience of this amazing phenomenon. These men mostly just squat in the dirt at the side of the road, each with a box of simple tools. Indian bikes are heavy-duty and tend to be poorly maintained, so they have an endless supply of work.

Sam's tube was crudely repaired in a heavy-handed manner but with great ingenuity, using recycled materials and a large club-hammer. All the tools seemed crude and industrial. I asked the man how much. "As you like," he told me with the characteristic Indian side-to-side wobble of the head. I fished in my pocket and brought out about half a euro in rupees. I wasn't yet sure of the money, but it didn't look enough.

"Yes, yes, this is sufficient," he said, smiling.

Sam and I left feeling we might have underpaid him. Later, I discovered that I had paid about five times the going rate. My good humour was not damaged – not even when the tube deflated again that evening. He was a nice man. Everything here remained beautiful.

However much you enjoy the variety of different places, I think you always know when you arrive in a place that suits you. Sam and me immediately realised that India, or certainly Kerala, was made for us. We felt calm and happy here. Even the filth seemed OK – nowhere near as bad as I remembered from previous short visits, anyway. Eating out for the first time, at a working-men's café in a grubby backstreet, seemed too good to be true: chicken biryani, potato cakes, puri, chapattis, divine banana and coconut fritters, and fresh lime soda, all less than fifty pence each (sterling).

Sam and I spent the next four days staying at a friendly little guesthouse in Fort Cochin, walking through the labyrinthine back streets of Mattacherry and visiting the nearby small city of Ernakulum.   It was a lovely place for casual walks in the evenings. We felt more relaxed than we had since Danube Nature Reserve.

One afternoon, walking through the rather unimaginatively named Jew Town looking at carpentry workshops, we came across a group of young boys playing cricket on a patch of waste ground by their shanty houses.   They ran to us as we passed and offered Sam the bat.   Sam accepted.   Soon he was battling the practiced skills of these skinny young boys, while I pretended to field at long-leg and chatted to their mothers and sisters over a wall.   It made an already lovely day just perfect.   We left promising that they would see their photographs on our blog.

Sam, not a bad cricketer himself, had been happy to be overrun by the skill and enthusiasm of these little boys and was their hero as a result.   I felt really pleased for him.   I thought how much I wished my father could have known him.   Making this trip would give Sam great stories to tell his own children and grandchildren long after I too was dead, I reminded myself.   I find these kinds of thoughts very difficult.

We loved sleepy Cochin, so we were happy to sit around in cafes drinking lime sodas.   Eager to see more of India, though, we soon agreed to head inland for the mountains of Tamil Nadu after a couple more days.   Sam felt he had been missing the challenge of mountain cycling and needed a boost to his fitness.   I was also eager to get out of the stifling heat that I remember hardly noticing as a child.   We liked the idea of heading for the small hill-station and tea plantation town of Munar for a night, then crossing over Mt Adai Mudi through a huge nature reserve into Tamil Nadu.

Our young guesthouse hosts in Cochin asked us how many days we were planning to take to cycle to Munar.   We were amused at their naïveté.   It was little more than 75km on the map.   To Indians, of course, that seemed a huge distance to cycle, we realised.

*

The day came to leave Cochin.   We had loved it here and enjoyed the contrasting cultural elements of India, the English Raj, the nuns and the Portuguese colonialists, all of which influenced the architecture as well as the food and character of the local people.   Eager as we were to get to Munar, we felt comfortable leaving late enough to have breakfast first and say goodbye to our fellow guests as well as our two young hosts.   Once past Ernakulum and out of the hectic traffic, we relaxed into the easy pace that had become our custom on our first morning after a big break.

After the rocky wilderness of Iran, we felt spoilt for choice by the number of cafes along the roadsides in India and also by the fact that after one village ends a new one soon begins. After 60 fairly level kilometres, we stopped for a basic lunch in Ootu.   When chatting to the owner over some rice and dhal, we felt sure he had made a mistake when he assured us Munar was another 82km away.   He rocked his head and sighed.

"I am sorry to say, my good gentlemen, but you will not be finding it possible to be reaching Munar tonight by means of a cycle."

Amused by this first experience of the Victorian Indian-English left behind by the colonial tea planters, we took him as an eccentric, ignorant of the potential distance that could be covered on a modern touring bike.   His less eccentric customers concurred, however.   It seemed that the map showed the roads as fairly straight when in fact they went around and around, cascading up and down each hill.   Sam and I resigned ourselves to stopping after 40 or 50 more kilometres. We cycled on only to find that after the next bend the road began to rise at an alarming gradient, spiralling around the lush green hills. We constantly doubled back on ourselves at hairpin bends without any sign of reaching a peak.

*

When climbing through long ranges of hills, you tend to get into a *cycling groove*.   Distance runners do the same thing.   It is a form of self-hypnosis aided by the repetitive motion of the pedals and the sound of the tyres at each downward pedal stroke.   Your breathing starts to beat out a rhythm and often you begin to chant a suitable song

141

in your head – one with a slow, steady beat usually.   It depends upon the gradient.   Rawhide is one of my favourites for hills, but I have many if I'm really going for it downhill, like Charlie Don't Surf or Police On My Back by the Clash.   Hold Tight by Dave Dee, Dozy, Beaky, Mick & Titch really helps when the going gets tough and I need to grit my teeth, whereas the Beatles' A Girl Like You or I Will are both good for calmly plodding along at a more sedate pace.   I am rarely tempted to use an mp3 player, however.   I find it too intrusive for cycling and potentially hazardous.

When not singing to myself, I am thinking.   Sam is the same. Long-distance cycling allows you plenty of time to think in peace and quiet.   It's one of the best things about it.   I have solved many a problem during a day on my bike.   This day on the Kerala hills, I drifted into thoughts about the game of cricket we had played with the little boys in Cochin.   Sam had loved it so much.   He had come alive.   I wondered if this was a message to me about what he needed. Should we carry a cricket bat, stumps and ball or a football so we could call together locals for a game each time we stopped?   It was an interesting idea.   But how long might it take us to reach Tokyo that way?   Did that matter?

I tried looking at it more objectively.   Was I being too literal? Maybe the cricket game was just an indication of other things – like Sam wanting to be with younger people, wanting to be in a position of people learning from him rather than the other way around.   I am a great believer in physical activity (team games especially) as a perfect way for dealing with, or highlighting, the root cause of psychological issues.   This may not be the primary intention, but the outcome – the potential for healing or unblocking barriers – can be immense.   I'm sure that is one of the reasons for sport and games in schools, a benefit so many children in recent generations have been denied.   Crazy!

This cycle trip, of course, was a perfect example of a physical activity (an expedition) that would provide us with far more than just a holiday or physical fitness.

*

After two hours of steady climbing in the sweltering heat, we were exhausted and in grave danger of overheating. So seeing a rock pool ahead, we stopped and I soaked myself in it. This felt much better, but as we cycled on I found myself dry again within only twenty minutes and there was still no sign of a summit. After another hour we had covered 40km since lunch and reluctantly agreed we might not make it to Munar that night.

Soon after this, we stopped at a rest station with roadside stalls to get a cold coke. The stall owner was busy killing a poisonous snake with a stick. We had begun to see a few of these squashed on the road. Adjacent to the stalls was a large waterfall – Adukkad Falls, I believe. As we sipped our cokes we saw that a number of young Indian men had climbed up and were standing under the thundering water. It looked very refreshing; reminding me of a Consulate menthol cigarette advertisement they used to show on Singaporean TV when I was a kid (cool as a mountain stream). With little hesitation we took turns to go in, wearing most of our cycle clothing. It felt amazing. So much so that after this we agreed to bite the bullet and keep going until we got to Munar.

After leaving the waterfall, it began to grow dark. We persisted doggedly up the steep hills and around the numerous hairpin bends at our steady, determined pace, counting the dead snakes as we watched the numbers tick over on the cycle computers. We had done this before and we knew that persistence and developing a trance-like state paid off.

"… will I wait a lonely lifetime, if you want me to I will …" I sang to myself, panting in between.

The climb continued without let up. Soon, I began to feel sick, and dizzy. It was as if all the energy had been drained out of me and only the weight of my feet was pushing the pedals around. I decided to keep quiet about it. It would do no good to tell Sam; it might make him less determined. The thing to do was to press on quietly, I decided.

I wondered whether my exhaustion was the price to be paid for caffeinated drinks. Sam seemed OK, though. I had not felt so utterly drained on the trip so far and I worried a little that I might be suffering from serious dehydration or altitude sickness. I was in a trance-like state now all right, but not one that I could snap out of.

My exhaustion was only momentarily forgotten as we cycled on a short downhill, through a village with loud jingly Indian music. Groups of people waved as we sped through. I called to Sam. With the background music it seemed like we were in one of those tacky Indian television advertisements. Moving in time with the music, we put on big toothy grins and theatrical Bollywood waves to fit the part. The people clapped with delight as we passed – a surreal moment.

It was a short-lived interlude of fun. Soon it was dark and the tight unlit roads became dangerous. We had lights but they were useless against the mad bus drivers screeching around the bends in both directions, using horns in place of brakes. We had to get off and walk and on several occasions jump into the ditch with our bikes to avoid being run down. I wondered at the wisdom of continuing along this treacherous road in such an exhausted state. With no sign of any guesthouses now, there was little choice. In an emergency, camping in the jungle at the roadside was always a possibility, but it was dark and the snakes were a good enough reason to avoid it.

Most of the last ten kilometres up to Munar had to be done on foot. Not so much because of the steepness of the hill as the fact that I now felt so weak. At one point, I told Sam I doubted I could continue any further. He looked at my pale face and seemed worried. His reaction gave me a bit of a fright. Despite this near acceptance of defeat, at around 8pm we finally saw the lights of the town. I managed to cycle the last mile or two on the flat, but was convinced I had imagined the lights. Quickly, though, we found ourselves taking directions to a guesthouse and were relieved to find a room available at the first one we reached.

After dumping our bags in the basic room, we locked up our bikes under the porch and headed straight for a restaurant along the road, fearful that it might close before we got there. I felt I would die if I didn't eat soon. The restaurant was open and we devoured a good biryani dinner, which revived me a little.

On the road that evening, I had remarked a couple of times that something sticky had leaked onto my thin baggy trousers. I had changed into them after the waterfall to protect my legs against mosquitoes. Finally relaxing after our meal, I noticed again the dark sticky mess on my trouser leg. Trying to identify what it was, I tasted it. Shampoo had come to mind, but it had no smell or taste. The restaurant lights were too dim to identify it visually. I pulled up my trouser leg for a better look. Sam immediately pulled back in horror. My whole leg was a mass of thick congealed blood. I must have been bleeding profusely for hours. I felt no pain, though, and couldn't remember injuring myself. Where had it come from?

We quickly paid and left, with Sam suggesting I get into a shower to clean it and see how severe the wound was. Still dizzy, I felt like I was in a dream, wondering how this had happened, as I stumbled anxiously back to the guesthouse.

"Maybe you cut it when we jumped into the ditch that time," Sam said.

I visualised a day wasted at a clinic, getting it stitched. As we climbed the path, I swooned and staggered.

"What if they have to bloody well amputate?" I muttered.

It seemed unlikely to be a cut, Sam deduced, since my trousers were not torn and I was sure there was no localised pain. This was more and more worrying, but I was beyond deduction.

Back in the room, I took off my trousers and immediately noticed something drop onto the floor.

"Agh, what the hell's that!" shouted Sam.

"It's a bloody leech!" I said.

Still feeling out of it, I remembered something my grandfather had told me about being in Burma during the war and having to burn them with cigarettes. We burned the fattened creature with a lighter from my bag – pointless, of course, now it had fallen off. Then I got into the shower to wash off all the congealed blood. There was so much it clogged the drain. Afterwards, I could see signs of several leeches having fed off me before dropping off. The wounds had obviously taken a long time before the blood managed to congeal and stop flowing, but owing to the effort of the climb I had failed to notice. We laughed uproariously. Used to pushing myself to the limit, I had put my dizziness and exhaustion down to all that uphill cycling in the heat and humidity.

*

Munar highlighted the attraction of hill stations during Indian summers.   It felt great to breathe cool oxygen-rich air and be out of that exhausting humidity.   We really enjoyed our mile walk into town for breakfast the following morning.   My leg ached a little and had only finally stopped bleeding a few hours after my shower, including an hour with it up in the air while we watched Premiership football.   There was so much congealed blood in the shower drain, the owner had to rod it to clear it all.

"I'm sorry – leeches!" I said.   Sam showed him a part-cremated creature.

"No, no, please, not sorry, sir.   I am hoping you will not be dead!"

I did not like the sound of that.   What did he mean exactly? He seemed unable to explain but neither did he behave like he might soon have a corpse on his hands.

"Does my dad need to see a doctor?"

"Well, sir, I do not think so.   I would recommend it if he were bitten by a larger animal.   A snake, yes, of course.   But I think leech will not cause death.   Maybe better to swim naked in waterfall, though, next time, sir.   Disregard your English reserve if I might say."

After our exertions, we agreed to stay an extra day in Munar.

"You need to make some more blood, Dad," Sam told me.

Next morning, we headed for the recommended Rapsy's Restaurant in the bazaar for falafel, banana lassi and strong black tea. I felt I needed a hearty breakfast to build myself up.   I had hoped for porridge but was to be disappointed by a menu that promised more than it was able to deliver.   This proved to be a common story in hill-towns with sporadic deliveries.

Sam kept asking about leeches and whether there might be any after-effects.   I said not but secretly wondered whether leeches could spread blood diseases like hepatitis or HIV.   No point asking our host, I thought; on the other hand, there must have been some explanation for him thinking I'd come close to death.   I was heartened, though, by how much Sam seemed to worry about me.

He seemed to enjoy this role. He didn't make a fuss but I could tell he cared. Of course, he may just have been concerned about who would pay for things if I snuffed it, but that seems unfairly pessimistic.

After our free day, recuperation complete, Sam and I headed off at around 8am the following morning, stopping briefly at a shack for banana fritters and falafel on our way out of town. Most meals here seemed to involve bananas, chickpeas or lentils. For me, this is a plus.

Both roads at the junction seemed to be signposted for Kodaikanal, our next destination, so we asked a good cross-section of locals which road to take before our decision. One road said 143km, the other 179km, but in mountain areas this can be deceiving. The longer route can often be quicker. In fact, the advice was unanimous and we headed on the higher (shorter) road up through the spectacular terraced tea plantations.

The views as we climbed out of Munar were really memorable. Bright green tea bushes formed into interesting organic shapes as they followed the contours of the hillsides. We saw an elephant being led up the hill, classic old buses with schoolchildren leaning out and calling to us, and tea pickers in bright coloured saris amongst the contrasting verdant bushes.

Our plan was to get to the summit village of Topstation for lunch after a long steep climb through the romantically named High Range of Travancore – some of the world's highest tea plantations. From there we needed to descend and then go back up around the edge of Mt Anai Mudi and through the large Adimali Nature Reserve. After this, we would descend again before climbing to the hill-station town of Kodaikanal, which towered over it all. We planned to rest there for three or four nights.

Sam seemed to have more energy in his legs after our rest day in Munar and I appeared fully recovered from my bloodletting experience, so we were in pretty positive spirits. Despite this, we made very slow progress. Not because the route was steep, but because the views were so astonishing that we were unable to avoid stopping to take photographs at every new bend in the road.

We moved on in fits and starts. By the time we reached the Maddapatty dam, we were stunned into silence by the beauty of what we had passed through.   It was too much for your mind to take in one day, we agreed.   We hardly noticed the steepness of the hills as we progressed through the lush forests, past troops of monkeys and leather-skinned lumberjacks leading elephants that were dragging huge logs.   An extended family of Indian tourists we had met in Munar waved to us each time they passed in their minibus.   Sam and I agreed that this day had edged ahead of our previous best day of the trip on the Danube.   And there was still so much more to come.

A large bus passed us and shouts resounded.   As a cyclist, it would not have been unusual if this had been people shouting in annoyance at being held up, but not here.

"Welcome to my country!" someone shouted.

"We will wait for you in Topstation!" called a group of smiling children.

Eventually we reached Topstation, surrounded by the beautiful Yellapatty tea plantations – once a British company but now owned by the huge Indian Tata Corporation.   There didn't seem much here. As we approached the small hamlet, the road turned into a mud track. We hoped it wouldn't be *one of those days*.

After stopping to take photos of the valleys miles below we walked to the centre.   This was a bend in the road with one shack-come-chai shop on the corner.   We were not too concerned.   Going over to an elderly man on the bend, we asked him if this was still the road to Kodaikanal.

"My dear friends," he began benevolently in what seemed like a practiced speech, "you cannot reach Kodaikanal by this road.   The road was destroyed in a storm last winter and it is impossible to continue by cycle, or even a Land Rover.   That is the sad fact of the matter."

He waggled his head about and held up his hands in apology.

I asked what the alternative was.   As expected, he said we needed to return to Munar (55km) then go via the other road (a further 179km).   He pointed out he could not guarantee with any certainty that this would be open either.

"OK, we'll walk until the road begins again.   How far until the road starts again?" I asked.

He stroked his large waxed moustache and raised his eyes to the heavens.

"Good sir, it is with a heavy heart that I must inform you that you may not even pass on foot much further.   The road does not begin again until the other side of the big mountain.   It is sad, but you find yourselves betwixt and between, gentlemen.   You will be wasting your time continuing, good sirs.   It is indeed without pleasure that I should be seeing you later tonight passing back this way immensely crestfallen, I regret to impart."

The old man clasped his chest, now wearing a pained look on his dark wrinkled face.   The tea plantations in this area were once the pride of British colonial companies.   We took the man to be a descendent perhaps of a batman to one of the bosses from that time.   The quaint language seems to have remained amongst many elderly locals and I have no doubt they could make a good living in British theatres.

Impressed by the man's theatrics but still sceptical, Sam and I agreed we would walk on a little way to see for ourselves.   A few hundred yards further on, we met another man whose manner and speech were more of our time.   He agreed that it might be possible to walk and thought the road returned after 10km.   But he confirmed that the road around the mountain had certainly been destroyed.   We walked on again to find a few winding, downhill sections where we could cycle and passed through a manned barrier into the Adimali Nature Reserve.   At the barrier, there was a wooden board with details of the area.   Mt Anai Mudi was 2695m high, it said. The next main town appeared to be Clourie in Tamil Nadu, on the other side of the mountain.

Incidentally, despite everyone calling this place Clourie, it does not seem to appear on maps.   This is never a surprise in countries like India.   Place names change, but many locals still use the old names.   On Google Maps, it seems it is called Kilavarai (a little too like *killer valley* for my liking).

A man in military uniform lifted the barrier with one hand and saluted us with the other.   We stopped to look at the board.

"Very beautiful," I said with a sweep of the arm.

"*Acha*, beautiful," he replied.   He pointed to the road over the mountain.   "Broken!"

We indicated that we understood this but would continue on foot if necessary.   He shrugged.   It was our own choice.   By now, we were feeling more confident of our own judgement , so we cycled on, enjoying the downhill run past women walking elegantly with cumbersome loads of thin logs in long bundles.   Beautifully dressed in colourful jackets with baggy skirts tucked up like shorts, they had lovely slim, healthy-looking bodies with straight backs and fine bone structure.   We called hello as we passed.   In each case, we saw the face of an old woman smiling back at us.   A meagre diet, mountain air and outdoor work clearly do wonders for your body.   We hoped it would do the same for us.

Leaving these thoughts behind we found ourselves on a steep, deeply rutted mud track where heavy construction traffic and manual labourers were busy rebuilding the road.   It looked like slow progress.   We walked the rest of the way to the nearby village, where we found a small dark chai shop perched precariously against the slope, selling bean soup, rice and deep-fried cakes.   We stepped inside to eat, drawing a large crowd who stared at us open-mouthed. Clearly, few westerners ventured this far, even before the road was destroyed.

The people were kind in their inquisitiveness but the café owner moved most of them on once he had determined who might be enticed in to eat or drink.   The food was basic but much tastier than it looked. The fried cakes tasted so good we bought four extra, along with some more water, just in case.

"We might need these, Sam.   It could be a tough day."

*

Riding and walking in fits and starts along the red muddy track, Sam and I began to consume water at a heavy rate in the heat and the dust. We agreed we should have bought more at the chai shop, but we hoped there would be another shop further on.   The road may have been washed away, but surely the settlements would remain.

We were coming closer to a small hamlet where there seemed to be some kind of fete, judging by the loud jingly music on the public address system.   Arriving at the village, however, we found it to be another one of those places way out in the sticks where loud music is played all day and evening to keep people cheery – or this was our deduction.   At that point, we met an elderly man with a long neatly trimmed white beard and an educated English accent.   We stopped to ask for directions.

"Upon my word!" he exclaimed. "You will not be able to get to Kodaikanal by this route – no, no, no!"

That same language again, I thought.   In the heat of afternoon, I hallucinated slightly, seeing the man as one of those Shakespearian characters on stage at the Globe Theatre in London who take themselves a little too seriously.   He had all the theatrical hand gestures.   Even his white robes were arranged about him like a costume.

"Yes, we know the road is broken," we said cheerfully.   "But we plan to walk along the bad sections."

Pointing up at the tall mountainside, with clouds hanging over the summit, he explained earnestly that the old road had passed around sheer mountain sections, held up with large logs.

"It was a most terrible storm, I assure you.   It seemed almost that the wrath of the gods was being brought down upon us simple folk."

The old man remained posed with his arm raised, pointing dramatically towards the mountain and the heavens, as if trying to ensure that his audience further back could understand, even if they could not hear him.

"It is talked of still in this village, sirs," he continued, adjusting his pose. "The entire construction was washed down the mountainside, destroying houses, great trees   all in its path.   Many died.   May my god strike me down if I have embellished the truth, sirs.   It would be impossible even to walk along the sections where the road once lay."

The old man clasped his head, gave a good impression of weakening at the knees and leaned heavily on his stick to steady himself.   Resisting the urge to clap, I reminded myself that this was in fact a serious warning and not a theatrical performance. He certainly seemed to know what he was talking about.

Sam and I looked at each other, reluctantly beginning to think again. Surely anything would be better at this stage than going back to Munar?

We questioned the old gentleman further about alternatives, finally establishing there was a steep goat track that went right up over the summit of the mountain, and that we would meet the remaining road down to Clourie over on the other side.

"But, mark my words, it is extremely steep," he warned us. "Very few people in this village would attempt it – only some shepherds, and alas, many of them have fallen. I cannot imagine it would be possible with cycles and luggage!"

We agreed it would be tough, but we were going to try anyway.

"We are very fit," laughed Sam.

The man joined him, laughing sarcastically as if he thought Sam might be talking about our mental state. I almost expected to see someone step out from behind a tree, holding up a sign saying

LAUGH

Knowing we were about to embark upon something momentous – maybe even ridiculous – we grinned to ourselves as we headed up the steep, deeply rutted track. It soon rose above the village almost at the angle of a ladder and became too steep to push the bikes on. Undeterred, we adopted a system whereby the two of us carried one loaded bike for about 100m then returned to collect the other. We continued like this in relays for about an hour, after which we felt that familiar sense of being sick with exhaustion. We laughed about the madness of it, kept drinking and continued on up. After another hour, we passed a mountain stream. Not knowing how long this would continue, I filled two empty bottles with water. It tasted clean. Not knowing what might be going into it above us, however, I poured in a few drops of iodine to purify it for later. This was the first time we had used it.

It was near this point that I almost stepped on a large green snake devouring a fat toad. We later discovered it was deadly, so we were lucky he had his mouth full.

The relay system was needed all the way up. We knew our time was limited to the remaining hours of daylight, so we didn't let up.

Five hours had passed by the time we reached the summit. Our legs ached and our shoulders were bruised from carrying the loaded bikes. It was now around 6:30pm. Utterly exhausted, we looked down through the cloud over the surrounding valleys way below us as the light faded. We had done it!

It was so beautiful. We felt like mountain climbers reaching the summit. In fact, of course, that day we were mountain climbers. Mt Anai Mudi may have been climbed by this route quite a few times before, but we doubted anyone had done it carrying two bikes with 24kg of luggage.

Sam and I had earned a break. We sat down, noticing that way up here we could still faintly hear the sound of the jingly music echoing in the valley below. We discussed whether to pitch our tent here for the night. I think it was at this point that I breathlessly recounted the insane story (and filming) of Werner Herzog's Fitzcarraldo. In this film, a mad European opera fanatic in Peru gets his crew of Native American Indians to carry a large steam ship over part of the Andes Mountains between rivers. Our achievement was not quite on that scale, but looking back onto the valley way below, it seemed to be in the same crazy ballpark.

We were physically drained. Even so, Sam declared himself happier on balance to get to the road and continue down to Clourie in darkness, rather than camp up here on a snake-infested mountaintop. It was downhill, so it wouldn't take long, he deduced (without complete conviction). I was happy to agree. We followed the track over to the dark side of the mountain and began our descent. The track quickly came to resemble a semi-dried-up waterfall. It was steeper than the other side, wetter and muddier, and as yet there was no sign of the road. We began clambering down, one of us passing a bike down to the other and clinging to the bushes growing between the slippery rocks. In the partial darkness, this felt dangerous and we hoped that it would not go on too much longer.

Progress was agonisingly slow as it became darker. I put on my head torch. What an unwise economy it had been to bring only one,

I thought. Sam's voice had become nervous behind me and I could see him quickly reaching exhaustion level again. Still sweltering, we drank the iodine water but wondered whether is was safe. Poisoning and parasites, however, seemed like the least of our troubles now. We were climbing with loaded bikes down a slippery dried up waterfall on a mountainside, in the dark. How stupid were we?

Our jovial mood now long gone, we adopted a nervous demeanour, as if we were clinging to life by our fingernails, which at times of course we were. Thoughts of Fitzcarraldo ominously made way to remembered scenes from Touching The Void. This time, I felt it better to keep my cinematic thoughts to myself.

After an hour or so of sustained climbing, the dried-up waterfall began to level out and could conceivably now be called a steep track. It was deeply rutted, with water flowing down and across it, but at least it was a track. What it certainly wasn't was a road. No vehicle, except perhaps a tank or an excavator, could pass along this. We had either missed the road or been misinformed. Shakily, we clambered over huge boulders and across fast-flowing water, still carrying the bikes most of the time. We were shivering. Not with cold, but with fear and exhaustion.

It was around this point that I was stopped short.

"My god! Dad, look!" Sam called out in a startled voice.

I was scared what I might see when I turned around. Eventually, I saw what he was pointing at. Highlighted by the torch, clouds of steam were coming off me in the darkness. I had generated so much heat that in the cooler night air it looked like I was on fire. I drank some more metallic brown water and we pushed on. Sam wondered if it might be the iodine that had caused me to steam.

"Was chemistry one of your stronger subjects?" I asked him.

In the darkness, we knew we must be nearing Clourie when we started to pass boys driving water buffalo home to a tiny collection of huts. It was an overwhelmingly reassuring sight. We also began to hear music. We pictured a busy hill-town like Munar with people sitting outside small cafes serving hot food, and a few small guesthouses with comfortable beds. This raised our spirits, although Sam had little left in the tank. Stepping up our pace a little, we began to talk and even laugh about how amazing this was going to be to look back on. Of course, this is always bad luck. Half an hour later, the music seemed no nearer.

The track remained treacherous and the promised road utterly elusive. Sam knew we must be near but really felt he could go no further. In the dark, he slipped a few times on wet rocks, scaring himself at not knowing where he might be about to fall. I reined in my irritation at signs of him giving up and tried not to make him feel bad about it. We didn't need an argument now.

We could pitch a tent in the trees if he wanted, I said. I knew full well this would not sound inviting. Unsurprisingly, he opted to keep going. Finally, we reached a shallow muddy river. This was getting harder. Cautiously, attempting to step from stone to slippery stone, we carried the bikes across with our last ounces of energy. I knew if we slipped and broke an ankle here, it could be disastrous. Moments later, though, we broke through a bramble hedge and collapsed onto what we could see was a *proper* road.

We looked up. Laughably there was a road sign indicating that we were entering Clourie.

"It must have been some storm that turned the road into that!" I said, pointing back.

We had no energy to ride. Pushing our bikes around a bend, we came into a small shanty on the outskirts of the town. The music seemed to be coming from a loudspeaker over a shack with a light at its door. There was another adjoining shack and a tin hut opposite. All three were in darkness. A man heard us talking and came out of the first shack in his *dhoti* (loincloth/sarong) to see who it was.

"Hello," I said. "Guesthouse? Hotel?" I pointed up ahead.

"No hotel," he said, then pointing at the small shack opposite, "This, Clourie hotel!"

We laughed. Humour was still welcome after our ordeal.

"OK, thanks. We'll go into Clourie to look for a guesthouse."

"This Clourie, sir," he insisted, indicating the three huts with a sweep of his arm. "Bus stop, chai shop, my house, my brother house."

"He can't be serious?" I said.

Where were the hotels, the busy restaurants with people sitting outside?

Sam said he would ride on around the bend to check. It was pitch black, so any sign ahead of the town would be fairly obvious. He returned with bad news: no town, just fields. The man walked over and opened the door of his chai shop.

"Please stay tonight in chai shop.   Eat, drink, no problem!"

Under the circumstances, this was what we wanted to hear, but our visual senses were less excited by that which lay before us – a leaky, corrugated iron hut with a rough concrete floor, two tables with broken chairs, and a counter with biscuits in a jar.

We ducked under a hand of bananas hanging from the roof. Our would-be host rushed to fetch a rush mat and threw it down on the damp concrete floor, then placed a dusty moth-eaten blanket on top.

"Bed!" he declared, like a magician, making grandiose presentational gestures with his arms.

"OK, good, but how about food … eggs, rice, *porotta*?"

A wide tombstone smile was his answer. He broke off four bananas, took some cookies out of the jar and placed a chunk of dry bread on the stained old counter.

"*Acha*, food!" he beamed.

"How much for bed and food?"

He rocked his head and waved away my question in what seemed like a savvy attempt at magnanimous hospitality. This was too obviously a ploy, I thought. And who could blame him? I doubted he got much business way out here with the road gone for a year.   But I was too tired for this.

"Pay tomorrow.   No problem now.   Pay tomorrow."

"No, no.   Pay now, please," I insisted. I was shattered and vulnerable to being ripped off, I realised.

Seeing he would not give a price, I knew I needed to offer him something.   An amount in line with what we would pay in a guesthouse for food and a bed, I thought. If I didn't get this sorted out now, I knew I would regret it in the morning.

"Two hundred rupees for all," I said, getting out my money. His bright eyes and teeth flashed in the moonlight.

"*Acha*, OK!"

We sat down at one of the tables to eat our basic supper. It tasted surprisingly good and he threw in a couple of extra bananas, to boost his reputation in case we should write a review of his hotel for the Lonely Planet India guide, I supposed. I thought about how in five years' time this shack might have grown into a big place named Clourie Paradise Hostel, with gap-year backpackers lying around in hammocks drinking Kingfisher beer.

After 15 minutes of chat about our journey over the mountain (he seemed to doubt its veracity), he said he was going to bed. He needed to open the chai shop for the bus passengers at 5.30am. No long lie-in, we realised. Our friend returned to his hammock in the small storeroom at the back of the shack. We retired to our mat on the concrete floor and unrolled our sleeping bags, then lay awake for some time thinking through what we had just done. It seemed an impossible journey, both physically and mentally. Just before falling into an exhausted sleep, I remembered how around midday we were both saying that this was the best day of the trip. In retrospect, the truth is that we still think it was. It had everything: beauty, healthy physical exertion, danger, camaraderie, humour, interesting people, a seemingly insurmountable challenge well tackled, and a simple prize at the end. It seemed fair to say that we had taken on the impossible and overcome it.

*

It was still pitch black when Sam and I were awoken by the sound of a kerosene stove being pumped. I opened one eye and checked my watch – 5am. In desperate need of more sleep, I turned over. The floor was hard. I gave up on sleep and sat up. Choking from the kerosene fumes made by our host, I woke Sam again. He had no idea where he was.

We managed to get up off our mat just as the first bus passengers arrived through the door. Not that finding a couple of people sleeping on the floor when you arrive in a cafe is anything unusual in India. God only knew where these bus passengers came from. They might have walked from three villages away. What was certain, though, was that they hadn't walked over Mt Anai Mudi from the Topstation side.

We bought a glass of tea and a banana each before thanking our host and heading off along the road. Cycling felt strange. Riding our bikes rather than carrying them felt like a bit of a novelty this morning.

The road was rough and narrow but it was a proper asphalt road. It would have been an unimaginable luxury last night.

I had asked Sam if he wanted to take the bus after yesterday, but he was quite sure he didn't. I was impressed. Throughout all the hardship and uncertainty of yesterday, he hadn't complained once. He'd looked like he was about to drop dead a few times, but that was all.

The tiny road took us through some lovely countryside, with more small tea plantations, a huge waterfall (Polur Falls, I believe) and some nut trees. We passed people walking to the bus stop with produce to sell in the next town and asked for directions to Kodaikanal. It was a main town only 53km away but nobody had heard of it, sending us the wrong way twice before we worked it out ourselves. It felt quite cold at 6am in the morning and we needed long trousers.

At the first main village, in need of a more substantial breakfast, we called into a blackened hole of a cafe. At the griddle, a man was cooking savoury steamed rice flour patties (*idli*). We became the morning's entertainment for the locals, eating idli with a large audience pushing at the door for a better view. It was cold at that altitude and the locals wore wads of raw cotton over their ears, held in place with pieces of string tied around their heads. They looked like wounded WW1 soldiers from the trenches.

The villages here seemed to be placed at the top of each hill. We were rather amused by how you could sit by the shop in one village and look across at the village on the adjacent hill only 250m away, yet it would be 5km to reach it, by a road winding all the way down one hill and up the other.

It was a tough 40km to reach the base of the mountain with Kodaikanal at its summit. To make it worse, Sam suffered three more punctures. I could see the problem: our tyres were pretty bald by now.   It reminded me to ask Lorna to order a bunch of things to bring for us when she came over at Christmas.

Despite the puncture-fest, Sam remained calm and seemed confident that we would reach Kodaikanal without too much fuss, if we just continued gently.   He would make a great explorer, I thought. I was less confident, since the boys at our B&B in Cochin had told me how long and steep the final climb was.   They had driven there in a car that had broken down three times going up the hill.

The countryside around here may have been beautiful, but drivers did their best to spoil the experience by constantly blaring their super-loud horns.   We found it a common habit/pastime across much of Asia.

The road up the mountain to Kodaikanal was certainly extreme. We saw several broken-down cars and trucks, along with plenty of crashed vehicles.   One local bus passed us several times and we became familiar with the driver.   Late that morning, as we rounded a bend, we saw the bus stopped in the middle of the road ahead of us. A traffic jam was forming and a large troop of monkeys sat in the road enjoying the entertainment.   As Sam and I cycled past, we were amazed to find that the entire engine had fallen out of the bus and onto the road.   More astonishing was the fact that the driver and a group of passengers were attempting to lever it back into place using a large tree branch, with the spare wheel as a pivot.   We laughed but were hardly surprised when the bus passed us, engine returned to its mountings, before we reached the top of the mountain.   Indian ingenuity is a wonderful thing.

At the lovely town of Kodaikanal we headed straight for a decent restaurant.   It was another of those *return to civilization* experiences. All we needed to cap it off was a tin bath of hot water, cowboy hat, small cigar and some women with garters and frilly underwear.

We celebrated with a delicious biryani lunch before seeking out the recommended Greenlands Youth Hostel, which we found easily and was indeed amazing.   It was basic but had the most unreal view from a steep terraced position at the edge of the mountain.   On arrival, we stood looking down in awe over smaller mountains and a world of eucalyptus forest with the odd shanty village, metal roofs glinting in the sun, way below.   There was plenty of activity: eagles soared over the jungle hillside and monkeys swung from branch to branch. On this first afternoon, we sat watching cockatiels fluttering around the terraces looking for crumbs. Words alone cannot describe the awe-inspiring beauty of this place.

Back at our room, a pair of fairly large monkeys climbed in through the open window, looked at us resting on our bunks and then scampered over to check out the contents of Sam's bag. We stayed as still as we could to observe them, Sam just moving enough to pick up his camera and get a picture. The leader took a pot of hair gel out of the bag and attempted to bite it open. His teeth looked pretty nasty and he made a point of showing them to us, in the same way a mugger might. Eventually, frightened by the camera flash, the monkeys scampered back to the window, followed by both of us with camera at the ready as they sprung up onto the roof. The villains threw the pot down at us in disgust and ran off along the rooftops shrieking. Monkeys may look cute, but I was beginning to see why most Indians dislike them. Fascinated by human habitats, they steal compulsively and seem to have a mischievous, even malevolent, desire to damage things.

One thing all visitors seem to agree on is that Kodaikanal is a very special place. It has a rather unusual international school and college, which are popular with Tibetans and Americans in particular. It is largely this that gives the town its unique character. In such a small hill-town, we were surprised to find numerous little restaurants and cafes of international varieties, full of students and teachers each evening. There was also an excellent English bakery, enticingly named Pastry Corner, along with many good hotels and guesthouses. What the Youth Hostel lacked in comfort and service, it more than made up for with the view and a certain amount of seedy charm.

The busy town of Kodaikanal is based around a large lake with a bridge across the middle and the whole atmosphere is like a magical place at the top of the world. We could, and maybe should, have stayed longer than five days, but as ever we were driven onwards.

*

At this point, Sam had really started to suffer with repetitive digestive problems. He felt hungry and would eat but the next day had the runs and cramps. After a day without food, he would be fine again for a day or two and then it would return. He was getting pretty fed up with this so when a lovely Spanish lady, staying at the hostel with her French partner, offered him a Kinesiology session he was glad to accept. Alicia said she felt that delayed shock from the mountain experience had caused Sam's upset. I would have suspected altitude sickness if we had driven or flown there, but with our slow progression by bike this seemed unlikely. Reluctantly, we accepted the delayed shock diagnosis. Whatever the reason, by our fourth day Sam was feeling better and we agreed to move on the following day, assuming it would be downhill for quite some distance.

We felt pretty positive as we set off on a steep descent from town after our hostel breakfast. Sam seemed OK and we coasted for about half an hour down through outlying villages. It was beautiful countryside, with dense tropical forests, bright flowers and banana trees at the sides of the road. Our free run did not last, though, and we were rather taken aback to find ourselves on a winding climb back up another mountain. I assumed we must have missed a turning, but a banana cutter we asked assured me that we were on the main road to Pollachi as intended. Somewhat despondently, we began a long climb uphill.

Hill climbing is fine when you are fit, and when you are prepared for it. Sam was far from fit today and neither of us was prepared for hill climbing. On the terrace of Greenlands Hostel, Kodaikanal had seemed at the summit of a big mountain, standing on its own with smaller individual mountains surrounding it. Pollachi was over to the northwest on the plains, so logically the road would go down our mountain then around the other smaller mountains, across largely flat land to Pollachi. In the real world, it didn't.

I remember once trying to argue this same logic with my geography teacher at primary school. Scotland is mountainous; the south of England is not. Therefore, obviously it would be uphill from London to Scotland and the reverse coming back.

"You should have paid more attention at school," joked Sam weakly.

It seemed that just out of our terrace view had been a range of mountains we needed to cross before we got to the plains. We had to come to terms with the fact that our easy run downhill and across flat plains to Pollachi was a pipe-dream. Sam seemed worried, since after only a few kilometres of climbing he realised that he was not up to it. We were out in the wilds again and the prospect of finding a guesthouse to rest up looked poor.

"We have all day, so don't worry," I told him, "We can take our time then find a nice guesthouse once we get to the plains."

This didn't seem to cheer him up much. It was occurring to him that we might have a repeat of the Mt Anai Mudi expedition.

Sam doesn't like to give up any more than I do. On this day, it might have been better if he had. Alicia, our new Kinesiology friend, had told us that Sam should not do anything demanding the day after his treatment, but he had not felt that a day coasting downhill then spinning along over the plains would fit into this category. How stupid, I thought – we could so happily have waited another day. We were on our way, though, so we got on with it, trying to tackle the hills using the least effort possible. Naturally, in the face of all this, another minor catastrophe seemed a little below the belt.

We had stopped to photograph some monkeys on a wall by the road. It seemed a great opportunity for some interesting shots, since we were still up high and the monkeys appeared to be sitting looking out over the plains below. Just as we were about to move on, though, I noticed the pressure in my rear tyre was a bit low. I gave it three or four pumps before there was a familiar bang and I realised another tube had burst at the valve. The sound left a sickening feeling in my stomach, bringing back all the misery of our week of punctures in Turkey.

We had one new tube left. Wanting to save this, I took up the challenge of cutting a hole in a patch and seating it over the valve. Although I had little hope of this working, it seemed to hold. But after only a few minutes riding, it deflated. We had to get off the bikes again, remove my luggage and put in the new tube.

I wondered what on earth was wrong with these tubes. Had they perished in the heat? Were they just poor quality, or was my pumping technique suddenly deficient? Fearing another burst tube, I didn't pump this new one up to normal pressure and we continued gingerly on.

Around midday, we emerged from a forest of trees and found ourselves looking down over the plains. The small town of Palani and a few lakes lay just below. Already imagining the taste of lunch, we sped downhill and before very long found ourselves sitting at a restaurant in town, eating dhal and chicken biryani. I tried my hardest to put the thought of punctures out of my head. I suspected Sam was doing the same.

As we left the restaurant, I recognised a now-familiar look on Sam's face. He was unsure whether lunch had been a good idea. I was concerned about this but at that point more preoccupied with the inner-tube situation. Why hadn't I let them drill out the bloody valve holes back in Turkey? We could then easily have bought Indian or Schrader-type tubes. I committed myself to getting this done in Pollachi the following day, but in the meantime my rear tyre looked very flat. After much agonising, Sam and I came down on the side of putting a few more pumps of air in it. We stopped and I gave a careful stroke of the pump, which seemed OK. So then another, and just one more … BANG!

I remembered again the grumpy man (a fireman, I'm told) outside O'Currain's bar in Dingle, and grimaced. It had seemed like such a trivial issue then, but now it seemed to threaten the entire trip (other cyclists, take note). This was paranoid overreaction, of course. I had always known we could just get them drilled out in any town on the way, or buy a drill and do it ourselves. But I still felt a crushing sense of defeat, and an overwhelming feeling that I was a complete idiot. We walked off along the Pollachi road looking for a puncture-wallah. Sam could see that his *calm supportive son* services were going to be required again.

As always in India, we had only to walk about half a mile before we were directed to a hut and a man sitting on the ground, grappling with a rusty old bike wheel. We showed him the problem. He shook his head and sighed a lot. Yes, we knew they were not Indian-sized valves, but was there anything he could do?

"Hmm, please wait one minute, sit down, drink tea," he said firmly, with a waggle of the head.

His wife brought tea, while her husband went to the mini-scrapyard he called his tool-shed and rooted around in wooden boxes. Unfortunately, he did not look confident on his return. I asked if he had a drill, but he didn't. He looked astounded – as if I had asked whether he possessed a laser micrometre or a CNC milling machine.

We were still trying to help, but he kept asking us to *stand back, please,* while he wrestled brutally with the tube. What came next horrified us – in fact, it had us shouting and trying to grab the inner-tube from his hands. Before we knew it, he had taken a large blunt knife and sliced through the tube on each side of the valve. This seemed insane. I wondered whether we had stumbled across a man with a grudge against the English. He pushed us away and eventually we gave up our protests, realising that whatever he did to the tube now would put us in no worse a situation than the one we were in already.

Sam and I looked on with increasing fascination as this man removed the valve, then placed a washer and a nut inside the removed section of tube, screwed the valve back through, glued a patch with a hole in it on the outside and placed another washer and nut on the outside before tightening it all up. Next, he sandpapered and glued the whole section back onto each end of the main piece of tube and hammered it with a mallet to get a good contact. All this was done with scrap parts.

"OK, now look, please," he said, like a father instructing small children.

He replaced the tube in the wheel and screwed on one of the rings that holds the valve in place. Then he pumped it up. Miraculously, it held. We were overcome with surprise and gratitude. He was immensely proud of himself, of course, with good reason. We asked how much we owed him.

"Twenty rupees," he said firmly.

"No, no, we must pay you more than that."

This was ridiculous, even in India. Twenty rupees was about 25p in the UK. I offered him 200 but he dismissed me, saying the repair would not last long and that he had only used two nuts and two washers. Also, it had only taken half an hour of his time.

He was not to be persuaded, so having paid the 20 rupees we went on our way.   As you can imagine, we were overjoyed to be progressing at normal cycling speed again.   If the world ever needs to be saved, I told Sam later, I would rely on an Indian puncture-wallah to come up with the solution ahead of all NASA's scientists.

By the time we approached Pollachi the tube was looking pretty deflated and I didn't want to chance putting any more air into it.   It had carried me the last 20km and we could now check into a hotel and relax.   Sam was certainly in need of rest after 132km of cycling on a hot day – much of it over a mountain range.   He looked pretty ill and confirmed this by leaving halfway through his dinner of plain steamed rice.   It was the start of a bout of vomiting that lasted for at least the next 36hrs.

*

We stayed at Hotel Sakti for two nights, all of which Sam spent between bed and bathroom.   I used this time to remove all four tyres from their wheels and take the wheels to an engineering company around the corner.   These charming gentlemen very professionally drilled out all four valve holes, then refused to charge me.   These absolutely superb people were, they said, *only too happy to help cyclists who honoured them by riding through their country.*

What was it with these people and not taking money?   They were obviously quite poor by anyone's standards, but they seemed to value friendship and goodwill more highly than money.   God, we loved it here!

The bread omelette (a variation on French toast) that we had found everywhere in Kodaikanal and had enjoyed as a basic breakfast at the hostel and at street stalls, was unheard of here in nearby Pollachi.   This is a common and surprising experience for westerners in rural Asia.   Few ordinary people seem to travel outside their town or village.   Knowledge of the adjacent town is the most you can expect.   For these two days, the street café next to Hotel Sakti was my spot for breakfast without Sam, and I found myself instructing their *chef* in how to make Kodai bread omelette.   He and his customers watched with fascination.   The second day, I noticed a number of people sitting at tables eating bread omelette as I passed.

It amused me that this must have been how regional dishes spread in Europe back in ancient times.   It is claimed that Chinese noodles were brought back to Italy by Marco Polo and became spaghetti.   I pictured someone like myself, except on horseback, riding around trying local dishes.   I felt pleased to have become a part of this region's future history.   Of course, I hope to do more in my life than the passing on of a recipe for bread omelette.   But if that is all I achieve, it will be fine by me.

Vomiting over after three sick days in Pollachi, Sam felt he would like to try a modest day's cycling.   Shoranur was only 50km away, back into Kerala.   Here, to catch up a little time, we planned to take a train journey up the coast so that we could spend Sam's birthday at a beach in Goa.   With Sam still looking very weak, we took it easy.   He refused breakfast, wanting to make sure that whatever bug he had picked up was well and truly gone.   This made the cycling very hard work, especially in 40-degree heat and high humidity.   He gritted his teeth, though, and managed to pedal along gently.   Thankfully, the roads here were quite flat.

Sam shakily kept himself going that morning with regular breaks and reviving drinks of Pepsi Cola.   Despite rarely drinking cola drinks in everyday life, both Sam and I found that there was nothing quite as effective when you were feeling really hot and tired on a bike. Freshly squeezed lime-soda came a close second and was our usual healthier pick-me-up, but iced Pepsi usually got there first at the end of a gruelling ride.   We later discovered, however, that there are long-term corrosive effects with this particular remedy.   We were warned about it later that day at one of our café stops.   An elderly gentleman with an important looking moustache came over and introduced himself.

"A charming afternoon, gentlemen, is it not?" he effused. "I am the headmaster in these parts.   And what would be your fine names?"

Sitting down to hear more about our trip, he asked us if we might be so kind as to tell him why we were drinking that *corrosive muck*. Headmasters are the same the world over, it seems.   He told us the old anecdote about hanging a piece of steak in a glass of coke and finding it eaten away in the morning. Always eager to take the contrary position, I suggested that if it ate away a piece of steak overnight, it must surely kill any bugs or bacteria in your stomach. I guess he realised I was not much of a scientist, but he was too polite to deride my idea.

Arriving late and very tired in Shoranur, due to roadworks and inaccurate maps, we headed for the station to find out about trains going north to Mangalore. We were further deflated when told by the booking clerk that we were in Diwali Festival month and therefore the next train north with available seats was in three weeks.

"Three weeks!" I spluttered. "That's impossible."

Silently, the woman turned her ageing computer screen for me to see. It would be the same situation with buses, she said. I broke the news to a disconsolate Sam, who had by now collapsed in a heap in the car park. We could rest here until he was better then cycle on, I told him. I was learning about India, though, and had not entirely accepted defeat.

At the station office, I asked to see the stationmaster. Seeing my cycle gear, he came out of his office with typical Indian inquisitiveness. I explained what the booking clerk had told me, and that my son was ill so we needed to get to Mangalore to see a doctor.

"Sir, it is only *bookable* seats and overnight sleepers that are unavailable," he said. "If you come to the station at 5am, you will certainly be able to buy a sleeper ticket for travel during the day."

Hugely relieved, I thanked him and relayed the news to Sam. As instructed, checked in our bikes as freight. This done, we walked off with our panniers to find a *tuk-tuk* (three-wheeled Vespa-powered taxi) to take us to a hotel.

Our trials were not over yet. Every hotel we went to said it were full. Diwali, of course. Finally, the driver took us to a luxurious Ayurvedic Resort Hotel on the outskirts, overlooking the river. It was expensive. Looking at the condition of Sam, I didn't care. The situation called for special measures.

We checked into our suite and after a long session in the bathroom, Sam settled himself in bed watching Premiership football. Meanwhile, I went for a swim in the pool, in advance of a much-needed meal in the restaurant. At the pool, I found myself unexpectedly an extra in a fashion magazine shoot with a couple of young Bollywood stars. They should have filmed in the changing-room shower – it was full of lurid tree frogs. I don't care for luxury hotels as a rule, but after a few months of basic accommodation, or when someone is feeling ill, they can be a great relief.

I enjoyed both the pool overlooking the river and the dinner that followed, but my mind was mainly on Sam and his seemingly worsening condition. I really did need to get him to a doctor.

Getting up at 4am was unwelcome but our ride to the station in the hotel's white Ambassador car made it quite special. Exactly as the stationmaster had said, we bought tickets with no problems and boarded the train.

Since reading Paul Theroux's classic The Great Railway Bazaar as a teenager, I had been looking forward to travelling on an Indian train, so I was excited about this first journey. We found our way through the crowds to our second-class sleeper carriage. Having booked top bunks, which remain available during the day (the lower ones get folded up or used for seating), we climbed up with our bags and settled in. We felt surprisingly comfortable.

The train was like a travelling village – families preparing food, reading newspapers, eating, cooking, laughing and arguing, children playing happily and old ladies telling stories to their grandchildren, while their old men snored loudly. Sam was asleep before the train set off and I prepared myself for a few hours of reading. I stopped, frequently, though, to watch the fascinating world going on both inside and outside the window.

I woke Sam just before we arrived in Mangalore, eager that he should get as much sleep as possible while he had the chance. Thankfully, he awoke feeling much better. I wished we were going further, but the train ended there and we disembarked with the hoards of families off to visit relatives over the long Diwali holiday. We collected our bicycles, which were already parked neatly on the platform, and marvelled at the efficiency of this system, with its carefully numbered tags and receipts. The railway is one of the only things that seem to work efficiently in India, although I must say that inefficiency is really a major part of India's charm.

Sam sat down on a bench while I went off to get some provisions. This was our first introduction to *chiki,* a kind of peanut brittle with far more peanuts and less toffee than the English equivalent. We found it all over India, but the Mangalore version remained the best.

Sam looked much better but seemed reluctant to move on to find a hotel. He was eager to return to sleep. It occurred to me that with nothing in particular to do in Mangalore but take him to a doctor (which he now looked less in need of), we could have continued to Goa and holed up there in a beach hut for a week. There would be doctors there. Sam could enjoy his birthday and fully recuperate.

When I shared these thoughts with him, I saw the worry lift from his face. It might be possible, I thought. I looked at a map, then went off to see if I could manage to buy a ticket to Canacona, a bit further up the coast on the Goan state border.

The Indian gods were smiling favourably upon us that day, I suppose. Although all the bunks were booked, I managed to get some un-bookable tickets in second-class seats. Sam looked delighted and I went off to the parcel office to book our bikes onto the train to Canacona later that day. By the time we boarded it, Sam was feeling he might eat something light. He tried some chiki and found that it really agreed with him. Later, after a banana and some more chiki, he began to look like a newly watered plant.

It was an extremely slow train but this didn't bother us. We were happy talking about Goa and chatting to families sitting close by. The conductor arrived and saw an opportunity for some extra cash, offering us the one free bunk left in our carriage for Sam to sleep on. After the conductor evicted the current squatter, Sam settled down to continue his recuperation. I concentrated on taking photographs. Out of the windows of the slow-moving train, there was no end of people busying themselves with various things. Some were tending crops; boys were playing cricket on a mown strip of especially lush field; people were wading across rivers with bundles of sticks, or herding buffalo in the golden evening light. Amazing illuminated scenes, filled with happy smiling people and unspoilt countryside. What a stunning place India is, I said to myself. All I had hoped.

Later, our conductor found me a bunk and I also managed to get some sleep before we arrived in Canacona in the early hours. We were a little shell-shocked getting off the train, and somewhat horrified to find that our bikes had been loaded behind a heap of vegetables and wooden crates in the luggage car. It was dark and the conductor seemed unwilling to help.

"Don't worry, sir. After these items have been unloaded in Mumbai, we will be coming back, you know. You can collect your cycles at the station here this evening. At your leisure."

Rather than see our bikes head off towards Mumbai, though, Sam managed to climb in through a small aperture and move things. He passed the obstructions out to me. Other passengers came to our aid, as they always do in India. The conductor remained good-humoured while the train was delayed. Eventually, we got the bikes out, and all that was lost in the confusion was my camping mat. No doubt it is now making an entire Indian family very comfortable.

After realigning a few bent parts on the bikes, we cycled off slowly in the direction of Palolem beach. It was early morning so there were few people about. We had jumped a few hundred kilometres, but Sam was ill. If we were to spend some time on a beach in Goa and still reach Rajasthan in time for Christmas, we needed to do it somewhere along the way. We hoped it would match what we had imagined.

SAM'S POINT OF VIEW

This period of time was a combination of stressed moments and periods of extreme calm. Our deliberations over a plan of action for getting past Pakistan seemed a last minute rush, but our visas were running out and we had to act. The decision was to fly from Tehran down to Kerala in the south of India. Given the unpleasant journey so far in Iran, this option was popular with me. Cycling through more desert past Helmund to the border of Pakistan and hoping to get a visa, was too risky and a major hassle. We'd been warned by the British embassy in Istanbul about the dangers of cycling through south Pakistan at that time, and had been told we wouldn't get a visa.

It seemed pointless to hope that the situation would change by the time we got to the border. In fact, we found out in Kerala that two trains had been blown up in Pakistan, along with a big hotel bomb, right at the time we would have been there. So our detour did seem to have been wise.

Eastern Turkey and Iran involved hard cycling with little enjoyment. What seemed like an eternity had passed and the trip really took a bit of a sour turn. Neither of us was enjoying ourselves; just helping each other get through it day by day. Flying to South India put an end to those feelings and gave us the bonus of time to cycle about, visiting interesting places before our family and friends met us in Delhi for Christmas.

Our arrival in India was really exciting. My dad immediately began reminiscing about his childhood in Malaysia, and how he felt happier now we were in India. I felt the same, but perhaps more due to arriving in a country with some freedom, and having people to talk to. India really cheered me up. Heavy rain greeted us on the very first day of cycling, but it was warm and in no way dented my spirits. My dad (Mr Puncture Avoidance) warned me to be careful of puddles in case of hidden debris. The inevitable happened soon after the warning and he seemed to flip completely. He probably thought he was being calm.

With all the rain and mud we decided to push the bikes until we found a puncture repair guy at the roadside. Finding a 'puncture-wallah' is far easier than you'd imagine. There's one every half a mile or so wherever you go. It sometimes seemed that every square inch of India was filled with people. Most of them have a few crude tools and the skill to fix anything, even buckled truck wheels. If someone breaks down, give it a few minutes and witness the swarm of helpers ready to assist them. They're just the best type of people

It's worth mentioning, though, that having people constantly trying to help you, even when you don't need it, can become very annoying. It took some getting used to. You can imagine the amount of people we attracted every time we stopped for a break – especially away from the main tourist areas. Indians would come over and point at our bikes asking, 'cycle, cycle?' Or they'd point at the water canisters – 'petrol, petrol?'   Often, my dad would explain to a large audience of Indians that our bikes were in fact time-machines; that he was named 'The Doctor' and that we were from another realm of time.   It was hilarious.

Although I was finding my dad a bit easier to put up with for some of this time, I still resented being with him.   Part of me wanted to be doing this trip on my own, although doing it with one of my mates would have been my ideal.   But at the same time, I really resisted his suggestions for me to take more of a lead in things.   I suppose it felt like even then it would be something he had suggested and therefore he would still be the one in the driving seat.

My mood wasn't helped by me beginning to feel ill and weak after Cochin.   I was loving the food so much, though, that I couldn't bring myself to miss meals, unless I felt really sick.   My dad, on the other hand, is really tough with himself about food poisoning.   He almost seems to enjoy the challenge of denying himself food for 24hrs. Purging himself.   What a loser!

Chapter 8

North to Goa and into Rajasthan – Sam the loner

"I am here to meet my father.   He's staying here."

"Are you seeking your god, young sir?"

"No, no, my dad.   He might think he's a god, but he's just my dad.   I think he's staying in this hotel – Hotel Dream Heaven."

"Ah indeed, sir, this is your mistake.   This is Hindu temple, sir. Hotel Dream Heaven, next to!"

Arriving in Goa we were struck by the difference in atmosphere to that of Kerala and Tamil Nadu.   The people here were still friendly, yet slightly more *knowing* with westerners, due to the tourism that has been attracted to the region over many years.   Seeing Palolem beach and the little thatched beach huts under the palms, facing onto an inviting sea, we could understand why.   It was really beautiful, especially at this time in the early morning, with people wandering along the sand or having a swim before a tropical breakfast at one of the many simple beach cafes.

"Oh my god!" Sam gasped. "Are we going to love it here or what?"

As it was early, I avoided conversation, but his unnaturally cheerful demeanour at this time of day didn't go without notice.

After a breakfast of banana pancakes and mango lassi, we walked along the single village track and met a sincere looking young guy, who seemed to know we were looking for a beach hut.   I was impressed with the modern conveniences inside his huts, despite the somewhat creative construction methods.   Having known about Goa in the early 70s, when the locals used to build you a basic hut to order for a few rupees on arrival, I was expecting something similar These ones had a toilet and a shower.   Well, the shower was a hose hung on a nail with a watering-can rose on the end, and the wastewater often just ran down into the sea, but at least the toilet waste was plumbed into some kind of drain.

We paid for a single night, in order to check out some other huts later.   After going on reconnaissance and satisfying ourselves we had a good place, we booked for the following nine days as well. Committing ourselves to a ten-day break seemed outrageous, but we felt we were due a bit of a treat.   It would take us up to just after Sam's birthday.   This would still give us time to cycle to Agra to meet Lorna, Scarlett, Hannah and our other friends who were coming over for Christmas and New Year.   Most importantly, it allowed time for Sam to recover or to see a doctor if he did not.

*

Our time in Palolem was a holiday really, although we did use our bikes a little to cycle into the nearby market town of Chaudi.   There we became daily customers of Hotel Udipi (big cafés or restaurants in Indian towns are often called *Hotel* something but don't have bedrooms).   Here we spent most lunchtimes eating tomato utappam with onion ravi masalla, before frequenting the small shops and market stalls that sold nuts, dried fruit and bananas for making our breakfast the next day, and buying vegetables for the odd picnic. Mainly, though, we hung out at our beach, body-surfing, helping fishermen and eating in cafes.

By a lucky coincidence, the bar-restaurant next to our hut (Mokcha) was one of the best in the area at the time.   This meant a bit of late night noise sometimes, but it was useful for watching English football.   Sam's birthday was spent at one of these local places.   Although there were still days I could see that I was really irritating him (and him me), in general we got on well.   The situation was helped by him being able to sleep late, while I went off walking along miles of white sandy beach, helping fishermen and having early morning swims on my own.

One particularly memorable evening we went to a restaurant in town named Cool Breeze for a bit of a treat, since it was comparatively expensive.   The restaurant was well known for gourmet burgers and steaks, which we had not eaten since Istanbul. As we were tucking into our delicious burgers, a large cow wandered in off the street and strolled along the aisle between tables.   It examined each customer in turn, along with their plate of food, before swaggering heavily along to the next.

As cows are sacred in India, the Indians in this restaurant were most worried about what this one might do. They did very little, though, since it is beholden upon Hindus to leave them to do as they please. Finally, the owner walked towards it, making veiled arm movements to encourage it outside, all the time checking to see if any Indian customers were watching him. Eventually, it condescended to leave. What was most amusing to me was how the cow seemed to be looking to see if anyone was eating beef – as if it had heard rumours and had come to check. I believe what we were eating, as is the norm for beef dishes in India, was in fact water buffalo. Anyway, the cow seemed to find this acceptable and left, causing no further trouble.

Mornings were my favourite time in Palolem. I would get up early, leaving Sam to sleep late while I walked along the beach collecting special shells as a Christmas present for Scarlett, my youngest daughter. Only a few people were around at this time, strolling along the sand like me or sitting reading their books on café decks over tropical fruit breakfasts. Most of all, I loved helping the fishermen to pull in their nets. These were simple dragnets that they spread along a section of sea at the edge of the surf to catch small fry.

Naturally, we were sad to leave Palolem after our little holiday. At the same time, we were a little tired of hearing English voices and being pestered by trinket vendors. Also, we knew that every day we cycled would bring us nearer to meeting our family and friends in Rajasthan. Sam seemed to be hanging on for this. He had lost his temper with me a few times in Palolem when it seemed uncalled for. I decided it was probably due to a gradual build up of resentment, as well as him not feeling well for so long. I was glad he would soon have the opportunity to discuss his problems with Lorna and to spend time with his friends, but I wondered if this would really solve anything. It might even make things worse.

*

On the 18 November, the day after Sam's birthday, we set off for Goa's state capital, Panjim.   I had heard about its Portuguese colonial architecture and riverfront but imagined a typical administrative centre, with tourist hotels to accommodate those flying to or from Europe via the nearby airport.   In fact, Panjim had a lovely relaxed atmosphere, friendly people and genuine charm.   The buildings gave it a nostalgic seediness and there were some great restaurants, largely specialising in seafood.   For us, the most notable of these was Viva Panjim, in the old Portuguese quarter where we stayed.   We found ourselves returning here for at least one meal a day and became really fond of Linda, the lovely lady owner.   On our last day, she persuaded us to order the most exotic dishes on the menu, then presented us with a bill with nothing written on it.

While in Panjim we were interviewed about our trip by the *Times of India* newspaper.   A couple of weeks later, we would be stopped by the police at the border going north into Maharashtra state. They kept us waiting, casually checking each item in our panniers.   We thought they suspected us of smuggling alcohol into (dry) Maharashtra from Goa (where it is allowed).   Finally, they gave up, smiled and shook our hands, then turned towards a lady who had just pulled up in a car.   She rushed up and took a load of photographs of us.   Laughing, the chief policeman banged us on the back and introduced us to the lady, who was from the Maharashtra state newspaper.   She had read the *Times of India* article, knew our planned route and had asked the police to phone her when we arrived at the checkpoint.   We wondered how long they would have been prepared to hold us while they waited for her to arrive.

Still in Goa for now, though, we cycled north from Panjim and west, back to the coast at Arambol.   This is a lesser-known, more laid-back resort, full of ageing hippies who often stay about four months to escape North European winters.   It is the complete opposite of nearby tourist resorts that are well known for high-rise hotels and raves on the beaches.   We enjoyed a further four days in holiday mode here, hanging out with a few interesting ex-pats.   They were not rich – just people who understood work-life balance. Eventually, though, we agreed we had better get back to daily cycling, before we forgot how to do it.

*

Somewhat nervous about the possibility of punctures to our balding tyres, we headed over the border into Maharashtra.   The state was all but untouched by foreign tourism, with the stark exception of recently renamed Mumbai, which locals still called Bombay.   Despite the amusement caused by being held up for the lady reporter, Sam seemed a bit down again.   I put this down to us having spent the last week with people of my age in Arambol.   Yet again he had expressed the feeling that he had found nothing useful to say.   I had tried to bring him into conversations – especially when we all sat around watching football matches on the old TV at the excellent Akram Café, which we made our temporary home – but it had not helped.   Despite his obviously superior football knowledge, Sam had remained unconvinced about the value of his contributions.   A great pity, it seemed to me, but not something I felt I could (or should) interfere in.

Maharashtra seemed less obviously friendly than Goa, but we still found people very helpful when approached.   Few people here spoke English.   There are now 22 national languages recognised by the constitution of India, among which Hindi is the official union language.   Besides these, there are 844 different dialects used in various parts of the country.   That may sound a lot, but as recently as 1961 there were 1652 languages in total.   In business circles, English is generally used as the universal language.   For this reason, the people of Bombay are said to see the rest of Maharashtra as an uneducated backwater, while largely rural Maharashtrans see Bombay people as arrogant and part of a different, more privileged world.

We were driven a little mad at times by the unhealthily loud horns incessantly blared right next to us as trucks and cars passed. Drivers just insisted upon leaning on their horns to say hello to us. We saw more road accidents here than anywhere on our whole journey.   Many drivers behaved like deranged children with a lethal new toy.   It was not our favourite part of the trip.

Our first night in Marharastra was spent in the small town of Talera.   Most towns along the main north-south highway appeared to cater to the movement of goods by heavy (and highly decorated) trucks. Sam and I got used to seeing these personalised vehicles at roadside halts, with the drivers generally sleeping in their cabs or under the truck. Consequently, despite the busyness of the one-street towns, there are few hotels. What we did find, however, were basic government-approved guesthouses aimed mainly at poor Indian travellers.   It was at one of these we stayed on our first night.

Prava Si Guesthouse (and seedy bar) was an extremely basic establishment even by Indian standards.   Popular mainly with mosquitos, it had the advantage of costing only 150 rupees per night (about £2 sterling) for two people but was comfortable enough for one night and the manager was friendly and helpful.   The big event of the day came, though, when my luggage rack snapped on the other side. This time, I was unable to fix it by myself.

The manager had a look and made some rather unhelpful attempts at repairs with a hammer and a pair of pliers.   Realising the job was beyond both his tools and skills, he sent us to the local truck repair depot.   Here, the extremely kind manager (Mr de Souza) found a mechanic who he said would be able to repair it, although this would have to be after the electricity came back on.   We were now in an area where daily power cuts were standard between 5pm and 7pm.

Sam and I went off for an hour to eat, then returned to Mr de Souza's office for tea while we waited for the power.   Mr de Souza and the other managers got out some chairs and a whole group of us sat around to chat.   Sam and I had to answer many questions about our trip and our lives in England – far more than we were able to ask them.   The whole experience turned into one of pleasure rather than necessity and we were quite moved when one of the men returned with an almond tree, which he planted next to the hut for shade in the future.

"We plant this tree in your honour," said Mr de Souza. "You must return in some years to see it fully grown."   We all clapped.

After a long but enjoyable wait, a cheer went up throughout the town to mark the return of the electricity supply and we went over to the workshops.   The mechanic had a selection of butchered metal panels and a very basic electric drill.   After asking me to sketch out my suggested method of repair on a scrap truck door, this kindly chap

Sam on a bike ride to Rye, Sussex, aged around 12 – Note 'speed hair.'

Looking east towards our goal from Coominole start point – Dingle, Ireland.

'Where am I, and why am I here?' Start line 26 July 2008 –
Only 9,570 miles to go. Onlookers from left, Colm Bambury, John Verling & Paddy Fenton.

Sam tucks into Maxi-burger – Café Noddy, St Quentin, France. Human cannonball & juggling clown in background.

Heavy-handed barber in Sisophon, Cambodia, goes too far. Son distraught.

Floating bridge near Csongrad, Hungary – Huckleberry Finn takes time out from fishing.

'Hey, she wants to marry you!' Generations of maize shellers, Nr Calafat, Romania.

Sam with cricketing friends – Mattancheri, Fort Kochi, Kerala, India.

Yellapatty Tea Estates, High Range of Travancore, Nr Munar, Kerala, India.

Mark carrying bike up Mt Anai Mudi, Adimali Reserve, Nr Topstation, Tamil Nadu, India.

Evening view from a train – Nr Mangalore, India.

Fishermen in Palolem, India – My early morning friends.

Happy truck mechanic repairs cycle rack – Talere Naka, Maharastra, India.

'Girly Milkshake.' Martin & Sam in Phanon Sarakan, Thailand.

Monks heading for lunch near Thalat, Nr Vientiane, Laos.

Martin in Vang Vieng, Laos. Bat cave in background.

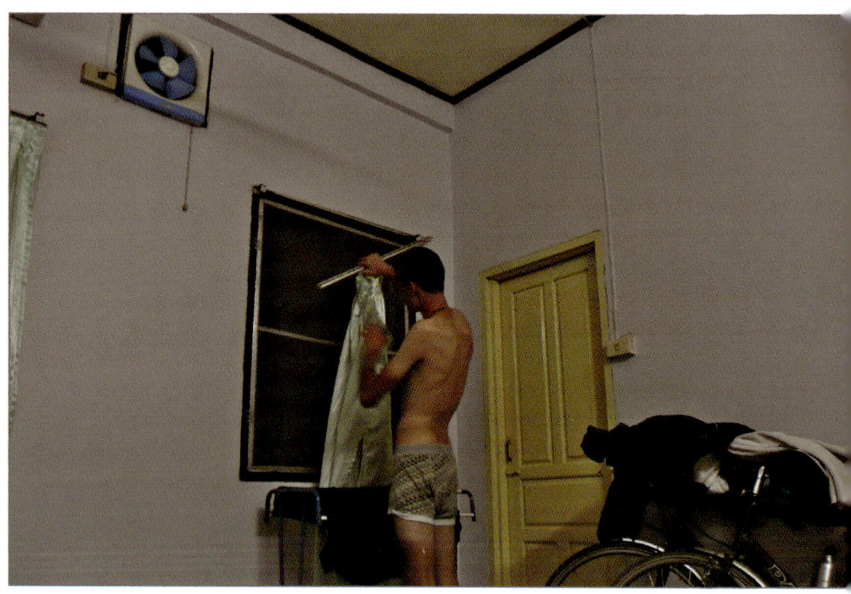

Sam fixes curtain - A typical guesthouse resting-place — Luang Parabang, Laos.

Typical happy children waiting along the roadside to slap our hands. Muiang Khoua, Laos

Tuan Giao Reception Committee – N.Vietnam.

Roast dogs for sale in a market – Quangzhuo, S.China.

Typically excellent café in Qiyang, Hunan, S.China.

Jenny giving instruction in Kung-Fu tea drinking – Wuhan, China.

S.Korean highways are spectacular but not open to cyclists – 'Such a beard sir!'

Rainy season begins — Harajuku, Tokyo, Japan.

13 May 2009 — Father & Son arrive at Steve's flat in Tokyo, Japan.

drilled a steel plate to clamp together the two halves (which were aluminium and he couldn't weld). It was quick and effective.

The charge was 10 rupees. I offered 100. He accepted 20. It is easy to develop a heartfelt love of this country and experiences like this strange but congenial form of bargaining, which seems to leave both sides happy afterwards, are one of the reasons for it. Indian mechanics, we discovered, regard work on bicycles as trivial and hardly worthy of a charge. As far as this man was concerned, he had only used three self-tapping screws and a cut-up bit of an old truck.

That night we sampled some Old Monk Indian rum to celebrate. It was served to us through bars in a hatch at our guesthouse. We thought at the time it was pretty good, but I'm sure it was horrendous. It was no worse, though, than the Thumbs Up mixer (local Pepsi substitute), with its aftertaste of weedkiller. The rum helped us sleep, anyway.

*

Sir, do you know Mr David Beckham? If you know him, sir, please say hello from Gurdeep Patil. I was his driver in Bombay. He was a good tipper, sir – oh yes. And he can play football almost beautiful like a cricketer, sir!

Two nights further on in Maharashtra, we found ourselves in an overpriced hotel (the only place available with glass in the windows) in a filthy hole of a town named Khed. Most crap towns have redeeming features. This town, not a single one! After coming a long way in two days over big hills, we needed a comfortable night, though, so we paid a premium. We also ate at the hotel restaurant.

In this near-deserted establishment, we were served at all times (to justify the prices perhaps) by two idiotic trainee waiters. The manager stood next to them, issuing instructions. The sight of the two beginners attempting to serve a dried-up old bread roll with a spoon and fork beggared belief. After the first clumsy oaf had tried for half a minute, the manager told the other to take over. The roll tumbled around the thumb-marked stainless steel platter, eventually falling onto my side plate, then bouncing onto my lap. The waiter

179

next attempted to retrieve the escaped roll from between my legs with his spoon and fork. Somewhat startled, I retrieved it myself without the use of utensils. I would love to have seen the manager slap him around the ear, as Basil Fawlty did with Manuel, but he restrained himself. Although the eccentrically cooked food that followed was not much appreciated by us, it was a very amusing evening on the whole and we went up to bed laughing.

I woke Sam at around 8am to get on the road and we left without indulging ourselves in further comedy at breakfast. After a few kilometres, Sam, silent so far as usual, remarked that I seemed very quiet and asked whether I was OK. I grunted. After covering a little more distance we stopped for breakfast, which I told Sam I would give a miss. He knew this meant that I was not OK, since I rarely miss a meal otherwise. At this point I admitted that I had been up all night with terrible vomiting and diarrhoea. The antics of the waiters seemed less funny to me now – no doubt they had also been responsible for the cooking. I felt utterly drained, dizzy and still sick. Sam, however, gave me confidence I would be well cared for if I keeled over.

I felt a little unwise for not staying in bed for a day, but I had hated that filthy town. The rubbish tip and stray dogs picking over it right in front of the hotel stank, and I couldn't face staying there a moment longer. In my haste to leave, I had abandoned finding a bank with a cash machine, deciding we were bound to pass one later.

After our breakfast break, we arrived at a steep mountain pass and the climbing immediately turned my legs to jelly. We stopped and I vomited more. I lay down on a stone wall with a shirt over my face, trying to make myself feel better, but I wanted to die. Sam managed not to laugh out loud and quietly took a photo while I lay there in a daze.

After a little while, we agreed that I would try to get up and over this pass in short stages, lying down in between. The plan was that if I passed out, Sam would put a wet towel over me and put up the tent for shelter. It felt that desperate.

We continued very slowly. I put the bike in its easiest gear and let my feet go around with no effort. Head down, I tried to think about something else and before long I was in a trance, not even answering Sam when he spoke to me.

"Lonely rivers flow ... to the sea ... to the sea..." I sang to myself.

By these means, with a fixated determination to get to somewhere cool and comfortable, I eventually found myself staggering into a small café at the top of the pass a couple of hours later. It really was steaming hot now.

Sam and I each drank a Limca (an Indian lemonade drink that tastes like Lemsip) and he put forward a new idea – he would ride on to the next town with my bankcard, get money from an ATM and cycle back (a hilly round trip of 45km); then we would find a hotel nearby for me to recuperate. Although this was extremely generous, I could not let him do it. Maybe it was my reluctance to relinquish control, but I could see too many problems. In particular:

1. There might not be an ATM, so he could cycle 45km for nothing.

2. We might not be able to find a hotel nearby – the café owner wasn't aware of one.

After my Limca, I insisted that I felt better and could certainly manage 25km to reach Mahad by nightfall. I worried silently about Mahad being midway on the unpleasant name scale (with Khed near the top), but this was no time to dwell on that particular prejudice. I believed I could make it; Sam, looking at the state of me, doubted it. Eventually he agreed to continue, with a *be it on your own head* look in my direction.

In fact, it was a little easier than I had anticipated. The roads got a little flatter and I stopped vomiting. Again, though, it was only by putting my head down and getting myself into the pedalling trance with Unchained Melody that I managed to keep going for those last 25km.

Arriving in Mahad mid afternoon, we found a cash machine and then a fairly acceptable hotel, although the 15 minutes it took to check in was about 14 too many for me. I went to bed while Sam went next door to eat lunch alone. It had been a horrendous day – perhaps my worst of the trip so far. I collapsed into sleep, not entirely convinced that I would ever wake up again.

After many nightmarish hours of sleep punctuated by sleepwalking trips to the Victorian mental asylum bathroom, I woke up early. Before loading the bikes, I washed some clothes and my sleeping bag liner.   Whatever bug it was I had picked up in that hellhole they call Khed, I wanted to be rid of any sign of it, however microscopic.

Sam was not at all convinced I should be up, let alone cycling, but after lining my stomach with a banana I was eager to set off.   I felt in a bit of a rush to get to Bombay.   Wanting to get to a city seemed to be our normal reaction if we were ill on the trip.   I suppose it somehow felt better that you could find some of the comforts of home, or a doctor if needed.   Despite a late start, around 9.30am, I optimistically hoped to make up a little of the distance lost the day before.

We decided to head for the port of Mandwar to take the little ferry across the bay into Bombay port.   Despite my weak condition, we pushed it hard all morning and all looked positive. The only minor annoyance was that of nobody seeming to know where Mandwar was.

At a roadside café for lunch, we were suddenly alerted to the television by the café owner.   We watched as dead bodies were carried out of Bombay railway station and flames leaped from windows of the Taj Hotel.   Accompanying the gory images was a soundtrack reminiscent of a James Bond movie.   At first, I wondered whether it was a new action movie.   The manager began to explain that there had been a terrorist attack.   We told him we were heading to Mumbai that night.

"No, no!   No Bombay tonight, boys!   Bombay closed!"

Back on the road, we did eventually find the turn off for Mandwar.   Although we were stopped several times on the road by police, none of them seemed to know about the siege.

After a pretty unpleasant 122km day, we were stopped at the village of Kihim, by a German catamaran-builder who had just put his parents on a plane back to Germany.   He told us the situation in Bombay was *mad confusion* and that all the westerners were clamouring to fly out, fearing further attacks.   He also told us that the ferries to Bombay were closed until further notice and kindly directed us to a decent guesthouse. This turned out to be full, so we ended up in an overpriced place that looked like nobody had stayed in it for years. At least now, though, we had somewhere to stay away from the trouble, a place we could rest until the situation returned to normal. We had always known that Pakistan was unlikely to be our only terrorist-induced delay or detour, so it did not unduly faze us.

On a more positive note, I seemed to be over my bout of sickness, so we walked into Chawnee to get dinner at the small town's main restaurant – Hotel Vaibon. After a good meal we walked quickly back, planning to watch football on TV. In most of India, we experienced daily power cuts and Kihim was no different. Our football-watching was interrupted and we were thrown into darkness at some crucial points. Inconvenient, yes, but nothing when set against the spectacle of Sam leaping up without warning and running to the bathroom to be sick.

This had gone beyond a joke. It seemed that we were taking turns. I felt pretty depressed, although not as down as Sam looked when he came out of the bathroom at the thought of being laid up here and not being able to eat for another day.

Fortunately, he felt much better by the next day. In town, we made enquiries about the ferry but these were inconclusive. I agreed with Sam that the next day we would cycle the two or three miles to the ferry-stage to check out the situation for ourselves.

*

The following morning, feeling inexplicably optimistic, Sam and I packed our bikes, checked out of the guesthouse and stopped at the restaurant in Chawnee for a simple, safe breakfast of tomato uttapam. As we left, I caught sight of a well-dressed Indian man leaving a hardware store and talking on a phone. It seemed to be a wireless DECT phone from his house, so I knew he must live nearby Thinking he looked like a reliable source of information, I stopped and waited for him to finish his call, then asked him about the ferries to Bombay.

"Yes, my wife is in Bombay and she just called me to say that the small ferry is running from Ravas," he said.

"Ravas?"

It turned out there was more than one ferry. Nobody had bothered to tell us. We would probably be able to get to Bombay that morning, he felt. But first, he insisted, we must follow him to take tea at his place. His place was a kind of plantation house. He explained that he was retired but in fact had owned tea plantations in Munar. He was very well educated, with an acute knowledge of history and politics, and spoke impeccable English. It was hard to drag ourselves away from his company and the cool, elegant sitting-room with its polished mahogany floor. Finally, however, after an instructive botanical tour of his garden, we did prise ourselves away and headed off to the small port of Ravas, with a swelling sense of anticipation. The city awaited.

On reaching the ferry stage, Sam and I were taken by armed guards into the police guardhouse and questioned.

"Do you know about the terrorist attacks?"

"What is your business in Mumbai?"

"From where have you travelled, and why haven't you a car?"

At first, it seemed that we might be detained or at least not allowed to cross into Bombay. After kindly buying us water and biscuits, however, the sergeant escorted us past the queues to the ticket office and then onto the jetty. This all seemed very well organised. Once the boat arrived, though, we witnessed the inefficiency and confusion the German catamaran guy had warned us about.

As our bags were being checked at the gangplank, one elderly gentleman objected to being searched, saying it was ridiculous and unnecessary. He refused to open his bag and said he would speak to his friend the commissioner. The policemen simply stood aside and waved him politely onto the boat.

Arriving in Bombay we sensed the typical aftermath of a crisis. The streets were a little quieter than they should have been, although they still fitted the description of manic. We headed down towards Colaba and the YWCA hotel. This was after being turned away from a hotel nearer the fishing port.   We later found out the terrorists had landed precisely at this point.

After cycling past the heavily guarded Stock Exchange of India and Central Railway Station – where many people had been killed – we stopped to ask a group of taxi drivers for directions.

The men had begun competing to give us directions when suddenly we were assailed by a crazy Australian woman shouting at us from somewhere over my shoulder.   We turned, slightly shocked, as she yelled and flung her hands about wildly.

"Get out, get out of Bombay!" she shouted, eyes bulging.   "It is NOT safe here – you are in great danger.   The advice from foreign embassies is that they are expecting more attacks.   Get out quickly!"

Clutching a hastily purchased carton of milk (worth braving *great danger* for, it seemed), she breathlessly explained that the international bank she worked for had instructed them to stay in their homes until they were taken to the airport to be flown home. Apparently all other ex-pats had been told to do the same.   The woman ran off.   I think we were more shocked by her behaviour than we had been seeing the siege unfold on TV the day before.   I turned to the taxi drivers, who also looked shocked.

"Is that true?" I asked. "Are we in danger here?"

They all clamoured to speak.

"No, no, it is not dangerous, sir.   Be careful, but if you are sensible, it is not dangerous.   Please enjoy our city."

We thanked them for their friendliness, took directions to the YWCA and cycled off saying that we would be delighted to stay and enjoy their city.

"That's right," shouted a spokesman.   "Don't give in to the terrorists!   Fuck them!   Fuck the bloody terrorists!"

We laughed at the rich use of the English language as they all echoed his feelings.   There may have been a serious attack two days before, but we felt little sense of danger in the air now.   Despite this, though, we did decide to remove our high-viz vests, which rather drew attention to ourselves.   We continued into Colaba and were reassured to find on our arrival that the YWCA was gated, with armed guards stationed outside.   Inside, we met a number of Europeans and Americans who had taken refuge there.

"So you knew about the siege but still came here – on bicycles? Jeez, you guys must be tired o' livin'!"

It may sound foolish but I can only say that we enjoyed Bombay and felt safe and welcome while we were there. We walked down to the fire-damaged Taj Hotel, site of the extended siege. A plume of smoke marked it out at a distance. Passing the Leopold Café we saw the fresh bullet holes in the walls and a TV camera crew interviewing customers and staff inside. Outside the Taj Hotel in front of the police cordon, groups of excited Indians were having their photographs taken. A couple of young men had dressed up in camouflage gear with dark glasses and had their girlfriends take photos as they struck action poses with the smoking hotel as a backdrop. The police seemed to see nothing unusual in this and allowed them to continue.

That evening we witnessed a large torch-lit procession with placards saying things like MR POLITICIAN, YOU DISGUST ME! and REFORM OR PERISH. These protestors were followed by a large group from a local Koran school, with placards saying PAKISTAN SHOULD BE DECLARED A TERRORIST STATE. We liked it here. We would certainly return, although hopefully under less hazardous circumstances.

*

Sam, feeling better after a few days of fasting and rest, now felt ready to attempt some cycling alone. We had talked about this back in Iran. Although a little apprehensive, I was in favour of it. I could understand the problem of Sam seeing the trip as just me looking after him, with that perceived reality devaluing his overall sense of achievement. He certainly seemed to have gained enough from the first half of the trip to enable him to cycle on his own. It would be over-protective to deny him.

Having worked out how much money he would need, we I got it for him from the bank on our last day. We agreed it would be better not to tell Lorna about him going it alone until afterwards; also, that he would text me every day to confirm he was OK.

186

These concerns about Sam cycling on his own, and Lorna being worried, took me back to one of my battles with my father when I was around fourteen. I informed my parents that I was going to cycle with two friends from our temporary home in Lichfield, to Derby and back – a round trip of about 60 miles. My parents were horrified, saying that it was impossible for three boys on basic bicycles to cycle that far in a day. My father strictly forbade me from going. His justification was that he didn't want to spend his Saturday evening coming to collect us by car when we failed, and that it was a dangerous road. He should have chosen his words more carefully. What he said amounted to the throwing down of a gauntlet.

In retrospect, I think his refusal was more to do with my mother being afraid of what might happen to me, and his desire to protect her from worry. Whatever the reason, it seemed outrageously unfair. As usual, I defied him, despite the likely consequences. It was tough on our heavy old-fashioned bikes, but we made it. Around 5pm, we returned from Derby and rode triumphantly to my front door, presenting my father with a copy of the Derby local paper and smug expressions. Of course, my father was less than impressed by this defiant showboating. Even so, he politely congratulated my friends, and then took me inside to begin a punishment of confinement to the house for the next week after school. I felt unfairly treated, of course, but it had been expected. In his defence, a week later my dad did admit he was impressed.

*

We left Bombay in the heat of the afternoon on 4 December, having asked for advice from the hotel staff about the road north out of the city. They explained it was a very busy highway for quite a way. I didn't want Sam beginning his lone journey under such risky circumstances, so we agreed to take the train out of Mumbai to Vadodara, the next main town; there, we would stay a night, before heading off on different routes to Agra, meeting in Udaipur on the way That made the timing of meeting the others in Jaipur about right.

187

We had problems finding a hotel in Vadodara because of a big local wedding, so we ended up staying in a dormitory and were kept awake by the Indian national snoring team.

The next morning, we serviced the bikes and had breakfast in a café. Outside, I waved Sam off, then headed away myself. I spent my first hour on the road wondering whether I had done the right thing. It felt really strange without him. After working through things in my head, however, I relaxed and resigned myself to texting him in the evening to see how he had got on. I also began to see some benefits to cycling on my own as I built up to a faster rhythm and spent time working out how far I could get that night if I kept it up as an average.

Despite a late start, I had covered 72km by the time I stopped for lunch. I was so raring to go that I was back on the road 45 minutes later. Pacing myself and calculating in my head kept me pretty busy all afternoon, but I was already thinking how boring it was without anyone to discuss things with on the road. It would be the same at the end of the day. During this time alone, I rarely bothered to take intermediate breaks, since these were normally an opportunity to have a chat about what we had seen, how we were getting on and where we might stop later.

At the one-horse town of Lunawada, I managed to find a working men's hostel with a simple clean room, and then made my way to the town's only restaurant. Both the room and the restaurant were basic but perfectly adequate and very cheap. The people here seemed very friendly. I phoned Sam, who seemed really happy and positive. It sounded like people were looking after him, responding kindly to such a young man travelling alone in their country and I felt reassured that his solo interlude had been a good idea. I relaxed for a good night's sleep.

The following day, I again decided to take advantage of my lone-cyclist situation and headed off at a stiff pace around 7am. The roads were quiet at this time and I enjoyed flying along, watching farm workers out in the fields, marvelling at the difference it makes to one's life to be waved at by a complete stranger. What lovely-natured people they were.

By 9:15, I felt in need of breakfast and was surprised to see I had already covered 52km. Eating my porata and sweet chai at a truck-stop, I worked out that if I maintained my 21kmh average from the first part of the morning, I could manage 160km by around 5pm. I realised this was unlikely in practice, but seeing me get back on the road so quickly seemed to amuse the truck drivers. I was up to speed again in no time, back into that mesmerising rhythm. The songs I sang to myself during this section had a faster beat. The Clash and Ramones predominated.

Lost in time and reveries, I found myself stopping for an early lunch with 105km on the clock before I knew it. The afternoon continued well and I began to calculate whether it was humanly possible to continue to Udaipur for a total distance of 232km. I could see that without a riding partner, I might easily push myself to the point of hardly stopping until I got to Japan. This may be satisfying in terms of breaking records, but it does not make for an interesting trip. I reminded myself of this as I reached an interesting-looking junction. I had agreed to meet Sam in Udaipur, I reminded myself, so there was little point in arriving two days early.

It seemed that cycling alone left me with little to concentrate on but making the best daily progress, working out averages and projecting targets. My mental arithmetic and physical fitness may have improved but not much else was gained; my life had not been enriched. During these few days, I thought a great deal about how different the trip would have been if I had ended up doing it alone. Sam's lone interlude was supposed to be for his benefit, but I was already beginning to see how it might help me as much as him.

Although I tried to make myself cycle with the same casual enjoyment I had with Sam, I found it very hard to achieve. With this in mind, though, I pulled off the main route at around 3.30pm towards a temple in nearby Kesariyaji. I was following directions from a pedestrian, who had told me I would find accommodation for pilgrims there. Wasn't I a pilgrim of sorts?

Arriving in this beautiful small town, I disturbed a huge flock of bright green parrots that took flight from a large banyan tree as I rode beneath. I stopped and stood looking up in wonder as they wheeled around in the sky, thrilled by the rushing sound of their wings as they returned to the branches of the tree above me.   Now my life had been enriched.

Moving on, I passed the lovely whitewashed Jain temple and found my way into the nearby courtyard.   What a great recommendation, I thought.   In this peaceful state, I was shown cool rooms and a communal restaurant.   The goodness of the man who took my paltry room fee seemed to radiate from his face and voice.

The facilities here were very old, dark and basic, as befitted the purpose, but a tremendous atmosphere of calm pervaded every corner of the place.   I had an overpowering sense I had been drawn here to learn something valuable, although I didn't know what it was.   My room was simple but also large enough to park my bike inside.   I freshened up, splashing water over myself from the large wooden barrel in the dark wash area.

Dressed for the evening, I had a walk around the town and visited the lovely temple, before returning and seating myself at the outdoor kitchen.   Other guests were starting to gather.   There was such beauty in all this.   People were friendly without saying very much.   I ate an excellent vegetarian set meal largely in silence, without any of the sense of awkwardness that a silent gathering usually brings.

I helped a man change a cauldron of dhal on the brazier for one of water.   He had asked me for help, and thanked me, without speaking.   I sat drinking chai, looking onto the old courtyard.   I felt utterly content just sitting there thinking, listening to bubbling water. A perfect evening.

After half an hour, people began to say good night.   It was early but I too felt happy to drift off quietly to my room.   Relaxing into my simple bed, I felt content in the knowledge that I had cycled over a hundred miles in a fairly short day, and found a lovely spiritual place to stay at the end.   I felt, somehow without anything significant to account for it, I had gained a lot from this day.   How Lorna would love this, I thought, or Sam, but especially Alex.

Beginning to settle down for the night, I reminded myself to send Sam a text to check how he was.   He replied that he was fine.   As he was some distance behind, I recommended that he try to stay here at the temple the next evening.   Drifting back into a calm sleep, I realised what it was that I had come here to learn. If I had followed my usual pattern, I would have missed these beautiful sights, only in order to prove to myself that I could reach Udaipur in one 232km day. I already knew I could achieve that, so what would have been gained from it beyond reinforcement of my own beliefs? Maybe it would have impressed Sam. But maybe not. I knew it was all about proving it to myself, not anyone else. But not to have come to Kesariyaji? What a great loss that would have been.

Still dwelling upon the revelation I had experienced at the closing of the previous day, I awoke early with the light and lay in bed thinking. Unusually, I felt no sense of urgency as I watched the sunlight gradually moving across the ceiling from the clerestory window above. What was it in me, I wondered, that made me need to set myself targets all the time? How had I got to fifty still not allowing myself to *fail* in my own eyes?

My wife tells me this is my *critical parent* talking to me – the person in my head. I'm sure Sam would never set himself crazy targets, then criticise himself for failing if he didn't achieve them, so why did I?

Looking back on my past, it seems that I was so determined to resist conditioning, authority and the conservative views of others, that I hardened myself against it all by setting my own ambitions then sticking to them as if it were a matter of life and death – driven as much by fear as anything else. I accept that this has resulted in a capacity to achieve worthwhile things, but at the same time I tend to oppress myself in a way that I totally resist from others. Stopping early in Kesariyaji had not cured me, but recognising it for myself as the sun began to fill my room, had begun a long journey to overcoming it.

*

Knowing I only had 69km to go to reach Udaipur, I set off calmly and soon pulled into a roadside truck café for breakfast. No rush, I told myself, still fighting my natural urge to race ahead. Some truckers were still asleep on the charpoys. These truck-stops were very interesting. They are quite large but extremely basic – truckers in

India are poor. Most of the cafes have a basic open kitchen amounting to a propane gas burner and a small work-surface. They rarely have a refrigerator, so the only drink is sweet milky tea (*chai*) all boiled up in one large pot. There are sometimes a few tables with chairs but in the main people take their food and drink sitting on a charpoy – a bed made of a crude wooden frame with lengths of truck inner-tube stretched across in a woven grid pattern. The truck drivers sleep on these at night using a blanket or their *dhoti* (short sarong) for a cover. During the day, customers sit cross-legged on the same charpoys, with a plank laid across the frame as a narrow table.

The food varies but the scope is always limited, with no menu or blackboards, so you must rely on asking the cook or the serving boy. For a foreigner, this is where it gets difficult. They are not at all used to foreign customers, so regardless of your ability in linguistics or mime, they are often incapable of helping you with food – mainly due to their surprise and a preconception that you will not like their food. Your best chance is to point at what someone else is eating. So the interaction on this morning was typical.

I get off and walk along the muddy, rutted pull-in, past the water hole where some semi-naked truckers are lathering their bodies with soap and washing their clothes at the same time. I park my bike and sit down on a free charpoy. Nobody else has come in for breakfast yet. The serving boy approaches nervously, assuming I have made a mistake.

"Chai!" I say purposefully with a smile, making a drinking motion then holding up one finger.

"Chai?" he asks doubtfully, wobbling his head from side to side. *An alien has landed.*

"*Acha*, one chai!" I confirm (I discovered early on that *please* only confuses them).

"OK, chai?" he says but simply stands staring at me open-mouthed. I point to the kitchen, repeat my order and thankfully he runs off to the kitchen. Five minutes later and there is still no sign of any chai, which is strange since there is always a cauldron boiling away on the hob. I get up and go to the cook at the kitchen area.

"Chai?" I ask, and then go through the same process, but this time I am given a glass of chai along with a toothless smile. Bolstered by this success, I use an Indian *food* gesture with my fingers to my mouth

"Porata? Dosa? Omlette?" I ask hopefully.

"*Nai naihm sah,*" he says, pointing to the adjacent biscuit shop.

I don't want biscuits, so I repeat my food question, listing some more typical truck-stop food items, but he shakes his head and eventually I return to my seat. After a few minutes, just beginning to come to terms with not getting any breakfast, I notice the cook has made someone a *porata* (fried Indian bread). I go back to him and point at the item, then at myself.

"Porata?" he asks with surprise – surely foreigners can't eat fried bread!

I smile, say "*acha*" and nod my head, amused as always by the way as a foreigner you can pronounce a word perfectly, at a place that serves little except what you've asked for, and they assume that you can't possibly mean you want to eat that.

Back on the saddle and weighed down by the greasy breakfast, I soon slipped into my rhythm on the potholed road. After snaking my way through a traffic jam caused by a horrendous coach crash, and a tar lorry on fire, I coasted into Udaipur around 10am. To make life even easier, I had a recommendation for a guesthouse named Dream Heaven just across the footbridge, and found it surprisingly quickly.

You might have noticed that I made little of the horrendous coach and tar lorry crash I passed on my way into Udaipur. Anyone who knows me at all would say I am quite an emotional person. The coach may have been empty when it crashed, but I think not. Although many people no doubt died in that crash in the early hours, I cycled on. It is a sad fact that the roads in India are a daily scene of carnage. I do not share the religion that helps many Indians view death as a positive move towards an improved next life. Nevertheless, like them, I had already come to see it as a commonplace feature of Indian life.

To my delight, Dream Heaven was the friendliest and most beautiful place, with a large roof-terrace restaurant overlooking the famous lake and palace. The view was stunning.

After checking in, I had a walk around the town and returned a little tired due to the heat and the persistent tourist touts. My little heaven on the other side of the river was well named. I settled down to a delicious lunch on the terrace. Having looked at the competition, I felt sure that Dream Heaven was the best place to stay in Udaipur. The luxury heritage hotels in town were mostly plywood pastiche anyway. I was sure Sam would agree when he arrived the next day. Thinking about this, I sent him a text with basic directions, before sinking into an afternoon sleep in my comfortable nomad's tent-style room.

Some time later, not knowing where I was or the time of day, I woke with a start after a deep sleep. One of the staff was calling and knocking on my door. Peering at my watch, I was surprised to find that it was 6:30pm and I had slept for nearly four hours. I got up, somewhat unsteady on my feet and a little bleary eyed. Why would someone be knocking on my door?

Opening the door, I met the man from reception standing there with Sam. I was amazed but also extremely happy. Undeniably I had enjoyed the freedom of a few days alone to decide my own schedule, but I had missed Sam's company more than I had expected.

"Please, sir, do you know this boy?"

"Certainly, he is my son."

"*Acha*. Have a pleasant evening. Dinner is served from seven o'clock."

Sam looked tired but was too excited to sleep. He had really pushed it, getting up uncharacteristically early without me to encourage him, and had managed to cover about 170km by 6:30pm. I felt delighted and really proud of him.

Feeling we deserved a good break after pushing it so hard these last few days, we agreed to stay three nights in Udaipur. Sam also said that he would prefer to cycle together for the last stretch to Agra and maybe do another section on his own later in China. I was glad to hear this. Both because I had missed his company and because he had got the desire for solitary travelling out of his system, at least for now.

Udaipur was a pretty place; there was no denying it. But it was a little too touristy for our liking. Although it looked very romantic, with its palaces on the lake and Raj-era style buildings, it lacked any real soul and you were hassled by touts every time you went into town. Many of the hotels, restaurants and cafes make a big thing of screening the James Bond movie Octopussy (it was filmed here). The fact this was shown every night suggested tourists only stayed here a night or two.

One of the benefits of tourist destinations in India is that there is usually a wider variety of food in restaurants. Despite searching hard, however, we had to agree that our guesthouse was also the number one restaurant in town.

I cannot move on from Udaipur without recounting one particularly memorable sight. Standing on our narrow footbridge one afternoon, we watched a gentleman from a local travel agent arrive at the riverside steps and empty several large sacks of office rubbish into the river. This was right in view of the tourists promenading and sitting on their hotel balconies and adjacent to where ladies dressed in colourful saris do their washing (a popular tourist attraction in itself). Much of this rubbish was not easily biodegradable and consisted of glossy tourist brochures.

Since the Bombay siege a few weeks before, tourism in Udaipur had suffered a collapse. It almost seemed to us that he was throwing the brochures into the lake – Udaipur's prime tourist attraction – as a symbolic gesture of despair. In reality, this was just a fanciful western view. All over India, rivers and lakes seem to be treated as standard receptacles for the disposal of rubbish. Despite our serious misgivings about Udaipur, though, we are still aghast at its beauty when we look back over our photographs.

*

As Sam and I made our way north through Rajasthan, we did start to notice that the people here were slightly less friendly than they had been further south. They are also more used to tourists, which in our experience often goes with surliness and a tendency to try and rip you off (forgivable in such a poor country).

At this point, I also reminded Sam about places with nasty sounding names turning out to be bad places to stay. I had noticed this first in Turkey. Although Sam had laughed about it then, in India he had given my idea more credence after Khed, where I suffered so badly from food poisoning at our so-called luxury hotel. Bhilwara was our proposed next stop after Udaipur. Sure that it sounded like some kind of unpleasant digestive disease, I felt quietly repelled by it.

As it turned out, we did go via Bhilwara and it was not really that bad. At our hostel, I revealed my prior suspicions to Sam. Did he not think it had a slightly aggressive, even sinister, air about it?

"Dad, I can't believe you're still pushing that theory!"

The following day, to make up some time, a short cut via a smaller road on the map looked like a worthwhile plan. Sam wanted to be sure I wasn't proposing this simply to avoid place names I didn't like. He could see the potential for this developing into some kind of debilitating Obsessive Compulsive Disorder and finding ourselves unable to move due to being surrounded by towns with unattractive names.

"Sam, get real! Look, I have no objection to Gulabpura or Bandawara, I can assure you. Even Jharwasa is fine!"

We agreed on the detour. As we progressed along the country road, however, it started to seem like a mistake. Smaller roads do carry less traffic but they are poorly maintained and drivers are less careful. In India, that can mean downright homicidal. Because these roads are narrow, truck and bus drivers blast their way along *lead boot* style, blaring their horns, intimidating smaller vehicles to pull over and pedestrians to jump into ditches. Bicycles are hardly noticed. Unless we'd pulled off the road, at some points we would have be flattened beneath their bald tyres.

I joked with Sam that the road was so potholed it must have been carpet bombed by the Indian Air Force. We had, in fact, seen them earlier, flying low overhead.

Kishingarh was our next overnight stop. It was a small but unbelievably busy Rajasthani town dependent on the marble industry. The traffic in the centre at night was reminiscent of the Thunder dome, in the film Mad Max II. At the junction near our guesthouse, Sam and I felt almost like the enemy being herded by huge numbers of roaring motorcycles and taxis wheeling around us in a choking cloud of exhaust smoke.

Later that evening, on our way out to eat, we were lucky enough to see a wedding party pass through the narrow streets on horseback. We heard the procession long before we saw it. Stretching up to find out where the booming music was coming from, we saw coloured lights and clouds of what we assumed to be incense.

"Looks like some kind of festival," said Sam.

Pushing our way through the dense crowd of pedestrians, we eventually saw a procession with a large group of elaborately dressed retainers and a pipe and drum band. Bizarrely, these smart tin-soldiers were followed by an old man with a sooty face and greasy overalls. He pushed a heavy cart with a large old diesel generator perched on it. A dangerous tangle of wires led from the generator, which was powering the candelabra on the head-dresses of the couple – no, really! It was also responsible for the deafeningly loud Bollywood-style music emanating from large speakers. The smoke was not incense but the fumes belching from the ancient generator.

*

According to my diary, it was around this time Sam started to develop an ache in one hip. This type of problem tends to be caused by incorrect geometry – saddle too high/low/far back, etc. We checked and Sam tried several changes to his habits. This seemed to help a little, but the problem always returned. I was concerned it could get much worse if allowed to continue, but I was also bothered by the suspicion it might just be me pushing him to ride further than he wanted each day.

I decided to ease up on the daily distance for a while. This is easier said than done for me, but I must have achieved some small level of restraint. My diary records that we only rode 107km to Jaipur the following day

We knew we would be coming back to Jaipur with Lorna in a week's time, so we were interested to check it out first. Fortunately, we discovered a superb restaurant on the roof of a guesthouse named the Pearl Palace. It was a truly great find.

Sam still seemed a little tetchy at this point and I longed for him to unload it on me so we could move on. The hip problem seemed to have brought on what I saw as a *can't be bothered* demeanour, although I may just have been seeing things that weren't there. Could it really be due to him feeling he had nothing to contribute in conversations or decisions about where we went? Or had he just come to loath being stuck with me so much that every day was a torturous effort not to tell me so? Perhaps I was just imagining everything. I hoped I would find out more once we were all together for Christmas. Maybe my friend Steve – who we had now arranged to meet in Delhi before the others arrived – would understand. If there was a problem, I wanted to put it right. But if I didn't know what the problem was, how could I? All typical male-pattern obsession, I know. Time to bring in the family psychologist.

The following night, we stayed in a so-called deluxe motel beside the highway to Agra. It was the first place we saw after leaving Jaipur and at 106km I didn't want to harm Sam's hip or his determination by trying to go further. We agreed to stay after negotiating a more reasonable rate. The extent of the *deluxe* tag, it transpired, was that we could get drinks served in our room and that there was cable TV showing only Indian stations, and no football. Criminal!

The lack of any curtains in a room facing east and right onto the highway, with a large lamp in front of the window, was far from luxurious and we got very little sleep. Due to the reported absence of any other restaurants nearby, we ate in the motel restaurant. It would have been better to starve. My suspicions were aroused when I saw no other guests. Another Khed? I checked the menu carefully. The waiter came to take our order.

"Sorry but I have to say this is the most expensive menu I have seen in all of India. It's even more expensive than the Hilton in Mumbai!"

"Oh dear," he said timidly. "Would you like me to fetch you the *local* menu, sir?"

I thanked him very much and he returned from the counter with another menu, written in pencil with even worse spelling. Neither Barf

Bourgingnon nor Crock Mesure filled me with confidence. Stake Diaphragm sounded positively indigestible.

The items were of course exactly the same as those on the first menu, but the prices were 50% less. We ordered something simple – vegetable biryani, I believe. The food came, although a little too soon for comfort. It was not great but restored our energy and sent us to bed vaguely satisfied. Halfway through the night, though, I felt far from satisfied. I was hit by a powerful bout of food poisoning. In places like India I always say it is safer to eat street-food than food in luxury restaurants. I learned this living in Asia. It's not quantum physics. Street-food is bought fresh each morning from local markets. It then needs to be cooked and eaten the same day, rather than as leftovers stored in refrigerators (which, unlike restaurants and hotels, dhabas don't have).

That evening we had been told there was no alternative eating-place for miles. I cursed this dishonesty the following morning as we passed a popular roadside café just along the way. It was 146km to Agra and I was determined to make it in one day. This was our last day's cycling before our three-week Christmas break, and it was a case of *the sooner, the better*. Food poisoning was not going to prevent us achieving it. I drank plenty of water and pedalled on weakly in silence, watching the kilometres steadily ticking over and focussing on a good rest in a decent hotel at the end.

"I look at you all, see the love there that's sleeping, while my..."

I was in the groove.

As always, Sam was very supportive. We made it to Agra by around 4pm, despite another road seemingly strafed by the Indian Air Force.

My relief was short-lived. I was tired and extremely weak but more than this I had deprived myself of food, which added up to a very short temper. I had hidden this all day by keeping my head down and saying nothing (except mumbled Beatles lyrics). Our plan was to check into the very exclusive Trident Hilton Hotel, for reasons that will become clear.

After managing to locate the hotel we found ourselves at a high security gate with armed guards. I explained that we wished to stay here but was told we could not do so without a prior reservation which technically we did have, but for three weeks later. We persuaded the chief guard to allow us to speak on his phone to the reception. Extremely politely, I explained to the duty manager that we would be staying with them for three nights with our family and friends in three weeks but that we would also like to stay for one night tonight, if possible, before beginning our tour.

I didn't mention it at that moment but we also hoped to leave our bikes there for those three weeks. With a party of ten booked for three nights at a fee more than the annual salary of the average Indian hotel worker, I did not think this was unreasonable.

The duty manager explained that they had no record of our booking in three weeks' time. Moreover, they did not accept bookings on the door (or *walk-ins*, as he disparagingly termed us). I was politely told to try booking via their website. I phoned home in a very irritated mood asking for *someone* to sort this out before I keeled over with exhaustion. Sam, seeing my face changing from pale yellow to purple, calmly asked for the phone and took over. Lorna was at work but would do what she could and call back. I sat hunched over on the neatly tended grass, which seemed to really bother the guards.

Gradually, sitting there feeling sorry for myself, I became aware of what an idiot I was. I felt embarrassed and grateful for Sam's support. I could see that he was actually extremely irritated by my manner and who could blame him? Luckily for me he was restrained, knowing how sick I felt.

Now I had calmed down, I thought sensibly about the situation.

"OK, Sam. We won't bother giving the Trident our money."

I sent Lorna a text apologising for worrying her and we crossed the road, checking into a perfectly pleasant local hotel at a third of the price. They put our bikes in their utility block at the back and agreed to keep them there for the next three weeks, with us returning for a night's stay the day after the Trident. Lorna and the others would have set off back to England by then. All seemed to have ended well in the end, I remarked to Sam as we did our washing in our comfortable room.

The next morning my digestion was back to normal, but I was still not totally recovered from the emotional trauma of the Trident fiasco. After a good breakfast we went to check out, asking at first to leave our panniers in their luggage room. A different manager was on duty and he told us the luggage room was full. He also told us we could not leave the bikes in the utility room. I was about ready to raise the roof when Sam stepped in and suggested he deal with this.

I sloped off disconsolately to sit in a leather armchair and try to decompress. Sam made a calm, painfully clear explanation of what we needed and why. I watched at a distance but couldn't believe this was going to make the slightest difference. Miraculously, however, at the end of Sam's explanation, the manager just said, "OK" – without any further objections. I was astounded, and delighted, of course. How different the day might have been without Sam there.

We were free for three weeks, without bikes or excess luggage, and our bikes were safe. It felt like a prison sentence had been lifted. I hugged Sam in gratitude as we walked out into the street to take a rickshaw to the station.

"Sam, you're a bloody hero!" I said, putting my arm around him.

"All part of the service," he said. "By the way, I don't want to be critical, but I don't understand how you can't see that your manner – your tone of voice, sometimes – just puts people's backs up."

There was no point trying to answer. I had never believed that to be true, but in the circumstances I had to accept he was right. Obviously, I needed to take more notice of how he dealt with these situations.

Sam, despite his troubled state of mind, had managed to save the situation several times of late. When my stress levels had sounded the *evacuate the reactor alarm*, he had come good. I was really glad of this, although at the same time rather ashamed.

SAM'S POINT OF VIEW

Getting to Goa for my birthday was such a relief. All frustration evaporated. The hot weather was awesome and I loved living in a thatched hut on the beach. I think getting up every morning, swimming in warm sea and eating fresh seafood all day is a dream for any Westerner. Cycling north from there to meet our family and friends was also pretty smooth and stress-free, apart from Mumbai when our arrival happened to coincide with the terrorist siege. We were delayed a few days but once in the city everything was fine.

Probably the best part of the year for me was the period of cycling I did on my own. The confidence I gained from just three days' cycling alone in India was amazing. I remember the excitement after asking my dad if he'd mind me doing it. I got the sense afterwards that he didn't enjoy it much, but there's no doubt that being independent produced a more positive, less grumpy side of me.

During those few days I met with such kindness from so many Indians. On the first day I landed in a tiny village with no shops, just farms and houses. I asked around and found myself staying in a house with a family. We shared stories, marvelling at each other's different worlds. They took me onto the roof to fly kites; the first of which I broke when it plummeted to the ground. I may have given them the impression I was cycling the whole trip on my own. OK, that wasn't true, but I can't say I didn't enjoy their response of shock.

"On your own! But are you not scared?"

The son of the family took me on his motorbike into town and bought me a delicious dinner. The following day I met a man with his son on a moped. We chatted for an hour riding side by side until they took me into a garage for tea. We discussed the problems of the West and how the Indian philosophy of life is so much more positive. Indians respond well to flattery as well as anyone does, but I meant it.

What impressed me about India was how they were all willing to help each other, communicate with one another. They always appeared happy. I find the English far too closed. People seem nervous about being themselves, worried about the judgement of others around them. This is so counterproductive and, it seems to me, leads to confusion or even depression. So many of us strive to conform – how screwed up is that? Surely there is no 'right way' to be. Everyone is different and we should allow difference to flourish, relishing what differentiates one from another. Surely it's what makes us interesting. Conformity is just so boring!

On the last day cycling on my own I managed to cover 110miles. I really wanted to see my dad and tell him everything I'd seen and all the people I'd met. I didn't let him know I was arriving that day, though. I wanted to surprise him. I arrived late, it was dark and the roads in Udaipur were really busy. Once I'd found the hotel, I asked if they knew of a man staying with a big beard and bicycle like mine. I was quickly ushered to my dad's room. He was having a sleep before dinner so he awoke a bit disorientated to answer the door. I felt amazing, especially noticing his shock and pleasure at seeing me standing there!

Anyone who has spent time in India will be unsurprised that I was suffering from a recurring upset stomach at this stage in our trip. At the time I thought it was to do with poor food hygiene in India. It turned out later that it was probably due to a parasite called giardia. Apparently you sometimes don't really recover for around three years. It was a total pain. Food had become such an integral part of my motivation to carry on. Eating a lot was also important to fuel us for cycling, so the lack of food combined with the heat of the Indian sun was really fatiguing. I felt fortunate that a big break was coming up during Christmas and New Year, but I knew that I'd have to hold off eating too much in order to recover properly.

I was really looking forward to the Christmas break by the time we hit Rajasthan. Although things with my dad at this stage were not so terrible, I was looking forward to spending some time with my friends and, frankly, without him. I'd spent the last six months staring at his backside on a saddle in front of me, dragging me along at his ridiculous pace, and I'd seen enough of it. At the same time, I could see how hard he was trying to be helpful to me. Sometimes I felt lucky to have him around and showing concern about my illness, but a lot of the time I just resented being stuck with him. Looking back on it, this seems stupid. I'd have gained a lot more if I'd stopped dwelling on all that and just enjoyed myself. The truth was whoever you chose to go on a trip like this with, you'll probably end up feeling annoyed with them quite a bit of the time. Most people my age could not even imagine having to spend ten months doing something with their father.

Chapter 9

Northern India – Christmas with family and friends

You cycled here from Ireland? Impossible! How many years did it take you?

The long-planned three-week Christmas break had been an alluring prize to aim at over the previous three months. We felt an overwhelming sense of pleasure at having reached it.

We still had a week before Lorna, Scarlett and our other friends arrived, but Steve from Tokyo was due to arrive the following day, so we took the train to New Delhi to meet him. No bikes to worry about. What luxury.

Finding a good basic guesthouse in the old Pahar Ganj area, we booked Steve and ourselves in, before meeting him in a rooftop café the following morning. These four days in Delhi were unexpectedly enjoyable, although Sam's pleasure was still tainted by the persistent stomach bug he was determined to starve out before Lorna arrived. He blamed his newfound love of exotic food for this but found it very difficult to resist eating, despite knowing his system needed a rest. This was being a bit harsh on himself, given that the cycling had demanded a significantly increased calorie intake for the past five months. For myself, though, a rest from the heavy intake now we were not cycling seemed a good idea.

Steve's arrival was a big boost for Sam and I. It seemed to help our relationship having him around. There had been a bit of friction between us again since Jaipur and I sensed the pressure rising in Sam. I think he was really dying to see his friends and how things were going to pan out with Hannah. I could tell he did not want to hope for too much under the circumstances. I wondered how he would feel about saying goodbye to her and everyone else after New Year, then setting off for a further six months alone with his annoying father. I hoped he would be more positive about that prospect by then, but doubts were creeping into my mind during these days leading up to their arrival.

Of course, my tendency as the father was to see it as my responsibility to make sure that Sam stayed positive about the trip, instead of letting him just get on with it and enjoying the trip for myself. The truth was, that if Sam was not enjoying the trip, it affected my enjoyment too.

My other worry at this time came when I discovered that somehow we had ended up with a tour bus, a driver and a navigator. These had been hired, and an extensive tour of Rajasthan organised, through an up-market tour company. Perish the thought! I vaguely knew about the program but not the mode of transport or the level of so-called luxury.

When the morning of their arrival came, Sam and I took at taxi to Lorna and Scarlett's hotel. We had half an hour with them and our friends Brendan and Velia before the tour company representative arrived to greet us and give a little talk about the itinerary. A very elegant lady in a sari duly arrived and explained the three-week tour, which would involve staying mainly in plush tourist hotels, in Delhi, Jaipur, Pushkar, Jaiselmer and Agra (Pushkar was a three-star exception that had been booked before we left).

A sick feeling overwhelmed me. I tried to fight it off, but memories of Istanbul plagued me. After enjoying cycling through backwaters and staying in friendly, basic guesthouses, the program this woman was proudly laying before us seemed like purgatory. Sam was not over-enamoured with the idea either.

"What's all that about?" he asked me afterwards. "It seems a bit over the top."

I did my best not to be critical and suggested Sam do the same, but he could read the feelings on my face. He had no problem with the luxury hotels, he told me, he was just a bit shocked. We agreed that it would be nice for Lorna. As with Istanbul, she deserved something special after staying at home and managing things. Reminding myself of Istanbul, I made myself a promise I absolutely would not voice any objection or criticism.

It was a real rush of happy emotions to see Lorna and Scarlett, and an enormous pleasure to sit around chatting to them in comfortable surroundings.   Sam and I managed to laugh about riding down to Jaipur in a minibus with *TOURISTS* written in huge letters across the front.   The converted old palace we stayed at turned out to be very pleasant.   Unfortunately, Lorna had arrived with a terrible bout of flu after the flight, but she at least found it a lovely environment in which to recover.

*

Sir, I must say that if ever there was ever an Englishman who was born to wear a turban it is you, sir.   Veritably, I feel this so strongly that I am bound to offer you a ten percent discount – something I have never done before. Jaisalmer Shopkeeper

Pushkar, where we were to spend Christmas itself, was the most superb place, with a lovely rooftop restaurant at our hotel where we enjoyed sunsets over the lake and the gentle sounds of chanting from a nearby ashram over breakfast each morning.   We watched monkeys being chased out of neighbouring gardens, escaping with bunches of bananas.   We wandered around the bazaars buying our Christmas presents and spent time watching people offering prayers by the lake, scattering flower petals.

On Boxing Day afternoon, we all took a long walk to the top of the sacred mountain.   Here we looked out over the town and the lake, with lands stretching out in all directions as the sun set.   The light was just incredible.   If you have to spend Christmas away from home, then this must be one of the best places on Earth to do it.

Sam seemed to have forgotten how annoyed he was with me. He was so much happier now that his friends were here.   I had underestimated their importance to him.   It also became more apparent to me at this point, that spending five months with any one person 24hrs a day is challenging, whoever it is – so what chance for a father and his teenage son?

It was really beneficial to have Lorna to talk this stuff through with for a few weeks.   It helped me to clear up a few unresolved issues in my mind and made me feel better prepared for the second half of the trip.   I felt so much calmer with Lorna now than I ever had: I could see that we were already benefiting from the time apart and my having left behind the pressure of daily work and home responsibilities. It was also nice to have Steve travelling around with us, casually joining in when he felt like it and catching up on reading when he didn't.

In retrospect this first week was perfect and I think we later wished we had just stayed in Pushkar. Easy to say, of course, but then we would no doubt have regretted not having seen the spectacular castle in Jodhpur, the walled city of Jaisalmer and the Taj Mahal in Agra. All three of these places that followed were special in their own right but the tourist bus and the opulent hotels took their toll on my patience. Shamefully, I broke my vow of not voicing any objections, which soured the end of the holiday for both Lorna and I. More work needed!

Thinking back over this period and how it should or could have been different, I realised how naïve I had been thinking it would be easy for us to break our trip in the middle. While I would not have wanted to miss Christmas with my family, I now felt quite convinced that it was all but incompatible with an expedition of this kind, where it is necessary to focus firmly upon the physical and mental challenge. It is very hard to switch off the focussed determination and then restart it again later. Or maybe it's just that I am too much of a control freak and too insistent upon things being done my way. Sam certainly dealt with it far better than I did. Whatever the reason, I felt glad to have been with them but wrong to have thought it would work. Worst of all, it had taken me back to being the person I thought I had left behind, and that was agonising.

Surprisingly, the Trident Hotel in Agra – words that I had spat out in furious distaste three weeks before – turned out to be a real pleasure, with lovely contemporary surroundings and cool, professional staff. Before we left, they were really helpful when we carried out a major service on our bikes to change the brake blocks, tyres, gear cassettes and chains for parts that Lorna and Sam's friend Luke had brought over for us in their luggage. The drivers in the car park where we did the work snapped up the offer of the old parts and we were only too happy to see them going to good homes. It pleases me to think that somewhere around Agra, our bald tyres are living a second life on a pair of Indian bicycles – if not holding up somebody's trousers.

*

Being back on the road again after three weeks felt really good to me and I embraced it like a long lost friend. Sam had slept for thirteen hours that night but was still too tired to wake at 8am. We needed to do a bit of preparation on the bikes before we started – mainly checks and lubrication – so I was keen to get up early to be sure of getting to a town with a guesthouse. What I didn't want to do was start off badly by pushing Sam. In the end, my fears were allayed, as he was really helpful in getting the bikes ready. Despite a dense mist, we set off in good spirits.

Our worries about reduced fitness seemed unfounded after a few hours. We were heading east at a good pace. This was India's busy Grand Trunk Road, though, which was not a great pleasure. One thing we were sure about: we felt glad to be back to basic Indian *dhabas* (road cafes) when we stopped for lunch.

Turning off the highway into Etawah after a good stretch of 130km, I felt a pang of reluctance due to what I perceived to be a slightly unattractive name. Sam saw me glance suspiciously at the road sign as we turned off. Behind me, I heard him mutter something like "no prejudice, then." The single fleapit guesthouse we found there confirmed my superstitions. Of course, as Sam pointed out, we had been spoilt with four- and five-star hotels for the last three weeks, so my judgement may have been a little biased. All I cared about really was that we were back in expedition mode with a singular focus on the route east. Both Sam and I were experiencing divided emotions, though, with another side of us feeling sad at the recent departure of our family and friends.

The following day really did confirm some validity in my prejudice about place names. After an unpleasant foggy day on the traffic-nightmare that is the Grand Trunk Road, we decided to follow a smaller road across country. We soon arrived in a town named Bognipur. Need I say more? Not only did the name instil trepidation but the road as we came into town might as well have had a sign saying WELCOME TO A LIVING HELL. Deep sticky mud led into a scene of catastrophic, and largely abandoned, attempts at roadworks. An ageing, incomplete flyover with concrete cancer rose above us but ended nowhere. It stunk. The most fume-belching un-maintained trucks in India seemed to be trying to pass through this cauldron of filth. After getting off to walk due to the red sticky mud, our eyes were drawn to roadside stalls where they seemed to be slaughtering all manner of animals. We realised that the mud we were walking through was actually diluted with gallons of animal blood.

A sly-eyed chicken slayer grinned at us as he clumsily gutted half-plucked birds and beckoned us in to watch. We politely declined. This ghoulish butcher, straight out of a Goya painting of purgatory, had rigged up a kind of demonic, beheading production line out of wires and string attached to a sewing-machine motor. Half-starved birds revolved on this contraption, heading towards a Black & Decker drill with a revolving saw blade, and their undignified demise.

Sam pulled his shirt up over his mouth and nose. The whole town stank and clouds of cement dust from the pointless, half-hearted attempt at ongoing road repairs, assailed our eyes and nostrils.

We laughed at the sheer apocalyptic vileness of the place and at just how bad a guesthouse located here might be.

Away from the noise of automated decapitation, we stopped to ask a smartly dressed man where we might find a guesthouse.

"One hundred twenty kilometre north, with disco," we were told. "Not possible by cycle."

A familiar feeling of resignation about communication with people in the countryside returned. We explained that we wanted a workmen's guesthouse not a luxury hotel. He seemed to understand, pointing to a new office-type building and indicating we should follow him. He brought out a couple of office chairs and told us to wait for the boss, who would be there in ten minutes. Bogville seemed to be yet another of those major mosquito breeding colonies and we passed the time in a seated killing spree.

To cut a painfully long story short, the man kept us there for an hour and a half. Each time we motioned to leave, he phoned his boss, reporting back that he would be just another few minutes. Finally, the boss arrived and unlocked the room we were to stay in. It was a bare office room incorporating a stinking hole-in-the-floor toilet.

Smirking now in disbelief, I asked about beds. The boss said he would go into town to get a bed. We were already out the door, furious at being kept waiting for nearly two hours for nothing. They seemed surprised. We asked them for directions to a real guesthouse, which they kindly gave us. We cycled off along what passed for a road on the look out for a motorcycle shop. Above this, we were assured, we would find a workmen's guesthouse called Mahindra Lodge. I liked the sound of this name better. My mood improved. I imagined a large weatherboard house on a prairie.

We found a motorcycle shop in the centre of a village. Sure enough, above it stood Mahindra Lodge. There had once been a sign in Hindi, but most of the letters were now missing. For all we knew, though, this may have been intentional and the remaining letters spelt an Indian insult.

Unable to find an entrance, we asked at the shop. A mechanic, greased up to the armpits, stopped his work and called his boss. Armchairs were set out for us to sit on.

"Oh my God, not this again!"

"Dad, stay calm," I was told. "Remember what we discussed."

He was referring to my promise to try and react calmly and politely in these circumstances. Sam was just doing his job, as I had asked him to following the incident in the hotel in Agra.

It was certainly an improvement on the last place. We were provided with good chai and friendly conversation while someone went for the manager. This time we waited only ten minutes before a man arrived carrying a bunch of prehistoric-looking keys. Doubles-up as a village prison perhaps?

After finishing our chai, we were taken upstairs. Here we were shown two floors of filthy semi-derelict rooms. Some, our grinning host proudly pointed out, had the luxury of decrepit air-conditioning units. All had vintage TVs and barred windows to keep the monkeys out. Glass in the windows seemed sporadic.

"Is glass extra?" I asked.

"Yes, glass extra," he replied seriously.

Sam shook his head in disbelief. The homemade beds were covered with stained brown sheets and filthy old blankets. In a contest between this and the room in Caldiran (Turkey), the Caldiran cell would win hands down. Scraps of newspaper or old clothes were used as curtains and everywhere there was the stench of un-maintained toilets. It was cheap, of course, but it made the heroin-den in Trainspotting look like a palace.

"Very nice," I said with irony to the permanently smiling man. "Is this a chain hotel? I wonder, do you have another hotel in Caldiran, Turkey?"

"No, no. Mahindra Lodge only in Bognipur, sir."

Sam covered his mouth and made a palm-down hand gesture, asking me to go no further.

"We'll take the non-air conditioned room," I said. "We wouldn't want to spoil ourselves."

After dining at a rather good hole-in-the-wall along the street, Sam and I came back and got into our luxurious silk sleeping-bag liners, using our shirts as pillowcases. It would be quite an effective deception once the light was turned off, we agreed. We switched on the TV. It failed to work. I turned the light back on to see why. It lacked a plug and there seemed to be no actual mains socket – just a minor detail.

Sam went downstairs and found Mr Smiley, who came up to fix it. He casually tore off some insulation from the wires with his teeth and then poked the wires into a hole in the wall. Sparks crackled and sprayed into the room, threatening to ignite the filthy blanket and Mr Smiley's greasy overalls. He continued unbothered, keeping his eyes fixed on the screen, waiting for something to appear. The likelihood seemed at the paranormal end of the scale. Something approaching success came, however, after several attempts to wedge the wires in place with a rag. After this, Mr Smiley declared the problem solved and left.

We found this all extremely entertaining until I approached the en-suite bathroom to clean my teeth. This facility consisted of the now-familiar filthy hole in the floor (no footprint pan here, mate), but the mess filling the room was quite unprecedented in Indian toilet history. Decency does not permit further description. I closed the door immediately and cleaned my teeth in the bedroom with my water bottle, even resisting Sam's suggestion to go back in to take a photo.

We settled into our sleeping bag liners on our shared bed, ready for an evening of watching Indian TV. Around this juncture, we were disturbed by a huge rat. Climbing through a hole in our wall up at ceiling level, he ran along the cornicing, then jumped down to floor level and scurried out through the large gap under our door. He seemed to know his way. I wouldn't have minded, but as he passed through, he managed to knock out the TV power cable.

Finding the stairway down now barred by a hefty steel security gate, I broke the news to Sam that our viewing of Terminator 2 – dubbed – was over for the night. Despite having seen this movie two days before, however, Sam was prepared to see me risk electrocution to watch it again. He lay there laughing as I somehow managed to repeat Smiley's magic trick of reconnecting the wires without killing myself or burning down Mahindra Lodge. God knows how we would have escaped if it had have caught fire. With monkey bars on the windows and a single padlocked steel door blocking the way down, we would have been stuffed. The words of a well-known song plagued me far into the night: *You can check out any time you like, but you can never leave.*

Waking early with noise from the street – there was no glass in our window, remember – I found myself eager to get away from Bogville and the Hotel California as soon as possible. I was not complaining. We had managed to get a decent night's sleep with no rat attacks. Sam had blocked the window with the photo-scrapbook his friends made him for Christmas. During the night, however, I had found myself needing a pee with no lights working. Feeling my way cautiously out into the corridor, I confirmed my suspicion that there was no toilet out there. With a sense of dread, I returned to the prospect of using our evil en-suite. Although knocked back by the powerful aroma as I slowly opened the door, I finally contrived a system of peeing from outside into the small blackened basin hanging off the wall just inside the door. My guess is that I was not the first to try this. I quickly discovered that the basin was not plumbed in anyway, so anything you poured into it ran out onto the floor, and therefore onto your feet.

*

The following three days saw us cycling through rural India on varying qualities of road and track. This played havoc with my luggage rack, which now constantly required tightening and re-bodging, but I was determined to try to help this sub-standard rack complete its tour of duty back to England.

The advantage of cycling through these rural areas was the absence of continuous traffic, and the wildlife. Parrots, vultures and wild cats stared at us from beside the roads. Now the weather was beginning to turn cooler, we frequently came across the bemusing sight of flocks of goats wearing hand-me-down jumpers or t-shirts. The downside was the obscenely healthy mosquito population. We began to question our plan of not beginning our Malarone tablets until arriving at the first known high-risk malarial area of Cambodia.

Sam and I managed to find fairly good accommodation in Fatehpur and Allahabad. The road for the last horrendous 80km into Allahabad was another work-in-progress resurfacing job that looked like it had been progressing haphazardly for years.

Our next break was to be in the ancient pilgrimage city of Varanasi (Benares). It was also a place we were expecting to be quite special, so it was no surprise that this last stretch seemed to go on forever.

The poverty we witnessed in the small towns and villages along the Grand Trunk Road to Varanasi was some of the worst we had seen so far. In one, I remember squalid little huts sited amid pools of sewage, surrounded by domestic rubbish and cows feeding off it. Naked children with filthy faces played happily in the pools while their mothers sat outside their huts sewing plastic sheeting together to replace their makeshift roofs. Meanwhile, their fathers were defecating publicly into the same water the children were playing in. A little further along the road we passed a recently dead cow being ripped apart by a pack of hungry dogs.

These desperate scenes stunned us to silence for quite a while. We pressed on without stopping – less due to concerns about hygiene than the stones and sticks thrown at us by children. We saw precious little sign of anywhere to eat. We were both suffering with digestive upsets again, however, despite having returned to a vegetarian diet, so there was no need.

Eventually, in the bustling, traffic-clogged city of Varanasi, Sam and I made our way to Hotel Ajaya, near to the centre. We planned to rest for a couple of days. A young *tuk-tuk* driver led us there. Expecting a demand of payment, I took out some coins, but he refused, handing Sam a card with his number on it.

"Please to call me when you need to go somewhere," he shouted.

So our first impressions were not all bad. We checked in with a sense of cautious optimism.

Time was moving on and we were aware of our visa expiry date looming uncomfortably closer. We needed to get to Calcutta to make a last-ditch effort at finding a boat around Burma to Thailand, rather than having to fly again. This was looking less and less likely, though, after our numerous internet searches, enquiries at travel agents and talking to other travellers. I had even asked a travel agent friend in London.

Back in the UK, we had clung onto a hope that the political situation in Burma might improve by the time we got there, allowing us to cycle through Burma and into Thailand that way, but the improvement had not materialised.

Sam's persistent digestive problems still seemed unresponsive to methods of natural treatment – 24 hours of fasting followed by light food for a few days. Although it got no worse, I was worrying about it again; not so worried, though, that I was prepared to suggest a course of Indian antibiotics. This was a naive prejudice.

We took advantage of being in a city to see whether a day or two of western-style food might settle his stomach. Pizza and ice cream certainly cheered Sam up and made him no worse, but sadly it was not the cure he had hoped for.

On our second day in Varanasi we visited the sacred Kedareshewara Temple. The bathing steps at Kedar Ghat on the broad majestic Ganges were as astounding as I remembered them in a geography book at school.   We were taken there by the crazy young tuk-tuk driver who had led us to the hotel the day before.   He careered down narrow pedestrian streets, at one point getting the tuk-tuk jammed between two buildings.   Finally, he parked right by the ghat, before escorting us along the steps.   The tourist police spotted him immediately and asked if this boy was bothering us.   He did not have a registered tour guide badge.   The policeman seemed infinitely more suspect than our driver, so we told him we were his friends.

On the way back, the boy pointed out a large black limousine that was passing us, followed by a pack of motorcycles with cheering riders.

"Who is that?" we asked.

"Baba-ji," said our driver with a big smile.

I knew this meant something like *The Daddy*, as I told Sam afterwards.   We guessed it might be a local wrestler.   On the TV news later, however, hearing the term *Baba Tibet*, we realised that it had been the Dali Lama on an official visit.   Now, every time I see him on TV, I can't help visualising him as a pro-wrestler in a leotard.

Varanasi seemed like a good place to hang out – and under different circumstances we might have done that – but we needed to move on.   Sam seemed weak and we were told by the hotel manager that the majority of the road to Calcutta was undergoing major reconstruction.   This would make it terrible for cycling, he said.

"In five years, it will be a road to be proud of indeed."

Sam was reluctant to take another train, but I was concerned about the combination of his health, the state of the road and our visa deadline.   If his illness got worse or something broke on the bikes, it could add up to a lot of stress.   Sam agreed that this seemed a pointless risk to take and would leave us with bad memories of India. We went to the station to check on trains to Calcutta.   Remembering the enjoyable journey from Karnataka to Goa back in November, we were relieved to find sleeper tickets available for the next night.

*

"Are you wishing to take weapons on the train, sir?"
"Weapons, no.   Why do you ask?"

When we arrived in Calcutta in the early morning, after a three-hour delay and a fitful sleep, we were surprised how busy the station was. Pushing our way through the crowds, we arrived at the goods carriage at the back of our train and were horrified to see an enormous heap of junk, coal and vegetables on top of a tangled mess of bicycles and motorbikes. A thuggish young goods porter was literally attacking this mountain with a lethal metal hook, ripping open sacks and spilling vegetables all over the platform. Meanwhile, the owners of the produce and station staff nervously remonstrated with him. Periodically, the porter paused to shout manically at these people, pushing them away and threatening them with the large lethal-looking hook. "Hey!" I shouted, worried about our bikes. He wheeled round on me with manic eyes, brandishing his hook and shouting in my face. His mouth was foaming.

From the submissive train guard, I established that the goods porter had felt it was time to go off duty.   First, however, he had been instructed to empty the goods carriage of this late arrival. No doubt he had some important appointment to keep, but he seemed mentally ill. It would not have surprised me to discover he had been bitten by a rabid dog. Only after he had uncovered the bicycles and motorcycles beneath – wrenching them off the train with his hook – did I realised our bikes were not there. My initial relief changed to a deeper concern.   Weighed down with our panniers, Sam and I hurriedly fought our way through the onlookers to reach the parcel office.

At the desk, we saw our bikes parked safely by the shelves of parcels. My luggage rack was broken again on both sides and would require further temporary repairs, but we felt lucky that the bikes had no grappling iron damage. In fact, we were surprised that they were there at all. Requisite papers signed, we began looking for bits of suitable discarded junk to bodge the rack with. There was plenty around.

A combination of hosepipe, duct tape and a butchered Thumbs-up cola-can solved the immediate problem. After this, we headed off across seething Howrah Bridge into central Calcutta. We were heading for the Red Shield hostel in Sudder Street, but we were to be disappointed. The building was missing.

At the Continental Guest House opposite, we were given a room and told that the Red Shield had been demolished a few months earlier. The Continental was really centrally located, with plenty of cafes and restaurants in the street below our small room. It was cheap and they were happy to let us carry our bikes up to the room. It was a relief to be here, on the doorstep of Southeast Asia – the next stage of our journey.

I knew this would feel very different. Sam seemed to know it too without me telling him. The climate and topography may be similar, but the mentality of Southeast Asians is quite different from that of Indians. I was looking forward to it. I like their efficiency. In particular, I like the food.

Although Sam and I had enjoyed eating Indian food, we had, like most western travellers, succumbed to food poisoning a few times. Sam was still suffering from the same sensitivity and repetitive stomach upsets that had been holding him back since Tamil Nadu.

The other big change for us would be that we were due to be joined by a friend from Canterbury for a few weeks. Cycling with another person might help the situation between Sam and I. Then again, having two older companions instead of one might make it worse. I hoped not.

Around the corner from our guesthouse we found a good internet café, although the post-Mumbai Siege anti-terrorist measures were annoying. Internet cafes now demanded the deposit of your passport before you went online. This worried us, since it was easy to leave without it.

Online, we made final checks about the possibility of a boat to Thailand, but our worst fears were confirmed. Reluctantly, we moved on to checking prices for flights. This was more fruitful. Later, we found a good flight-booking agent on a street stall. Here we got a good budget flight to Bangkok leaving a few days later – just before our visas expired.

Sam looked unhappy about flying, but there was no choice unless we waited until spring to ride north via the Himalayas. Although a boat was available from Chennai, that would be a major detour back south and I suspected we might get there and find this had also been suspended. I reminded Sam that at least we could make up the distance, as we now we planned to detour up into Cambodia from Bangkok.

I also emailed Brian, a friend of a friend from England, who lived in Bangkok and had kindly invited us to stay with him for a few days. Things were shaping up well for our next leg and my enthusiasm was mounting. Sam did his best, but he still looked reluctant. I think his poor health at this point must have been a large part of that.

I feel Calcutta would have been very different if we had arrived there at the start of the India leg rather than the end. It makes a big difference to get to a place just before you move on to another country. Although we enjoyed Calcutta, our minds were constantly on our arrangements for moving forwards and it was hard to avoid thinking about Thailand.

*

Back in Canterbury, we had discussed the possibility of our friend Martin Ashton joining us. A few weeks in Thailand or Burma might be possible, he said. He was due to take early retirement. Sam and I had both cycled with Martin before and felt fairly confident it would work, although Martin had expressed his concern about the inevitable gap between our fitness levels at that stage of our trip. He had not bargained on Sam being ill, though, any more than we had.

Over Christmas, we received final confirmation from Martin that he would meet us in Thailand and cycle for about three weeks with us through Thailand into Laos, before flying home again. It was at that point we agreed to detour via Cambodia if Burma was a no-go.

In the last few days before we left India, I talked with Sam about Martin coming. He did seem to be looking forward to it, agreeing that it would change the pace and dynamics for a while. Sam pointed out that if I was going to write a book, it might also be beneficial later on to have had a third-party observer to report on the interaction between him and I – things we might not recognise ourselves. There was also the small thrill of Martin having asked for a shopping list from us. This largely consisted of special luxuries we had been craving, such as wine gums, jaffa cakes, liquorice and Lindt 85% chocolate.

We thoroughly enjoyed our five days in Calcutta. Steve had recommended it highly from his own Indian trips. We did manage to fit in a little cultural tourism too. At the internet cafe, I asked Sam to research places to visit and he came up with a list of the highest-rated attractions. I was sceptical about the Indian Museum – the largest museum collection in Asia – being listed as the number one thing to see but I was pleasantly surprised. The collections of plants, bones, stuffed animals, pottery, sculpture, etc. were displayed within a stunning example of British colonial architecture and we hung about there far longer than we had expected.

In the city centre, we found some excellent restaurants and cafes, along with Mother Theresa's mission. Relaxing over an Indian buffet lunch at our favourite Malgudi Junction afterwards, we agreed that Calcutta had made it onto our list of places worth coming back to.

The only thing that put a downer on this time was the prospect of having to fly again. As I have said before, this creates a sudden jump between cultures; also, it would be stressful getting the bikes onto the plane and hoping they didn't get damaged. But there were no other options.

Getting to the airport started things off with stress, due to a lack of road signs. Most visitors go by taxi, we supposed. As in Iran, we turned up at the check-in desk with our bikes and were met with open-mouthed incredulity from the desk staff.

"Sir, I regret to inform you that you can't take these cycles on the plane. It is…"

I had prepared for this in advance.

"Thank you," I replied, smiling calmly. "Don't worry, it's fine. We've done it before."

Luckily, they immediately rescinded their objections. Two of the staff casually wheeled the bikes onto the plane, this time without any packing, and an hour or so later we found them parked by the baggage carousel in Bangkok Airport. In the end, it couldn't have been easier.

SAM'S POINT OF VIEW

The Christmas break was really great.   I released a lot of the tension that had built up with my dad, by talking to my friend Luke and my then-girlfriend, Hannah.   Being able to have sex again was pretty fantastic.   We stayed in really expensive hotels from the moment my family and friends arrived.   Mum, Hannah, my younger sister Scarlett, Steve, my friend Ellie, Luke and his family all helped to make a kind of party atmosphere.   I knew then that Christmas was going to be really sweet, and it was.   I couldn't believe we'd got more than halfway.   New Year was brilliant as well.   The firework display was delayed until ten past midnight, but that's pretty good going for India.

I remember being really pissed off with my dad telling people stories about his own experiences, which on reflection is weird.   There was nothing wrong with this, but it made me livid at the time.   It's an indication of how short-fused I was with him.   I feel bad thinking about it now, but at the time I was certain I was in the right and he was just a massive pain in the arse who didn't deserve my company. Hah!   What an absolute tool I was!

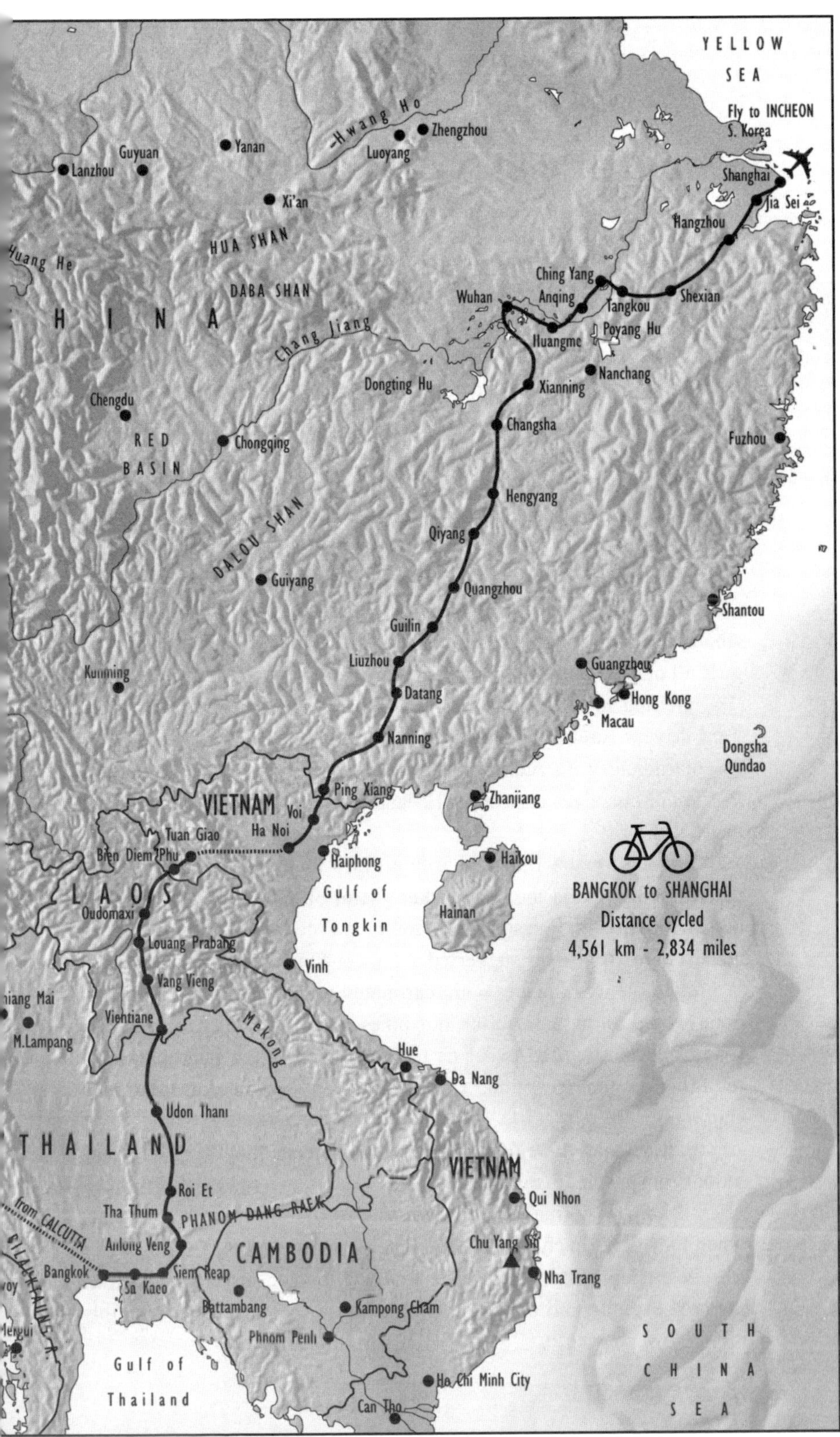

YELLOW
SEA
Fly to INCHEON
S. Korea
Lanzhou
Guyuan
Yanan
Hwang Ho
Zhengzhou
Luoyang
Shanghai
Jia Sei
Hangzhou
Xi'an
HUA SHAN
Ching Yang
Anqing
Shexian
Tangkou
DABA SHAN
Wuhan
Huang He
CHINA
Chang Jiang
Huangme
Poyang Hu
Nanchang
Chengdu
Dongting Hu
Xianning
RED
BASIN
Chongqing
Changsha
Fuzhou
DALOU SHAN
Hengyang
Qiyang
Guiyang
Quangzhou
Shantou
Guilin
Kunming
Liuzhou
Guangzhou
Datang
Hong Kong
Macau
Nanning
Dongsha
Qundao
Ping Xiang
VIETNAM
Voi
Zhanjiang
Tuan Giao
Ha Noi
Bien Diem Phu
Haiphong
Haikou
LAOS
Gulf of
Oudomaxi
Hainan
Tongkin
Louang Prabang
Vang Vieng
Vinh
iang Mai
Vientiane
Mekong
M.Lampang
Hue
Da Nang
Udon Thani
BANGKOK to SHANGHAI
Distance cycled
4,561 km - 2,834 miles
THAILAND
VIETNAM
Roi Et
Qui Nhon
Tha Thum
PHANOM DANG RAEK
from CALCUTTA
Chu Yang Sin
Anlong Veng
CAMBODIA
Bangkok
Siem Reap
Nha Trang
Sa Kaeo
Battambang
Kampong Cham
Phnom Penh
SOUTH
Gulf of
CHINA
Thailand
Ho Chi Minh City
SEA
Can Tho

Chapter 10

Southeast Asia – Joined by a friend for four weeks

Mister, we like your son, please.   You give me money.   We take him very good time.   No problem for you; my mother come here three or four minute.

Arriving abruptly in Thailand, we were prepared for a sudden change in culture after eastern India.   The first thing we noticed was how clean it seemed.   I felt more comfortable, despite not really minding a bit of dirt.   For Sam, it was another big first.   He had never visited the Orient and was immediately intoxicated by it.   The perfumed smells, faster pace after India, quick-talking people and sweet-natured girls all made a powerful impression on him.

Getting into Bangkok from the airport was bound to be a pain. Taxi drivers, street-stall vendors, policemen and pedestrians all gave us contradictory instructions before we finally got on the right road. We found ourselves on a busy 12-lane highway leading right into the heart of the city.

Having visited Bangkok a few times many years before, I felt determined to avoid the backpacker ghetto of Khao San Road, so we began looking for guesthouses around the central Sukhumvit Road area, where Brian had suggested we meet him.   This was not easy. We found plenty of places with reasonably priced rooms available, but none would allow us to bring our bikes inside.   Finally, though, we found one that agreed to let us put our bikes in the bedroom.   On returning to the reception, I was pleased to see a dog-tired Sam smiling.

"OK, Sam, we've finally persuaded someone that bringing a bike indoors isn't weird – we can stay."

"Dad, is it normal here for women to stroke your arms?   I mean, when they don't even know you?"

We telephoned Brian, who arranged to meet us along the road the next evening and transfer us to his house.   He seemed incredibly pleasant, and happy about us coming to stay, so I felt pleased I had taken up the invitation of contacting him. Like anyone, I have doubts about such situations with people I don't know.

Brian turned out to be a great guy. He and his wife had just moved into a spacious new home on the outskirts of the city with their two bulldogs – Ketchup and Pork Leg. After a 45km bike ride through the densest of traffic to the suburbs where Brian lived, we relaxed into a more sedate pace of life, watching UK TV and being well looked after by the maids. We also heard details of the global financial meltdown that was to dominate the news well beyond the end of our trip. At the time, it seemed a million miles from our world.

Brian and Gik's house gave us a calm base from which to organise our China visas and plan our onward route through Cambodia, Thailand and Laos, most of which Brian had cycled through himself on various expeditions. A few days later, we collected our visas for China without any of the anticipated problems. Martin arrived the same morning.

We had booked a large three-bed room in a very friendly hostel in Bangkok's Chinatown district and had agreed to stay there for three nights after Martin's arrival. This allowed him to acclimatise and hire himself a bike from a company recommended by Brian. It all went off very smoothly, enabling us to spend the rest of the week enjoying ourselves as well as fighting the temptation to eat all the treats Martin had brought in one depraved session.

Discussing our plans for the following weeks and listening to Sam's descriptions of our typical cycling days so far, Martin wanted to make one thing quite clear.

"I'm sorry, I signed up for cycling 100km a day, so 100km is the most I'll be doing. If you two want to go further than that, you're welcome, but you'll be leaving me behind."

"Oh no, that sounds great, Martin," said Sam, delighted, "I'll be sticking with you."

During Martin's acclimatisation days, we took river taxis way upriver to wander around street markets, checked out Chinatown restaurants and met Brian and his friends for home-food and Guinness at the Dubliner before a surprise low-key tour of Patpong clubs. This last interlude had been arranged for Sam's cultural education, Brian said. In fact, Sam found it all a bit unpleasant – a point I felt was a good learning experience in itself.   This was one of the only negative elements of Thailand for Sam.   Although he enjoyed the friendliness of some of the hostess girls, he found the whole sex-consumer fixation of ageing Western men just too unsavoury.

*

And so the cycling recommenced.   Surely Martin was not serious about the 100km a day?

Heading out of Bangkok in mad traffic after collecting Martin's bike, we kept going until lunchtime, when finally the Thai countryside began, and stopped at a wayside cafe.   After vegetable fried-rice, Sam and I perused the large menu of soya-milk shakes.   Surprised at this, Martin teased us that it was a bit girly.

Although not big on desserts back home, Sam and I had developed a penchant for this kind of thing and no amount of macho ribbing was about to make us feel shy about it.   The bizarre twist in proceedings came when Martin, in sudden defiance of his rather traditional masculine eating habits, ordered a shake for himself. More surprising still was that what arrived in front of him was the most lurid girly-pink shake imaginable.   Through the parasols and whipped cream, he proceeded to drink it through the straw in a most coquettish manner.

Having Martin around certainly made life more interesting. Along with his non-negotiable rule about 100km per day, we now found ourselves drinking beer at lunchtime, buying Thai whisky most evenings and partying on guesthouse verandas well into the night. This seemed to cheer Sam up a lot.   He even came to thinking that strong alcohol improved his digestive troubles.

Sam liked the 100km per day schedule for a while too, although in the first week this often meant him hanging back to keep Martin company while I impatiently tore off ahead.   This was a job Sam did very well.   It brought out the compassionate side of him that I remember most when Scarlett was little – Sam was the only one she would allow to do things for her.   After a week of short cycling days,

I certainly came to see there was some pleasure to be gained from Martin's more relaxed approach, especially in such beautiful and culturally interesting locations.

In India, a Canadian couple on bikes had warned us that the road from Bangkok to Siem Reap in Cambodia had been so nightmarish for them they turned back soon after the Cambodian border and took a bus from Bangkok instead. Apparently, even the bus (up to its axles in mud) had struggled to make it. We asked a few people and were told this was only true in the monsoon season. It seemed plausible. Probably another traveller's tall tale, I concluded.

It is about 215km from the Cambodian border to Siem Reap – the main town adjacent to the famous temples of Angkor Wat. The halfway point is the small town of Si Sophon. Here, we spent a comfortable night in a modern guesthouse. Up to this point, the road had a pretty good asphalt surface. Then, 20km out of Si Sophon, we arrived at signs saying "Roadworks" and the surface turned to yellow dust (mud, of course, when it rains).

Reminiscent of India, the roadworks seem to have been here for as long as most people can remember. It has all the hallmarks of a political feud. Each day, huge road-rolling vehicles arrive and flatten the dust that has become rutted by cars, trucks and buses. The curse for bicycles, though, is that they flatten it with a kind of square-toothed roller. This creates a compacted, deeply indented surface designed to provide more grip for cars, etc. moving at speed. For a cyclist, the surface is hell, mercilessly shaking your nuts and bolts, teeth and bones, eyeballs and balls, for hours on end. After the Roadworks sign, we tried to bear it patiently, waiting for it to end, looking constantly at the horizon for an asphalt road that never materialised. Why had nobody told us about this in Si Sophon or at the border?

Stopping for lunch we asked a coach driver at a café how much further the roadworks went. We were not entirely surprised when he told us that they continued like this for another 60km - all the way to Siem Reap. It seemed impossible to bear another 60km of this without walking, but the prospect of camping by the side of the godforsaken dusty road seemed worse, so we kept going. By the end, despite some pleasant countryside, we had come to detest

Cambodia.   I began to prepare a case in my head for heading back to Thailand after Angkor Wat rather than continuing through up the Mekong River to Laos.

The road really took its toll on all of us.   Once installed in our Siem Reap hostel, we found ourselves suffering collective sense-of-humour failure.   Over the next day, each of us separately talked to the guesthouse manager and other travellers about the state of the roads in Cambodia: whether the one north via Anlong Veng into Thailand was surfaced, whether this northwestern border was open to foreigners (Lonely Planet said not), and whether there was enough to see to warrant taking the chance.

Martin and I concluded from our research that it was best to take a bus back to the same Thai border then head up to Laos through Thailand.   Sam insisted this would be copping out and that Cambodian roads would be fine if we took the boat south through the lakes.   Martin and I pointed out that we didn't have time to go south if we were to keep to our schedule.

This seemed to exasperate Sam more than anything else on the trip so far.   He felt Martin and I, as older people, were ganging up on him, treating his opinions as naive and irrelevant.   It felt likely that Sam would insist on going off on his own in Cambodia, which seemed an unwise prospect.   So Martin, who missed his vocation as a diplomat, suggested we go and put our options to the guesthouse staff, pin them down about critical things, listen to their advice and then make a group decision, if we could.   This seemed a good plan to me. If it still meant Sam going off on his own, then so be it.

All of this had distracted us from the primary purpose of detouring into Cambodia in the first place – the mysterious temples of Angkor Wat.   Switching our focus, we took a day off from worrying about our next move and spent it at these fabulous ruins.

Part of the attraction of these temples is the fact that they have not been over-restored.   In fact, many of the ruins at Angkor Wat are rapidly being absorbed by the surrounding forests.   Anyone who has fought ivy in their garden should imagine the same thing magnified to 100 times the size.   With powerful roots growing down between the huge stones of Angkor Thom and the hypnotically beautiful faces of the Bayon statues, it seems like the whole beautiful place is about to be devoured and returned to the earth.   Sam secretly seemed to enjoy this day.   Although photographs taken at the time are marred by his grumpy expression, by the evening he appeared to have thawed a great deal.

Siem Reap is a town that depends almost entirely on western tourists – most of them flying in from points worldwide.   This means numerous good-quality restaurants in the small centre that have a feel more like waterfront San Francisco than a town in Cambodia.   One such restaurant is named the Red Piano.   Despite the high prices, it was so good we ate there two nights running.

We ate at this kind of place more often with Martin around.   It may have been an underlying sense of missing out on treats like this that brought Sam around to the idea that it might be better to stick together.   When we approached the guesthouse staff that night, he seemed a lot less confrontational and inclined to go it alone.

Trying to pin down whether the northwestern border with Thailand was open to foreigners, and how bad the road was, proved to be worthwhile.   The manager assured us that he had dropped several groups off at that very border in recent weeks, and also received email confirmation of them getting through.   That was all we needed: we agreed to take a chance on the road north.   The manager described it as mostly a dusty dirt track but not rolled with a studded roller and not muddy at this time of year.

*

In the evening, when Sam was out on his own, Martin talked to me a bit about him.   I felt disloyal complaining.   Martin had plenty of parenting experience of his own, including a fairly long spell bringing up a young son alone.   He helped me not to feel I was being unreasonable but still remained sympathetic to Sam's difficulties.   He must have talked to Sam on his own later as well, because Sam certainly seemed much calmer about things by the time we came to set off upcountry.

All of this took me back to my struggles with my own father in my early teens.   I remembered that I used to be infuriated by what I saw as arrogance over his opinions, even though I knew at the same time what he was saying was right.   I can see now that these feelings in teenagers are in fact a longing to feel that their opinions count for something – a desire to feel like a grown-up.   They accuse the adults close to them of being arrogant, when in fact it is about them experiencing frustration at their lack of comparative knowledge.

In my case, I have no doubt now that my own arrogance as a teenager far exceeded that of my father.   Not a criticism that could be made of Sam, I'm glad to say.   My emotions over my wrangling with Sam must have been influenced by these memories, since my mood became overwhelmingly sad.

By the time I was fifteen, I believe my father, having reached an extreme state of frustration in his failure to guide me in the *right* direction, had reluctantly accepted my abnormal personality as incurable.   As he began to back off from his determination to direct me, I began to see just how much stress this had caused him. Despite remaining resolved to fighting authority and conditioning, I longed to apologise and to try to help him see that my difference from him and from other people was only *different*, not *wrong*.   After a troubled summer holiday, my dad drove me back to boarding school and I struggled to get the words out, but they would not come.   I was not quite ready.   It was the last time I ever saw him.   He died of a burst artery aged only 37.   For many years, I believed the stress I had induced in him had killed him.   Worse still was the resulting sense of guilt about feeling free of his control.

I didn't feel like I deserved the vitriolic criticism I was getting from Sam.   Then again, perhaps I did, on the basis of having been the same with my own father.   With Sam, I felt at a loss, not knowing how to respond for the best.   Having Martin around certainly helped, though.   Since then, I have come to the conclusion that it is usually best to go out of one's way as the adult to ask for the opinions of a teenager more than might seem warranted.   It is difficult, though, to get the balance right without seeming patronising – a bit of a parenting tightrope, to say the least.

"Just because I'm only 19, you think I'm automatically wrong. I can understand why you guys would think that – after all, you've been around a lot longer than me.   But in this case, you're both wrong."

*

Due to the dust, the ride up to Anlong Veng was fairly tough, but it was far from unpleasant. More worrying were the large areas of burning forest, where local farmers were clearing the forest to grow cash crops. It looked, in a sinister way, too much like scenes from Apocalypse Now or The Killing Fields. Our main problem was misinformation and the lack of proper maps. Everyone we asked gave a different figure for the distance from Siem Reap to Anlong Veng: 120km, 128km and 140km were all given as firm assurances. Using his un-detailed map, Martin concluded it was 160km, supporting his case for it not being possible to cycle in a day. I certainly felt it would not be possible to find anywhere to stay on the way, unless three full-sized men were happy to squeeze into a small two-man tent. Unsurprisingly, I was determined to do it in a day; but I didn't want to be seen as in any way dogmatic about it. Nor did I want to risk reigniting Sam's sense of being railroaded. As it turned out, we managed to reach Anlog Veng as the sun set. We found ourselves a rather good guesthouse too.

The locals seemed to take great pride in telling us that the Khmer Rouge had their camps in this area, but I suppose they have little else to attract tourism. We encountered a more unpleasantly mercenary atmosphere here, all the more noticeable after the excessive generosity we had found in rural Thailand. At one of the many street stalls, run by a mother and daughter, we were presented with a staggeringly inflated bill at the end of a meagre snack. It was more than we had paid for our rooms.

We had bought a few other things in shops along the road so we knew the value of money and objected. Cursing ourselves for not checking all the prices first, we asked the daughter to itemise the bill. It seemed the expensive item had been the tough scrap of meat. This had been forced on us and we hadn't actually eaten it. The women immediately became very aggressive and refused to negotiate. When I suggested they fetch the police, the daughter went berserk banging bowls and cutlery and pointing fingers in our faces. I noticed the old woman fingering a large kitchen knife. Finally, not in the mood for

229

an argument, or having our heads cut off, we paid up and left with further bad feelings about Cambodia. The two women laughed mockingly. They had clearly watched too many American war films.

"Hah, you don' like lose your big money, Hollywood! Cambodia people, no *stoopit*! You come back, give me more, tomorrow."

It always surprises me how overland travellers find themselves arguing over what are relatively small sums of money back home. I think it's about a sense that you will be bled dry if you let your discipline slip. Whatever the cause, the two women were responsible for some serious damage to Cambodia's reputation.

Our return to Thailand the next day was as pleasant a contrast as we expected it to be, with generous, friendly service at the very first café, immediately after crossing through the tiny border post. It was a hot day (44 degrees) and the road had become rather hilly for the first time in months.

We were no longer used to big hills. That evening, pulling into a modern roadside motel we remarked on our tired legs. After a good dinner, we agreed that we deserved a few Chang beers and a bottle of Sangsom whisky to celebrate our happy return to Thailand. The shaky scrawl in my diary betrays an evening of merriment. We apparently lost hold of reality, enough for me to extract a pledge from Sam and Martin that from now on they would achieve an easily achievable minimum of 60km per day, regardless of start time or terrain. The punishment for failure – which seemed reasonable at the time – would involve the offender having to return to England in a dress, with the name in their passport changed to Martina, Samantha or Marcia.

It sounds like something from a stag weekend or Animal House movie, but we needed to let off steam after the conflict and resentment built up in Siem Reap. We ended this little celebration with a late walk around to the petrol station's 7-Eleven shop, where we purchased three Blueberry *Teascake* cornettos – sadly never found again after this day. The memory of our failed sense of humour had, thank goodness, been left far behind in Cambodia.

The following day continued in a positive vein, cycling along a small road through attractive countryside. It ended with us being taken to a nice motel in pleasantly named Tha Tum by a Belgian guy on a motorbike. The motel was run by his German friend, Hans. We guessed he was a bit of a joker when we saw the large poster of the New York skyline in reception. On it was stuck a Lufthansa airliner, heading for the twin towers.

Taking a cooling swim in the pool, we began to get a clearer picture of Hans' usual clientele – the surrounding tiles featured explicit sexual silhouette designs. At the motel, though, we met a French cyclist named Clement, who had peddled to Thailand from Lyon in France nearly a year before and certainly did not seem like a sex tourist. He had stayed there on and off since his arrival, he told us, passing back and forth to Laos for visa purposes. We met a number of Europeans like him in Thailand. Most had come on an extended holiday and not wanted to leave. We could see why. For every one of them, however, we met many single older men who had come on the short package holidays known locally as *Shag 'n Go* and stayed on (*Shag 'n Stay?*).

After the infectious negativity of Cambodia, things certainly seemed to be going much better for us back in infectiously positive Thailand. Sam had also returned to his happy if slightly sceptical self.

The opportunity to get Martin's perspective on things was a big help for me, and I suspect it was for Sam too. It helped me to see things in a more balanced way; I certainly felt more proud of Sam than I had before. As Martin pointed out, at least he was not just going along with everything I wanted to do. Sam's view is that Martin's presence increased the fun level of the trip and also helped him to understand my perspective better. I think we all gained.

*

One of the main towns in northeast Thailand is Roi Et. It is not on tourist maps and Lonely Planet credits it with little beyond a very tall, slim Buddha. Even so, the town became one of the highlights of Thailand for us, although the reason for extending our stay was unwelcome to Martin.

We had looked around for a guesthouse or cheap hotel for an hour or more and were shown some truly abysmal rooms. Finally, irritated by these repeated disappointments, we followed a professional-looking sign to the Roi Et City Centre Hotel. On arrival, we found a seven-storey five-star hotel. Although doubtful, we agreed to go in and see if they would give us a deal.

Offered a good discount on an already reasonable rate, along with satellite TV and buffet breakfast, we agreed to live it up here for the night. By late that evening, though, we were worried. Martin had shunned the offer of a glass of whisky in the room, so we knew something must be very wrong, even before he took up semi-permanent residence in the bathroom. Not even Manchester United vs Everton followed by Liverpool vs Chelsea on TV could bring him around. In the morning, he broke it to us that he would not be cycling anywhere that day. At this point, it would have been unkind to remind him about the dress.

With good feelings about Roi Et, we needed no encouragement to stay longer. Sam and I booked a further night for us all and we went off to explore, leaving Martin to sleep (suffer in isolation). Nearby, we found excellent traditional self-service restaurants, as well as a kind of Rocky Mountain Cabin-style restaurant by the river, where we decided to have dinner. Meanwhile, Martin had been out looking for a chemist shop but found a clinic instead. Here he received some medication, along with instructions from the doctor to eat only plain rice for 24 hours. His enjoyment of the Cabin's menu that night was therefore somewhat restricted.

The following morning, Martin felt he needed a further day's recovery, so we agreed that Sam and I would continue on up to Vientiane, the Laotian capital. Martin would meet us there a day or so later, assuming he lived. After a decent breakfast, we headed off along a good road to the small rural town of Kranuan, where we arrived after 112km around 4pm. Sam and I had discussed the possibility of pushing hard to reach Tha Khanto in the hills by a lake, but I was keen not to regain a reputation for slave-driving. When I suggested we stop in Kranuan, Sam's face told me my concern was well founded. I was learning. I was also eager to dispel any suspicion that without Martin, I would immediately begin pushing him to go faster and further.

The following morning, we encountered a strong headwind and some fairly hilly countryside. This combined with the 42-degree heat to seriously wear us out. Despite everything, we managed to get to the small city of Udon Thani after 112km by around 2.30pm. Dodging traffic on the outer ring road, we found it impossible to resist following a sign saying, AUSSIE BAR WITH ACCOMMODATION. The bar was fine, despite some seedy Shag 'n Stay types. The most notable, and deplorable, of these was a swearing three-toothed Gollum-esque ex-plumber from Blackburn. This freak of nature lisped his way lasciviously through descriptions of the young women he could *pull* here. He honestly believed they wanted him for his rugged good looks. Martin is originally from Blackburn, so I was cruelly tempted to text him and suggest he meet up with this delightful chap on the way up. As it was, the Aussie hostel's rooms were full, so we took up an offer to be shown some hotels by an English guy from Eastbourne. He was with his elderly mother and father, and seemed less lascivious. Looks can be deceiving.

There was a Harley Davidson rally in Udon Thani that weekend and, after visiting every establishment the man knew, we had to settle for a fleapit by a busy crossing with no glass in the windows. I cursed the magnetic attraction of signs saying Aussie Bar that had pulled us off the road early to end up in this dump. Unsurprisingly, we got little sleep in our grotty room, and set off at crack of dawn. On our way out, the hotel night porter proudly informed us that Udon Thani has the reputation of providing most of the *best* girls in Bangkok's Patpong clubs. This dubious accolade did nothing to enhance its already poor image in our eyes.

We had not rushed to get to Vientiane – partly because we knew Martin needed to catch us up, and partly because we knew that the Vietnamese Embassy would be closed until Monday. We pedalled off along the highway with the same easy pace of the last few days, crossing Friendship Bridge at the Laotian border around midday and arriving in Vientiane around 2pm.

Just after the border, our first Laotian lunch experience gave us positive feelings about the weeks to come. As in many theoretically poor countries, the food in Laos is limited in range, relying on what can easily be grown or reared in people's small gardens. This, however, means everything is usually very fresh and pretty cheap.

I say *theoretically poor* for good reason. Some months later, I was showing someone some of our photos of Laos – small villages with people sitting outside their small wooden houses on stilts, kids cycling back from a day fishing in a nearby river with homemade spear guns, etc – and they said to me something about the people being poor. I was immediately confused. They were not poor, definitely not, I replied.

This was not any kind of politically correct statement. It was my immediate reaction before I had given any thought to the country's economic standing. In reality, if one looks at economic statistics for Laos – GDP, how many people own cars, how many can afford to travel, etc – then they are certainly very poor. In fact, though, people live fairly comfortably in their little wooden houses, growing their own vegetables, keeping a few chickens and a small pig, maybe even a cow. So they eat well and smile most of the time. They have most of the things they need in life. They are all nicely dressed and mostly they have a television and mobile phones along with a small motorbike to get around locally.

Immediately we arrived in Laos we liked it. You could feel the calm atmosphere and we were constantly warmed by the sincere smiles on people's faces. They all seemed happy. Not something we are used to in Europe. They gained pleasure from different things. Shopping was not a big pastime here. I discovered that what the Laotians can't buy they generally make themselves. You see very little disease, vagrancy or misery and they do have basic public healthcare. From what I could understand, they have very little crime or divorce. They are also seldom in a rush and there is almost no stress or pressure. There are noticeably few factories so there is little or no drudgery in these people's work and the children go to low-pressure schools. Poor? I don't think so. I honestly feel that Laos is one of the nicest countries I have ever visited. I am not naïve enough, however, to believe that it will stay this way.

*

Our first lunch was the standard Laotian meal of feu (pronounced *fur*). This is a bowl of noodle soup with a varied basket of delicious green vegetable leaves that you place, one bunch at a time, into the hot broth. It is delicious, always super-fresh, and usually very nourishing. Along with this, we ate some chicken fried rice and drank an excellent Beer Laos – pretty much the only beer in Laos and the company seemed the country's most successful by far. Almost every bit of merchandise you see in Laos appears to have a Beer Laos logo on it.

Vientiane, the capital city, is not large or densely populated, and is similar in scale to Canterbury or Stratford-upon-Avon, with wide streets and some excellent multi-cultural restaurants, due to the international diplomatic staff at the embassies. It must be one of the best postings in the world for a diplomat. Many backpackers come through Vientiane but only stay a night or two before heading up country. It also attracts wealthier culture-oriented tourists, however, as well as diplomats, so there are a number of good-quality hotels and prices are generally a little higher than in Thailand.

We were lucky enough to find a reasonably priced guesthouse near to the centre. Later, we received a text from Martin saying he had survived and would arrive the following afternoon. With relief I threw away the draft *How your husband died – not our fault* letter to his wife.

It was great to see Martin smiling and looking well (though rather gaunt) the next day. He didn't look like he had a day's hard cycling in him. I realised we would need to stay another day or so to build him up before we headed off into mountainous Laos.

Up early that morning, I had walked the mile or so to the Vietnamese embassy to apply for our visas with their next-day service, so my work for day was done. Sam and I were eager to take Martin to some of the places we had discovered so far. After he'd had a post-ride shower, we headed off for an excellent lunch of feu followed by beef (water buffalo again) fried rice and a few Beer Laos at one of the riverside beer-garden restaurants. A few afternoon beers extended into the evening and we found ourselves sampling our first bottles of Lao Lao, the powerful national clear spirit.

Eventually, noticing the time, we left and took a tuk-tuk a little way along the Mekong river to Bunmala restaurant for an excellent dinner. It was great to have Martin back. Now all we needed was to put some weight back on him before we hit the hills.

After collecting our Vietnam visas the following morning with the characteristic ease we were already becoming used to in Laos, Sam and I cycled back to meet Martin for the luxurious Riviera Breakfast at the rather chic Café Vista. There we planned the rest of the day.

Full of get-up-and-go after two cups of world-renowned Laos coffee, I was eager to get moving. Martin, however, persuaded me we should first watch England beat Italy in six nations rugby at the guesthouse. We then headed out to Vieng Savan, a popular Chinese/ Laos street restaurant, where we were served delicious steamed dumplings and excellent feu with huge baskets of the fresh green leaves I had come to term English Country Garden. Martin was looking better already and confirmed this by suggesting we return to one of the beer-garden places for a relaxed few Beer Laos. Here, we lazed around drinking safe in the knowledge that Sam and I at least would be burning all this off tomorrow on Laos's notorious mountain passes. Martin looked like he'd just come out of a prolonged spell in a Viet Cong POW camp and had nothing to burn.

*

Told in advance how beautiful the Laos countryside is and how steep the mountain roads are, we were anticipating a tough day in full sun. The morning, however, proved fairly easy. The countryside was certainly beautiful, with neat bright-green rice paddies, banana trees, little teak and mahogany houses on stilts and a backdrop of mountains on the horizon. By this stage, however, Martin had become rather sick of feu for every meal. He may even have blamed the Thai equivalent for his stomach bug in Roi Et.

"I never liked it," he proclaimed. "I only ate it to be polite."

This was unfortunate, since out in the countryside it was often the only food you could get. To make matters worse, he was also having a problem swallowing rice. That morning, his supermodel breakfast at the Happy Girls Café consisted of a couple of tired old biscuits from his bar bag and a cup of black coffee.

We studied the map and talked about the best route to Pong Hong with the Happy Girls, who seemed to be recovering from a happy night (they were still asleep on benches when we arrived). After this consultation, we agreed that the long loop around a huge lake/reservoir would be more interesting. The map, of course, failed to indicate it would also mean climbing over some very big hills, since the lake was nestled high up in the mountains. Fortunately, we stopped for a good lunch just before reaching the hills, so we were at least well fuelled.

Just before arriving at our roadside lunch-spot, we passed a group of saffron-robed monks cycling along with umbrellas to keep the sun off. We commented that we needed to learn to cycle as serenely as them. Quarter of an hour later, as we sat outside the café waiting for our lunch, the monks parked their bikes and strolled inside. They sat there laughing and joking over their Beer Laos, tucking into their lunch while we waited. Clearly, they had phoned ahead or were daily regulars. We envied their lives we decided.

The sun blasted us on the way up the long pass that followed lunch. The sweat poured off us, stinging our eyes. These were real hills – mountains, in fact – but I was pleased with the chance to push myself. I stopped at the top of the pass to wait for Martin and Sam and take photographs of their exhausted faces as they struggled up the hill. Taking out my camera, I noticed that the thermometer attached to my bar bag read 50 degrees – hot enough to fry an egg on the pavement, I believe.

The road kept rising up and around the sheer rocky cliff it had been cut through. The view back down and across the flatter land towards Vientiane was too stunning to be true: miles of variegated forest, little winding roads, blue sky, large technicolour dragon-flies buzzing around, one or two small wooden houses and the odd 1950s-style truck carrying timber. All of this was either undeveloped or at least sustainable, and certainly unspoilt. Seldom have I seen a view more worthy of the title paradise.

After another few steep climbs, we reached the lake at Thinkco (near Thalat), where the road ran along above a large fast-flowing river.   Overlooking the river was a perfectly located wooden-decked restaurant we all agreed we should stop at for a cold beer before completing the last 30km to Pong Hong.   We were parched.

It was around 2.30pm when, relaxing with our beers, we noticed that just below the deck on the riverbank there were four nicely furnished huts.   After discovering they were also pretty cheap, we needed no enticement to have a slightly short day of 93km and leave the Pong Hong stretch until early next morning.   Martin needed this, we agreed.   We finished a second round of beer and unpacked. Sam and then I headed off down to the riverbank to check out the swimming potential.

In a little inlet just away from the raging white water, a few young locals had come down to wash their clothes and take an afternoon dip.   This told us it was safe to swim, although it was sweltering hot and even the threat of leeches wouldn't have deterred us.   Having finished their washing, the two young guys swam out towards us.   Caught by the fast current, they were rocketed downstream, where they grabbed onto a small islet.   They were pretty strong swimmers and had clearly done this before.   We sat in the water, cooling off for a while, then walked along to watch them jumping off the rock into a roaring gulley of water.   This carried them over some smooth rocks and a waterfall before dumping them into the bubbling water down below, leaving them swimming for their lives to reach the bank before being dragged off towards a far bigger waterfall further on.

They had several shots at this and sustained no injuries, so when they beckoned us to swim over to the rock, I agreed.   Sam, always more sensible than me, said he'd rather stay behind to watch.   I walked further back upstream and dived in.   I was amazed at the speed and strength of the current; I am a strong swimmer but there would be no swimming against this.

Moving at a hell of a speed, I was swept along towards the rock. I could see that keeping hold of the small islet was going to be hard even if I hit it straight on.   Largely from sheer fear of going over the steeper part of the waterfall, I managed to grab hold and clamber out onto the rock, heart pounding.   That was bloody stupid, I thought. But amazing!

Back on the bank, Sam appeared very worried. The young guys, about to leave, waved to tell me to try sliding over the waterfall. This looked incredibly scary, but I realised I needed to get back to the shore somehow. I jumped in. Before I could think, I was rocketed down the gully and over the waterfall, bumping into the smooth rocks on the way. Finally, I was spat out over the edge and down into the foaming pool at the bottom.

Head still spinning, I immediately felt the current trying to pull me out into the faster water. Quickly, I began swimming hard for the shore. It seemed to take a long time to cover the short distance, but I got there eventually and climbed out with exhilaration written all over my face.

Sam, seeing my childish glee, was now thinking about having a try. I walked upstream and dived in again. Once more, I just managed to grab onto the small islet. If Sam needed help, I would be in a better position here. Noticing that Martin had arrived on the bank, I clambered onto the rock. Sam came hurtling downstream towards me. I could see the growing terror on his face, given his speed as he approached, and stood at the edge waiting for him. I grabbed his hands as he hit the rock, but he was still being pulled by the raging current. A comical pirouette followed, leaving him on the rock and me in the water fighting against the current.

Failing to grab onto another rock, I was thrown out of sight and over the waterfall, narrowly missing some rocks below. Sam, seeing I had survived the fall, now forgot his own fear and was in stitches. Meanwhile, back on shore, Martin was filming with his phone and chuckling nervously. I encouraged Sam to slide down over the waterfall while I was still down below, so I could help him if he had any problems. In a few minutes, we were both back on shore watching the pirouette on Martin's phone, before climbing the bank to the bar for the cold beers that awaited us. It was the best of endings for a blistering hot day – and no leeches.

*

PLEASE NOTE – THE SUPERMODEL BREAKFAST OF DRY BISCUITS AND COFFEE IS ONLY SUITED TO SUPERMODELS AND THOSE LEADING A

Having ascertained it was only 105km further to Vang Vieng, we had a relaxed 7:30am start the following morning and stopped to buy some bananas and pakora by the road.   Martin, now extremely averse to all Asian staples, had already eaten an egg on toast with coffee at the café.   Sam and I felt he was still looking unhealthily thin and were concerned about him returning to Canterbury an emaciated shadow of his former self.   I considered the possible contents of a new letter to his wife, Judith.

There were some fairly serious climbs and descents this day. At a bridge at the bottom of one long descent, we met a 63-year-old Dutchman named Kase.   He had cycled up from Bangkok. Watching the rushing water beneath the bridge, we shared our body and cycle breakdown experiences over a ten-minute rest break.   Kase had started cycling for fitness after a heart operation.   After getting the bug, he now cycled all over the world.   It was a surprisingly familiar story.   We took particular note of his advice on guesthouses he had stayed at on his previous trip to Laos, including one special establishment we came to know simply as the Hot Spring Place.   He also advised us on the dirt-track mountain routes from Laos into North Vietnam, which sounded far from comfortable.   Martin pronounced himself glad he would not be with us for that particular experience.

After arriving reasonably early in the so-called backpacker paradise of Vang Vieng, we worked our way along the riverside thatched guesthouses until we reached Le Jardain Organique, the furthest one from the centre.   A beautiful spot with jasmine, palms and flowering bushes, it seemed friendly and well priced.   We settled for a couple of huts overlooking the river and small wooden road-bridge.

Backpackers are drawn to Vang Vieng by the promise of wild party times and the so-called white-water experience.   A few miles upstream, local entrepreneurs have hacked back the riverside jungle and built a large deck with a muddy car-park and a hut serving powerful Lao Lao cocktails.   The cocktails can apparently be fortified to order with drugs of various types.   All this is in marked contrast to the peaceful organic silk farm and café next door, which seemed most unhappy about their neighbour.

Martin and I walked to the café one hot afternoon, heard the loud rave music and strolled along to the deck to have a look what was going on. Sprawled on the deck were about a hundred spaced-out kids, some no more than teenagers, in Bermuda shorts or bikinis, downing booze like water. Many were already badly sunburned. There was a tall wooden crane-like structure that turned out to be a kind of lethal cross between a bungee jumping tower and rope swing. Every minute or so, the structure would deposit a drunk whooping twenty-something into the river, while his or her friends screamed and made lewd signs to comment on the performance. Still slugging beer from bottles, showboating boys were throwing topless drunk girls into the river. Meanwhile, off to one side, the two local guys running the party were busy taking people's money then shoving them off in truck inner-tubes to float downstream back to town. You couldn't fault their business acumen.

On the right day, I'm sure I would have found it fun, but my overriding feeling on this day was sadness over what Laos was set to become. My prior plan to try tubing went out the window at the sight of this chimp's teaparty. Particularly as there was nothing remotely resembling white-water in sight.

Apparently, as you float stoned at a snail's pace downstream, men on the riverbank wave ready-rolled spiffs or bottles of Beer Lao, then stretch out a hooked stick to pull you in and do the deal. The idea is that by the time you float into Veng Vieng you are completely smashed – that is, if you don't drown on the way. This explained the floating beer bottles that collected at every river inlet downstream. The general management style (or lack of) at this place also explained why a girl had drowned there that week. The Irish Pub manager in town told me this is a regular occurrence. The internet bears this out.

The small single dirt-street town was a similar story. Bar-restaurants had signs boasting, NON-STOP FRIENDS DVDs. The menu in most places remains the same – pizza, spag-bol, ring-burner curries, fish-n'-chips and kebabs. All are offered as standard or *happy*. Waitresses ask, "Would you like to make that happy, sir?"

Meaning: would you like marijuana, or something stronger, sprinkled over it?

Sam could see this was spoiling a beautiful country and giving Laotians a very bad impression of westerners, but he could also see the attraction of returning there one day with a bunch of his mates. In truth, I would have too a few years earlier. Even now, Martin and I were not immune to the saner end of this exploitation. The Steak & Guinness Pie with mash hardly needed *happying-up*, nor did the excellent chocolate cake. Martin, of course, was glad to be anywhere he didn't have to eat feu, noodles or rice – food he had by now developed a positive hatred of. With free draft beer with meals and Chelsea vs Hull on a decent screen, we toned down our criticisms of Vang Vieng. At least they were keeping it to this one town so far, and the natural surroundings remained stunning and unspoilt.

The view from our huts was certainly spectacular. That night, as we shared a bottle of Lao Lao on the riverside terrace, watching rickety old carts and trucks gingerly crossing through the shallow river to avoid paying for the bridge, sharp-eyed Sam drew our attention to something strange silhouetted against the red sunset. We looked harder and saw a huge flock of bats taking off from a big cave in the mountains. The waitress explained that this happened every evening at exactly the moment the final sliver of sun passed below the horizon. "Paradise!" I told her. "Now, could you make *that* happy?"

*

Moving on, we agreed we should try to stay at the Hot Springs Place that Kase, the Dutch cyclist, had told us about. After Vang Vieng, we imagined a kind of famous resort hotel (with pink champagne on ice, as the song goes). We asked our guesthouse manager for directions but received only a vague "between here and Luang Prabang – you can't miss it". This made us fairly confident of finding it. Kase had said the road passed right through it and there was nothing else for miles.

After a steady morning's pedalling and a good long lunch in Kasi, we climbed for a couple of hours up a long steep road through jungle, watching out for somewhere resembling an early Las Vegas. Near the top of the pass, we stopped to look back over the valley and saw a forest fire below us that was beginning to eat its way noisily through the jungle. We wondered whether this had been started intentionally. The noise was incredible.

Still tired from the hours of climbing, we hoped the resort would not be too far. There seemed no sign of any development, so we assumed we must have quite a way to go. Just around the first corner, we heard the unmistakeable sound of children's laughter and slowed to see where it was coming from. Perhaps we could get directions? Through the trees, we could just make out some kind of pond in which the children were swimming. Cycling on a few metres, were surprised to see a group of five lovely little mahogany huts on stilts and someone mending a bicycle.

We wondered whether it a small hamlet where the children lived.

Pulling over to check, we saw that the bicycle repairer was European He called over to us.

"Hello, you guys must be shattered!"

"We're looking for the Hot Spring Place," I replied.

"You found it!" he laughed.

Thankfully, the place was not what we had imagined.

Finding the old lady who ran the place, we enquired about accommodation and were delighted to find there were two huts left with a double bed and WC/shower shoehorned into each.

We parked our bikes, paid the old lady and scurried off down through the trees to the large stone-sided water tank surrounded by jungle, where several other cyclists were soothing away the day's aches and pains in the steaming water. The small glistening brown children had now got out and were sitting at the edge watching.

In the heavenly pool, we started chatting with a rather forthright German lady. Sonja took pains to explain that the older man who had just gone back to the hut was not her husband or boyfriend

"I don't have sex with him, oh *mein Got*, no!" she assured us, frowning. "And anyhow, he is having a bad back problem."

He was just a friend and a very annoying man to travel with, apparently. After she got out, the man returned and seemed far from annoying. In fact, he had cycled almost everywhere in Asia over many years, between being a landscape gardener back in Germany. He proved to be a fascinating source of information and had a great sense of humour – especially, when pressed, about her.

The Hot Springs Place (its only name) was in a hamlet named Ban Nam Oon. Far from being the casino resort we had imagined, no one really stayed there except cyclists or motorcyclists. According to the guidebooks, there was nothing of tourist interest in the area. If this place was not an advertisement for the advantages of going *off-piste*, I don't know what is.

On the opposite side of the narrow road lay a small cafe serving pretty good food beyond the standard feu, bush-meat and rice. Herman, the amusing German gardener, had adopted us after our solidarity over his difficulties with his female travelling companion and came over to share a few Beer Lao with us. He reiterated Kase's warnings about the terrible unsurfaced mountain roads from northern Laos into Vietnam. We were so grateful to Kase for guiding us here. The Hot Springs Place was superb and certainly deserved its reputation among visiting cyclists.

Herman was great entertainment.

"I tell you, be careful about taking passengers. This woman was visiting a house where I was working in the garden. The householder introduced us and told her I travelled very much in Asia. This woman (he pointed towards her accusingly) told me she always like to visit Asia. She calls me later to invite me for drinking. She made me quite drunk, then captured me with nice behaviours." He fluttered his eyelids and stuck out his chest. "This is how I am now burdened with this such difficult woman in Laos – a woman who is complaining from waking until sleeping. Believe me, many times I think death is better and think to ride over the mountain edge!"

Herman also repeated Kase's warning about how long and steep the hills were to Kiou Kachun, our next stopover point. Martin listened carefully and announced after dinner he would get up an hour earlier than us to get a head start.

The following morning, Sam and I got up at seven and left fairly quickly. The staff were asleep on the tables at the café, so not bothering with breakfast for once, we set off after Martin on a gentle slope that surprisingly, just around the corner, became a steep, winding downhill run. We were too experienced now to celebrate this and were neither surprised nor disappointed when it all too soon became a long steep climb.

After about half an hour, we met Martin sitting at the side of the road eating a sickly lardy-cake he had bought from an old woman in the previous hill village. I imagine she had managed to kill her whole family with this arterial glue. Thoughtfully, Martin had bought one for each of us and was waiting there to invite us for breakfast. The food was not great, but it was all that was available. Martin's thoughtfulness made up for whatever the *gloop* lacked.

After a further two hours of serious first- and second-gear climbing in rising heat, we were rewarded with a modern rest station at the top of the mountain. Here, we had a proper breakfast of buffalo and vegetable rice. Although the spot seemed to be at the peak of a mountain, we continued to climb for half an hour after our feast, before settling into a more familiar pattern of ups and downs. There always seemed to be more of the former than the latter. In a common-sense world, we should not have been cycling. On the unsheltered mountain road, the sun after mid-day was absolutely blistering. That day, the heat hit 46 degrees.

Eventually, we did reach the mountain village of Kiou Kachun, where we found a basic cold-water guesthouse. In the cafe next door, we chose veg fried rice in preference to the array of charred creatures in the glass display cabinet. While we sat there quaffing our beer Lao, a boy arrived with some kind of large gopher hanging on a string by its foot. He showed this to our rotund host, who examined it and sent him to the kitchen. The squealing from the kitchen soon after was followed by high-pressure selling from our host.

"We have good meat now. You try! *Werry, werry* tasty! Cheaps price. Luang Prabang restaurant, ten thousand kip!"

We were not persuaded. By the time we came to leave, a roasted version of the same creature had been proudly placed in the glass cabinet.

"You come, breakfast," she said pointing at it. *"Derishus!"*

After a good sleep and a bracing cold wash, we returned to the bushmeat café for omelettes with rice. The woman did try once more to interest us in the selection of charred fauna gracing her cabinet.

"Nipper, no?" she asked, pointing at the cabinet.

It sounded something like nipper anyway.

"Nipper, no," we assured her.

Finishing our breakfast quickly, we thanked her, checked over the bikes and mounted up. Soon, we were speeding off downhill into the dense jungle. The view was incredible. A blanket of thick cloud hung over the forest way below, which we soon descended through.

With sparsely located misty villages and suspicious people, it was a tough day for mountain cycling. It reminded me of the mission upriver to find Kurtz in Apocalypse Now.

"The horror, the horror!" I whispered as we approached one spooky hamlet with mist hanging over a muddy river. Martin and Sam knew what I meant.

After a day of seemingly endless climbs and would-be head-hunters, the three of us relished the long winding downhill off the mountains near the end. The pleasure soon ended, though, due to our dizziness and the potholes (trenches) we found at every bend. You could never get any decent speed-up, and the smell of smoking brake rubber lingered around us throughout most of Laos. As always, there was a long climb saved for the end of our day, just to catch us out when we thought we were there. The very small city of Luang Prabang did arrive eventually, however, and we found two pleasant rooms in the first recommended guesthouse we called at.

Martin had been subdued during the second half of the day. Of course, he had found the hills hard going, but that was not the reason. He knew today would be the last day he would cycle with us on this trip. Although the growing mountains had made him start to look forward to this day, he felt sad about it now.

At nearly sixty, he had regained his previous physical fitness quite dramatically and felt justly proud about not copping out of anything during the month. He would not be going home in a dress and I could probably now throw away my draft letters informing his wife of his untimely death. He longed to continue with us, knowing now that he was still capable of it (he had cycled the length of Vietnam about eight years earlier), but that was not possible.

We were sad to be losing his company too. We had laughed more with Martin around and it had been good to have the personal dynamics changed for a while. But deep down, Sam and I both knew that it was right for us to continue alone and be able to look back on this month as something different, and special. Anyway, Judith had a banister back home waiting for Martin to strip and paint.

*

Luang Prabang was a far call from the backpacker playground of Veng Vieng. In fact, there seemed remarkably few backpackers compared with the number of mature, well-heeled tourists. Many of these came on side trips by small prop-driven plane from Vientiane, Bangkok or Hanoi and left the same way. For backpackers, it was a long way to come by bus over the mountains. The more conservative atmosphere, coupled with a midnight curfew, probably did a lot to put them off anyway. This left a relaxed, relatively crowd-free atmosphere, with pleasant local people and some surprisingly up-market restaurants and hotels.

On his last night, Martin took us to a lovely tropical garden restaurant, the cheesily named Blue Lagoon. He and I enjoyed the most exquisitely cooked fish straight from the Mekong, while Sam ate an unusual concoction described on the menu as a pizza. It looked more like trifle. Wrong choice, Sam.

It may have been the pizza-trifle that reawakened the sleeping demon in Sam's insides, or the stress of knowing he was back to only having me for company. His digestive system protested badly in the night. Of course, we had failed to discourage him from drinking rather a lot of Lao Lao that evening on our charming veranda, but common sense had told us this would do more good than harm. (For the idiot's guide to self-medication, go to markmartinremedies.com)

The next morning, Martin and I searched the internet for a diagnosis of Sam's very specific symptoms. Each time, it came back to giardia – *a rather persistent intestinal parasite which few long-term travellers to the Indian Subcontinent fail to play host to at some point.*

According to the web, about two-thirds of sufferers bid farewell to the parasite after a few weeks of diarrhoea, while the other third find the insidious visitor reluctant to leave. These unfortunates suffer repeated bouts, sometimes for up to six months.

Sam was clearly one of the latter cases and needed help. Later that morning, we woke him with news we had managed to track down at a Luang Prabang chemist, a course of the antibiotics advised on the internet. I have brought up my children never to take medicines unless all else fails. Sam refused the drugs, saying he'd rather keep them until he had tried everything else first. This seemed laudable, but after the parasitic guest's two month overstay it seemed unlikely to work. Nonetheless, we left it up to him.

*

We discovered an excellent place for breakfast in Luang Prabang. This was a small traditional café beside the road and opposite a small luxury hotel. Luckily, it was just five minutes along from our guesthouse. One very special morning, we enjoyed an extended breakfast here watching life go on in the neighbourhood, constructing stories and suppositions around what we saw. During the hour and a half we sat there, we watched a somewhat overdressed American lady waiting for someone on the pavement in front of the hotel. She wore thickly applied lip-gloss over her pink lipstick, which she reapplied at several points during the twenty minutes that she paced anxiously up and down.

We each offered different theories about what or whom this lady could be waiting for:

She was waiting for her husband to go with her on a tour, but he had run off with a waitress;

She was single and had met a man in a restaurant the previous night who had thought better of his promise to take her for breakfast;

She was booked onto a tour bus that had failed to show up because they had not understood the address delivered in her deep-south accent.

The lady made a number of calls on her mobile phone, becoming more animated and irritated with each failed attempt or rebuttal.

Each call was followed with the application of ever more lip-gloss. Eventually, a local man in a suit turned up. We picked him out as he walked towards her, conspicuous by his reluctance to arrive despite his apparent quickness of step. The lady began by explaining her plight with excessive use of hand gestures and soon began remonstrating with him. The man made several phone calls, each time pointing up the street, assuring her that whoever or whatever she was expecting was just about to arrive. Nothing did. He offered her a piece of paper but she seemed to scorn this, placing her hands on her ample hips.

"It's a voucher for a free massage," Sam said.

"Free botox lip-treatment," replied Martin.

Many calls and several aggressive applications of lip-gloss later, the man finally accepted defeat. He peeled off a large number of notes from a bundle he seemed to keep up his sleeve.

"He's a bloody drug dealer!" I said, attracting the attention of our lady café proprietor. "I've seen that money-up-the-sleeve thing in movies. There we were, thinking she was on the phone saying, *Where's the Goddam coach to take me to the waterfall?* Really, she was asking, *Where in hell are my three kilos of smack?* And threatening someone with waking up to a horse's head in their bed!"

Around 5pm, we said a sad goodbye to Martin and he cycled off towards the bus station. He was to take a gruelling bus ride back over the rough mountain roads to Vientiane, a train from the border to Bangkok for an overnight stay and a game of golf with an ex-colleague before flying home to England.

Sam and I went quietly out to get an early supper at the street market in the centre of town at a stall with numerous vegetarian dishes laid out for a self-service buffet meal. It felt strange being out for dinner without Martin and we forewent the usual bottle of Lao Lao on our way back. This had become a ritual with Martin.

Back at the guesthouse, the man on reception stopped us. "Your friend like to find you my house, you no stay my house She go by walk someways, please."

We deduced that Martin had returned for some reason but had gone out to find us. On the other hand, it may have meant that a known prostitute who Sam had innocently chatted to at breakfast had come looking for him and as a result we were now being asked to vacate the premises. Either way, we went back out to look for our visitor, who – maybe to Sam's relief – did prove to be Martin, carrying a large bottle of Lao Lao.

Although there had been a seat for him on the bus as booked, there was no space for his bike on the roof, so he had been bumped onto the bus the following evening. It sounded like a poor excuse to spend another raucous evening on the veranda with me and Sam, but this was no great hardship for us. The night before, Martin and Sam had been doubled-up in painful hilarity when, very much the worse for Lao Lao, I had sneezed halfway through telling one of my tall stories. As a result, I had spilt my drink in my lap and filled my overgrown beard with a mountain of mucus. Martin had rushed to photograph this on his phone but had dropped it off the balcony. He then disturbed an amorous couple downstairs while he groped for it drunkenly in the grass outside their window.

*

Risking happiness-overload, the three of us did benefit from another entertaining evening of Lao Lao and stories on the balcony, during which Sam insisted he had finally killed his giardia. We also enjoyed another breakfast at our café along the road. As this began, our attention was drawn by the chink of bottles. Through the haze of dust in the morning sun, we looked up to see an old woman with a handcart collecting discarded bottles and sorting them meticulously by type on a small patch of waste ground adjacent to the hotel. OCD was not far off for her, we felt.

There was a solitary kitchen cupboard dumped adjacent to her bottle store and I put forward the idea that she lived in this. It seemed like a comic story until, after messing about with the bottles for half an hour, she climbed inside the cupboard and slid the door shut. Silenced, we waited for her to come out, but she stayed put. A little while later, a policeman passed and went over to knock on the cupboard door. Rather than move her on as we expected, he passed her a paper cup of coffee and offered her a cigarette. She took both and the policeman departed, tipping his hat to her.

Later, as we left the café and walked past the bottle lady's camp, we noticed smoke rising from the cabinet.   She seemed to be blowing it out through the plug-hole of the inset sink.   We strolled off wondering whether we had ordered a happy breakfast by mistake.

Over breakfast, we had agreed we should try to mark Martin's bonus last day with a trip out.   After Martin bade farewell to our café lady, we wandered along the street and found a tuk-tuk driver to take us to see the famous waterfall and Bear Rescue Centre.   It was an interesting trip, despite the irritation of mixing with outsized tourists squeezed into uniform Beer Lao T-shirts.   All too soon, though, the time came for Martin to set off again.

Leaving us at the front steps of Thavi Souk Guesthouse, Martin cycled off into the sunset towards the bus station.   This time, despite us waiting around for a while in hope, he did not return.   Sam and I slouched off into town to find somewhere to eat.   Stupidly, we decided to eat at an Indian restaurant for the first time since India.   It was Sam's idea!   It felt completely like being back in India.   The waiter was pleasant enough but couldn't really be bothered.   He came to the table and cleaned the street dust off our plates with the tail of his grubby shirt.   Two minutes after our food arrived, the electricity went off, leaving us to eat in the pitch black.   Within two hours, Sam's giardia was far from history.   The prospect of antibiotics for him loomed ever closer.

SAM'S POINT OF VIEW

Thailand was really interesting - another major change of culture and of food. We met Martin, a family friend from home, who flew in to cycle as far as Laos with us. To be honest, his presence was needed at that time. He really helped calm me down and stopped me from getting so angry. Getting back to mountainous terrain after the relative flatness of eastern India was beautiful and a joy to cycle. When you get to the point you can cycle two hours up a steep mountain and hardly notice any pain, you feel pretty unstoppable.

Thailand was perhaps even more colourful than India. In northern Thailand and Laos, we ate a lot of feu, which is basically a bowl of stock with root vegetables, the odd mushroom and a pile of leaves to throw in at the table. It provided plenty of energy for cycling. Martin quickly got tired of it, though. Having to make a quick transition from western food to Asian peasant food probably wasn't easy, not when it's often all there is to eat each day. I was surprised how well Martin kept up with us really, given that we'd had months of training and he'd had very little.

On our way up to Laos we took a wide detour through Cambodia. The temples were amazing from what I remember, although I wasn't that interested at the time. It just wasn't the right time for me, I guess. Angkor Wat was the most spectacular place, though, especially the main temple with its turrets and carved faces. It reminded me a bit of Gaudi's cathedral in Barcelona.

We got our heads shaved in Cambodia. It seemed a good idea at the time, especially with the heat. There is a horrendous photo on our blog of us standing outside the barbers (butchers!). Can you imagine my dad with a full beard suddenly having a completely bald head? Ridiculous! I didn't look much better, though.

Laos was a brilliant country. Unfortunately, my stomach was bad at this point. I was certain Lao Lao, a local spirit (rice vodka), was the cure for it. That turned out to be a short-lived experiment. It was just so frustrating and meant I was tired all the time, which was not great for cycling through such mountainous countryside.

Laos was probably the most stunning of all the countries to cycle through. Only some places in southern India (Kerala and Tamil Nadu) were better. There was one spot I will never forget. Right at the top of a tropical mountain range five mahogany huts amongst the trees were kept mainly for cyclists. These were tiny but comfortable, with a superb view. Next to the huts was a natural hot spring in which you could sit chatting with other cyclists while overlooking an astounding view of jungle and mountains stretching into the distance. It was unbelievable. There was even a bar at the other side of the little road where we could eat and drink in the evening. If I ever go back anywhere that we stopped on this trip, it'll be there.

It was sad to see Martin go. The last few nights on our balcony in Luang Prabang were absolutely superb and hilarious. He really made this section a lot of fun for me. Beyond doubt, having him around helped things between my dad and I, and that was sorely needed.

Chapter 11

Northern Laos & Vietnam – Life after Rolling Thunder

This village, old-time Viet Cong camp, my friend.   Many head cut off. You come, look.   I show you bones.

On 20 February, the morning after Martin left, Sam and I got up, paid, cleaned and oiled our chains, then headed off to our breakfast place with loaded bikes.   We were alone again, and we felt it.

Sitting down at our usual table, we looked at the empty third chair.   The lady pointed at the chair and made a grimace.   We nodded and ordered breakfast, opting for Martin's hated feu rather than the fried egg and salad baguettes we had kept him company with over the last few days.

We ate quickly and wasted no time staying on for tea or watching for entertainment on the street outside.   There was smoke rising from the bottle lady's cupboard, but we did not wait to see her begin work, or the policeman to bring her coffee.   Hanging around with Martin gone just didn't feel good and we were eager to depart, despite how much we'd enjoyed it here.   We waved to our café lady and peddled off.   The small road over the wooden bridge took us to the main Pak Mong road north.

The road in southern Laos (yes, there was really only one) had been small but pretty well surfaced, but it gradually deteriorated as we came further north.   From here on, it became quite bad, with frequent un-surfaced sections and deep potholes.   At one point this day, we reached a huge crevasse where the road had collapsed into the river below.   We were expecting mountain roads, and that was what we got: up and down all day long, with the beautiful big Nam Oon River flowing below us most of the morning.

Wherever there is a river in Laos you find activity, amazing wildlife, and in particular, people.   There were invariably groups of women in colourful traditional dress washing clothes, men carrying logs across in shallow handmade boats and people fishing.   In a number of places we saw young boys on bicycles carrying homemade spear guns, flippers and goggles. We watched carefully to see how they used them. It seemed they crouched in the fast-moving water immediately following a weir, watching for fish to swim over. They seemed to catch plenty, hanging them on loops of string over their handlebars and proudly displaying them to us as they cycled home.

The kids around here seemed the epitome of good children. Wide, open smiles were shown to all. They needed no electronic gadgets or other luxuries to keep them happy; they played games of marbles or draughts together, fished, told stories and played football. Encountered along the way, these kids stood in the road in a row holding out their hands for us to slap as we rode past. They were confident but never cheeky. Maybe the simple subsistence way of life, with what seemed like minimal schooling and no factory or building site to go to when they graduated, was responsible for their happiness. In place of an academic education perhaps, they looked forward to joining their fathers fishing or cutting down a few trees, or growing vegetables and tending a few chickens. Whatever it was, it seemed admirable, for now at least. I reminded myself that the temptations of a western consumer lifestyle could not be far away.

For me, this seemed one of the best cycling days of the trip, mainly due to the stunning riverside scenery, the peace and quiet, the flora and fauna and the lovely smiling people we met along the way. Sam tried to see it that way, but his feelings were marred by the giardia still at work in his intestines – his whole day needed to be one of unhappy restraint. I felt sorry for him and said I really felt the time had come to take the antibiotics. He agreed, saying he would take them during our planned two-night break in the next main town, Oudomaxi.

Pak Mong was a one-horse town. In fact, it was a no-horse town. It had two cafes, a provisions shop, a greasy filling station and a very basic guesthouse. The elderly guesthouse owner was really friendly – too friendly, in fact. Sam had to try hard to see the stroking of his young lycra-clad thighs as merely an interest in his cycling athleticism. Bizarrely, Sam was not the only subject of his affections. I found myself laughing out loud as the old guy repeatedly hugged me and told me how much he admired my explorer's beard.

Since Sam had been sharing his nourishment with his giardia, he was hungry and eager to find somewhere to eat. This far off the beaten track, though, bush-meat of uncertain types was all they had in the cafes apart from rice and eggs, so we stuck to that, for fear of adding to the endangerment of a species. As a treat, we bought some biscuits at the shop on our way home.

*

The landscape had noticeable changed now. It was wilder and more extreme. We had found the south undeveloped and attractively simple, but this was tougher. Finding places to eat had become harder and what they had to offer was more limited. Nothing like as bad as the wilderness in Iran, of course, but still challenging. We would need to remember to stock up in each town again, in case we couldn't find anywhere to get food later.

I realised at this stage, probably after discussions with locals, that we were now in territory fought over during the Vietnam War. The US Air Force ran major bombing sorties from this area as part of a campaign theatrically named Rolling Thunder. The Tet offensive and Khe Sanh operations were also run from here. The Viet Cong had guerrilla camps in the hills around the Vietnam border that remained in use well after the USA pulled out of Vietnam. Probably the US Army secretly did too. People in the area still talked about the Vietnam War as if it were a recent event. You could see the powerful influence it had made on their lives.

Sam and I both had a reasonable night's sleep in our small basic room. We got up fairly early and enjoyed a decent bowl of feu at the truck-stop café. The lady tried to persuade us to go for something more substantial, showing us a selection of familiar charred rodents.

"Nipper, no!" I said firmly.

Wanting to set off before it got too hot, we began what promised to be a relatively short 86km ride to Oudomaxi. After the fabulous cycling experience of the previous day, this was to prove one of the hardest days of the trip. No sooner had we left the town boundary than we hit the first hill. As we often did, we stopped at the bottom to look up at what lay ahead. It was a rough, steep, winding road with a really bad surface. We could see large smoky old trucks way up ahead, struggling up the hills into the mountains.

"Please, no!" said Sam as his eye followed the telegraph poles marking the road. These were clearly visible winding back and forth around the verdant hills right up to the sky.

I was concerned. Sam was not physically up to the climb, especially in this heat. I told him not to worry: we would take it slowly and stop frequently. But unless we were going to turn back, we did need to get going now before the sun got too hot. Sam thought about the old man back at the guesthouse – I had named him Uncle Ernie, remembering the rock opera Tommy. We set off uphill. The first hill continued for 30km with deep potholes and sections under long-term repair. Slowing us to walking pace in first and second gear the whole time, it went on for over three hours. The temperature was close to 50 degrees.

We saw no sign of cafes or a shop for those first 30km, so when we reached a poor hamlet at the top of a pass around 11.30am, we decided to stop and try to find something for lunch. There were still no cafes or shops, but when asked about food a lady ushered us into a small wooden house and sat us at a large table. About six or seven other people were eating there. We took them to be her customers. In fact, they were her extended family. We ate a bowl of woody feu filled with gritty forest roots, a few leaves and some fungi along with a noodle or two. It was almost tasteless but we were glad of it.

"Maybe we should have said yes to the Nipper," Sam suggested as we filled our water bottles and paid the lady.

We were dreading what lay ahead, and were right to – it was a further 50km of steep climbing on rough roads in intense heat, with just the odd downhill. At one point, Sam looked close to collapse and I thought he may give up, but he kept on going in silent determination.

Fortunately, we had some rice crackers and bananas from the evening before. These managed to keep Sam going until we finally reached a flat road for the last 8km into Oudomxai. What a sense of relief!

Riding into Oudomaxi at sunset felt sweet; we both revelled in the glow of what we had achieved. Not wishing to give up anything now, we cycled through the whole town looking at guesthouses before we settled on one in a side street.

We could see Oudomaxi was a staging-post for long distance travellers. There were guest-worker coaches from China and lots of backpackers in the cafes. They wore the air of people proud of reaching this far up into the backwoods of Laos, or making it over the mountains from China.

*

After a long night's sleep in our dingy room, we felt thoroughly rested. Sam felt too well to consider the need for the antibiotics. From the instructions on the pack, it seemed that for amoebic dysentery the patient needed to take one pill per day for four days, whereas for giardia you needed to take all four in one deadly hit. Sam didn't fancy this and insisted he was on the mend. Sadly, after an excellent light meal of rice, vegetables and sweet and sour tofu in a clean restaurant, he spent half the night in the bathroom.

The following afternoon, Sam gave in to the four nasty-looking pills and collapsed into bed. We were supposed to be leaving that day but I could see we were going nowhere. The results of the antibiotics were worrying. Painful stomach cramps doubled him up in agony every few minutes and he suffered raging diarrhoea for most of the morning. After that, he just slept for hours bathed in sweat. I asked whether he thought something was wrong and I should get a doctor. He just shook his head and lay back down.

That night and the next day were spent watching movies on TV, with Sam just sipping at water. The diarrhoea had stopped but he now seemed incredibly weak and subdued. I was worried about whether we had misread or misunderstood the instructions on the antibiotic pack. Taking all four pills at once did seem extreme, although I remembered the various medical websites Martin and I had researched had said the same thing.

Sam said he thought he would be well enough to ride gently the following day once he had eaten something for breakfast. I doubted this but agreed cautiously, thinking we could stay another day if he didn't look good in the morning.

After a long night's sleep, Sam seemed OK by mid-morning the next day, so we packed and set off. Within a few miles, though, he admitted to feeling very weak and said he would not be able to do hills.

We did encounter some in the first few kilometres, but after that, following an attractive river with lovely views, we found the road pretty flat, so we didn't turn back straight away.

Other issues compounded our problems. Something was not right with Sam's bike. We stopped and both felt completely gutted to discover his main gear cable had begun to fray at a sleeve point. Although I had fortunately brought two spares, I had never changed a gear cable with this kind of (Shimano Tiagra) combined brake-and-gear housing before. Sam said he would manage by just using the front chain-rings until we reached our next stopover. He had clearly decided to continue.

Luckily, the road stayed flat. With the positive effects of breakfast working their way through, Sam started to find a little more energy. Things continued to improve slightly. After a good lunch, we managed to make it all the way to Muiang Khoua – the last town before the Vietnam border. It looked like a nice place to stop.

Sam had been really amazing that day, never complaining; in fact, he apologised for holding us up. I remembered cycling on no food, with no strength in my legs, after the disgusting town of Khed, and again the day we cycled to Agra, so I knew what it was like. I saw Sam focussing on a point on the road ahead and keeping his legs going around with minimal effort, just like I had. You don't want to talk. You don't look at anything around you. You are a machine that goes slowly in one direction, until it stops – or until you fall off.

At Muiang Khoua, we found the roads all dug up and the Lonely Planet-recommended guesthouse full. The manageress offered us a storeroom adjacent to the kitchen, but nobody could find the key. She made lunatic attempts to open the door with a large carving knife, but thankfully to no avail. Instead, we found a cosy basic guesthouse nearby. The friendly owner brought our loaded bikes into his living-room for safety.   While Sam had a sleep, I headed off down to check out the so-called floating bridge across the river.

The place had a different sense about it to other small towns we had encountered in Laos.   It felt further from civilisation – like we were on the fringes of dense jungle, which in fact we were.   The people also seemed different; a little more closed and secretive maybe. Although it was another 56km to the Vietnamese border, it certainly felt like we were out on the edge.

The floating bridge turned out to be a roll-on roll-off barge on a cable that took traffic across every hour.   Down by the ferry-stage, I met a French-Canadian couple with mountain bikes who were also leaving the following day.   Like us, they had come via India and Thailand.   This was not all we shared: Pierre and Gen (Genevieve) had suffered a few stomach upsets in India as well, and hers, like Sam's, had continued intermittently since then.   Also, they had come to the conclusion she was harbouring a giardia parasite.

Well informed about this section of the route – far more than us, it seemed – they told me the 56km of road from the other side of the river to the border was a rough muddy mountain track all the way to Vietnam.   This was just as Kase and Herman, our German gardener friend, had said.   That day, the couple had spoken to an experienced mountain-biker who had just ridden the route in the opposite direction. He had described it as nearly impassable, even with full suspension and no luggage.   They had therefore booked two seats on a 4x4 minibus to the border the next morning and advised me to do the same.

I wandered back up to the house to see if Sam was awake.   He was and seemed in fairly good spirits, all things considered.   Sam accepted we should follow Pierre and Gen's advice on taking the bus – if not because of his weak state, then at least to avoid trashing the bikes.

We had a pleasant evening at one of the two cafes in town. Here we spoke to a few people who had been around a while.   They confirmed what Pierre had told me about the road, which made the decision easier.

*

Catching the bus meant getting up early. We were awake by 6:30am, then quickly out the door and down to the floating bridge. It was by no means certain the bus would have places for us. This was the only way to find out at short notice.

The bus was waiting at the other side of the river. The boatman tried to extort an unreasonable amount of money from the four of us cyclists to cross. We hadn't come across this kind of behaviour so far in Laos. After much haggling, we eventually crossed for double the foot-rate. The price clearly went up when there was a bus to catch. I could imagine this kind of behaviour had been going on for centuries.

There were plenty of people waiting for the bus with big bags of vegetables and other heavy luggage, so we were concerned at first about there being space on the roof for our bikes, let alone seats for us inside. I sought out the driver and paid him quickly. The price seemed high for such a short journey, but Pierre and Gen confirmed it was the price they had been told. No mention had been made about paying for the bikes at this point. Sam was hopeful they were included in the fare. Based on the behaviour so far, I thought this unlikely and anticipated a further haggling battle.

Eventually, when all 25 passengers were squeezed into the 20-seat bus and the luggage strapped on top, the boss-man told us that each bike on the roof would cost double the price of a passenger ticket. Pierre's eyes nearly fell out. He had seen the other passengers pay a few coppers for putting their huge sacks of fruit and vegetables there, so he was not expecting this. On the basis it was only a starting point for haggling, I advised Pierre to put away his wallet and offered the guy about one-tenth of what he had asked. The man threw up his hands and immediately became angry and belligerent – the first aggression I had seen in Laos – shouting that we could take the bikes off the roof if we didn't want to pay.

The local passengers then seemed to tell him to be fair. He came back with an amount the same as the passenger price, which we refused. Never back down when you're winning, I reminded myself.

The bus was getting ready to go now. The guy had taken to yelling in our faces, but we just sat there. I knew Sam was remembering the Lake Van incident in Turkey. Finally, smiling, the boss-man accepted a price of half the passenger fare per bike. It was still ridiculous, but we set off.

Within a couple of miles, we could see that the *impassable* description Pierre and Gen had received was more than justified. There was no road; it was a dirt track. Steep, with deeply rutted mud, this wound through the mountainous jungle. Wrecked vehicles lay dumped or under repair at every turn. Within an hour, we had replaced two punctured wheels and repaired a suspension strut smashed by a rock. This was crazy. Everyone felt sick from the constant bouncing around, roaring engine, thick dust and acrid fumes. In many places, we could not believe it was possible for a vehicle to get through. To think these guys did this every few days.

If we had tried to cycle, we realised, we would have ended up walking the whole way caked in mud and red dust, taking two days minimum. We even saw Land Rovers that had failed to make it. Walking, we could certainly have managed it, but why?

In this challenging terrain, it took six hours to cover the 56km to the Vietnam border – six hours of rodeo-riding in an overcrowded bus, punctuated by roadside repairs. I could see now why the bus operator was so much more stressed than other Laotians. In fact, I believe we later discovered he was Vietnamese. I could see Laotians would be far too laid back for this job. We began to wonder if walking would have been easier.

After the punishment of the drive, it dawned upon me that the border crossing might be the final straw. There had been reports of officious guards sending people back just for the hell of it. Luckily, though, we got through without any hitches and by early afternoon had found a decent guesthouse in the small city of Bien Dien Phu. I tipped the bus boss as we got off and got a toothy smile.

"You're just trying to feel better about yourself," laughed Sam.

Pierre and Gen checked into the same guest house, needing to rest up for a few days due to Gen's giardia. Sam seemed a little better but remained averse to alcohol and any thought of heavy food.

It took us a few hours to get over the motion sickness from our journey. Finally, though, we felt able to get off our beds and go looking for an ATM, to get some Vietnamese cash. Dinner that evening was spent at a basic café in the very atmospheric central fish market. Despite the basic surroundings, the food was good and so was the service.

A table of Vietnamese guys who had over-ordered sent over all their untouched dishes and bottles of beer before leaving. On our first evening in the country, this was a really positive introduction and in stark contrast to stories other travellers had told us in Thailand and Laos. They had warned us that the Vietnamese were unfriendly to westerners and a big shock after the kindness of the Thais and Laotians. With the possible exception of the bus boss, this proved to be totally untrue in our experience.

The following morning, eager to experience Vietnam, we set about servicing the bikes in front of the guesthouse before setting off. I had all the tools and spare cables ready to repair Sam's frayed gear cable, but try as we might we could not get the old cable out. I was worried about being too rough; it was a high-quality, delicate mechanism and no parts I broke could be replaced locally. Finally, for fear of causing irreparable damage, we reluctantly gave up. We would leave it until we could find a proper modern bike shop in Hanoi – our next major stopover.

*

After servicing the bikes, Sam and I tucked a note with our email into one of the bar-bags of the still sleeping Pierre and Gen. After this we returned to the fish market for a late breakfast to cheer ourselves up before setting off on the busy road towards Hanoi. Pierre and Gen did find our note, but only when they returned home two months later.

At the fish market café, two truck drivers told us the road to Hanoi was a complete disaster of mud, dust and roadworks.

"Road to Hanoi, no funny. Take too many hour in car, in truck. With cycle, you die one hundred time!"

This was not a complete surprise. Fifty percent of people had told us the same thing, although the other half told us that the road was fine now. We hoped luck would be with us on this one. Sam was getting stronger each day, but he was still far from being back to full fitness and cycling was still a major exertion. Aware he didn't want to slow us down or cause me any worry, I needed to try to give him an easy time without him realising I was doing it.   He would not want to be treated like a kid with his dad looking after him.   I was happy not to treat him like one.

Sam, though, could have done without the added handicap of cycling all day in fifth gear with only the front chain-rings to help him on hills.   I felt pretty annoyed with myself for not asking to be shown how to deal with Tiagra mechanisms on our bike mechanics course back in Canterbury.   Unknown to Sam, I punished myself for this omission by also riding in fifth gear all day.   How screwed up is that?   Fortunately, it was only 80km from Bien Dien Phu to Tuan Giao, our next planned stop.   Despite a number of hills, we managed to reach it without too much pain.

I remember this day being one where negativity started to creep into my head.   The gear cable had started it.   Examining my own behaviour as we cycled along, I saw how stupid this was.   I spend most of my life being annoyingly optimistic about everything, but when some minor problem occurs I treat it as if it is the beginning of a total disaster.   This is anxiety neurosis, apparently.

Of course, at this stage nothing that bad had actually happened. In my mind, though, I had seen an indication of impending disaster. To others, there may be no strong evidence of any problem to come, but to me it will seem almost certain.   In fact, if anyone tells me it won't happen, I will argue it will until I am blue in the face, presenting all sorts of crazy evidence, approaching it from every critical angle.   I become a veritable prophet of doom.

Unfortunately with people like me, this sets up a self-fulfilling prophecy.   Because we are sure something major is going to go wrong, it does.   This then reinforces our belief we can anticipate disaster.

"See, I told you it was all going to go wrong," I say.

This kind of thing doesn't happen to me that often, thank goodness.   When it did on the trip, you can see why it exasperated Sam – although only slightly more than my more usual excessive optimism did.

The people we met or who waved to us along the country road from Dien Bien Phu were a sheer delight and we wondered how the backpackers we had talked to could have thought Vietnam was unfriendly. We concluded again this was due to groups of young people who visited only the main towns and sights listed in backpacker guides. Local people can't help but be affected by the constant influx of westerners and their money. The net effect is negative for all concerned. Such experiences seemed to have a profound effect on Sam. So much so, that he was determined to remember it when he came to travel on his own later in life.

*

As always, arriving in a new country was exciting. We immediately set about writing down and learning our standard list of key words and phrases. This usually meant asking an English-speaking local to tell us the words we needed to know. The standard list was built up from our experience in each country along the way. This provided us with a fairly short number of essentials to learn:

Yes / No / Please / Thank you / Delicious / Which is the road for XYZ? / Where can I find a guesthouse/café? / Father / Son / How much? / How many?

These and others were followed by the names for rice, egg, vegetables, fish, chicken, beef, prawn, squid, tofu, coffee and tea. Beer was ubiquitous. It was not a lot to learn. Sam and I could usually manage it within a few days by testing each other at random times. The surprising thing was how we almost completely wiped this vocabulary from our minds as soon as we moved on to the next country. Only my travel diary now reminds me of how much of so many languages we learned.

After this first section, we felt more confident about the road to Hanoi and rounded off the day nicely by finding an excellent luxury guesthouse in Tuan Giao with a restaurant in the garden. During the night, we had plenty of time to consider our next section, due to the apparent love the Vietnamese people have for karaoke. The caterwauling from the bar downstairs until the early hours was hilarious at first, but soon Sam was asking about earplugs. They certainly would have been a useful addition to our trip equipment list.

Unfortunately, our first day's cycling on the road to Hanoi was not representative. The road out of Tuan Giao was a confusion of dust, concrete, construction vehicles and jammed traffic – the truck drivers had been right. We stopped and discussed the best course of action. As Sam only had fifth gear and his front triple, it seemed sensible to take a bus if there was one. We cycled back into town and negotiated two seats on a minibus, plus the back seat for the bikes. This was annoying, but it was a relief there was a bus. One way or another, we would get the gear cable sorted in Hanoi.

This gave us twenty minutes for breakfast at a cafe opposite. Cafes near bus and train stations were usually good in our experience and this was no exception. The staff were friendly and we were served an excellent breakfast of noodles with vegetables and prawns.

"*Huan giap!*" the lady kept saying, poking Sam's stomach. *Eat more*, apparently.

The healthy breakfast put a better complexion on things. Looking out the window as we drove through the roadworks in relative comfort, Sam and I smiled, thankful we had made this decision. The roadwork hell was short lived, however, and the road improved once we had climbed into the hills. We looked at each other in resigned disappointment. No good asking to get off now, we agreed. It had taken fifteen minutes to squeeze our bikes into the bus.

Up at altitude, we found ourselves being driven through dense damp mist, catching glimpses through holes in the cloud of forested green hills below, until we descended back onto the plains. This would have made great cycling and frankly we were gutted. From there, it was fairly flat with a better road surface than expected most of the way to Hanoi. The heavy traffic became the greatest hazard.

About ten kilometres from Hanoi, the bus driver pulled over at the side of the busy suburban street, got out and crawled under the bus. I went to see if I could help. He had found something wrong with the clutch mechanism and the hydraulic fluid had leaked out. A very Asian event followed, with all the passengers getting off and pushing the large minibus along the road until we reached some kind of chicken-farm-cum-garage. Here, they eventually managed to manufacture a new seal from a bit of inner-tube and refill the reservoir. The bus then limped into central Hanoi and deposited us.

The place we had been dropped seemed to be a poor quarter of Hanoi. We had no city map, which was bad planning. But by sheer luck and an inexplicable sense of direction, we found ourselves reaching one of the lakes I knew to be near the city centre. Spotting a fairly luxurious looking four-star hotel, I asked where we could find a good hostel. As I half expected, the duty manager offered us a discounted rate to stay with them for four nights. I felt Sam at least deserved a bit of comfort for a few days and also hoped the friendly staff might help us to find a cycle shop to repair Sam's bike.

We were soon installed in a comfortable room, watching English Premiership football on an unfamiliar modern flat-screen TV. Things were looking up. Sam seemed more cheerful than I had seen him in a while.

The place had a homey feel about it and the guys on reception were kind enough to let us use the desk computer to access the internet and update our blog. It was our first opportunity to do this since Laos.

*

The Hanoi Lake View Hotel was a good decision. Sam was much happier, the staff were really helpful and we met some interesting people at breakfast. One ageing Californian playboy-type named Steve made a particular impression on us. His speech and mental faculties, it seemed, were a testament to either a brain damaged by drugs during his hippy youth or of something he was on now. He seemed incapable of retaining any information in his short to medium-term memory.

"Maybe he had an accident," suggested Sam.

"Must have been a bad one," I replied.

With an unbuttoned shirt displaying a gold medallion and a chicken neck, Steve was the friendliest guy. He was astounded by our journey, rushing off to tell the staff and other regular guests to come and meet us. It seemed he stayed here regularly on trips from Los Angeles, but it was hard to ascertain anything for sure. One problem was that he was incapable of remembering our names or any of the details of our trip. It meant that he introduced us with different names each time. Naturally, this became most amusing and we finally settled upon two of the mistaken names as aliases.

"Have you heard about Stan and Chester's amazing adventure?" we heard him ask some people on the next table.

Stan and Chester – it had a kind of a ring to it.

It was difficult to establish what had brought Steve to Vietnam so many times over the years and why he spoke Vietnamese. Whether his confused and contradictory explanations about business, military service and tourism were an attempt at a cover-up – or just the fact that his brain was fried – was hard to confirm, but it certainly made for some surreal discussions.

Over our four days in Hanoi, we met Steve a few times in reception, where he was invariably accompanied by expensively dressed Vietnamese beauties he always described as *friends*. Eventually, we decided he was a wealthy work-shy heir to a Hollywood movie fortune whose only real motivations in life were recreational drugs and beautiful young Asian women. He seemed to have little interest in anything else, or at least no ability to remember.

On our first day, one of the receptionists told us where to go to find bike shops. Fortunately, Hanoi is one of those cities that retain a kind of ancient layout of trade establishments that all operate in one quarter. By sheer coincidence, the bicycle area was very close to our hotel. Less fortunate was our discovery that derailleur-geared bicycles had yet to reach Vietnam. The people in the bike shops stared at ours in wonder. It did not bode well.

Sam and I went from shop to shop and saw a lot of head shaking. Finally, one rather arrogant shop owner called his mechanic out of the workshop. The pair looked over Sam's bike together and said they could fix it. We were apprehensive but agreed to let them try.

The mechanic returned to his workshop and came back with some agricultural-looking tools. He told us to stand back. Memories of an Indian puncture-wallah returned. Even before he began yanking and prising off coverings, we were already worried. Next, he took his large pliers to the cable and began pulling. Nothing gave, so he pulled harder. Sam and I pleaded with him to stop. The two men told us to stand clear and joined forces pulling at the cable. It was like a Tom and Jerry cartoon. We waited nervously for the cable to snap and send the two of them cascading head over heels into the gutter. I was already thinking about the options once they had wrecked it.

My father used to describe such behaviour as *brute force and ignorance*. As if reading my thoughts, the two men stopped pulling. One, it seemed, had suddenly had the wild idea of pushing the cable rather than pulling it. It popped out easily. He yanked the cable out and in no time had the new cable in place. The gears were miraculously set perfectly first time and we were on our way only a few quid the poorer. Despite this eventual success, we felt unable to adopt their approach to cycle mechanics in future.

*

After four days' rest, our minds were now positive and clear of worry. We had certainly been lucky with Sam's gear cable. The day of our departure for China came and we wheeled our bikes outside purposefully. Just as were oiling our chains, however, a further mechanical problem came to light. This revealed itself to be slightly more serious than a worn gear cable.

While running a cleaning cloth around my back wheel rim, I noticed that my rear brake-blocks were binding. Spinning the wheel, I could see a bit of a buckle in the rim. As I *pinged* my spokes to check for tension, I suddenly felt one go soft against my fingers. With a sick feeling, I looked more closely, expecting to find a broken spoke. I gasped in horror – three or four spokes had pulled right through the alloy rim. This effectively rendered the rear wheel completely useless, at least within a few miles.

I cursed myself for not noticing this four days before. Then I praised myself for checking the wheels before we started out of the city, where there would be no decent bike shops. Having already been around the bike shops, though, I knew we were unlikely to find a 700c-sized wheel inside the shores of Vietnam. I was determined not to slip into a negative frame of mind this time, however. This was not a crisis, I told myself, just a small barrier thrown in my way to test me.   I could deal with it . . .

I was already thinking in terms of how long we would need to wait for a wheel rim to be couriered over from UK and whether we could afford to stay in the same hotel that long.   Nonetheless, we headed back to the bicycle district and called in at some of the same shops.   It began raining quite hard, adding an atmosphere of misery to proceedings, but I would not be negative.   This was not a sign of doom on the horizon, I told myself.   There was still hope.

Absolutely no dice, was the obvious response to our enquiries at every shop.

Sam pointed out that today was the first proper rain since Cochin back in October.   I swallowed hard.   Indians would think nothing of this.   They would come up with a solution.   But I was not an Indian.

We were just about to give up and head back to the Lake View Hotel when a young guy called us over.   He seemed to be saying he knew a mechanic who might fix the wheel.   I pointed at the numbers on the tyre to indicate the odd size.

"OK, OK!"   He waved me towards an alley.

I knew it was next to impossible to repair an aluminium alloy wheel, but we followed him to a tiny workshop.   Out came a wiry guy in shorts and a tatty vest to look at the wheel.   He was clearly an extra from Apocalypse Now, Platoon, or Full Metal Jacket.   After nodding, he got on his mobile phone.

"New wheel come my shop thirty minute; 400,000 Vietnam dollar, OK?"

It sounded like a big number but was no more than £16.   I nodded happily.   It would be a cheap and heavy old wheel but might get us to Naning or Guilin in China.   What unbelievable luck, we agreed.

The mechanic – who in the movie would have been referred to as *Charlie* – took us into his workshop, made us tea and sat us in front of a small TV.

"Like football?" he asked.

Yes, we loved football, we told him.

Once he was sure we were comfortable, he set to work.   First, he unscrewed all the spokes and removed the rim like a true master.

At the same time, he chatted to us about Manchester United, Chelsea, Arsenal and Liverpool. He was extremely knowledgeable.

"*Totten-ham* good style," he told us. "One day, *Totten-ham* number one!"

Fortunately, he also seemed expert at dealing with foreign bikes. We could see several quality imported mountain bikes in his small workshop. As far as bicycles in Vietnam were concerned, we had clearly been brought to *The Man*.

The new rim arrived. Our man asked me to approve it before he began replacing the spokes and truing the wheel on his special homemade jig. In fact, it was not a bad rim. Miraculously, we were back on the road in an hour. The bucket-load of stress I had taken on over the morning seemed to have gone. I felt proud of myself for staying positive. It had been a good lesson.

The moment of victory was short-lived, however. Half an hour down the road, I found my gears didn't work. My self-control immediately went out of the window. In a very grumpy and pessimistic mood, I removed the cable from the sheath before I realised Charlie had simply pinched the cable in the wheel clamp. Feeding the cable back in, which had now frayed at the end, looked an impossible task, though.

Not realising quite how bad I was feeling, Sam laughed at my downcast mood. When I looked up angrily, he was really critical about me losing my temper. This was not constructive but incredibly rude, I felt. For the first time on the trip, I failed to restrain myself, telling him to either fix it himself or shut up – or words to that effect. His silence told me how angry he was. Eventually, motivated by sheer pig-headedness, I did manage to reinsert the cable, but not before a great deal of frustration, swearing and grovelling in the wet dirt at the side of the road. The whole experience, though, had shattered and disappointed me. I rode off feeling seriously weakened, with a very dark cloud over my head.

It seemed all too easy for Sam to tell me to keep calm and say "it's only a cable" when I was always the one left to sort these things out. Of course, looking back on it later, I could see he had a point. But he could have dealt with it helpfully rather than critically – advice I needed to follow myself much of the time. What had really made the morning tough and put me in a sensitive mood, though, was that I was suffering from an explosive and debilitating case of diarrhoea. This was the last thing I needed on a morning with so many problems – especially away from a hotel with a clean modern toilet.

*

After two frustrating breakdowns in a few days, Sam and I now felt nervous about the possibility of something else going wrong. We had been fortunate with bike problems so far, especially compared with most other cyclists we had met on the way. We feared that the balance might be about to be redressed by the law of averages. Yes, that smug, self-righteous law of averages – the curse of economists, scientists and gamblers down the ages. You think you have discovered something useful, a great idea, and develop a system that proves your idea right; but just as you are enjoying the rewards and starting to feel proud of your achievement, it all goes wrong. You realise your success was just part of a bigger cycle, and you are now on the downward part of that.

I realise now, that at this point I was in danger of taking life a bit too seriously. I continued wrangling over it as we cycled in a communication blackout. After no broken spokes or wheel rims up to Hanoi – and thinking we had earned this by things like regular maintenance and not overloading our bikes – were we now going to suffer multiple breakages? Were our mechanical problems going to average out at about the same as those of other riders? The thought agonised me so much I did not share it with Sam, even after we had begun speaking again.

Missing lunch on account of my digestive problems, I re-bodged my rack with a nut and bolt to replace a self-tapping screw and we managed to reach Voi by 4pm. I felt bloody awful, both physically and mentally. Only achieving 70km, due to the late start, felt like a failure for a start. I told myself I was being pathetic. Yet, given the problems that had been overcome in just the morning, I should have thanked our good luck for getting anywhere at all that day.

For the first time I could remember on the trip, it started to feel cold in Voi. Going out for dinner, we had to put fleeces on under our jackets. In my negative state, I wondered if it was a sign of harder times to come.

At a basic street café where two women cooked noodle soup on a brazier, Sam and I ordered everything they had. I was now hungry after fasting all day. We were served several things we couldn't recognise in the dark. One of them was easy, though, and we sliced the tops off a boiled egg each. The woman had asked us whether we wanted one kind or another, but our Vietnamese food language did not run to understanding the details. Confident you couldn't go far wrong with boiled eggs, I asked for the second and more expensive type. Probably duck eggs, I thought. Eating them, we noticed that they were kind of stringy and chewy in parts and tasted a little odd. Not exactly unpleasant, just odd. The following day, at the same place for breakfast, we discovered we had eaten embryonic eggs, which have soft chicks inside just prior to hatching.

"Mmm, interesting!"

Getting up early, we felt excited knowing we should be in China that afternoon, but I was still a little out of sorts. As long as we made decent time and are not held up at the border, I thought. It was a miserable grey morning, a little cold and raining steadily; the climatic novelty had already worn thin and we gritted our teeth. At the planning stage, I had been aware we may hit the start of the south China rainy season but hoped we would be lucky. Sam was already remembering what poor circulation he has in his hands and feet, and I was remembering how miserable it made him.

I was still in a negative frame of mind when we approached the border. This was mainly due to the fact that the numbskull boyfriend of our guesthouse manageress had busted my plastic rear mudguard by trying to bend it straight. It didn't help my sense of doom to remember being told that Chinese Customs were confiscating copies of the Lonely Planet China guide. After hesitantly buying this in Hanoi, I was now worried. Although it was a reluctant purchase (it was heavy and often talked total bullshit), it had cost quite a bit and I didn't want to lose it.

As we approached the border, I took the large book from my pannier and stuffed it down my lycra shorts with my shirt hanging loosely over to cover it. Sam laughed, rather too loudly. The shirt may have covered the enormous and strangely angular bulge, but it made me walk like I had suffered a serious mishap. As it was, our panniers were thoroughly searched. Questions were asked about maps, novels and foodstuffs, but fortunately my shorts remained unrumaged.

SAM'S POINT OF VIEW

After Martin left, our trip continued right up into the mountains of Northern Laos and across the border into North Vietnam. The roads up there were not much more than tracks.

The hills north of Luang Prabang were huge and the weather was really not great for cycling during the heat of the day. Also, there were less places to stay or to find food again, and this made things a bit tougher. Food was a big issue for me, since I kept having to avoid it after stomach upsets from bouts of giardia. Once we got to Oudomaxi I decided to take the antibiotics. Four of them in one go absolutely knocked me for six. I thought I was dying! Soon after this, struggling on to the next place, my bike developed a frayed gear cable. My dad was really good at helping me deal with the weakness brought on by the antibiotic bombardment and despite all this hassle I did enjoy Northern Laos.

Getting over the border into Vietnam was tough. Basically, there was no road. Bien Dien Phu was a great place once we got there and I loved the café we found in the market. Moving on from there, my gear cable proved a problem to fix, so when we encountered a massive chain of roadworks we decided to take a bus 50 miles into Hanoi. As it turned out, this was another mistake. The bus broke down and we ended up pushing it.

Resting-up in Hanoi was excellent. It was a great city and we found a nice hotel with a decent TV to watch football and movies. It's a great way to relax and recharge. We met a crazy American there, who seemed brain dead from drugs or something, and we became his friends Stan and Chester!

Getting the gear cable sorted in Hanoi was a relief but discovering my dad's broken wheel just as we were leaving seemed like a disaster. Luckily, Asian ingenuity came to the rescue and we were only held up for a couple of hours. Amazing!

Cycling on from there into China seemed to me to be a turning point in the trip. It was the first time I really felt we were getting close to our ultimate destination.

Chapter 12

China – Austerity causes conflict but eventual harmony

My father is one doctor for make healthy the sick animal.   But, more time people pay him money for to kill them.

Cycling out of the smart frontier reception area, we turned down the offer of money exchange by street hawkers and headed off on a decent new dual-carriageway towards Ping Xiang – the first main town after the border.

I had spent a month in China with Lorna on our way back from Japan 23 years before, when the country first reopened for tourism after the Cultural Revolution.   It already looked very different.   Judging by the roads, buildings, vehicles and the clothes people were wearing, a whole age seemed to have passed.   More noticeably, people seemed friendly and polite – politeness having seemed utterly alien to them the last time I was there.

Getting to Ping Xiang had been slightly worrying, due to the dual-carriageways, but nothing too tiring.   By starting out at 7am that morning, we managed to cover the 130km by 4pm.   We felt excited about being there.   After eventually breaking through the language/cultural barrier, we located a cash machine and were then directed to an excellent small guesthouse.   This was a kind of converted shop or office.   It was still raining steadily and, as always in China (some things had not changed in 23years), the streets had become filthy as a result.   We felt embarrassed wheeling our dirty bikes across the lady's sparkling clean floor.   Politeness was clearly not alien to this lady.   She could not have been more welcoming.

"Ah, no problem, please," she beckoned us forwards with the bikes.   "No problem.   Clean later, very easy."

Indicating that we could leave our bikes in her small reception, the lady took us upstairs.   We felt good about this place already. On the first floor of the building she led us into a nice spacious room. She then demonstrated how the hot water heater worked, found an

English TV channel for us and made us tea.   On our way out to eat later, this kind lady insisted on lending us her own umbrella to protect us from the continuing rain.   It was a world away from the China I once knew.

In town, the good omens continued as we found a selection of friendly restaurants and cafes with reasonable prices and great food. The smile hadn't left Sam's face since we arrived here.   That was a wonderful thing to see.   The waitresses in the restaurant were really pleasant.   They made us feel most welcome and helped us to choose some delicious food.   Even the local beer (Li-Q) was excellent.

Well-fed and feeling content, Sam and I walked through a smart new shopping-mall back to our warm guesthouse, wondering what the hell the Lonely Planet guide was on about, saying that this town was merely a place to change buses and not worth stopping at.   These things are so subjective.   Even on a windswept rainy evening, we liked the atmosphere here so much we wished we were staying longer. Our compulsion to move on was annoying.   We did need to reach Shanghai by a fixed deadline, though, and I was hoping we might somehow get ahead of this seasonal rain.

Ping Xiang was certainly a good introduction to China, especially for Sam, who had not been to the country before.   I only hoped the rest of China would be as enjoyable.   The bloody law of averages thing was still gnawing away at me.

*

Next morning, I made a bodged repair to my rear mudguard with some duct tape and a butchered coat-hanger.   Across the street, we bought a couple of dumplings to give us energy for the morning and stood under a shop doorway to eat them.   People smiled as they passed us with their morning newspapers covering their heads to shield them from the persistent rain.   An elderly man stopped and put a small plastic bag over Sam's saddle to keep it dry, waved, then walked quickly on.

"God, I love it here!" said Sam.

After checking our map again we cycled off, following directions for Nanning and hoping we had read the Chinese characters correctly.   We were in a more adventurous frame of mind today.

The map was not very detailed so we were really only heading in a general direction and hoping to find a good road at this stage.   We had cleaned and lubed the bikes before we started, but with the rain and mud on the roads they were soon a mess again.   Despite all this, we remained in high spirits.   It did seem like the start of a bad day, though, when our chosen road led to the tollbooth of an expressway and we were greeted with a loud siren.

Pulling over at the sentry box, we had our passports checked by the army.   Rather surprisingly, we were waved on without any fuss, so we remounted and cycled on to the end toll kiosk.   Before we knew it, though, a uniformed woman in one of the tollbooths began waving frantically.   She seemed to be in a total panic about us being there.   The deafening siren howled again and we stopped, waiting until the chief toll-lady arrived.   She marched over from her booth and attempted to explain the problem to us.

"*Er, mayo!*" she said, pointing at the bicycles. "*Mayo!*"
I knew the word well from many years before.   It could mean all manner of things, but all with the same inference: *No way, Jose!*

It didn't need much working out.   Obviously, bicycles were not permitted on Chinese expressways.   Fine, so where was the alternative route?   Seeing we were not about to make a break for it, she made a signal and stopped the siren.   The lady smiled, but I wasn't getting my hopes up.   It turned out she spoke some English.

"No alternative, er *lute*.   Better you take, er bus."

We insisted that surely there must be a smaller road.   Trying to communicate this with our map and sign language was a challenge, but she seemed to understand and was perhaps even sympathetic. We had not enjoyed our last bus trip and were determined not to use them again unless absolutely necessary.   It was a relief, therefore, when she finally accepted our preference and directed us back through town to a small road heading east.   It obviously seemed a strange choice to her, though.

"*Bery* smaller *load*, you like a bus too much more!" she laughed.

What a nice lady, we thought. She really made us smile. Despite the rain, we kept smiling all the way back across town until we were on the *bery smaller load*. It was just the right size for us and the surface was not bad at all.

The small road took us through simple Chinese villages and muddy agricultural countryside, which provided us with some interest for the morning. We stopped for lunch in a superb pick-your-own street restaurant in busy Ning Ming and had our first experience of rural Chinese eating. To our great amusement, local people came in to stare at us as we ate, like we were a theatrical performance.

"Not many western travellers coming through here, then," I smiled.

"Not many aliens landing here either," replied Sam.

I had expected cycling in China to be tough. The rain during the morning and the muddy roads it brought with it had not been particularly pleasant, but it had still been a fairly relaxing ride so far.

After lunch, things got tougher. The road surface deteriorated markedly. Smoky old trucks precariously overloaded with sugar cane struggled to pass us as the hills got progressively steeper. I reminded myself that China is a big country, so this could go on for a long time. The outlook was bearable for me, but I was worried how Sam would deal with it. Although his fitness was clearly still under par, he had seemed much better since Hanoi and I really didn't want anything to spoil that. Thankfully, his stomach problems seemed to have improved. Perhaps the giardia had been evicted at last.

After 120 challenging kilometres, we arrived at a poverty-stricken workers housing collective named Banli. This was more like the China I remembered. There may have been a village here once, but now it was simply a miserable, grey street of concrete terraced buildings and a dirt road between. The shop units sold cheap bits of cut-up animals, packet food that was not really food (synthetic crisps, puffed rice biscuits, etc), plastic bowls and cheap ironmongery. It was very much what you'd find in a Pound Shop on most British high streets these days.

Fortunately, there was a large guesthouse. The front door was unlocked and we went inside. The reception was empty, though, and nobody seemed to be around to rent us a room. We finally searched upstairs and found the staff all eating at a huge banqueting table. Seeing us, a young woman in a trendy bright-red coat jumped up to help us. This rather lovely young woman found us a room and helped us put our bikes on the balcony, before returning apologetically to her meal.

After washing our muddy wet clothes and taking a shower, at reception we asked two spotty young men about food in the town. There was nowhere, they shrugged.

"*Mayo!*"

Old China again, I thought. Remembering how to deal with it, I persisted doggedly until they phoned our diminutive lady in red, who came back from home to sort out the problem.

"*What the hell do you mean, telling them there is no food?*" she seemed to say. "*Get to the bloody kitchen and tell the chef to cook them something! Useless self-gratifiers!*"

The two men scuttled off in shame. Our little saviour sat down with us at a table and translated a number of things on the menu that we liked the sound of. She phoned the chef to tell him what to cook. We asked her to not worry and to go home to her family, but she was insistent. She waited until our delicious food arrived and then said goodnight.

"I think I love this woman," whispered Sam.

"I saw her first, Sam."

"You're married and too bloody old, you greedy bastard!"

"Young women like old men here. Have you seen the way she looks at me?"

"I have, Dad. It's called pity."

*

The rain had stopped when we set off the next morning. We were in the heart of the Chinese sugar-cane belt. All day we marvelled at the outrageously overloaded trucks, which frequently blocked the entire road. No sooner had we claimed one truck as the worst we had seen, than another even more precariously loaded example passed us to snatch the trophy.

"They could give Indian trucks a good run for their money," Sam laughed.

This section was tough going, with badly surfaced narrow roads and primitive small towns displaying little that looked appealing in their shops and cafes. Intestines seemed to be the main protein on offer, but nothing they did to it in the preparation or cooking seemed to make it any more appetising than it looked. Sam's stomach proved itself to still be a little sensitive and the hills hurt his weakened legs, so our troubles were not entirely over in that department. I hoped China was not all going to be like this.

Despite the predominately rural landscape, the views were far from uplifting. In fact, they were rather ugly and the people looked far from contented. I knew there would be times like this on the trip; I was surprised there had not been more so far. It was a far cry from the bliss of rural life in Laos and Vietnam, or even India.

Sam seemed miserable too now and lagged behind, despite my attempts to ride at his pace. Our two maps gave different distances between towns and invariably neither was correct – it was nearly always significantly further.

It is probably hard to imagine quite how depressing it is for a cyclist in a place they would rather get through quickly, to continually discover the next stopping point is further than they have been told. Despite all efforts to remain positive, it is punishing and you start to feel like the world is laughing at your pain. This was our experience in much of rural China. Fortunately, though, there were regular up-sides that compensated.

The irritation I had felt with Sam and his awkward behaviour a few months back had now turned to worry. His stomach problem appeared to be getting better, but suddenly and for no good reason it had returned. He had taken the antibiotics. I wanted to get something done about it but lacked faith in any doctor we might be able to find. It added to my frustration that Sam consistently told me he was much better and not to worry. More than anything, it seemed a shame that Sam often felt too rough to enjoy the journey or the places we stayed. I knew that if Lorna were here, she would get him straight to a doctor whether he liked it or not. On this trip, however, I felt I had already learned Sam was ready to make his own decisions in life and resented parents trying to make decisions for him. So I continued quietly worrying and treading cautiously when we talked, due to the fragile temperament that seemed to accompany his fragile physical state.

*

After such a miserable few days, Sam and I were overjoyed to arrive in the modern and surprisingly large city of Nanning. We had a recommendation for a good hotel in the centre. After a long ride through the heavily trafficked urban streets, we were shown a comfortable and spacious twin room. We agreed to book in for three nights in order to allow Sam's digestion time to recover again.

The hotel was one of those huge 1950s places built for Communist Party cadres, with long uniform corridors and dull furnishings. It was comfortable, reasonably priced and well located. Nearby, I found some great Moslem cafes serving noodles they made by hand in front of you, plus many workers' kitchen-type places with pick-your-own dishes from a multitude of trays.

Sam was on a strict light-food diet for a few days – a prospect that irritated him, since he was eager to try all of these delicious-looking dishes. After a day, though, he started to feel better. Soon, we were back to organising ourselves around where, what and when we would eat.

As I have emphasised, food becomes a bit of an obsession when you are exerting yourself so much. Not only is it your fuel but often a main source of interest, with the cuisine always changing as the journey progresses. Stomach upsets make life much harder, since you have to cut food out of your day, or at least cut down to light basics, and you lack the energy you need. More than anything, though, such problems just make the day boring, with nothing to look forward to. Similarly, on a well-earned break for a few days, you want to sample a few treats and it is miserable if you can't. By this stage of the journey, Sam's life much of the time involved finding himself in constant dilemmas over whether to eat something he liked the look of or not.

After three nights in Nanning, Sam felt well enough to continue and we headed off for the town of Datang.   Back in the countryside again, we were soon slowed to a monotonous pace by roadworks. This was all the more annoying when we discovered this was nothing more than a couple of elderly women each with a bucket of stones that they were treading into potholes.   Then it started to rain.

Rain on Chinese country roads is hell.   All the dust quickly turns into mud and gritty dirt seems to get into everything.   This has a really abrasive effect on your bike as well as your willpower.   Add to the cocktail large amounts of black smoke belched from tired old trucks and you have a recipe for a very miserable day.

What made things even harder was that the people in this area couldn't seem to understand us when we asked the way to Datang. We knew it must be our incorrect pronunciation (a common problem with Chinese for westerners) but we tried every conceivable permutation until we were nearly mad with frustration, somewhere between laughing and crying.   Finally, we discovered, by exaggerated mimicry, that they understood if we shouted the word and kind of spat at the same time.

In retrospect, I think it was the same syndrome we encountered in rural India of rural people assuming they won't understand you, waving their hands and blocking out what you say.   In today's case, we gained great amusement from the ridiculous shouted pronunciation necessary to be understood.   To this day we insist on referring in conversation to it as *DaaahTTTang!*   Surprisingly, this *shout and spit* pronunciation system worked for other place names in China, so it was a great step forward in our Chinese linguistic abilities.

Datang itself was another grey, poverty-stricken one-street town and, judging by our dining spot, yet another favoured spot for fly breeding.   Despite being told by the police there was no accommodation, we found a kind of workers' hostel with a tiny damp room.   Small and cold though it was, we felt lucky to be there.

*

In the new China, being poor and stupid is not good.

Luzai, our next stop – 108km, not 67 as indicated on my map, or 62, as on Sam's – came at the end of another filthy wet day on a terrible potholed road. We had planned to reach Lippu that day. Our shouting and spitting of its name met with universal recognition, so we were progressing with the spoken language at least. Lippu is pronounced as by a man with no hands trying to blow a feather off his nose. Our advances in pronunciation, however, was not matched by our progress towards reaching Lippu. On arriving in Luzai, after a gruelling 60km, we saw a sign. Instead of a further 52km to Lippu, the sign said it was another 97km. There was nothing to discuss. We agreed to stay in Luzai.

Fortunately, we found a really nice hotel staffed by trendy young people who took us out to find a good place to eat. Luzai was a rather upbeat town really; one of the new cities, it seemed, with good shops and happy-looking people. If you were a poor Chinese person in this region, you would want to live here. This made me ponder the future of China.

The country had modernised so much since I'd been here 23 years before and most people seemed much happier. Now, though, there was a huge disparity between the lifestyles of those in large towns and cities, and those who lived in the countryside. Country-dwellers eked out meagre existences on minimal diets, huddled around crude coal stoves, working long hours for minimal reward. In cities fairly nearby, however, one could now find Chinese living in the lap of luxury, driving expensive cars and working reasonable hours in air-conditioned offices. These are the ones we had started to see on holiday in Europe.

The improved living standards did not appear to be spreading to the countryside and it seemed to me that it would not be long before the simple countryfolk became fed up with this. Surely, before long they would down tools and revolt. In such a large country, this would be hard to control. I shared my thoughts with Sam as we were selecting cakes in a bakery after dinner.

"Far from growing as a stable economic miracle, mate, China could face major socio-economic problems in the future."

"Sorry, cakes are the issue right now," he replied.

We had a really enjoyable evening, but fate was balancing things out again.   Back at our hotel, we received some bad news.   Chatting to one of our new friends at reception, we discovered the small road via Lippu to Guilin was closed for repair.

"Closed?"   It didn't seem possible.   How could they just close it?

"This China, government decide.   People not important in China.   Politician say close *load*, so *load* close.   Car, bus and truck can use highway.   Bicycle people, poor and *stoopid*, so no problem. Ah yes, Mark and Sam poor and *stoopid*.   Ha, ha!"

We could not cycle on the highway, of course.   We'd tried that. This had become too familiar of late.   Cyclists were second class citizens here now.   In the new China, being poor and stupid was not good.

*

In the morning, Sam and I rode up to the start of the road just to make sure, but our fate was confirmed when a man with a red flag sharply turned us back.

"*Mayo!*"

It was still bugging me.   It seemed crazy, I told Sam, that in a predominantly rural country like China, you only had the option of a motorway when the old road was closed.   No doubt the government felt it was sound economics.   Farmers with horses and carts or peasants with only bicycles would have to buy cars or motorcycles – Chinese cars and motorcycles, of course.   This would continue to drive the economic miracle that is China.   And that, as they say, is progress.   Sam grunted.   My mistake, it was before lunchtime.

Reluctantly, we headed to the bus station to take a bus.   It rained incessantly.   On the highway, from the window of our bus, we saw the small dug-up road and accepted it would have been impossible for cycling, even if we had been allowed on it.   We sat back to enjoy the two-hour ride in relative comfort.   A little further along the highway, we noticed a man pushing a broken bicycle through the quagmire of mud at the side of the old road.   A construction worker with a whistle was ordering him away from the track.   I tapped Sam's shoulder and pointed.

"Him, poor and *stoopid*!"

A woman in the seat opposite looked across at me disapprovingly.   There was no point trying to explain.

Surrounded by spectacular karst limestone peaks, the tourist city of Guilin was made famous by the Chinese paintings and silk screens you see in Chinese restaurants all over the world.   You might think the representations of these mountains are a wild exaggeration of the real thing.   When you come here, though, you realise they aren't. Individual fingers of rock tower into the sky, with trees clinging to the tops like something from a fairytale.   As a visitor, you never quite get used to this landscape.   It seems to defy reality.

It was pouring with rain again now and it didn't look temporary. This was not a shower, it was an entire rainy season.   After finding a good backpacker hostel near the centre, Sam and I agreed it was worth resting-up here for a few days.   This would get us out of the rain and give us the chance to wash some clothes.   Until recently, we had enjoyed the very effective system of washing clothes at night, then drying them on our panniers as we rode along in the breeze the next morning.   The arrival of the miserable south China rainy season had curtailed this, however, and we had to rely on the less effective traveller's system of stringing washing across our room at night. This drove home to us how important the whole clothes washing/drying issue was on a trip like this.   One could just avoid washing them, of course.   That had its downsides, though.   Apart from the likely fungal complaints in the groin and underarm areas, I feel we would not have enjoyed such good luck with people if we had smelled like a couple of hobos.

Our hostel was pleasant enough, despite the holes in the roof that allowed rainwater to pour into buckets in the main lounge area.   We met nice people here and found a useful large bookshop to buy some better road maps.   But Guilin's shopping malls and tour buses were not so pleasing to us.   By the time we had done the rounds of a few restaurants and shops, we were eager to move on.

Sam seemed to be coming out of another digestive disruption phase, and his renewed strength prompted him to suggest we try to cover the 1,000km to Wuhan over the next seven days without another break.   I was always up for a challenge like this and held out some forlorn hope that it might yet get us ahead of the rain belt.   There seemed no point staying longer anyway.   The rain was not going to stop.   After only two nights in Guilin, we set off back on the road again, heading for the mega-city of Wuhan.

*

Looking at our new road maps, our route from Guilin would take us via Quangzhou, Qiyang, Hengyang, Changsha, Yueyang and Xianning.   None of these places seemed to hold any great promise, according to the Lonely Planet China guide, but we knew by now not to put much store by that.

In Quangzhou (or Guanzhou), we found a good hotel overlooking the modern town square and fountains.   Here we also saw roasted dogs for sale in the market for the first time.   The three unmistakeable creatures were placed on top of a cage containing a live dog.   We wondered if this one was aware of what misfortune had befallen the others, and what he might be thinking.   His behaviour certainly seemed fairly normal.   It was as if he was unaware, or existentially resigned, to his fate.

We were making good progress, unlike the poor dogs of Quangzhou.   Arriving in Qiyang the following night, I noted in my diary that we ate the best food of the trip so far, in a cheap pick-your-own place.   The food we selected and placed in our baskets was so fresh and was cooked so well for us, we felt tempted to return for breakfast before leaving the next morning.

In these pick-your-own restaurants, the drill is to select what you want from a raw selection outside, placing it all in a plastic basket. You give this to the chef, then point to the protein that you want – meat, tofu or sometimes fish (no, never dog, in my experience) – and the whole lot is cooked for you.   The cook determines which items need to be cooked separately and which together, then woks them up and brings them to your table.   Customers help themselves to steamed rice and tea as they need them.

This is an excellent system that enables you to enjoy really fresh food and avoid anything you don't like. These places are always cheap (which is why they don't have dog – too expensive) and full of friendly happy people swigging beer or Chinese spirits and generally making a hell of a mess and racket. I can't tell you how much I would rather eat in one of these places than any five-star hotel or Michelin star restaurant. Absolutely no contest.

As we progressed further north from Guangdong into Hunan Province, the food and the people changed markedly. Things became gradually more modern and the people seemed generally friendlier. Horn abuse from traffic, though, was some of the worst on the trip and it took its toll on our nerves. I recounted this to Lorna in a phone conversation and it seemed to amuse her far more than it did us. I wondered whether I was taking things a bit too seriously.

Since India, I generally now phoned Lorna every few weeks but sent emails in between. E-mail was more satisfying in some ways, since on the phone we often forgot the things we wanted to say until just after we had hung up. Around Hengyang, I phoned her and was worried by how physically and emotionally drained she sounded. She seemed to be working really hard, going out to theatre and cinema with Scarlett, eating out a lot with our friends and dealing with the emotional traumas of many of them. She was clearly enjoying her life but getting totally worn down.

An old friend of ours, she told me, had tragically taken his own life and another was suffering from the recent death of his wife to cancer, so Lorna was adopting her usual supportive role with the families involved. This would be enough to exhaust anyone, I thought. She sounded really relieved when I told her Sam and I had set a definite date for our return of 11 June.

*

At the end of a long, dark stormy day, through areas of heavy industry and rural poverty, we arrived in Changsha. It was a shock. Changsha was a large modern city with luxury high-rise hotels and a riot of neon. Unable to find a cheap hotel that admitted foreigners, we were forced to stay in one of the four-star, high-rise places. We had a superb view from our comfortable room on the twenty-first floor, but we felt strangely isolated. It was so far removed from the blackness of primitive industrial landscapes and dank villages we had ridden through all day. We washed all the dirty, moulding clothes that had mounted up since Guilin and turned up the room thermostat. From adjacent apartment buildings, our luxurious room must have resembled a Chinese laundry or refugee camp.

In the morning, Sam valiantly struggled not to overeat at what was a banquet of a buffet breakfast, before we headed off into Hubei Province for a strenuous 150km day. These days were not scenic or particularly interesting, but there was entertainment to be had. Occasions when we needed to ask for directions were often either humorous or infuriating and went some way to breaking the monotony. Food was frequently the only highlight of our day. In the main, we found ourselves slogging along for hour after hour on poor but fairly straight roads against bleak open landscapes. This Orwellian world was semi-dark all day, probably not helped by the industrial pollution.

There were quite a few hilly sections, although even these were rather dull. The weather didn't help. Every day was either rainy or misty. If it wasn't raining it was threatening to rain. We did not complain. All of this helped us to make progress. There was little to stop for and Sam was feeling much stronger, so we just kept at it, thinking and singing in our heads as our feet went endlessly around.

One positive experience stands out from this leg of the trip. In Xianning, we found a spacious room in a nice hotel overlooking the main square. It was a slightly larger, more open kind of place than other small towns we had stayed in since Changsha. The sun also shone during the latter half of the day, lifting our spirits.

Out for the night in a tented market area of the square, we came across a good pick-your-own restaurant, which immediately seemed like a bit of a find. Here, as more wind and rain battered the canvass walls of the tent, we witnessed a veritable chimp's tea party of an event. At the table next to us, a group of businessmen seemed to be out for the evening, chaperoned by an extremely tolerant young woman. This must be a party with money, or some local importance, we deduced, since they were being serenaded by the restaurant's lovely singing guitarist.   The five or six businessmen were completely drunk, collapsing face down into their food, pathetically fighting each other, spilling their drinks and coughing food over everyone.

At one point, a waiter came and asked us if we would like to move.   That was the last thing we wanted.   It was entertainment of the finest quality and we didn't want to miss it.   Having a bit of food or drink showered over us was well worth the trouble for a ringside seat, we felt.

The men got gradually worse, but we just sat back and enjoyed the show.   The lady singer was pretty good and played the guitar well.   Before long, the men began joining in with hilarious attempts at singing, and it was soon after this that they began falling off their chairs.   We felt sorry for the poor young chaperone, who was knocked off her chair several times as the men fell, but she seemed rather well practiced.   It was a truly brilliant evening's entertainment for Sam and I.   We did remind ourselves of how much Lorna would have hated it.

*

Finally, at the end of only six and a half gruelling days, we arrived in Wuhan, averaging more than 100 miles a day over the final three days. After consulting the Lonely Planet guide, we headed for the old city of Hangkou but found the hotels there very expensive.   Looking for something more in our line for a four-night stay, we asked a young couple on a scooter for directions.   Young city-Chinese often speak English, and theirs was rather good.   They kindly gave up the rest of their afternoon off to help us, explaining that the government did not allow basic guesthouses to take foreigners in big cities like Wuhan. This explained our experience in Changsha.   They helped us get around such problems by using their own identity cards.   While we waited around at the corner, the two of them checked into a perfectly comfortable place on our behalf, and at a very reasonable price.

Our two new friends – nicknamed Snowy and Jenny – sold English courses for a nationwide language school and took it upon themselves to make sure we had a good time in Wuhan over the next four days. Although this was extremely kind of them, it became rather oppressive at times.

One particular afternoon, close to the end of our stay, they took us to a street of specialist teashops with licensed tea vendors. As a self-proclaimed expert (at 24) Jenny took us from shop to shop, asking to see the credentials of the proprietors, scrutinising each certificate like a detective. Finally, he selected one. We were then served Kung-fu tea outside at tables on the pavement, whereupon Jenny explained the history to us and demonstrated in infuriatingly doctrinaire terms, how the tea was to be drunk.

"Ah, with, er, the kung-fu tea, you must, ah, first pour the hot water at the correctly temperature, then wash, er, water around pot. After this you *must*, ah, throw away the tea. Then you pour in more water and wait for five minutes. *Only* after this time, can you drink, er, the Kung-fu tea!"

We sat outside this kiosk, having to order pot after expensive pot of kung-fu tea, in order for Jenny to demonstrate exactly how this was done. After about three hours of this tutorial, I felt I might strangle him. Fortunately, I think Snowy threatened to do it for me. Whatever it was she sternly said to him, he was suddenly eager to move on. We breathed a sigh of relief.

Tea was not the only instrument of torture in Jenny's arsenal. Often, when we would rather have been getting some rest, Sam and I found ourselves overeating in restaurants and drinking beer.

"This one is good to eat. It will make you vomit. Then you can, ah, eat more foods."

Even so, we learned a lot from Snowy and Jenny and the experience did leave us with some good memories: Jenny's comic three-hour tutorial on how to drink tea, of course, as well as the beautiful Snowy riding side-saddle on Jenny's scooter and smiling back at us as we followed.

We suffered a sobering experience while in Wuhan. One day, out with Snowy and Jenny, I darted into a bank to get more money from a cashpoint machine. Minutes later, I rushed back out to catch up with Sam, who was following their scooter. A few hours later, after a mammoth feast in a well-known local restaurant, I went to pay and found my credit card missing from my wallet. Going back over the morning in my head, I was horrified to realise I must have left it in the cash dispenser at the bank.   After paying with a different card, we rushed back to the bank, only to find it closed.   It seemed pointless anyway.   The card would be long gone.

The following morning, I returned to the bank to explain my loss and ask them to put a stop on the card.   A very kind man asked me to sit down with tea while he made some checks.   Sam and I expected to be there for half the morning dealing with the bureaucracy, so Sam took out the book he had brought to read.   He had hardly opened it, however, before the man returned with my card.

"Is this your card?"

"Yes, it is," I gasped, hardly able to believe my luck.

"Card was inside machine.   No need to cancel card.   Enjoy your time in China, please," he said with a huge smile.

"We love your country!" we told him.

*

After Wuhan, Sam and I headed east towards Shanghai, detouring south a little to stop off at the sacred mountain of Huang Shan.   I had read about this place in a guidebook and thought it worth the extra effort.   Sam was not convinced, at least not until we reached the beautiful surrounding scenery.

One night, on our way to Tangkou, we reached a town named Qingyang in Anhui Province.   It was late and the whole town seemed asleep.   Fortunately, though, on the outskirts we saw a small run-down guesthouse on a corner, with a light on in the foyer.   I knocked. Someone was asleep down behind the reception desk and surfaced to let us in.   The old wooden building was like a rickety old galleon, with narrow gangways and creaky, sloping floors.

We were shown a small room, which we accepted gladly since we were extremely tired.   Next door, we made use of a dangerous-looking gas boiler with a shower attachment.   A woman in a dressing gown was waiting outside as I came out and I apologised for keeping her waiting.   We got into bed at around 1am and switched on the TV. A film or something would help us sleep, we agreed.

Both of us must have dropped off, because around 2:15 we were awoken by knocking at our door.   We sat up and stared at the door for a moment.   The TV must be disturbing someone, we agreed. This is probably the guy from reception, I thought.

Sam got up and opened the door.   Immediately, a woman in pyjamas slipped in and shut the door behind her.   Her finger was held to her lips.

What the hell was going on?

The woman switched on the dim room light, seeming to know where it was.   Sam, still by the door, backed up a little in surprise. Our visitor was around 40, fairly plain, with hair wet from the shower. I recognised her from earlier outside the shower room.   A perfumed scent had wafted in with her.

"*Masaji*?   You want *masaji*?   Only 50 yuan for two peoples."

She began making hand gestures in case we were not yet aware of what she was offering.

"Er, this is my son, Sam," I replied.   "I am his father, Mark. Pleased to meet you."

Sitting up in bed, I held out my hand formally, thinking she would get the message, but no.   We were now this woman's only chance of business for the night.   She tried other gestures.   She certainly didn't need language.   The gestures were most explicit.

"Sorry, it's kind of you to offer, but I am *Baba*.   This is my son."   I made my own gestures.

"Fifty yuan too much for two peoples?" she asked.

I made a sleeping gesture and tried to help her out of the door. She was reluctant but with a little more encouragement did eventually leave.   By now, Sam was laughing, and so was I.   I locked the door and got back into bed muttering.   We dropped back off to sleep, but woke each other again several times, with spontaneous laughter in the dark.

*

The ride to Tankou was pleasant.   There were lush green fields and the road followed a lake for part of the way.   As we approached the town it got very hilly and rain started to fall.   In fact, it rained most of the time we were in Tangkou, down at the foot of the sacred mountain. It was a strange town, with an abandoned feel to it. No doubt it was busy with tourists the rest of the year, I thought, when it wasn't pissing with rain.

Our day walking up the mountain was wet, with a shroud of dense mist. Luckily, there was a TV screen in a reception centre half way up that showed the beauty of the place on a clear day. The video was no doubt there to persuade tourists that the price of about $50 per person they charged to let you walk up to the summit was worthwhile. On such a cloudy day, however, many like us made do with watching the video.

Sam seemed at bit miserable at this point. His stomach was complaining again and the cold rainy weather did not help his mood. I tried my best to cheer him up, but it remained an emotionally flat period. Much of the time, we were just looking forward to reaching Shanghai for a rest and seeing friends. What a difference weather can make to a place.

*

Moving on from Tangkou we travelled across country via Shexian, with its multiple bridges over the river, to Chang Hua in Linan Province. The area was mountainous and the temperature was now down to about 10 degrees centigrade. At one point, we watched snow falling on the mountains to either side of us.

With only fingerless cycling gloves, Sam's hands began to suffer, so we stopped and bought cotton gardening gloves for a few pence each to get us through this section. Never good with cycling in cold weather, Sam had refused to bring warmer gloves for cold weather. We recalled our agonising ride from Canterbury to Ghent. Given that he had never forgotten the cold of that long weekend, why the reluctance to bring warm gloves on a ten-month bike trip?

In Zhejian Province, we arrived in the most touristy of Chinese tourist centres – the lakeside city of Hangzhou. Here, astounded by the cost of hotels and restaurants, we stayed in the youth hostel, where we shared a dormitory room with a Taiwanese couple and their mother.

The mother was barking mad, sitting on her bed the whole time reading aloud robotically from a book and hanging her big washed knickers over the ends of everyone's beds. Day and night. she chanted something like *"Bolla bolla ching sam sapor"*. Sam, in the bunk below, joked that she was putting a spell on him. We thought that perhaps they had brought her to Hangzhou for treatment at a mental hospital, or to have her sectioned. I think the son took pity on us and made several generous gestures by way of compensation, like offering us the use of his laptop. We were too politely English to embarrass them by putting in earplugs, although we came close.

Hangzhou was a pretty awful place really. Apart from the high prices, we were constantly harassed by well-dressed old beggars, who virtually queued up to ask, "Hello, money, money?" In our eyes, the place was only narrowly saved by excellent doughnuts and some very good Moslem noodle-shops. Good food could make up for a lot.

On the leg from Wuhan, I think Sam began to remember his desire to cycle another part of the journey alone. He had promised himself to do this in China, but now he felt too fragile. He also told me later that his previous experience had taught him how much harder it was to be the one who had to make decisions every day about which way to go, where to stop and where to stay the night.

It was a pity that Sam did not feel up to this when the opportunity was there. It would no doubt have given him more of a sense of achievement at the end of our trip.

*

On the home stretch now, before a three-week break at my friends Doug and Tomoko's house in Shanghai, Sam suffered his first puncture since India. It was easily fixed, but we were less calm when we noticed a big split in his rear tyre. It took me several minutes to work out it had been caused by a badly adjusted brake block rubbing against the tyre wall. When you are covering 1000 kilometres a week, it doesn't take long for this kind of damage to occur. Determined to stay positive, we told ourselves that at least in Shanghai we would be able to find a European-sized tyre to replace it. Despite managing a passable temporary repair with duct tape,

295

however, we were with left a sick sensation in our stomachs, knowing it might go at any moment.

After a night in the large industrial new-town of Jia Sei – so new it was not on any map – we found ourselves entering the modern metropolis of Shanghai and heading for the old French quarter.

Doug and Tomoko's house was big, comfortable and located centrally in the excellent French Concession area. We felt really lucky to be there. I had known Doug in Tokyo 23 years before, when he was a pallid teenager, and it seemed bizarre to see him now, a successful lawyer with his Japanese wife and four children.

We had timed our arrival in Shanghai to coincide with the birthdays of me and Steve (Tokyo Steve), which are a week apart. Two weeks early, we had time to relax with Doug and his family for a few days, before making a trip by train up to Beijing. We would be able to see some of the sights around Beijing and then return to Shanghai as Steve arrived. That would give us four more days there and a birthday party at renowned restaurant, 'M' On The Bund.

*

Our trip to Beijing and the Great Wall was really enjoyable. It was good to have a break from the saddle and explore a bit without having to worry about the bikes or riding on to the next place. We also met a couple of guys nearer Sam's age at our hostel.

I remember a particularly amusing incident on the fast sleeper train back to Shanghai. Around 2am, a Chinese man in the bunk above Sam began snoring so loudly things fell off the table. Sam tried everything to encourage him to stop but nothing worked. Finally, in exhausted desperation and fury, Sam banged the fibreglass underside of the bunk. It made such a bang that the man fell out of his bunk in shock, thinking the train had crashed.

Back in Shanghai, we enjoyed hanging out with Doug's family. Seeing Steve for a few days was also really nice and Sam certainly benefitted from a few discussions with him. It was during his visit that Steve, heading out to eat wearing a Godfather (movie) t-shirt, was told by Sam he had never had a godfather of his own. The vacancy was filled by the time we reached the noodle shop.

Immediately taking on the responsibility for moral education, Steve began tutoring Sam in seventies and eighties music, as well as identifying gaps in film and literature.   This helped Steve to plan our itinerary for our four weeks in Tokyo at the end of the trip.

Our last night in China was somewhat extreme.   Our timing was such that we spent the night watching Manchester United vs Everton live at O'Malleys Irish pub until 4am, then cycled straight off to Pudong airport to fly to South Korea.

We had planned to take a boat, but despite assurances from several local sources that it was still operating, we had gone to the dock to find it out of service and been forced to fly.   This was a sadly familiar experience for us by now.

Tired and wet, we took a ferry across to Pudong harbour, then cycled amongst the new skyscrapers, looking for airport signs. There were none to be seen and my compass steamed up in the rain. Much to the amusement of locals, we were reduced to seeking directions by mimicking aeroplanes taking off.   They just looked at us like we were crazy.   I followed my intuitive sense of direction, but it failed me completely on this occasion, taking us miles out of our way.   Despite being way ahead of time initially, we found ourselves pedalling like crazy along a busy motorway at 6am, having given up on finding a smaller road.

In Shanghai, the airport planners had assumed everyone would travel there by motorway, or using the 300mph magnetic levitation (Maglev) monorail train – both of which are banned to cyclists.

By some super-human effort, covering 36km in an hour, we managed to arrive at Pudong airport 25 minutes before take-off, running up a disused stairway from the road and banging on the glass doors to get workmen to let us onto the walkway between terminals. Exhausted, we cycled through the walkway and into departures, ran up the escalators and, heart in mouth, to the departures desk.

"Do you have luggages?" asked the young man quickly, seeing that my tickets were for a plane leaving in 20 minutes.

"Yes," I said breathlessly, pointing to the bike and panniers. He gasped loudly, clasping his hands to his head.

"This is impossible.   You cannot take this bicycle on a plane!"

"Yes, I can, it's fine; we've done it before."

"Uh, OK. But where is your fellow travelling companion, Mr Sam?"

I looked around … no Mr Sam! Disaster! I asked the man to put out an alert on the public address and ran to look for him while the guy puzzled over how he was going to get bike, luggage and two passengers onto the plane in only 15 minutes.

As I returned with Sam, the man at the desk, now weighing my panniers, looked up.

"Another bicycle!"

I acknowledged that we did indeed have another bicycle. He scratched his head as I told Sam in uncharacteristically defeatist fashion that there was no way we could make it now. I resorted to the hope that if we managed to check in, we might not have to pay for another flight.

"Bring your bicycles with me!" the man said rushing towards an outsize luggage scanner.

Thank God – we had picked a guy who wanted to be a hero.

We knew from previous experience the bikes would only go through upright with the front wheels off. After removing them quickly, we shoved the whole lot through with Sam's panniers still loaded on his bike. The officious woman operating the machine demanded a second pass. Furiously, I grabbed my bike and tried to run back to the beginning of the unit. Disaster 2! I kicked the wheel leaning against the wall and tripped. Seeing I was about to put my big foot through the wheel, with my own weight and that of the bike I was carrying, I dived through the air to avoid this. It was one of those slow-motion moments. I flew slowly through the air then came down with a huge crash, tangled in the bike. I had landed heavily on my head and shoulder, both of which I presumed I had broken. I lay there dazed, looking up into the face of a very concerned Sam and the check-in desk clerk, who looked at me like I was completely insane.

"We've missed it, Sam," I whimpered – or stronger words to that effect. Sam was not deterred.

"It's fine, Dad. We can still make it if you'll just stay calm."

Somehow, all this had happened in the space of about two minutes. A minute later, the bikes were wheeled off to the plane with a security label on.   I hobbled in agony along the walkway to the plane.   It didn't seem possible, but at our departure time we were in our seats, surrounded by tutting fellow passengers.   Breathing hard, we watched them put the bikes into the hold.   I had probably never been closer to a heart attack.   As the plane roared off into the sky, we burst into relieved laughter.   An hour later we were at Incheon airport collecting two undamaged bikes.   God knows how, but we had made it.   My beard had turned grey at the ends overnight, but at that moment we seemed like the luckiest men alive.   It would be an understatement to say that in future I would avoid travelling by plane with bikes if I possibly could.

SAM'S POINT OF VIEW

I loved China from the start, despite experiencing the hardship of the first bad weather of our trip.   China was fascinating.   Every country before had possessed its own unique qualities, but China was a quantum leap.   The best thing for me was once again the food.   I struggled to eat responsibly given my stomach problem; there was just so much to try.   At the side of every road were stalls selling snacks, noodles or dim-sum, all with different fillings, depending on what was available in the region.

The basic eating-places frequented by workmen out in the sticks, were the best.   These usually had two chefs with massive woks at the front, with up to fifty trays of different ingredients.   There is a great system where you pick what you want and place it into a small basket for the chef to prepare and bring to your table.   Somehow it was always delicious and a great way to provide you with all of your vitamins and minerals.   I learned quite a bit, watching those chefs. I was looking forward to trying out some Chinese cooking myself when we got back home.

Maybe better still were the noodle bars run by Chinese Moslems. It's hard to explain if you've never seen noodles being made by hand, but it looks very hard.   Almost like a magic trick.   The chef pokes his fingers through the dough then stretches it, repeating this several times with his arms wide.   The action looks a little like someone playing a giant accordion. He repeats the splitting and stretching process over and over until finally a mass of long thin noodles appears and he slices off the ends. The noodles are then put straight into a large pot of boiling water before being served into bowls with your choice of sauce. It's an awesome trick!

More than just getting well fed, you get to enjoy a fascinating performance several times during each visit. These guys really are like magicians. I once joked about how you might find an audience of customers sitting watching one of these chefs, as he appears to pull noodles out of his arse!

Perhaps the most surprising thing about China was the wealth and development we found in the major cities after cycling for days through such primitive rural settlements. It was a startling contrast. All the major cities were clean, often powered by high-tech green energy, which considering the amount of neon advertising plastered all over the skyscrapers, was very impressive. Arriving out of the rural wastelands into one of these cities was a bit like stepping onto the set of Blade Runner.

My favourite places in China numbered around four – Guilin, with its stunning green peaks and good food, then Wuhan, which is really three cities joined into one, then Beijing, and finally Shanghai, one of the most outstanding cities I encountered on our whole trip.

Shanghai was so massive, with such a vast range of cultures. Doug, an old friend of my dad's, took us to some amazing restaurants serving expensive wine and sophisticated cuisine. 'M' On The Bund, with its stunning views over the Bund, where we celebrated Dad and Steve's birthdays, was outstanding.

At the other end of the price scale, the tiny Chinese steamed dumpling cafe down the road from Doug's was an awesome place to hang out once Steve arrived. We used to stay there chatting for hours, drinking beer, ordering more and more bau-zi (pronounced bauzer) until they closed in the early hours. I was still pretty quiet, though. I felt unconfident. I thought that anything I said would be of little interest to my dad or Steve, and as a result it seemed easier to just listen. It was a pretty crappy feeling, I remember.

My dad and godfather Steve enjoyed their birthday week together. Shanghai was where Steve actually became my godfather after coming out one day wearing a 'Godfather' t-shirt and me realising I hadn't actually seen the film.

The day we left for the super-modern Shanghai airport (in Pudong) to fly over to South Korea was a complete nightmare. For a start, we had wanted to go by boat but the ferries were all closed down. We left from a football bar in the early hours with plenty of time to spare, but we got lost. Eventually we had to use the motorway, which was highly dangerous and illegal, but we had no choice. As we rushed into the airport, I got lost when my dad decided to cycle along the internal walkway. He sent a message out over the airport public address system to alert me of his position, but I didn't even hear it.

Eventually 'Manic Mark' came in a major rush and found me. We talked our way onto the flight – initially, they wouldn't let us on. It was 15 minutes before take-off and we were in bits. My dad was completely hyper. They hurried our bikes over to a machine that was big enough to x-ray them. By this time, the plane was due to leave and in all the panic my dad darted round the machine to try and help, then fell over the bike, crashing down and badly hurting himself.

All of this was completely over the top and unnecessary – the kind of scene you could imagine taking place in Fawlty Towers, with Basil and Sybil going on holiday. They eventually took the bikes through and gave us our boarding passes. We didn't speak for ages, even when we were on the plane. My dad was limping badly and I could see his shoulder was giving him pain. We just sat there, trying to get our breath, in a complete haze of shock and disarray.

My dad's way of dealing with situations like that is, bluntly, nothing short of terrible. He literally loses sight of all rationality. Ironically, though, it was probably his stress, panic and falling over that made the officials let us on the flight. I think they were eager to get rid of him before he had a heart attack! I can say without doubt, it was one of the worst days of the trip.

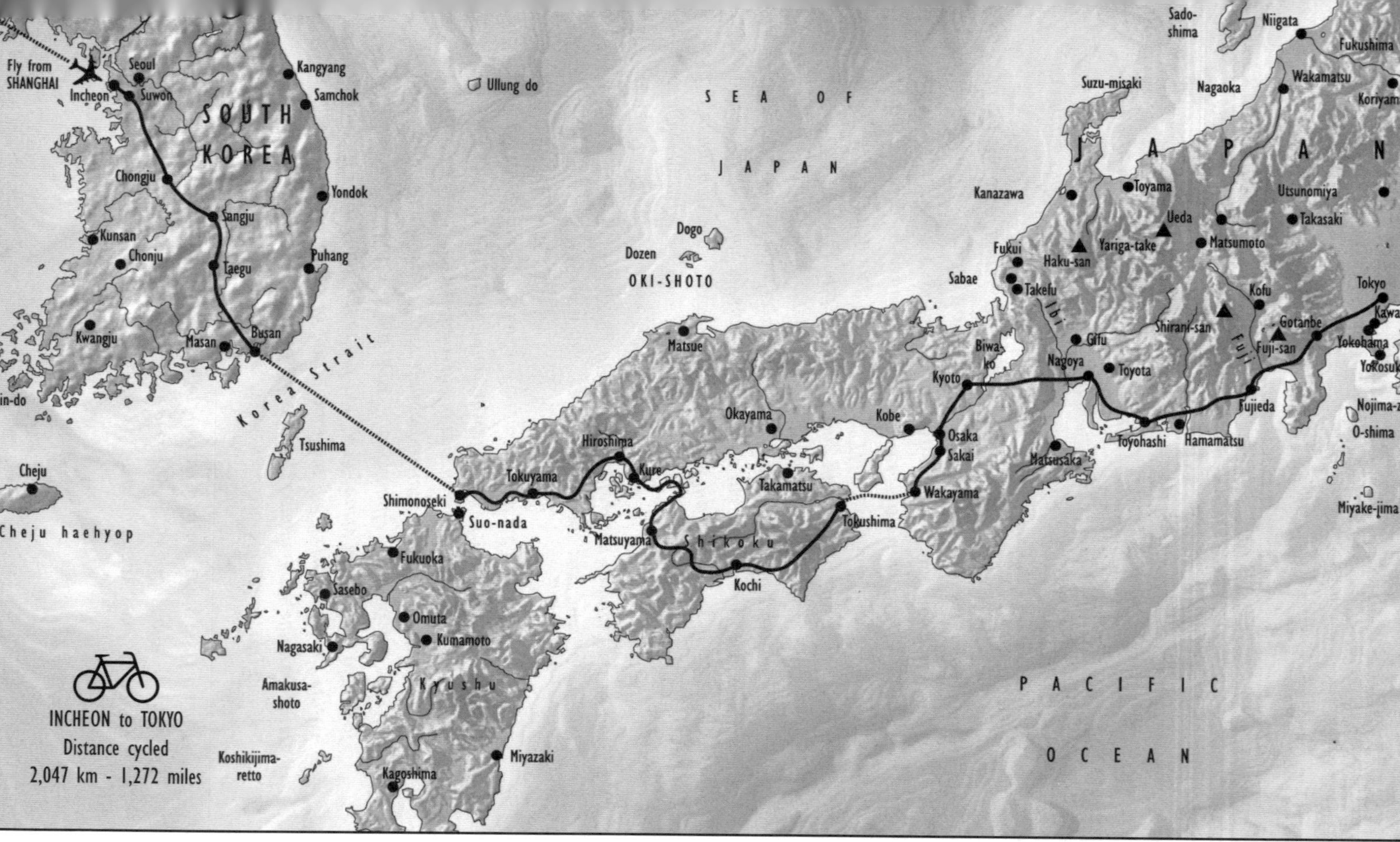

INCHEON to TOKYO
Distance cycled
2,047 km - 1,272 miles
Fly from SHANGHAI
Incheon
Seoul
Suwon
Kangyang
Samchok
SOUTH KOREA
Chongju
Sangju
Kunsan
Chonju
Taegu
Yondok
Puhang
Kwangju
Masan
Busan
Chin-do
Korea Strait
Tsushima
Cheju
Cheju haehyop
Ullung do
SEA OF JAPAN
Dogo
Dozen
OKI-SHOTO
Matsue
Okayama
Hiroshima
Kure
Tokuyama
Shimonoseki
Suo-nada
Matsuyama
Shikoku
Takamatsu
Kochi
Tokushima
Fukuoka
Sasebo
Omuta
Kumamoto
Nagasaki
Amakusa-shoto
Koshikijima-retto
Kyushu
Kagoshima
Miyazaki
Kobe
Osaka
Sakai
Wakayama
Kyoto
Biwa-ko
Nagoya
Matsusaka
Sabae
Fukui
Takefu
Haku-san
Yariga-take
Kanazawa
Toyama
Ueda
Matsumoto
Ibi
Gifu
Toyota
Shirani-san
Kofu
Fuji-san
Fuji
Gotanbe
Fujieda
Toyohashi
Hamamatsu
Suzu-misaki
Nagaoka
Sado-shima
Niigata
Fukushima
Wakamatsu
Koryama
Utsunomiya
Takasaki
JAPAN
Tokyo
Kawasa
Yokohama
Yokosuka
Nojima-za
O-shima
Miyake-jima
PACIFIC OCEAN

Chapter 13

South Korea and Japan - Elation and deflation

Don't worry. My mother and auntie are pretty damned rich, and they like your sensual outfits.

Sam and I felt incredibly lucky to have made it at all to Incheon airport that morning.   By rights, we should have missed that plane and had to wait until the next day at least.   My shoulder and upper arm were killing me, my ankle was sprained and I certainly had concussion, but we were here and I felt sure nothing was broken.   It was pouring with rain and blowing a gale.   We had not slept and had pushed ourselves harder on the way to Pudong airport than Lance Armstrong on the last stretch of his sixth Tour de France.   We were not about to cycle anywhere beyond Incheon that day.

We sat in the airport café eating breakfast and discussing our plan.   This amounted to finding a hotel and sleeping for a very long time.   We headed to the airport tourist information desk – this was South Korea, they have things like that.   The lady gave us a leaflet for a cheap apartment hotel nearby, on the island.

"On the island?"

She explained that the new Incheon airport – it certainly looked brand new – was on a small island connected to the mainland by a large suspension bridge.   I knew what was coming next. Unfortunately, the suspension bridge was prohibited to cyclists and we would need to cycle around the island to take a ferry to get to the mainland. How quaint And how bloody typical! Just when you think your luck has made a turn for the better, you get more bad news. We thanked her and finally braved the driving wind and rain to find the hotel.

Located inside an apartment building, it was not easy to track down, but in the end we stumbled on a simple paper sign affixed to a door on the seventh floor. Somewhat shattered and disorientated, we checked in and descended into a deep afternoon sleep. After about eight hours, we emerged from our room bleary-eyed and hungry. Shoes left to dry, we headed down in the lift wearing our complementary disposable slippers to find a Korean restaurant in the basement.

Now we had slept, we managed to make some sense of where we were staying. Basically, we were in a block of flats with some individual rooms rented by the day. In the basement was a small shopping mall. Even the hotel office and reception was run from one of the apartments.

The food downstairs was good and saved us from going out in the wind and rain in our slippers.

*

Next morning, feeling slightly more human, we were up at 8am cleaning the Chinese road-dirt off our bikes before eating a breakfast sandwich outside the 7-11 opposite. We cursed the no-cycling signs leading up to the huge new bridge as we passed under it. The ferry was miles away and we had a bit of a wait at the jetty. When the ferry finally arrived, it was a slow old tub. The groups of old ladies travelling with us shared their rice crackers and chatted to us in Korean, which by some surreal means we thought we understood. They clearly thought so too.

It was already apparent to me that South Korea had developed a great deal since I last came here with Steve – updating our Japanese visas back in 1985. We had loved it back then, with its kind-hearted, hard-working people and its undeveloped mountainous countryside. Although the cities were developing fast, it had still seemed a poor, relatively inefficient developing nation. Now it was clean, modern and as well organised as Japan, with an even greater sense of optimism.

On our first night in mainland South Korea, we searched for a guesthouse in Suwon, about 45km inland from Incheon. We were directed to a busy, somewhat seedy district near the central railway station. It was obvious to me that this was an area of *love hotels* – generally rented to couples by the hour, half-day or overnight. As in

Japan, travellers sometimes use these for convenience and economy. I received some strange looks: a heavily bearded 50-year-old man arriving at the reception in lycra shorts and shirt, with a similarly clad teenage boy lurking outside. We were turned away from the first few before I realised what the problem was.

It was at this point I learned to put on long trousers before entering a hotel and to show them mine and Sam's passports, saying the words *nea adeul* (my son) to pre-empt suspicions. These love hotels were extremely well equipped with big flat-screen cable TVs and computers with free internet. In the rooms were cutesy dressing tables loaded with cosmetics, frequently in a theme of Snow White or a Victorian dolls-house. On the practical side, there was usually a fridge, often stocked with complementary energy drinks.

Our other big discovery was a newly opened restaurant chain, named Seafood Ocean. These places had large seafood buffets, a huge variety of fish, seafood, salads, vegetables and puddings, all fresh each day. The healthy Japanese-style diet that eating here encouraged did wonders for Sam's ailing digestion. I had promised that he would be all right once he was eating Japanese food and this proved to be true. It had come earlier than expected.

*

We worked our way south through the country, stopping mostly at large towns like Cheyongju, Sangju and Gyeongsan, before reaching South Korea's second city of Busan, on the southern tip. Without exception, we received the best hospitality in all of these places, found comfortable hotels and ate great food. The roads were invariably pretty hard work, often winding up and down steep mountainsides while overlooking spectacular raised motorways cut through the mountains and spanning large rivers. Steep hills and cold weather, however, were no big deal to us now. We knew we were on the home stretch and we had started to see everything in a positive light.

I remember back in Shanghai saying to Sam that we had 2,000 kilometres to go, and us both feeling that this was no distance at all. Those planning long cycle trips for the first time should take note that before this trip 2,000 kilometres had seemed to us like an enormous distance to cycle. My belief is that there is seldom any physical problem in cycling a great distance, as long as you take it easy at the start and build up the daily amount gradually. The biggest barrier is your own perception about what is possible. Obviously age and physical fitness have some bearing, but in reality far less than most people think.

The hotels and guesthouses we stayed in across South Korea reflected the obsession of Koreans with technology. There were usually numerous satellite channels available, many with English language films, and my diary records that during our eight days in Korea we saw 12 movies. It is a pity that by this stage of our journey we were beginning to gallop towards the finish line, because South Korea was a really pleasant and interesting place. Still, we consoled ourselves afterwards that getting a positive taste of a place and being drawn to go back later usually leads to a satisfactory conclusion.

I am often aware that when you return to countries that hold special memories, nostalgia for the place as it was is not matched by what you find there now. Things will have moved on, the country and the culture will have modernised and what you remembered can't be found there anymore. Take heart, though, the place you remember can often be found in other countries nearby that are a little further behind in development. This was my experience when I went back to Singapore at 22, having left when I was 11. I was disappointed to find the place I had grow up in was gone. But when I went to Thailand, I felt a flood of nostalgia for old Singapore. The same applied in southern India with Malaysia.

On this visit with Sam, South Korea had become like the Japan I remembered. I was taken back to the great times I had with Steve when we first arrived in Tokyo 23 years before. No doubt Sam will feel these same emotions in years to come when he returns to some of the places we visited on this journey.

*

We had some memorable experiences as we cycled down through South Korea. One, in particular, stands out. In the small rural town of Heung, between Cheyongju and Sangju, we stopped for an early lunch at a small family-run restaurant. It seated ten people at a squeeze. Being quite early, we ordered a relatively light meal. Once our lunch arrived we began eating, but more dishes arrived. We tried to explain in minimal Korean that we had only ordered one dish each with rice. The waitress pointed to a couple of older ladies on the adjacent table who smiled and bowed towards us. It seemed these rather maternal ladies thought we had not ordered enough. Two skinny guys away from home – we needed looking after, and it was down to them to provide for us, we supposed.

We shook their hands and thanked them, then withdrew, feeling rather embarrassed. After a few moments, one came over and handed me her mobile phone. I took it and said hello. The young woman who answered spoke excellent English. She explained that her mother and aunt had wanted to make sure we had a good experience in Korea, and that we needed to try a good selection of Korean dishes.

"Don't worry," she told me. "They are pretty damned rich, and they like your sensual outfits."

We hadn't been worried before she said that, but we were afterwards, especially when the two grinning ladies asked us to dance.

A little later, I spoke to the young woman on the phone for another 20 minutes, hearing about her having lived in Canada (I will do anything to avoid having to dance). At the same time, we found ourselves working our way through a vastly enlarged meal. While I was on the phone Sam had been talking to the two old ladies through sign language. They were showing a good deal of interest in his lycra shorts. I imagined it going something like:

"Ooh, feel them, Mee-Yon, they are so smooth!"

"Mmm, yes, they're very silky, Hae-Won. I would like to wear them. Good for winter under a dress and they would hold your bottom in quite firmly."

The conversation continued as we ate. Now, though, every time one of us failed to understand something, the daughter was called to translate. She didn't seem to mind. Strong alcohol arrived and the planned snack lunch ran on for about two hours, with the daughter in Seoul on the phone most of that time. It is hardly surprising that we only managed 92km that day, or that most of it was achieved before lunch, but the kindness and the hilarity we experienced in Heung was well worth the delay.

We arrived in Busan two days later. It was my 51st birthday. We were devastated to discover, though, that Seafood Ocean had not yet opened an outlet in the city. Sam had been guarding a secret plan to take me there for my birthday dinner. Instead, we went to a raw fish place run by more friendly old ladies at Hyundai Beach across the bay. These three exercised more restraint than Mee-Yon and Hae-Won in Hueng, though.

After two enjoyable days of rest in Busan, we bid farewell to South Korea and took the ferry across to Shimonoseki on the southwest coast of Japan. Shimonoseki was a port I had sailed to and from a few times more than 20 years earlier. It felt strange to be arriving by bike. As we sailed into the harbour, Sam could see that I was being gripped by nostalgia. I think this sense of me coming back to a country that meant so much to my past gave him a special feeling too. It was, after all, the main reason for him having wanted to cycle here as a little boy nearly nine years before. I hoped he wouldn't be disappointed after all that time and effort to get here.

*

It certainly felt good getting off the boat and cycling into a typical Japanese street. I was in a country I knew well, where I could still speak a fair amount of the language and knew we would meet with unrivalled hospitality. My enthusiastic smile said it all, Sam told me later. It was a permanent fixture for most of the next 16 days as we travelled across Japan. At the same time, though, Sam and I were poignantly aware that we were now very close to the end of our trip and before long it would all be over. In a long expedition, it is unavoidable that you are eager to move forward towards your ultimate destination, no matter how much you may be enjoying where you are. In this sense, there is a constant conflict. I have always found it a struggle to get the balance right.

I felt really close to Sam at this time. I was so impressed that he had made it here as a 19-year-old with so little fuss. I had always wanted to bring my children to Japan, but I never expected to do it by bicycle.

Sam still seemed a little distant. It was obvious that even towards the end of this long trip, he remained in turmoil over his inner feelings, what he wanted to do after our return and what all of this really meant. I had given up thinking he might experience a sudden overwhelming revelation that would answer all his questions, and I think he had too. I had come to the conclusion that what he had learned was locked away in his head and the answers would probably not be revealed to him until later in his life. This had stopped me from thinking it was my responsibility to help him find meaning in it all now. It was a weight off my shoulders.

Cycling through southern Japan was a constant contrast of concrete urban sprawl dotted between old temples, beautiful green mountainsides, shimmering bright green or red maple trees, and delicately perfumed flowers. Everything was suddenly noticeably neat and efficient: immaculately manicured tea bushes, people who never think of crossing on a red light, dazzlingly clean trucks and delicious, beautifully presented food. After living here for two years in my twenties, I had been completely spoilt by the politeness, generosity and helpfulness of Japanese people and by how efficiently everything was operated.

Returning to England from Tokyo in 1986, I remember being horrified by the indifferent service I received in shops and by the general acceptance of inefficient transport systems and business operations. The day after getting home, I was taking a train from Folkestone to London. I bought a ticket and was told to go to platform two for the 11.05 train. At 11.05, there was no sign of the train. After half a minute more, I rushed back to the ticket office to check whether I was on the right platform. They looked at me in astonishment, perplexed to see that I actually expected the train to arrive on time. I soon adjusted but still wonder how the Japanese can manage to do it consistently and we consistently can't. In my experience, six months in Japan changes people forever. Afterwards, they can never accept the kind of inefficiency or lack of attention to detail they find elsewhere.

*

From Shimonoseki we headed east along the hard shoulder of a highway to Tokushima.   Although I have been waxing lyrical about how efficient the Japanese are, I am now about to contradict myself.

The roads in Japan are good and all numbered, which should make them easy to follow.   This may be the case for motor vehicles, but for cyclists the legendary efficiency of the Japanese goes haywire. Told by the tourist office in Shimonoseki to follow the R2, we later discovered that around bigger towns, bypasses share the same road number as the old road that passes through the centre.   It is not uncommon to find three or four roads going around or through a town that all share the same road number.   This is not a big problem for cars I suppose, since they will get there one way or another.   But one evening, heading towards one of the long R2 bypass road tunnels, we found ourselves the target of a spectacular roadblock, with three wailing police cars used to corner us.

My point that three roads with the same number was confusing was received with amusement by the police.

"Please tell me what to do!   I don't want to put my son in danger," I protested.

My concern about the safety of my son allowed us to get away without a large fine.   Fortunately, the understanding of Japanese cultural values – in this case, paternal responsibility – drew their sympathy.   When I first went to Japan I found you could get away with almost any misdemeanour by admitting you had been drunk at the time.   I doubt whether that would have worked on this occasion!

Overnight stops in Japan became a constant search for sushi-bars as Sam discovered that he was becoming as dependent on sushi as I am.   We were directed to an especially good one on the outskirts of Hiroshima, by the staff of our excellent city centre hostel (K's House Backpackers Hostel).

Despite our eagerness to get to Tokyo, we were still able to enjoy visiting some places on the way.   We were really moved by Hiroshima's peace park, built near the epicentre of the atomic bomb that was dropped on the city.   It was somehow completely chilling and yet at the same time overwhelmingly joyful.   The city of

Hiroshima was left unreconstructed for two years after the bomb, with a consensus that it should not be rebuilt after such a terrible experience. It was also believed at this time that nothing would grow there for hundreds of years. But after only a year, green shoots began to come through, right at the epicentre, and in typically poetic Japanese fashion they took it as a sign: renewal, cleansing, good should come out of bad. It is now the loveliest city with a strangely serene atmosphere and we really enjoyed our time here, before cycling on towards the large southern island of Shikoku.

*

I never visited Shikoku when I lived in Tokyo and had not been there on any of my subsequent return trips, but I had heard what a lovely place it is and how it remains like *old Japan.* In recent years, a string of spectacular suspension bridges have been built from the Kansai mainland. Ten of them hop between little islands across the large bay. The bridges are a feat of engineering and I remembered being shown a film about their design and construction while I was studying architecture.

Sam and I spent the first night of this leg camping in a small public garden by the road down onto the little island of Innoshima. This tiny island supports the towering concrete column of the first suspension bridge. Camping on this garden roundabout was not technically allowed. Typical of the polite Japanese, however, nobody bothered us and we were back on the road at 8am, after a picnic breakfast at the table and benches provided. The view from the bridges was breathtaking early in the morning – small forested islands floating in a vivid turquoise sea. The sun shone and several large groups of immaculately uniformed schoolchildren waved to us as they filed by on bicycle outings.

There is a kind of brave new world perfection about Japan that even extends to nature. It always seems to me that the whole country has been efficiently designed, constructed and maintained from scratch, rather than there being any sense of evolution, or nature's haphazardness. Lorna used to find this rather sinister – like bonsai trees.

Hopping from islet to islet on the chain of suspension bridges, we reached Shikoku Island by lunchtime and stopped to eat at a Joyful family restaurant. Here we spent hours talking about the world of work, university, marriage, raising children, etc. over complementary coffee and endless glasses of iced *macha* green tea with soya milk. Sam realised that I came to Japan and met Lorna when I was not so much older than he was now, and I think this made him start to see his life in a wider time perspective. It seemed to reassure him anyway. I got a sense that he had passed a major hurdle.

Fuelled by coffee and enthusiastic thoughts of beginning his working life upon our return, Sam flew through the remaining miles to Matsuyama city. His remaining dilemma seemed to be that most of all he wanted to be an entrepreneur, running his own business, but he recognised he first needed to gain some experience in the world of work.

If he needed an introduction to the world of work, he was certainly in the right country. The Japanese tend to approach everything they do with extreme dedication, their work most of all. I remember when I first lived here in 1984 that businessmen used to introduce themselves by the name of their company before they told you their own name. Such tendencies have faded over the last 20 years or so, with young people no longer handing themselves over to a company for life, but it is still a fundamental part of the Japanese psyche. Pride in doing something well is an art-form here and I like that. Everyone can be bothered.

We found a good hotel in Matsuyama by asking at the Tourist Information desk in the main station – a reliable system we repeated often in Japan. Due to the poor quality of what was on offer in Shanghai, we had decided not to buy a replacement tyre there for Sam's bike. Fortunately, the repaired one had held up through South Korea. By this point, however, the split had started to grow and we realised it wouldn't last much longer. The efficiency of the people at the Tourist Information desk had impressed us so much that after checking in at our hotel we returned to ask for advice on cycle shops. Unbelievably, the lady got out the phone directory and phoned most of the bike shops in the city, listing our specific requirements and taking down details before she found one that had the perfect tyre in stock.   We were amazed and felt really warmed by her kindness and dedication.   Words still fail me, when it comes to these people.

Sam replaced the tyre that evening, so we left Matsuyama the next morning feeling far more confident.   Heading towards the southern city of Kochi, we climbed our first big Japanese mountain pass on a demanding 125km stint.   I was pleased we had decided to detour to Shikoku.   Japan had modernised a great deal since the mid-1980s and I wanted Sam to get a feel of what the country had been like when Lorna and I lived here.   So far, this seemed about right. Shikoku was pretty similar to how the main island (Honshu) was back then.

At Kochi, we had been told, we would find a really traditional small Japanese city with a kind of brash air (for Japan anyway), probably due to fishing having been its main industry.   We enjoyed the mountainous riding conditions and the lovely forested countryside on the way there and arrived in the late afternoon.

We made several failed attempts to find a hotel in Kochi involving some rather convoluted processes.   The management of each hotel unable to accommodate us was so regretful that they phoned around and escorted us to the next place, where they implored the hotelier to find space for us, explaining about our cycle trip and how it fell upon the people of Kochi to look after us as special guests. This was very kind but proved to be futile and time-consuming.   It was difficult to extricate ourselves from these embarrassing situations without making up excuses.   One smart hotel actually gave us a large, boxed present by way of an apology for not having a room.

Eventually, we reached the Tourist Information desk at the railway station.   They came to our rescue.   It was the Golden Week public holiday, they explained, and everywhere would be full.   But these were Japanese – and did not do failure.   Eventually, after many phone calls, these kind people found us a really friendly family-run ryokan (traditional Japanese inn) in a quiet street, near to the centre of town.

It wasn't cheap, but we were totally spoilt with generosity. Sam enjoyed getting to grips with traditional Japanese living: the Japanese bath (*o-furo*), where you washed before getting in and then left the water in for others; the leaving of shoes by the front door and wearing of special slippers to protect the traditional tatami-mat flooring; and the futons that were unfolded each night, with quilts (*kake-buton*) that were hung out of the windows to air during the day. Like me, he quickly came to see this as a superior way of living.

The young couple that ran our ryokan spoilt us with daily treats of traditional Japanese rice cakes, chestnut buns and seaweed wrapped savouries, bought from a local specialist store. When we got home from dinner on our first evening, the old mother (*oka-san*) had washed and ironed all of Sam's clothes. On the morning we left, the young couple gave us each a picnic lunch full of treats. We had paid the evening before, but as we left they came out to wave us off and the old mother gave us 2,000 yen back as a present. Need I tell you how sorely we missed this place after we left? There are not many places in the world where you will enjoy this level of kindness.

*

I was glad that Sam loved Japan as much as I did. I knew this would have a bearing on how he remembered the overall trip. As I had promised, the food also had a beneficial effect on his digestion and therefore his general sense of wellbeing. He was already talking in terms of coming back here in the future. Sam's irritation with me also seemed to have reduced a lot since China, but this may simply have been because he knew he didn't have to put up with me at this level of intensity for much longer. Whatever the reason, it was certainly nice not to feel his eyes burning into my back as we cycled.

By this point, I had started to feel the benefits of us spending so much time together in such extreme circumstances had largely been fulfilled. For things to settle in our minds, we probably needed some time apart. Clearly, it would be some time before we recognised what we had really gained from the experience as a father and son. Going by my own experience, perhaps Sam would only really know once he had children of his own.

On our way to Tokushima from Kochi, we found ourselves on another challenging but beautiful mountain pass. We stopped at a mountain spa for a lunchtime rest and after a meal of traditional Japanese soba noodles with tempura, had the pleasure of a long winding downhill road at the other side of the pass. The pleasure was short-lived, however: close to the bottom, I pulled onto a grass verge with a puncture.

After more than 9,000 miles of cycling over some pretty rough terrain, this was my only actual puncture of the trip (not including the two burst tubes that perished around the valve). In fact, the puncture was only caused by my nervousness about putting more air in my rear tyre after the exploding-valve experience in India. Leaning around the sharp mountain bends at speed had pinched the under-inflated tube against the rim and punctured it. I tried to tell myself it didn't matter, and that 9,000 miles without a puncture was virtually as good as 9,600, but it still irritates me, even now.

That night, Sam and I camped by a large river, unwilling to wear ourselves out at this stage of the trip by pushing hard to reach Tokushima in one 198km day. It was a good decision, I think. Although it rained heavily in the night – which meant the annoyance of packing-up a wet tent, knowing we would need to get it out again later and dry it – but we still felt happy in the morning as we snaked off along the mountain road following the spectacular bolder-strewn river towards Tokushima. We phoned Ken (Kenichi) Harada, a friend and work colleague of Tokyo Steve's.

Ken met us in town and welcomed us to stay at his apartment. He did a great job of taking us around the area to see the sights: strange swirling currents under the huge suspension bridge; surf beaches; old temples, etc. We also visited the first three of the 88 Shikoku island Buddhist temples, which are part of a popular pilgrimage for the Japanese (it takes about four weeks to walk to all of them, spending nights in temple accommodation). The temples are beautiful, well kept and very calming, and we found these days a very de-stressing experience. Many Japanese people promise themselves to do the pilgrimage at some point in their lives and do it in their sixties after retirement. We saw quite a few of them walking along the roads in traditional pilgrim's dress, with a long stick and a pointed woven bamboo hat. I have a vague plan to return to visit the other 85 when I am older, maybe with Alex, my eldest daughter.

The Japanese do not regard themselves as very religious people, but they certainly have a strong spiritual element in their lives – more than in most cultures, I would say. Their ceremonies are both Buddhist and Shinto. The minimalist philosophy these encourage can be seen everywhere in Japanese life. Japanese architecture, paintings, calligraphy and other traditional arts are obvious interpretations, but there are many everyday examples.

Go shopping in Japan and you will see them. Vegetables in a greengrocer will be displayed with great care: polished, with colours and sizes enhancing those of each neighbouring vegetable, creating a beautiful picture for the eye. A simple bag of rice will be beautifully wrapped for you in lovely handmade paper: the shopkeeper regards it as his responsibility to honour the sacred nature of the rice, give it due reverence and demonstrate this in the way it is presented. These items will be handed to the customer with both hands, rather like the awarding of a great prize, and most shopkeepers still bow. The same thing happens with the presentation of food in a restaurant or even in a humble cafe. All of this traditional reverence still exists, somehow in harmony with what is now a high-tech modern country.

To further enhance our traditional Japanese experience, Ken took us to his friend's excellent *issakaya* (simple traditional bar/restaurant), where he meets regularly with other local journalists, writers and theatre performers. The restaurant was specially opened for us by the *mama-san* (landlady) – many local bars that depend on business clientele close during Golden Week. I just can't imagine anyone doing this in England.

*

From Tokushima, we had to take a boat back from Wakayama over to the Kansai region on the mainland. The huge suspension bridge forbids cyclists and it would have been a very long way around to go back over the ten bridges we had arrived by. Early in the morning, we left Ken's apartment in torrential rain to take the ferry. The rain only got heavier, which quite honestly didn't seem possible, and continued all day on our way up through the city of Osaka to our next stopover, the historic city of Kyoto. I reminded myself of the Confucian proverb: *A wet man does not mind the rain.* No rain could dampen our enthusiasm for Japan, however, and we still arrived in Kyoto feeling we had enjoyed the day.

Kyoto was the ancient capital of Japan during the era of the shogun. It is a beautiful, traditional city full of temples and historic narrow streets, and a place where the geisha tradition survives. It is also notoriously expensive.

The mature parks and traditional Japanese gardens in Kyoto are world-famous. You couldn't fail to be impressed by them. With so many special and unique things in a relatively small city centre, it is no wonder you find hoards of well-heeled tourists everywhere you go here.

Arriving in Kyoto, we headed for the centre and were struck by its spectacular modern central station complex. Nearby, we stayed at another excellent K's House Backpackers Hostel, the same as in Hiroshima. Plenty of young backpackers stay here, but we found many more were mature tourists this time. It was not difficult to see why – it is centrally located, clean, modern, friendly and well staffed, with an excellent buffet breakfast. Arriving back from a walk in heavy rain on our first day here, we found shoe-drying machines in the foyer, which proved most effective. No charge was made for their use. It was pleasant surprises like this that made cycling in Japan so pleasant.

Our dormitory beds at K's House were good value rather than cheap, but nothing is cheap in Kyoto. During our two-night stay, we met some really nice people, underlining again the benefits of staying in a decent hostel rather than a hotel. We could have stayed in a hotel for a week and never really got to know anyone; this would be almost impossible in a hostel. It is also a good way to find out about less touristy things to do.

I think we spent more time visiting cultural and religious buildings in Japan than anywhere else on the whole trip. Kyoto has some of the most astounding Buddhist temples in the world. The tranquillity Sam and I experienced during our days in Kyoto, visiting Ryoanji Temple (with its rock garden) and the Golden Temple (situated on a peaceful lake) really seemed to affect our mood for the rest of our ride to Tokyo.

Food was still one of our main focuses, though. Japan was superb for making sure we ate good healthy food at regular times. There was rarely a time that we couldn't get something we wanted. Even outside normal shop hours, there are usually 24-hour supermarkets. At the very least, you find sophisticated vending machines at stations and street corners.

Our favourite gastronomic treat was the *kaiten* sushi bars, where you help yourself to sushi on fixed price plates from a conveyor belt. Most visitors to Japan seem to like these places, and they are increasingly popular in the West. I think the convenience of seeing the actual food rather than having to chose things blind from a menu is a big factor. Most establishments are fairly basic, although they do vary in quality. The fish is usually at least fresh that day. As in all Japanese restaurants, freshness is the deciding factor for quality.

I think it would still be true to say at the time of writing that the worst sushi found in Japan would generally be better than what we get in Europe or elsewhere.

Kaiten sushi bars were so convenient that our break times while we were cycling were often determined by when we saw one. They provided us with a quick, nourishing meal that left us feeling fit and healthy all afternoon. I have dreams about kaiten-sushi, and I think Sam is now well on the way to the same level of obsession.

*

Kyoto was great, but we felt driven forward and cycled on. Over the coming week, we passed through Yokkaichi, Toyohashi, Fujieda, Numatzu and Gotanbe in a progression towards our goal – Tokyo. Mainly commercial centres, these cities were not especially beautiful but authentically Japanese and therefore still interesting. While following the main route, we mainly stayed in Tokyo Inn hotels – a chain of fairly standard business hotels found in the centre of many Japanese towns. They seemed extremely luxurious to us after most of our trip.

A big attraction with this chain was the communal Japanese bathhouse (*sento*). Guests can always be seen wandering through the hotel in the evenings wearing the *yukata* robe and slippers provided, on their way to or from the hotel sento.   The communal bath (separate ones for men and women) is rather like a small swimming pool or a traditional footballer's bath, except that the water is piping hot and you wash yourself before you get in.   For the Japanese this is a strict daily regime.   You will rarely feel as clean as when you come out of a sento.

Despite feeling pulled towards Tokyo, we were trying hard not to race through this beautiful country.   I wanted Sam to have plenty of opportunities to meet Japanese people and learn about the culture. But the thought of being in Tokyo with Steve, visiting my favourite places and seeing people I knew, built up a strong impetus.   I think Sam was also looking forward to the opportunity to meet more people his own age.

After a night in mountainous Fujieda, we passed close to iconic Mt Fuji.   Disappointingly, we saw only the base of this extinct volcano, since it was shrouded in threatening back clouds.   This signalled the impending arrival of Japan's rainy season.

On a clear day, you can see Mt Fuji from central Tokyo, I reminded myself.   I shared this thought with Sam, since, more than numbers on a road-sign, I felt it gave a real sense of how close we now were.

We avoided the discomfort of another soaking on our final few days towards Tokyo, but we still had mountain roads to contend with throughout much of each day.   On the plus side, the steep roads provided us with lovely scenery.   Fortunately, our legs, after nearly 10,000 muscle-building miles, felt no pain from the exertion.   Never one for intentional bodybuilding, I must say that the sight of the muscle definition on my calves often shocked me during the trip.   It sometimes made me feel quite ill – as if they were not really my legs.

*

We did spend the last couple of days counting down the kilometres on the road-signs as we neared Tokyo.   The outskirts spread further than you can imagine and we were well into urban sprawl for the whole of our last day.   Tokyo is the world's largest city.   We needed to get used to it.   The city has relatively little green space.   Even back in the 1980s, I can remember it feeling at times like we were living on a huge space station.

Cycling between heavy city traffic down Shibuya's Omotesando Dori in the southern part of central Tokyo was nothing short of surreal. I know Shibuya well from when I lived in Tokyo and have been there a number of times since. This time, though, I found it difficult to get my head around the fact that I had travelled here on my bicycle rather than by plane. It is almost more than the mind can take in.

Darting in and out of traffic, we rode through the large crowded streets of central Tokyo: down Meiji-dori; through Higashi Shinjuku; past Okubo-dori (where Steve and I lived when I first came to Tokyo); past Takadanobaba station and down Waseda-dori to Nakano – all familiar places to me, steeped in nostalgia.

I cannot describe the feeling as Sam and I finally arrived at the foot of the stairs to Steve's flat. It was a strange combination of exhilaration and deflation, if that is possible. We were earlier than expected and Steve was still at work, so it was just us, with no reception committee. We thought this would be a relief, but it did make things seem a bit *normal*. We took a photo of the moment, using the timer on the camera. Then, having retrieved the hidden key, we unloaded our bikes and baggage into Steve's homely apartment. That was it, then!

Sadly, it all seemed a bit of an anti-climax now. We had expected to experience a huge physical relief, like one feels at the end of a marathon. In fact, we felt fine, not at all overcome with emotion. 9,600-odd miles. We were here. I made a cup of tea.

Looking around, I could see Steve had spring-cleaned and arranged plenty of cupboard space for our stuff. This came as something of a surprise – we are talking about a man who lives alone here! Sam and I stowed our baggage and took turns in the shower, then drank our *genmai-cha* tea. After sitting down for a few minutes, we checked our emails on Steve's computer and spoke to Steve on the phone.

What now? We felt we should be doing something, but what? We sat for a moment, trying to relax but it was no good. Dressed for relaxation but feeling anything but relaxed, we headed off out for our first kaiten-sushi in Tokyo, at Steve's excellent local establishment. We were greeted by the proprietor.

"This is more like it," I said.

By our second plate, we were well and truly *in the zone*.

I had visited Steve every three years or so of late, so it felt good walking down the familiar streets, pointing out places I knew. At the same time, though, I remained troubled by feeling a little underwhelmed. It was not how we wanted to be feeling at such an important time. We had waited for this moment for nine months, and now what? Had we really done it? Was that it, over? Did we really not have to get up early and cycle to the next place any more?

I was in a familiar place but felt disorientated. Dizzy almost. The world was all a bit of a blur, and judging by Sam's behaviour he felt the same. It felt like I was looking down on all this from a distance. Unexpectedly, we realised this was going to take some getting used to.

SAM'S POINT OF VIEW

After grounding ourselves in South Korea, our spirits quickly picked up. The disorganised, chaotic lifestyle we'd become so used to in China was far from the norm in South Korea. Everything was clean, everyone was polite and the food was exquisite.

We made two great discoveries while we were in Korea. The first was Seafood Ocean. How they made any money, I'm unsure. The buffets were beyond gourmet. OK, it wasn't cheap, but for what you got, there was no way you'd say it wasn't worth the price – rows and rows of California rolls, sashimi, sushi, dim-sum, dumplings, gyoza and delicious salads as well as some superb puddings. And all of this was replenished as soon as someone put something on their plate. Since it was a buffet, so you could try a little of everything, then eat until you dropped! The quality and freshness were just amazing.

The second great discovery was the love hotels, which seemed to go down a treat with locals. We discovered that they were always conveniently located near the centre and very reasonably priced. You can imagine the look on a love hotel receptionist's face as a 50-

year-old man (with large beard) and a very skinny boy, both in lycra shorts, rock up to the reception asking for a room. We were turned away quite a few times before we worked out why. After that we made sure we established our 'father-son status' and assured them we just wanted a place to sleep! For cheap places, they were very well kitted out so they became the obvious place to head for in each main town.

The other thing that sticks in my memory are the amazing freeways that cut through the mountainous landscape. They hardly ever go over the hills; it was just tunnel after tunnel. The only problem was that they don't let bicycles on the freeways. The alternative route was always extremely hilly.

I felt a lot more positive at this point in the trip and my health was far better. It was probably the excitement of being close to finishing that was helping me to feel so positive. It had been a tough nine months for both of us, but it was only around this time I started to realise how difficult the time must have been for my dad as well. I'd been so grumpy for so long.

Arriving in Japan was so exciting. We were very close now and the days were going really quickly. The pain of cycling had evaporated; I was just enjoying the super-clean, organised, honourable lifestyle of the Japanese. The food was once again amazing. The landscape was beautiful, especially on the island of Shikoku, which is linked by ten impressive suspension bridges. It was really mountainous and so beautiful.

Hiroshima was a very memorable city for me. Obviously, it was very modern, having been totally rebuilt after the US almost entirely wiped it out in their effort to end the Second World War. The peace memorial museum was very moving, with kids' shoes and people's hair sometimes all that survived the blast. It was a big eye-opener and something I think we could all benefit from seeing.

The hostel we stayed at here was so Japanese. As always, everything was spotless and worked perfectly. Most impressive was the shoe-dryers they placed in the reception and on each floor when it rained. The Japanese think of everything to make you comfortable and feel welcome. We went out into the city to find some food and were met by a very unusual downpour on our way home from a 'kaiten' sushi bar (conveyor-belt style). On our return, we saw how useful those shoe-dryers were when you only had one pair of shoes. They dried them out in minutes. I think you'd struggle to find such levels of customer satisfaction elsewhere, least of all for a hostel.

I drunk a lot of coffee in Japan – more than I had in the whole of the rest of the trip. There was a chain of family restaurants called Joyful, or 'Joyfooru' as they pronounced it. They offered unlimited coffee and tea so I used to have about six coffees after food, while my dad got his gentler caffeine explosion from green tea. After leaving the restaurant, we'd bomb it to our destination and then crash. We made really good time some of those days and being so close to finishing was really exciting for me. Eventually, we began seeing signs for Tokyo. I couldn't imagine how I'd feel when we actually finished.

We started eating a lot of doughnuts in Japan too. You couldn't go many miles without seeing a doughnut shop; they just love them. We were soon eating about six a day, which was fine when we were burning it off with 100-mile cycling days.

My mood was far better, from what I remember – largely because we'd gotten used to managing each other. The demands of being around each other day and night never really left my consciousness, but I dealt with it by remaining relatively quiet. This kept me calm throughout the day and was easy for me to do. The only daunting thing at the time was socialising with other adults. On my own, I was calm and found it easy, but add my dad to the equation and I felt I couldn't get into the conversation. I felt embarrassed and didn't really want to be spoken to. The fact that my dad kept trying to bring me into the conversation was really unhelpful, despite me realising his good intentions. Not being allowed to remain silent and simply listen to others talk felt irritating. I could see my silence made other people uncomfortable and probably even confused about how a boy who has just been exposed to such a variety of cultures and exciting experiences could be so troubled, quiet and rude.

After two days of counting the signs for Tokyo, we finally arrived. We'd actually cycled from home and arrived on the other side of the world. Nine thousand seven hundred miles of cycling! I look back and feel that what we did that year was amazing. But I'd have to say that the moment we arrived in Tokyo was a massive anti-climax. I'd looked forward to it for a whole year, but now finishing just felt like any other day.

Looking back nearly two years later, I remember both of us feeling it – that what we'd done didn't seem that amazing. I spent a long time waiting for it to sink in. People told me it would take time. I just didn't realise it would take over two years. Perhaps the worst of my memories have finally been filtered out.

<h1 style="text-align:right">Chapter 14</h1>

Tokyo - Four weeks R&R and the return home

Eventually, all things merge into one and a river runs through it. The river was cut by the world's great flood and runs over the rocks from the basement of time. On some of the rocks are timeless raindrops. Under the rocks are the words, and some of the words are theirs. Norman Maclean.

It took a day to sink in. Yes, we had indeed done it. We had cycled nearly 10,000 miles from Ireland to Japan. Then again, we never doubted that we would. Others may have doubted it, but we never did. We are both a bit single-minded (simple-minded?) in that way. Yes, we had taken a couple of flights and train rides, but we knew at the start we would have to do that. We had made up the distance elsewhere along the way anyway.

Having arrived, Sam's main motivation for the time being was to catch up on some sleep, with plenty of all-day lie-ins. But for our first night there, he was happy to stay up and celebrate with Steve and I when Steve got back from work.

Steve works as an editor and English language advisor for a large Japanese press agency. He has a number of other freelance jobs, which is quite common for foreigners living in Tokyo. In the main, he works in the evenings, returning home around 11pm. This fitted very well with our ideal lifestyle as non-working men. Coincidentally, this also allowed us to get onto UK time a month in advance – by getting up around midday and going to bed around 5am.

In Tokyo, these hours are really not that unusual and we found that it fitted well, enhancing the kind of *Bladerunneresque* quality that Tokyo already has.

Steve kindly dropped all of his other freelance work over the four weeks we were in Tokyo to help us to enjoy the fruits of our labour. Each night, we went out to a local *issakaya* to eat, drink and calmly discuss life.   Sam was sceptical about this.   If it hadn't been for the fact that he liked Steve so much and that Steve was so easy going, I think it could have been problematic.   He was really not in the mood for discussing the meaning of life.

Brunch was generally spent in a kaiten-sushi bar, although Steve and I did have quite a few late breakfasts in Japanese coffee shops on the days he worked.   On re-charge for most of these four weeks, I don't think Sam made it up for a single breakfast or brunch.   We did of course do some serious cultural things during the day, but the important matter of hanging out all night in issakayas generally took precedence.   This lifestyle suited Sam.   It is after all very similar to the life of a student and he had been looking forward to that.

Four weeks gave us time to get into a comfortable routine.   It was also long enough for Steve to enjoy having us there, but (I suspect) to be glad to see the back of us when we had gone.   He is sociable enough generally, but he rarely has guests staying, so it must have put some pressure on him having us there for a full month.

I remember us calling in at a supermarket to buy some sliced bread for snacks one afternoon.   I was well aware of Steve's intense dislike of *nato* – a stinking Japanese fermented soya-bean product, that some Japanese eat for breakfast.   Knowing this sticky delicacy has great health-giving properties, I had gradually become accustomed to it when living there back in the 80s, and I took some childish pride in being the only westerner I knew who liked it.   Steve had said to me a few days after our arrival that I was absolutely not to eat nato in his flat.   This was said in a bar somewhere in the early hours, so I had taken it simply as a kind of demonstration to Sam of how disgusting the stuff is.   Misguidedly working on the assumption he was not really being serious, I bought a few packs at the supermarket. Steve, a man renowned for his naturally calm state, was dumbfounded, demanding that I get the evil substance out of his fridge and *out of his apartment*.   Sure it was an act, I laughed and said not to worry, I would eat it out on the balcony.

Later, Sam told me Steve had turned to him, steam metaphorically emanating from his ears, and asked him what on earth had happened to me on the trip to have rendered me so unbelievably stupid. I finished the second pack on the balcony the next morning before anyone else was up – and I bloody well enjoyed it, I might add.

This was probably the unique moment of friction with Steve and one of the few in all the years I've known him. Friction between Sam and I, however, was still a regular facet of life. Despite Steve being his newfound godfather, Sam was back into a state of irritation about being with old farts. Supposedly, we were not interested in anything he had to say. Steve took this on board seriously. I was a little tired of hearing it.

This open wound was regularly inflamed by our weekly visits to a longstanding venue in Takadanobaba (northwest central Tokyo), where we met various old friends for food, drink and intense alcohol-fuelled debate. Sam enjoyed the party atmosphere, good food and serious drinking of beer and sake, but he always awoke the next day feeling unhappy. He'd had nothing valuable to say, he insisted again – but the opposite was true. People thought him *naïve*, he assured us, although Steve and I knew people were fascinated by him and were glad of the opportunity to talk to someone his age on this level. Apart from anything else, this poor kid had cycled ten months across the world with his father. On that subject alone, it was worth hearing his thoughts. People even valued his opinions. But he wouldn't hear any of this from us.

Steve and I felt sorry for Sam and remembered our own growing pains around that age – in fact, Steve had been about the same age when we first met in Tokyo. But when we made an effort to bring conversations around to things Sam could talk about with authority, he told us that he was aware of what we were doing, even though sometimes we weren't. In the end Steve and I agreed we should just act naturally and leave him to get on with it. That was easier for Steve. Although significantly younger than me, he has always been a great mentor to me with his *live and let live* philosophy, especially when we were first in Japan

Fortunately one of our friends at the bar in Takadanobaba had a close friend with a son around the same age as Sam. The young guy, named Dowd, was studying at nearby Waseda University. He shared a house with a few other students in Nakano, where Steve lives. So John arranged for Sam to meet up with Dowd. They got on well and

Sam spent a few nights out with him and his housemates, crashed at their place for a bit afterwards and went to baseball games. This seemed to make a big difference and he always seemed happier to see me after one of these sessions. This helped me feel confident about how he would be once back in England with his friends around.

When Sam wasn't around, Steve reminded me how hard it must have been for Sam to be away from his friends and people his own age for so long. I knew that but perhaps had nothing to compare it with – no equivalent experience in my own youth – to help me understand what it really felt like.

Taking all this into consideration, I could see maybe Sam had really been very tolerant with me. I wondered how I would have been with my own father and whether the experience had taught Sam anything. It had certainly taught me something, but I still wasn't sure either of us had rationalised any of it yet. At that point, I think Sam might still have put his feelings down to his dad just being a very annoying person – which I'm well aware I can be. He sees it differently now.

*

A few days after arriving at Steve's, Sam and I cycled into central Tokyo to meet the Irish ambassador at his embassy. We had arrived in Tokyo towards the end of the Golden Week holiday. Until fairly recently, the Japanese were engaged in a quest of intense effort to bring about a spectacular economic recovery after the country's collapse following WW2. They still work long hours and take relatively few extended holidays compared to people in the West, but this is balanced by having a large number of short cultural holidays. Once Japan became more prosperous, the Japanese Government decided to bridge two consecutive long weekend holidays to make a 10-day break. This became known as Golden Week.

Tokyo is a very urban city with very little green and not a great deal of space per person. This is part of what makes it so exciting, although one inevitably becomes worn down by it, craving open space, quiet and clean air. Golden Week, therefore, is a prime time for the Japanese to get away and rediscover nature. The Irish ambassador had abandoned Tokyo, bizarrely, it transpired, to go to Dingle where he hung out with his brother in Paudy O'Shea's bar – a place I know well. So we had to wait a few days for his return before ceremoniously completing our journey as planned.

Sam was really unhappy about this on the day. He couldn't see what difference it made turning up at the embassy on our bikes to meet the ambassador or being photographed by the press. To him it must have spelt more of his dad organising everything without his input. Finally, I agreed that we would not repack the bags onto the bikes, although I held out for the cycle clothing. He agreed without a big argument. I was convinced the early wake-up time of 10am had been the problem. In the end, Sam turned on his youthful charm once we arrived, which was a bit of a relief. The ambassador and the press presence made us feel pretty special – more like we had expected to feel on our arrival – so it was probably worth the effort, even for Sam.

One unanticipated big difference about being in Tokyo was that we were able to have meetings with Lorna and Scarlett via Skype on computer. It was amazing to be able to sit and chat to them, seeing them in our Canterbury living room looking natural and happy. The time difference did mean these sessions often took place around 4am Japan time when we had just come home from Orenji, my favourite local issakaya, so it caught us at our worst, or best, depending on Lorna's perspective at the time.

Lorna still seemed worn out by the pressures of her work but exhilarated by all the theatre-going and other cultural outings she and Scarlett had immersed themselves in while their lives were their own. I could see that this was very positive on the whole, although I was still worried about her energy levels. She seemed worried a little about mine too.

"Don't you think you might be hitting it a bit hard?" she asked. "Do the celebrations really need to go on this long?"

Scarlett seemed as indefatigably full of enthusiasm for life as ever a whirlwind of baking, researching gadgets, watching quirky American comedy series and listening to music. She had been a great companion to Lorna but was now really longing for our return. She had missed Sam more than she, or he, had imagined possible. I could see signs that she might even be missing *me*.   Lorna confirmed this later, and I can see that our long absence must have been a little confusing for Scarlett.   Amongst the people she knew, having your father go away for nearly a year without it being due to a relationship break-up was very rare if not unheard of.

Ending our journey somewhere that is a bit of a second home to me certainly added poignancy to the trip.   For Sam, it was also a special place to arrive – somewhere mystical he had heard about as a child, the place where his mother and father had met.   I hope it lived up to his expectations.   At the time, he seemed unable to rationalise things.   I can see now that by then he needed to be away from me and out of the expeditionary situation before he could to start to make sense of any of it.   In fact, so did I.

We really enjoyed our four weeks in Tokyo, while at the same time we longed to be home.   In truth, the trip was not over yet for either of us.   We longed for the sense of achievement we now felt would only come when we arrived home in Canterbury.

*

During the trip Sam and I spent many a night lying in our tent, in seedy hotel rooms with brown sheets, or on the rooftops of hostels, planning our homecoming.   We had fine-tuned the plan as the trip progressed and in Tokyo we now knew exactly what we wanted.   We asked Lorna to organise a party at our house on the afternoon of Saturday 13 June.   She told us that over 100 of our friends and family had confirmed they would be there, along with the press.

We wanted to cycle from Heathrow airport down to Canterbury, so we decided that in order to be sure of arriving back on time, and not keeping our reception committee waiting, we would secretly spend a night at a B&B in nearby Faversham.   We could then have a lie-in and cycle the last ten miles home after an English pub lunch.   Our hearts had raced many times at the thought of it.   In fact, it was one thing that absolutely made us feel close and in harmony.

While we were pretty pleased with the plan, we had failed to take into account Lorna's eagerness to see us.   Lorna said she would come to the airport to meet us before we did the last stretch.   Sam thought this would destroy the special experience and would result in his friends all turning up too. I could see his point, so finally we agreed to tell Lorna alone of our plan. We agreed that she, Scarlett and Alexandra would come and have dinner with us in Faversham on the night of the twelfth, so we didn't have to have the press and everyone else along when we met for the first time.

I could tell Sam was dubious about this change of plan but he could see it was unfair to ask more of Lorna. This was one of the parts of the trip she wanted to play a big part in. Sam agreed it seemed a reasonable compromise, so we built it into the plan.

The next day, our Faversham B&B host emailed me to ask if we wouldn't mind sharing a double bed to allow a lady and her daughter to have the twin. We agreed, of course, realising that this mother and daughter must in fact be Lorna and Scarlet. Or so we thought. In fact, they turned out to be someone else entirely. It amused me, though, that the planning of our return home day was turning out to be more involved than the planning of the rest of the trip. Later, it also amused Sam that I might have bowled into the other mother and daughter's room straight from my shower.

*

At the end of our month in Tokyo and after several celebratory leaving nights, we set off for Narita airport. Narita is a fair distance east of Tokyo, and we felt decidedly out of condition after a month of eating and drinking, with no exercise and living at the opposite end of the clock. We were by no means confident about the modest 87km ride to get there. In addition, we had agreed to detour via Ikebukero in northern Tokyo, where our friend Nobuko and some other very hospitable Japanese businesswomen had asked us to call in to say goodbye. These ladies had taken us out to a wrestling bar just a few days before and seemed particularly fond of Sam. On the day, we managed to get up at 9am and cycle off calmly. Steve came down to see us off, waving goodbye in his pyjamas and overcoat before returning back up to bed. Heading off uphill to meet the ladies in Ikebukuro, we felt light-headed.

"Dad, you're still pissed!" Sam called out as I snaked along the road.

I didn't try to defend myself. It was nothing that a sandwich and a Japanese energy drink from the mini-mart wouldn't put right, I assured him.

Ikebukuro was a steeper uphill climb than expected and we found it a bit off a challenge after a month.

"Oh, you look a little tired," one of the ladies told us. "Hadn't you better to take the train?"

We were not so tired we wanted to take a train. We were on the road home now, we told ourselves as we sped back down through central Tokyo.

This was familiar territory to me. We found ourselves passing many offices where I had worked and taught as a young man. Eventually, we reached the endless sprawl of the eastern suburbs. It took forever to reach countryside, but in the end the familiar paddy-fields, chain-cafes, and simple hardware stores told us we were out. A flicker of nostalgia ran through our hearts for a moment. We wondered whether we might find one of our favourite Joyful restaurants for lunch. Sadly, were to be disappointed. The Joyful experiences would have to remain a memory.

Sam and I had booked to stay that last night at a hostel somewhere right under the flight-path of Narita Airport. We followed directions provided by the manager but assumed we were lost when we found ourselves in an arable field, approaching a small pre-fab house. At the door, a very pleasant young manager invited us in. He spoke very good English. Later, he explained that the guesthouse had been his first business idea after university. There had previously been no backpacker hostels near Narita Airport. He had spotted a gap in the market.

"So far," he said with resignation, "it is looking like an elephant of whiter shade."

Despite my years as an English teacher in Tokyo, I resisted correcting this lovely piece of accidental poetry.

*

332

Just to remind us life has a way of doing such things, the rain poured on us the next morning and we arrived pretty damp at the airport. Yet again, we cursed the idiocy of planners, even Japanese ones, who fail to imagine passengers arriving at an airport by bicycle or on foot. It took forever trying to find a way in on a road that allowed cyclists. Finally, we were shepherded by baffled security guards through gaps in the security fences and pointed towards the terminal building.

"You must to go very *quickery* across the road of the airplane. They don't stop for the bicycle hardly!"

Sam and I already knew what to expect when we got to check-in with our heavily laden bicycles, and those expectations were immediately fulfilled.

"Hello, sir. Do you have any *ruggages*?"

"Yes, we do have luggages." I pointed to our parked bicycles.

"You will take only the luggages, yes?"

"No, no, we will take the bicycles too."

"Aagh, no, sir. I am so sorry, this is impossible, we cannot take them, they are too largely!"

"No, it's quite alright. We have taken them before. When I booked the flight in London, I was told it would be fine. They said if we had any problems to speak to the chief supervisor."

The British Airways duty supervisor was called and a charming Japanese man arrived looking very smart in his uniform. I spurred my brain to think ahead. What would I say? I explained that we had cycled to Japan from Ireland. Slightly embellishing the truth, I said we had been assured by his company's global marketing director that we would be able take the bikes back on the plane.

"Do the bicycles break up to pieces?" he asked. "If no, we cannot take them on the plane. Sadly impossible."

The man made a firm cross sign with two fingers. This was beginning to look harder than I had expected. Again, I racked my brain for a solution.

"Yes, I understand your problem, but I contacted your company to sponsor us before our trip and Mr Steve Beardsley, your marketing director, said that although BA could not give us a free flight, he would make sure our bikes were flown back without a problem."

Sam was looking at me quizzically – he knew that I had done no such thing. Moreover, he knew that Steve Beardsley is a friend of mine who is in fact a construction safety manager.

"Mr Beardsley said that if there was any problem, I should ask to speak to the chief supervisor and that if necessary he could be telephoned at BA's head office in London," I said, knowing full well it was now 3am in London.

The supervisor scratched his head.

"OK, you can take the bicycles on the plane. But you must pay extra baggage charge and …"

"Mr Steve Beardsley told me that we ..." I began. At the further mention of Mr Beardsley, however, he accepted defeat.

The charming man told the stewardess to please check in the baggage and label the bikes. After the familiar outsize luggage scanner, the bikes were loaded into a specially ordered van. All was done with beautiful efficiency and we were soon relaxing in the departure lounge.

"Dad, you are an unbelievable liar!" Sam said as we walked away.

I smiled, reminding him that the Japanese are not daft and the supervisor had probably guessed I was making it up. The key thing, I told Sam, was that I had appealed to his sense of pride in his country and company, which had made him want to help us. That's not exactly lying.

"So you did him a favour really!" smiled Sam.

It had certainly done no harm anyway, I felt. At least I hadn't asked to be upgraded.

*

After five in-flight movies our plane deposited us at Heathrow. It was still afternoon and we had managed to get some sleep. Our month on UK time in Tokyo really seemed to have paid off. The other passengers all looked shattered, in agony at the prospect of the afternoon ahead while their bodies were telling them it was the early hours of the morning.

We arrived at the baggage carousel to find our bikes already parked at the far end.   In very little time at all, we were cycling out of that familiar airport.   I sniggered at the idea I was doing this on a bike.   Other road users seemed less amused.   Braving bendy-buses, baggage transfer trucks and baffled foreigners driving unfamiliar right-hand drive hire cars, we headed out along the appallingly surfaced A4 dual-carriageway into London.

Blaring their horns and shouting obscenities at being held up for a few extra seconds, local car drivers immediately reminded us we were home.   A gang of lads on their way home from school detention kicked a can at us as we passed by.   Others pretended not to see us, intentionally blocking the cycle path, which we soon abandoned due to all the broken glass.   We had seen nothing like this in ten months across the world through poverty stricken third-world countries and political trouble-spots.   Here in affluent England, yobbery was thriving.

I chastised myself for grumbling, determined not to return to the grumpy old man behaviour I had indulged in before our departure. Sam was more able to laugh, saying that it made him feel at home. To enhance his nostalgia, I stopped at the first rough old pub we saw alongside the main road.   Here we bought two pints of Guinness and a couple of packets of stale cheese and onion crisps.   Leaving the local unemployed and long-term sick to the comfort of the bar, we sat outside by the dirty, thundering traffic, immersed in a scene of urban decay and economic despair.   Not the best reintroduction to England, but it certainly made a powerful impression upon us.

Continuing the reintroduction theme, we decided to take a busy route right through central London, passing many of the great landmarks: Buckingham Palace, Westminster Abbey, Big Ben, St Paul's Cathedral and Tower Bridge followed in close succession.   On the positive side, there did seemed to have been a large increase in the number of cyclists on the roads going in and out of central London since we had left.   It turned out this was due to another great English institution – a London tube strike.

After all those hours thinking about our return home, we were able to enjoy this first day without any sense of pressure.   We had planned it that way.   I was determined Sam would not end the trip feeling that he was being pushed to go further or faster than he wanted. Consequently, we were able to pootle along through central London before heading over Tower Bridge, and on to Greenwich, where we had booked a hostel for the night. It was almost too easy.

Checking into the hostel felt strange. At 55 miles, we were near enough to cycle home by dinnertime. I didn't share this thought with Sam. It would have sounded painfully familiar to him. Instead, I got onto the subject of what we would do that night. It could have been any other night on the trip: check into the hostel; secure the bikes; shower and change and then go out to eat. It felt very different, though. Apart from anything else, we were coming to the end of two days of continuous daylight. It felt confusing. I think we were also both experiencing mixed emotions. I felt excited about our return home with everyone waiting for us, but at the same time I felt sad to be ending the trip. I think I was also dwelling upon the fact that after the next day I was unlikely to spend so much time with Sam ever again. That made me sad, despite the slight sense of distance he now seemed to have placed between us.

Our ride down to Faversham the next day was as relaxed as we had intended. It began with breakfast in the pub downstairs and a 9:30 start. Sam seemed to be in a bit of a dream world, rather like he used to be as a little boy when we were going on holiday. I thought back to that time and how endearing his dreaminess had been. I felt it was worth risking a joke, even though it was still before lunchtime.

"Any Idea where we are going today, Sam?"

He thought about my question for a moment in silence as we pushed our bikes out onto the street. Then I saw him smile.

"Are we back on the England planet yet, Dad?"

*

Heading out across familiar Blackheath and up never-ending Shooters Hill, we felt glad to be approaching countryside again. Speeding down the other side, the shoulder strap of Sam's pannier, left loose due to what I saw as a determination to ignore fatherly advice, caught in his back wheel. Fortunately, he managed to stop before it got entirely chewed up in the back wheel or broke a bunch of spokes.

He knew what I was thinking, although I fought with myself not to show a flicker of criticism in my look or my voice.

The old A2 route from Greenwich to Faversham could only be described as scenic if you were someone nostalgic for decaying, largely poverty-stricken dormitory towns. I remarked to Sam as we passed through Gillingham and Rainham that it was like a post-apocalyptic view of Britain. Takeaway detritus, broken beer bottles, dumped washing machines, dog mess, and second-rate graffiti littered the roadside. Hugely obese disenfranchised young people, pallid white skin and spots peeping out from under hoodies, tossed chips at us as we passed. Cars with racist stickers in the back windows cut in front of us as girlfriends or teenage boys shouted abuse out of the passenger windows.

"Get off the f'kin road, y'tossers!"

"Next time we'll flatten yers!"

A whack around the head with a maize stick seemed infinitely preferable to this. Could it be that the people of the Medway towns hated cyclists more than people anywhere else on our route across the world?

The degradation of the Medway towns behind us, we were comforted by green and pleasant English countryside as we approached Faversham. Despite our very relaxed pace, it was still only 3pm. We coasted around looking for our B&B, but not trying too hard. After a little directional help from a youth with a chip lodged in his beard, we checked in and had showers. Force of habit prevented us from relaxing before we had washed our socks and shorts. Trying to pass the time, I read for a while, ate the complementary shortbread biscuits and watched some news. Finally, we set off for the Sun Hotel to meet Lorna, Scarlett and Alex for dinner. Surreal!

It was amazing to see the three of them, of course, but really quite odd. These were strange circumstances. We were only ten miles from home but not going home until the next day, and they were not staying with us. It almost felt like some kind of prison visit. It had seemed like a good idea when we talked about it in Japan, but now we were here it felt a bit like torture. As the evening went on, though, we got used to the idea.

Sam and I went back to our B&B and watched some TV, as we had done on so many nights while we were on the road, but it felt very different. It did give me time to get back to the final chapter of the book I had been reading (*Far From the Madding Crowd*). It would have felt terrible to get back without quite finishing it.

*

I woke very early on our final morning. At 5:30 I was sitting up reading the last few pages of my book, the emotion of which, according to my diary, I was quite overwhelmed by. No doubt this was my mind's way of trying to deal with the emotion of the end of the trip and returning to my family, while at the same time I was about to lose my close daily contact with my son. My emotions felt strange – they did not feel like my own. I sat in a chair watching the sun slowly rising on what would be a memorable day for our family.

Even Sam was awake earlier than I expected – certainly earlier than he needed to be. After fortifying ourselves with our first English breakfast for about a year, we busied ourselves packing. We delayed as long as we could, since we knew we were not due at our house until around 1:30pm. It seemed a long time to wait, but it was too late to change it now. What the hell had we thought we would be doing all morning? Waiting for Sam to wake up, I guess.

Sometime before 10am, we set off for Canterbury. It was a short ride but one with a long steep hill in the middle. We took our time. Even so, we arrived on the outskirts, in Lower Harbledown, before 11am. Trying to ride slowly and arrive later was a strange reversal of behaviour for me.

The village of Harbledown is about half a mile from our house. Conveniently, it had a good pub. Coincidentally of course, Martin, who had cycled with us in Thailand and Laos, lived there.

We parked our bikes, bought ourselves a couple of pints of cider and went to sit in the garden. It was a lovely sunny day and the view south across the hop fields was stunning. An intensely more beautiful reintroduction to England. This was a really good idea we agreed – a good way to calm everything down before all the fuss of the reception that awaited us around the corner.

"Sam, shall I phone Martin and see if he wants to join us for a drink?"

Sam was not sure. Right from when we agreed our plans in Japan, he hadn't wanted to make any changes.

"Do you think he'll be able to keep it a secret? It would be terrible if people found out after we arrive at the reception that we'd been sitting around the corner in a pub for three hours."

Half an hour later, Martin told Judith he was slipping out to buy some things to take to the party. After enjoying a nostalgic hour and a half with us, he returned home, saying someone he knew had waylaid him. Economical with the truth perhaps, but hardly a lie.

At 1:30pm, Sam and I swerved nervously into our road.

"Bloody hell, there are loads of them, Sam!"

Sam laughed. He was beyond worrying about that now. We put our heads down and tried to look like two men at the end of a hard day's ride.

"Hold your breath, Sam. We need to be gasping when we arrive."

Sam was still laughing. He swerved again – he was going to to fall off his bike if he wasn't careful.

"Come on, Dad. Shall we cycle straight past?"

I remembered for one hazy moment the unending questions we had been asked in Dingle at the start of the trip nearly a year before. Then I heard cheering. There was a finish-line tape across the path and we were chicaned precariously towards it. We were going too fast! I gulped. My mind had gone blank. What on earth was I going to say?

"Sam, just act normal," I said, trying to be serious as we juddered to a stop. "Smile a lot."

SAM'S POINT OF VIEW

Looking back on it now, I am able to fully appreciate the work my dad put in for this trip and how tough it must have been to remain calm with such an ungrateful teenager constantly around. That's not to say that I was being nasty, or that I was a bad person; I was just ignorant of the situation. I shouldn't forget how amazing the challenge was, and that we overcame it.

Two years later and I've just planned a cycle trip with some friends to Poland for next summer, so it didn't put me off. I feel more excited than ever about what we did and what trips I'll make in the future. I suppose most of us have experienced that buzz you get looking ahead to an adventure, or thinking back on it later, but it's weird that you often don't feel it when you're doing it. There's no doubt now the Japan cycle trip is over that it seems epic, and I feel really proud of myself.

Tokyo was surreal. Arriving had felt so normal. In hindsight, I had envisaged soaring levels of pleasure and relief but I felt nothing. We arrived at Steve's, and that was that. Bizarre!

Still not feeling like talking much, the pressure of being silent was often too much. People wanted to know what I felt about the trip. I found myself responding vaguely to questions or conversations, but feeling annoyed about it. The exhaustion really started to kick in after a few initial days of rest; that feeling you get when your body knows it's time to recover and you just kind of shut down. I would've slept for days in a row if I could have. My dad is pretty adamant I spent more than half my time in Tokyo asleep, but I could've done with a lot more.

Steve took on his role as godfather by educating me on music and film with lots of trips to the DVD hire shop. I'm pretty sure he almost wet himself when I told him I hadn't actually seen the Godfather films.

Hanging out with Steve and my dad was hard. They tried their utmost to accommodate me and get me involved, but I'd had my fill of being with middle-aged men. I felt I was being really ungrateful and a bit of a nuisance. The two of them had loads to talk about and my lack of knowledge on almost any of their topics of conversation meant that making a contribution was difficult. Regardless of my state of negativity, though, Tokyo was a great place to be. My friends would kill to spend six weeks in Tokyo, living comfortably without needing money. I couldn't have had it much better.

The bars and the food were just amazing – so many different types of cuisine produced with absolute perfection, and everything operating so efficiently. Tokyo might be expensive but I could see that the end product justified the cost. I will definitely be going back.

Arriving home felt like I was in a dream. Nobody I spoke to was even close to understanding what I felt about the trip and I still didn't feel able to explain it to them. Everyone seemed to expect such positive responses to their questions, so they were surprised to hear me say I was glad it was over. I think now I understand why. They saw what we'd done as a major physical challenge. We had been successful in overcoming that challenge, so surely I would feel positive about it. But you mustn't forget that cycling for ten months across the world is seriously hard work mentally as well as physically. When the local press ask you to sum up your feelings in two or three words, you feel like your head might be ready to implode. Even weirder were the people who said it seemed we'd 'just left yesterday'. It felt like ten years for me!

Two years on, and I've become much more positive about the trip. It was an amazing thing to do with my dad, and the memories are now generally positive, even though I know how hard it was to get through and how angry I felt at times. When I look at the pictures on the blog www.bugbitten.com/father_son_cycle, I can't believe some of the places we saw. So many breath-taking images of things that seemed so normal at the time. It was an amazing experience and, yes, I'll be doing it again.

Chapter 15

Why?

Always go too far, because that is where you will find the truth.
Albert Camus.

I think most people would agree it is fortunate that we all seek different things in life. Bees, ants and lemmings may not, but I think most human beings celebrate their difference from one another. At the extremes, what inspires one person will seem mind-numbingly pointless to another, and what is painful for one man may be a pleasure for his friend.

For me, cycling nearly 10,000 miles across the world was an enormous pleasure, whereas my wife and many of my friends can think of few things they would like to do less.

"But what's the point?" several of them enquired, with irritatingly puzzled expressions.

Many were fixated upon the idea that people do these things to break records or raise money for charity (see final page for details). Quite a number were the same people who exclaimed – as if they had found some fundamental flaw in our plan – "Ah, but what about when you have to cross water, like from China to Korea?" As if by taking a short boat ride we were *cheating* and therefore destroying the point of our trip. Sadly, these poor souls uniformly thought they were the first to spot this *flaw*. We learned to humour them, saying that we planned to cycle up and down the deck during boat crossings.

We were not attracted by the need to break any records, or prove anything to anyone. Instead, we agreed that we were determined, most of all, to enjoy ourselves. If that meant taking a boat ride, or even flying ourselves out of danger or an intolerable situation, then we would do so. Judging by some travellers we met en route, we made our trip more satisfying by deciding this in advance. Others we met had made determined pledges about crossing the world without flying, and then felt their entire trip had *failed* when they were faced with no option but to fly over Pakistan or wait in Iran until the situation improved (impractical, given the visa situation there). I would not criticise them for that – nothing wrong with deciding to cycle every mile – but that was never our quest.

Ferries from the United Arab Emirates to India have disappeared due to impossible competition from low-cost airlines, and the option of going around the north of the Himalayas in November would have meant us missing all of India and Southeast Asia, let alone Christmas with Lorna and the others. Our flexible approach allowed us to fly to Kerala in the very south of India and make up the Pakistan distance by cycling up through India, rather than just cycling across the top of it as we had originally planned. This turned out to be one of the best parts of our trip, and that is how we tried to think about things all the way through. If something went wrong, maybe there was a good reason for it? Perhaps it was leading us to a better place? I find this a great maxim in life that works in all kinds of situations.

Lorna and I had given Sam a copy of Voltaire's *Candide* to read on the trip, and he of course found it amusing to liken my excessively optimistic outlook to the disastrously deluded Dr. Pangloss. I can take that. Yes, I am something of an optimistic idealist. I believe in a limitless possibility to physical achievement and that our limits are set largely by what we believe them to be. Sam finds this very annoying – or he did before completing the journey. Some people I express this belief to seem determined to find an example where it doesn't work (like the people who felt the need to point out that we could not cycle across the sea). This is not so hard to do, but little in life is a hundred percent true. The fact is that if you stick by the principle, you will always achieve more than other people believe is possible, and one day it might even save your life. It has probably saved mine on more than one occasion.

At the risk of flogging it to death, I would point out that I have seen this philosophy used to great advantage in sport as well as in business. It is what enables people to achieve things way above their perceived ability and against all odds. Some call it a can-do philosophy (a particularly useful expression to come out of America). Sadly, I find it to be in short supply in Britain these days.

*

Sam and I both enjoy physical endurance challenges. My wife says that I have a faulty gene, which when we travel places causes me to say things like, "OK, we'll stop soon. Let's just see what's over this next hill." I admit that she is correct: by *hill*, I mean horizon, and even those who still believe in a flat Earth know that the horizon has yet to be reached. It can be infuriating to others, but it works for me.

So what do we gain from travel? The adage that travel broadens the mind is somewhat out-dated, I feel. You can probably do more to broaden your mind these days by watching the Discovery Channel than by travelling – especially if travel means a round-the-world flight, stopping off at western-style hotels.

Increasing numbers of young people take a gap year, backpacking around the world. Unfortunately, most of them seem to want to follow a comfortable, well-trodden route, staying in the same places as each other, in the same hostels, and eating in the same restaurants serving home-food. Their experience of the world is predefined within the pages of backpackers' guides and they see little in between. The places they stay have become backpacker ghettos – with cliché cafés serving banana and peanut butter pancakes, playing endless DVDs of American sit-coms on wall-to-wall TVs. Guidebooks and backpacker buses encourage this happy band not to bother with the places in between. *Nothing to see here* is a common subjective entry in various editions of Lonely Planet guides, and maybe that is fortunate in the grand scheme of things – keep the rest of it unspoiled.

But we wanted to experience the less visited places in between. Cycling really is the best way to do that, if you can put up with a little discomfort. Basically, it leaves you no choice. On a bike, you see, hear and smell most things as you pass through. You cannot avoid it. You have to eat local food and you have to manage to communicate with the people, who (in contrast to many in the main towns) rarely speak your language and have little experience of foreigners.

It is this full immersion nature of cycle touring that makes it so special. Walking may be even more full immersion, but it will only take you a relatively short distance each day and is very wearing on the feet and joints. Cycling has the benefit of being easier on the body if you take it sensibly, and enables you to cover a decent distance. A touring cyclist will usually pass through a good selection of countryside, villages and towns in a day. This gives us plenty to think about when we lie down at night for a well-earned sleep.

My reasons for making the trip were different to Sam's, and so were the things we feel we gained from it. Sam said he hoped the trip would give him a wider understanding of the world and at the same time bring him closer to me as a friend. I looked forward to the physical and mental challenge of cycling 10,000 miles through widely varying terrain, languages and cultures. I also hoped it would bring me closer to my son, and to a large extent I wanted to do it for him – to give him a great start in his adult life, and also give him something to remember later in life.

Obviously, for Sam at 18, the trip helped his transition from boy to man. That was not his conscious aim, although Lorna and I very much felt that the trip presented an opportunity for the transition to occur naturally and smoothly. I witnessed it as we went along, but for Lorna it came as a shock to see how much Sam had changed when we returned. She stood agog when she came back from work to find that not only had he emptied the dishwasher and made his own bed without being asked but he had also washed all his own clothes. It slowly dawned upon her that she no longer needed to encourage him to study or get a job; he just did things quietly on his own.

*

I think all our aims for the trip were achieved in different degrees. But at the same time, important things were learned that neither of us had planned, or were aware of until later in the journey or even after our return home. I think It is probably true to say that in life it is these unintended things that often prove to be the most valuable of all. It is as if they have been invisibly locked inside us, held back by the pressures of daily life and prejudices about what is important or what we *think* we need. Our subconscious looks for a way to allow these deep-set issues to surface so we can resolve them. I feel, now more than ever, that we need to trust in the unknown.

Having completed this expedition, and looking back on this and other demanding experiences in my life, I can see that such challenges, especially physical ones, bring about revelations and then allow us to find solutions to problems that we don't realise we have. To a certain extent, Sam and I cycled into the unknown and unexpected things happened to us – especially psychologically.

Physical challenges allow us to focus upon basic, simple, easily understood issues. *We have to achieve this much today; we need do this and that to achieve it.* On an expedition, we eat because we need energy and we sleep because we are physically tired. There are few complications to preoccupy us, so we simply focus on getting the job done. Meanwhile, stuff happens.

*

Any long-distance runner, cyclist, lone-sailor or walker will tell you that such activities provide a great opportunity to meditate upon things; to see them clearly at a distance and therefore to resolve difficult issues. For one thing, you have plenty of time, something most of us rarely allow ourselves these days. Secondly, you are away from the things that usually preoccupy or distract you – the telephone, television, computers, work, people, children, bills, etc. Thirdly, you are involved in a rhythmic, repetitive physical activity. At first, you consciously focus on this; but after time it induces a kind of trancelike state. It is the long periods in this state that present such fertile ground for deep thought, seeing things from a distance, making breakthroughs and getting your life sorted out in your mind.

For me, keeping a daily diary really helped in this process. Sam, on the other hand, found that writing down his thoughts and feelings, after spending all day absorbed by them, really became too much, so he stopped. It may be due to our different personalities, or to our difference in age, but my diary quickly became structured, with a table at the beginning of each day. Here, I inserted information like start time, distance cycled before and after lunch, amount spent on food, dead dogs on road, amount spent on accommodation, repairs and servicing, etc. Sam's diary focussed primarily upon what he saw, what he did and how he felt. Mine contained these elements too, but the focus, as well as the main purpose, was markedly different.

So, although Sam and I realise that not everyone is inspired by the same things in life, we both see that everyone has a lot to gain from putting themselves into tough situations, pitting themselves against difficult odds and dealing with demanding physical and mental challenges. Sam and I are unlikely to reach the end of our lives saying, "I could have done without cycling across the world." But if we hadn't done it, we would always have regretted it.

For anyone who has read this book with the idea that they could take a similar demanding expedition with one of their children, or a friend maybe, in order to achieve or learn something in particular, I would say, "Great, do it!" But a word of caution: it is unwise to have any set ideas about what can be achieved or learned. I would say that all you can do is set up the circumstances for something to happen – lessons that might be learned, improvements made in relationships, things discovered, etc. Most likely, something major will happen, or be learned, but it may not be what you were expecting.

*

Back in Canterbury, we initially put our dreamlike state down to jet-lag, but it was months before any kind of *normal* mental state returned, and in truth it never really has. This was less true for Sam in the beginning. He seemed to slot happily back into life with his friends, although he consistently said he felt different. He went off to university knowing he had been changed, but unsure what it was that had changed. Several years later, he is just beginning to recognise it. For me, I don't think my normal state of mind will ever return. And that is fine.

A few weeks after appearing on BBC Breakfast TV, we were sitting in a local restaurant when a lady at the next table said to Sam, "I think you've been somewhere exotic. Did you enjoy your cycle trip?"

Unsurprised now by the number of people who had seen the program, Sam thanked her and said we had. The lady then

347

whispered to her children about who we were and what we had done. All of a sudden, her little boy's loud voice cut through the hubbub of the restaurant:

"But can you do that with your dad?"

SAM'S POINT OF VIEW

As has been said, although my dad felt all the way through that he was doing this trip for me, I actually felt I was doing it for him. Even back when I was ten, I wanted to cycle with him because I could see how much he loved it, and I suppose I wanted to please him. Not that I didn't enjoy it too, but I think that pleasing him was the primary reason. Even the choice of Japan was about my dad. He thought I chose Japan because he and my mum had met there, but in fact I chose it because I could see that it meant so much to him. This was not exactly conscious when I was ten, but I feel quite sure of it looking back. All of this helped make me annoyed during the trip of course. He thought he was doing the trip to benefit me, whereas at the time we left a large part of me would rather have been with my friends, thanks very much!

Leading up to the start of the trip, I think my mum realised that I was not looking forward to it. My efforts to sound enthusiastic didn't convince her. She was sympathetic and tried to reassure me about what a great opportunity it was for me, and how I would come to see the benefits later. I knew that really. But I think my dad started the trip still thinking he was doing it for my benefit – which I can see in his mind he was.

I sometimes feel rather embarrassed now about how grumpy I was during the trip. How many 18 year olds get a chance like that? It does seem ungrateful. I don't regret anything about the trip, though, regardless of my mood at the time. It was clearly necessary and natural for me to be like that, so I have to accept it.

It was a massive challenge for me, and one that would have been a total failure if my dad hadn't been so patient and understanding. It's amazing to think how ungrateful teenagers can be, especially if their upbringing has been largely without pain or anguish. All you can ask for is guidance and support, and I've had more than my fair share of both. But not to take anything away from who I am, or was at the time – I think teenagers behave badly/negatively due to being naive or ignorant, not because they're bad people or want to annoy others. Blatantly, those teenage years are difficult ones for the teenager as well as the parents. Young people are primarily selfish, but they grow out of it, and it is this that gives me hope that good will eventually prevail within almost anyone, even if it takes time.

Looking back now, I feel so positive about it all. It's really given me a taste of what life can offer if you make the effort. Cycling long distances is hard work, but worth it for the experience, the people you meet, the places you see, etc. It was unfortunate timing – unfortunate that I wasn't in a place within myself to really thrive on all the experiences we had. But by the same merit, the timing couldn't have been more perfect for me to get away from home. I had been really depressed before we left and the trip completely sorted me out. Ending up engrained in you that you can complete a momentous challenge like that would set anyone up for life, no matter how difficult it was to see the benefits at the start. I'm 22 now and have a great life ahead of me. I really feel I can achieve anything I want. That's what the trip did for me.

Chapter 16

What we learned - and how we might have done it differently

Man is the only creature who refuses to be what he is.
Albert Camus.

What I really learned were things that didn't occur to me needed learning.   Naturally, this came as a bit of a surprise.

Call me smug, but by the age of 50 I thought I pretty much knew how I ticked.   I had put myself through a wide variety of extreme life experiences and come out the other side wiser – yes, and all those clichés you read in magazines and see movies about – so I had a good idea of what I would learn from this trip, and I planned it accordingly. In fact, on a practical level, I feel I may have planned it too well.

I have a tendency to plan any kind of expedition with military precision: researching, working out what I will need, choosing the best equipment, keeping weight and encumbrances to a minimum.   I enjoyed working out mundane stuff like average distances we might cover per day, how often we needed to wash clothes, the best food supplies to carry (weight vs. energy), the best routes, what spares we were most likely to need.   I enjoyed the research and planning almost as much as the trip itself.   Of course, I still like to leave some things to chance, but even that is a measured decision for me – an opportunity to discover a delightful hidden village, or find that a piece of kit is surplus to requirements and can be given away.

Sam was happy to let me do all of this obsessive stuff, and he said he was really impressed with how well that planning worked out. This was a satisfying vindication of course, but towards the end of the trip I did start to think that less planning might have created a few more interesting incidents and taken us down more unexpected paths. As I said earlier, trust in the unknown.   The counter argument, as people have reminded me, is that this is like wishing accidents on yourself.   You don't get to choose how serious those accidents might be, so you'd best do what you can to avoid them.

As always, moderation is the answer, and I would just say that it is worth leaving some things to be decided along the way. Assess the risks (but not too obsessively). At least consider the possible consequences of not preparing, and perhaps make some contingency arrangements for when the worst happens.

*

"What did you learn from the trip, Sam?"

This question plagued Sam after the completion of our expedition. Everyone wanted to know the answer, but he was unable to satisfy their curiosity with a simple sound-bite. Sam insisted he didn't yet know what he'd learned from the trip, but for those who were prepared to dig deeper, to listen and interpret, there was plenty to learn from him. Years later, he may still not entirely have formulated his thoughts into conclusions for himself, but surely at his age we can hardly expect him to have. Of course, he knows he learned a lot of practical stuff about cycling, food, washing clothes, trip planning, digestive ailments, and so on, as well as a good deal about foreign cultures and geography. He knows that all this knowledge will be useful to him, but he expected to come home having learned more about himself and what he wanted to do with his life, perhaps even the *meaning of life*. In this respect, he came home feeling surprisingly empty. He says he has a sense that he has learned a lot about life and about himself but that he still can't quite say what.

So what does that tell us?

It is clear to Lorna and I that he now knows what he doesn't know. It may even be true to say that he now knows the things he needs to find out. Realistically this is the best one can hope for from a 22-year-old. Knowing the meaning of life at twenty-two would almost make the rest of one's life pointless. It is that lifetime's search that makes life worthwhile. Surely, the right answer to the question "What did you learn from the trip, Sam?" (if there is a right answer) is "Time will tell". And in fact these days that is what Sam says. Sam also says he thinks more clearly now. My own opinion is that perhaps neither of us will ever know. And maybe if we don't, it doesn't matter.   Time *may* tell.   I hope that if Sam has children he might be awakened unexpectedly to some of these things when he does something challenging with them, as I was.   Life is still a mystery to me, and I certainly feel glad of that.   I do share Sam's slight disappointment, though, that there was not a big revelation for him at the end.

*

So what was it I learned that I didn't expect to learn? Two things stand out for me.

Firstly, when I look back on my life from where I am now, it is clear that it can be divided up into phases, or what one might pretentiously call eras.   It's the same for all of us of course.   I can see now that at certain key points in my life, crossroads were reached where I chose a certain path and passed a border into my next era. Mostly these crossings were forced by an event, but always there has been an important personal choice involved over which road I took. I know now that making the cycle trip to Japan with Sam marked the passage across a border into another era of my life.   Maybe it will turn out to be the same for him; maybe not.

I think there are certain times in life when it is possible to predict that a certain event will mark the end of one era of your life and the beginning of another.   My father's death at an early age is a typical example (for him as well as me), although his early death was not predictable.   Most of the time, immersed in the detail of our everyday lives, we tend to see things as a gradual progression.   It is only when we stand back and take stock, usually later in our lives, that we can see the distinct boundaries between the eras.

Pondering these kinds of issues usually brings me to thinking about the subject of destiny.   How much are we in control of our future lives, and how much will turn out a certain way, no matter how hard we try to steer it in the direction we want to go?   If we want to change our lives radically, can we bring about a new era?   Many of us try – a change of job, partner, home or country.   But isn't it true that all too often people make big changes in their lives expecting problems to be left behind, only to find that their problems follow them? And that far from having moved into a new era they are just in a different facet of the same one?

I see this happen often in people's relationships. One partner leaves the other, maybe seeing them as too lazy, angry or un-ambitious, then finds themselves in the same situation in the next and subsequent relationships until (hopefully) they realise that the problem lies within them – their attraction to a certain type of partner, for example. So on balance, I suspect that trying to bring about a new era simply by changing one's circumstances will often fail. Without a powerful life-changing experience to bring underlying issues to the surface, it is too easy to stay in one's comfort (or discomfort) zones.

This is the key to what I feel Sam and I gained from our challenging ten-month expedition. As I have said, we embarked upon the trip with certain expectations about what we would gain from it, but what we really gained were the unexpected things that we learned (dare I say) by accident along the way. If my requirement for this expedition had been only that I gain a better relationship with my son, and if Sam's requirement had been that he would know what he wanted to do with his life by the end of it, we would both have been disappointed. Neither of us would have moved into any new era.

In fact, Sam and I were open to any possible outcomes from making this journey, and some surprising ones arrived – for me anyway. My relationship with my wife changed (for the better, although it is a challenge sometimes), as it did with my other children. My relationship with work also changed. But most of all, the whole way I see and live life changed. I moved into a new, more relaxed stage of life. I would not be exaggerating if I said that in fact I now feel the trip may have saved my life. Not being able to escape from stress in my life before the trip might have killed me. It may sound melodramatic, but it is probably what killed my father.

The point is I would never have accepted that I was stressed, or that I could change it even if I did. I would not have done anything about it directly unless I had collapsed with a heart attack – and only then if I survived it. But something in my sub-conscious was driving me to make this journey with Sam. It may have been Sam's idea to make the trip, when he was still too young to understand the implications, but it was me who needed it most, not him.   He now says that he chose Japan as a destination because it meant so much to me (not him) and that the whole reason for wanting to do a cycle expedition was because he could see even as a small boy how much I loved cycling, and he wanted to share that with me.   So from that perspective it may have been Sam, as an un-knowing but intuitive young boy, who saved me.   That really is a nice feeling.

*

The second major thing I learned that I didn't expect was related to work – how to let go of the reins.

I was never wedded to work, although when I do it, I always work hard.   I left school on reaching 16, while most of my friends studied hard to get into good universities and well-paid careers.   The major obstacle to my freedom to opt out had been suddenly and heartbreakingly removed – my father.

I spent my mid-teens hitchhiking; later, I hitched all over Europe.   I loved it, especially the discussions with travelling businessmen who gave me lifts.   They told me how they envied my freedom, and how they wished they had not put themselves into situations where they had to work all the time to fund mortgages, family ski holidays, second homes, yachts, etc.   Many of these men (for they were mainly men) were rich and successful, and I was amazed to hear them say this, since it was their lifestyle to which we had all been encouraged to aspire.   I learned a lot from this and vowed not to get caught in that trap myself.   In general, freedom from oppression or inability to exercise my free will was all I sought. So for me, like a primitive man, work needed only be a means of getting food, warmth and shelter.

As Sam entered his final year of school, my commitment to the bike trip – brought about by his boyhood request – created a tormenting challenge for me.   But I was determined to go through with it, to the extent that I would close the business if necessary.   I decided that the trip came first.   I had enjoyed years of prosperity and happiness as a result of the business, but now was the time to move

354

on. Money, I reminded myself, is not everything – indeed, I was happy enough before I had any.

What I didn't realise then, and what I came to recognise by the time I returned home, is that the trip was just a means of me learning to let go of the reins. I needed to make a major leap forward in my relationship with work in order for me to get the best out of my business, and I realise now that under normal circumstances I would not have been able to make that leap (unless, like so many people, I made myself ill with overwork). I had become just like the guys who gave me lifts as a teenager.

Sam unwittingly created a situation that pushed me to make a leap into the unknown, and Lorna encouraged me not to fear it. Of course, I see now this was the main purpose of the trip. It wasn't about what I could do for Sam; it was about what I could enable Sam to do for me.

*

Generally, I come down on the side of not believing in destiny. I like to think we are the authors of our own futures, creating our own luck. And yet I can see a kind of symmetry in all of this.

I see how, out of love and a sense of responsibility, my father couldn't allow me to take my own chances in life, which made me fight passionately against him and all authority, and made me a wild risk-taker. I see how the stress of this probably helped bring about his death at the age of 37, despite him seeming to possess excellent health. I see how I learned the value of life from my father's death but how eventually the same sense of responsibility and need to control my family's security, which had helped to kill him, began to ensnare me too. And I see now how my own son and my wife worked instinctively to save me from the same fate, or at least from a sense of major failure. I have spent years since my father's death wishing I could have done something to help him, rather than being the source of his frustration. Finally, it was my own son who helped me to put it right by teaching me not to repeat the same pattern.

Three years after we cycled into Tokyo, I look back and I see clearly how we can learn as much from our children as they can from us. Getting locked into conditioned roles, where parents think they need to instruct and *get it right*, leads at best to a one-way learning experience. More often it leads to angry teenagers who refuse to listen. At the same time, poor work-life choices are the curse of many families and I hold out some hope that we might move towards a better future, where it becomes the norm to keep life and work in a healthy balance.

Most of all, I hope for a future where we listen to the instinctive wisdom in our children.

Thanks, Sam. I'm listening now.

Addendum

What we took and how it performed

Tent – Terra Nova Laser Large
This tent was chosen for quality of manufacture and its incredible lightness balanced with being fairly spacious for two grown men (1.7 Kg). It had space for us and our overnight backpacks inside plus our four Ortleib panniers, handlebar bags etc in the entrance vestibule. It had good ventilation (very important in hot climates) with mosquito protection. It performed superbly, was regularly put up in the dark while tired and weighed almost nothing. We never minded carrying it even during long periods when we weren't using it.

Head torch – Petzel LED
Tiny, powerful and batteries last for ever!   There are cheap versions but this was invaluable, especially for putting up the tent in the dark. Ten months of almost daily use - same batteries were still fine at the end.   Should have taken one each.

Wind-up Torch / Charger – AA
Charges all phones etc. Sent this home when Lorna visited us after 6 months. It wasn't worth the hassle carrying it.   Made only minimal impression on charging phone battery. Better to take spare phone battery.

Tools & Spares
Crank Bros Multi-tool 19.   Gerber Multi-tool Pliers. Cassette Removal tool. 2 Spanners + Allen Key set. Screwdrivers. Spare nuts & bolts, spokes & cables. Cable-ties. Puncture kit & 2 innertubes. Duct tape. Tupperware box to contain all.   <u>Should have taken</u> 4 better quality innertubes + 1 folding tyre & drilled out rims to take large 'Shrader' valves. Otherwise a good kit.

Chain Lubricant
(Wet) Prolink . 1 x 250ml bottle.   Superb performance in mostly dry conditions resulted in minimal wear and smooth changes. One bottle lasted nearly 10,000 miles.

Compass – Silva Junior
Very useful when there are no clear signs – even in cities.

Mobile Phone & Charger – Nokia (for reliability).
1 phone each with one 2 pin charger (much smaller & was the right type for the whole journey).   Never let us down but be warned, some PAYG SIMs in foreign countries will only last for a month in an 'imported' phone - anti-grey import measure.

Maps & Itineraries – distance / stopping / spending log sheets.
Very useful for checking back and ahead and for working out averages etc. Log sheet also helps to remember where you did what and pass on advice to others you meet.

Books
Rough-guide excerpts, Maps, Dorling Kindersley Bicycle Maintenance Manual, Novels (The Alchemist, Raymond Carver Short Stories, Checkov Short Stories). Lonely Planet guides bought along the way when we were staying long periods in one country – they are heavy but useful so long as you don't take them as gospel truth + they are opinionated. Maps usually bought on arrival but limited choice, can take a couple of days to find map shop and then in local language (good & bad) so restricts prior planning. Fortunately took Turkey, Iran, India, SE Asia & China maps with us.

Stove – MSR Pocket Rocket
Large gas canisters & homemade windshield (tin-foil + wood barbeque skewers – shop bought ones are way overpriced).
Excellent performance and weighs nothing. Titanium model not worth the extra. Didn't use often so could have left it behind, but great when we needed it.

Cooking pot – 1.5L Primus Eta
Good price to weight ratio and best size for two. (+ Wooden cooking spoon).

Food storage containers – 2 Litre Tupperware type.
1 each to store food and eat out of instead of plates / bowls + use lid as chopping board.   Invaluable for the whole trip. Multiple uses.

Emergencies
Fire-striker – Swedish. Small, light, effective but never used. Whistle – never used.   Space blanket – never used

Food
Dry food – Couscous, Pasta & Lentils.
Tinned   & fresh food etc – One tin of tuna and one of kidney beans kept in panniers at all times was the best arrangement - Heavy, but worth it when

there are no shops. Bread, tomatoes, peppers, onion & fruit bought regularly. Salt & pepper, soya sauce, stock cubes, ketchup sachets picked up in cafes. Mostly ate out but when you are out in the wilds you really need food when you're tired.

Toilet paper & antibacterial wet-wipes
Wipes were very useful for washing face and body when no facilities around, then used same wipe for quick cleaning of bikes. Use sparingly; Alex says they are an environmental disaster.

1st Aid kit etc
Sudocrem, iodine (liquid), sunprotection cream, anti-malarial tablets, deet mosquito repellent lotion (Boots). Sewing / mending kit. Multi size basin / bath plug. Sudocrem was one of the most important things we took; it worked like magic.

Computer USB memory stick
With scanned copies of passport barcode pages, birth certificates, PC address book, internet banking site, passwords etc.   Invaluable.

Camera
Lumix DMC TZ3 with 10x zoom.   Memory cards (4 x 2mb).   Memory-card reader (camera & phone).   2 pin plug cable. Sam's Kodak camera worked with the same charger so took one for both. Good balance between size / weight & performance.

Touring Bicycles - Dawes Super Galaxy (1x 2006 model, 1x 2008)   Double sided Clipless pedals, Brooks B17 standard leather saddle (Sam's is a B17 narrow), Marathon Plus tyres (Sam's had plain Marathons until India). Catseye simple F&Rear lights, Catseye F11 Cycle computer, Ortlieb Back Roller Classic panniers, Ortleib Bar-bags. 3 bottle carriers (2 each with 750ml large aluminium bottles + 1 smaller), bungees & cargo nets. Could have done without the clipless pedals most of the time was our verdict for this kind of touring. Bikes were absolutely the best – would definitely use the same again. My rear wheel rim was all that broke due to unseen pothole. Marathon Plus tyres well worth the extra – my 1 puncture to Sam's 15 proves it. Brooks saddles were great after 200 miles breaking in.

Sleeping Mats
1x Thermarest inflating & 1x dimple folding type (larger but more comfortable and lighter). Vital if you want to sleep and awaken feeling rested.

Sleeping bags
Blacks Quantum 500 (down) Stormshield 1100 (polyester).   Both equally
good although my polyester bag didn't smell like Sam's after he'd slept with
wet socks on in Wales (no amount of airing got rid of it).

Silk sleeping-bag liners (made by my mum with silk provided by our friend
Judith).
Also for use alone in hot weather. Another vital item. We used them in dirty
hotels a lot too.

Padded lycra cycle shorts
Sam 2 pairs DHB Earnley.   Mark 1 pair DHB + 1 pair Pearl Izumi Microsensor.
Worn next to skin. DHB as good as Pearl Izzumi at a quarter the price - £18
from www.wiggle.co.uk). Also vital and easy to wash. Dry very quickly when
stretched over your bar bag in the morning sun.

General clothes
Lightweight surf shorts for use as trunks or casual.   Convertible lightweight
trousers - North Face (high wicking). Lightweight Waterproof jackets - Endura
Crosslite.   M&S cotton & lycra t-shirt vests (black, 2 each). All excellent
choices that performed superbly for wear and washing.

SPD Cycle shoes
Specialized Soma. Very comfortable on the bike and off. I wore them all day
every day for ten months and they are still serviceable. Spare lightweight
shoes (1 x Crocs 1 x imitation) - don't make panniers & clothes smell, like wet
trainers do. My imitation Crocks not comfortable after a few weeks. Made do
with cycle shoes which were enough.

Cycle shirts – 2 High Wicking cycle shirts each
Specialized   + 1 long sleeved football shirt each. Long sleeved more useful in
full sun all day.

Microfleece
1 Protec short zip, 1 O'Neil short zip. Both performed well and useful even in
warm climes. Don't need thicker in cold climes, just wear more layers.

3 Underpants each – M&S Lycra & Cotton mix (for off the bike).   Easy to dry.

Hats
1 warm fleece hat (me), 1 jungle sun hat each, 1 Cycle helmet each – Giro
Indicator.   Fleece hat never used but good for emergency. Jungle hats very
useful. Cycle helmet comfortable with good ventilation.

Sunglasses
DHB with 3 lenses (wiggle again £28) – Mine broke after 1 month. Cheap Indian alternatives were fine (£2).

KF&Spoon Titanium set (from Blacks).   1 Penknife - Swiss army (Camper)   - Both excellent and used a lot. Cups - Lexan (from Blacks) – rarely used but light and survived well.

Wash-kit – Bag, Tooth Brush, Tooth Paste, Facewash / Showergel, Shampoo/conditioner, Disposable razor (to trim round my mouth as I grew an 'explorer beard'), Travelwash. Hair-gel for Sam. Replaceable from hotels or shops.

Passport + visas photos (8 each) & photocopies – rather necessary

Bum Bag - for money and passport etc   - Very useful, never lost anything and always had the important things with me when out and about.

Diary – Moleskine (A5)   - A key memory of the trip for evermore and useful for checking back on details during the trip (sketches each day also). People have often since asked me for information which I've found in here.

Money – 2 bank cards (go for cards with no commission on exchange worldwide) + 2 credit cards (1 visa + 1 mastercard – important to have both as in many places ATM machines take one or the other). Cash - $500US (not enough – remember you can't get cash from machines in Iran) + some East European Currencies.   US Dollar was still the most useful but the Euro was getting more widely accepted.

Websites - Most useful were:

www.hostelworld.com
www.lonelyplanet.com/thorntree/
www.google.com/maps
www.fco.gov.uk   (Foreign & Commonwealth Office)
www.google/mail
www.warmshowers.org (hospitality for touring cyclists)

Our own Blog, covering each stage of our trip and various other facets plus more photographs, can be found at: www.bugbitten.com/father_son_cycle

DOING GOOD

While we never set out to make this trip in order to raise money for charity, we did decide upon a very deserving cause. Sam and I decided to ask people to donate money to 'The Rising Sun Domestic Violence Project'. This organisation does excellent work running a refuge, crisis support and therapy service for women and their children who are the victims of domestic violence. They receive no state funding and do an amazing job with limited resources. As most of the perpetrators of domestic violence are men, Sam and I felt it logical that we two men should help RSDVP, and at the same time help raise awareness in other men of how they might achieve better family relationships.   They   can   be   contacted   via   their   website   at: www.rsdvp.co.uk

Mark Swain, through his company *Systems2 Consulting Ltd*, works (not exessively) as a Management Consultant, specialising in the area of risk.   He is interested in how humanbeings percieve and approach risk and how we can manage our lives to get the best from them.   In a business context, this often means helping companies to see how the management of risk, far from constraining their key commercial interests, can enhance them.

Mark says:

"The ridiculous, *Health & Safety Gone Mad* stories one reads in the press, about the law forcing schools to ban conkers etc, give the impression that risk management is all about banishing risk from our lives.   This is a myth.   The law only requires organisations to demonstrate that they have assessed the risks and made sensible efforts to control them – nothing wrong with that.   It is in the over-zealous interpretation of the law, that things go wrong.   Risk is a healthy part of life and the law allows us to embrace it.   Don't let anyone tell you otherwise."

As a Chartered H&S Practitioner, Mark Swain delivers training on subjects relating to Risk Management, Safety by Design etc.   In addition, he now delivers talks on the experiences of his Ireland – Japan trip with his son, along with motivational training courses for managers and entrepreneurs.

Details are on his company website: www.systems2consulting.com or via the publisher at: www.tinderboxpublishing.com